THE EVOLUTION OF BRITISH HISTORIOGRAPHY

From Bacon to Namier

THE EVOLUTION OF BRITISH HISTORIOGRAPHY

From Bacon to Namier

EDITED BY J. R. HALE

MACMILLAN
London · Melbourne
1967

First published in the United States and her dependencies by The World Publishing Company, Cleveland, Ohio, and simultaneously in Canada by Nelson, Easter & Scott Ltd.

First published in the United Kingdom by Macmillan & Co Ltd. 1967.

MACMILLAN AND COMPANY LIMITED
Little Essex Street London WC2
also Bombay Calcutta Madras Melbourne

Grateful acknowledgment is made to the following for permission to reprint previously published material:

Longmans, Green & Co. Limited for "Malplaquet," from Volume 3, *The Peace and the Protestant Succession*, of *England Under Queen Anne*, by G. M. Trevelyan, published in 1934.

John Murray (Publishers) Ltd. for "The New Medicine for Poverty", from *Religion and the Rise of Capitalism*, by R. H. Tawney, first published in 1926.

Hamish Hamilton Ltd. for "King George III: A Study of Personality", from *Personalities and Powers*, by Sir Lewis Namier, published in 1955.

PRINTED IN GREAT BRITAIN BY
LOWE AND BRYDONE (PRINTERS) LTD., LONDON

CONTENTS

PREFACE

However selective the aims of individual historians may be, their collective aim is to climb to an increasingly comprehensive view of the past. This anthology is designed to show by what feats of imagination and technique the hairpin turns in the road of historical writing have been engineered. The men represented here all possess certain qualities in common: literary ability, intellectual power, broad vision, a reflective, "philosophic" cast of mind, a scholarly and critical attitude toward their material, and a concern for the purpose, as well as the content, of history. None can be removed from the story of the development of historical writing in England without leaving a conspicuous void; all except one were pioneers. The exception is G. M. Trevelyan. I include him as the noblest example of those historians who were content with the straight road.

In the Introduction I attempt to give a brief account of the evolution of English historical writing. Historians use the groundwork of many—philologists, antiquarians, archaeologists—who are fine scholars without being themselves historians. They are moved by influences from abroad—Humanism, Rationalism, Marxism—and by currents of thought in their own society—romanticism, nationalism, the withering of faith in progress. A history book is itself a historical document and means most when most is known about the age in which it was produced. These points should be borne in mind when reading my bald account of the subject's inner laws of growth. The Introduction's purpose is to provide a background to the passages quoted in the anthology. The notes prefaced to each series of extracts are designed merely to give references, explain obscurities, and show how the study of a particular author can be followed up.

ACKNOWLEDGMENTS

I am greatly indebted to Mr. Christopher Hill for encouragement and much careful advice; and to Mrs. Frances Walsh for preparing nearly the whole of the bibliography from which I worked. For checking the texts I am grateful to Miss Ann Stallard and Mrs. Rosalind Dale-Harris.

INTRODUCTION

Modern British historical writing begins with a constellation of important works which appeared at the end of the sixteenth and the beginning of the seventeenth century. In addition to Sir Walter Raleigh's *History of the World* (1614), William Camden's *History of Elizabeth* (1615), and Francis Bacon's *History of the Reign of King Henry VII* (1622), extracts from which are included in this book, there was John Stow's *Survey of London* (1598), the first scholarly history of an English town, and John Selden's *History of Tithes* (1621), the first detailed history of a particular institution. As in the growth of the drama from Marlowe to Webster, this sudden burst of activity, seeming as it did to blaze from darkness and die away again, while owing most to the accidental existence of men of genius, owes much to particular social and political conditions, and to the subject's previous development.

Medieval historians were the product of a lively interest in events and a desire to relate them to divine Providence; God played the game, while man watched and learned. The chronicler wrote *à longue haleine,* often going back to the Creation, when the board was first divided and the pieces fashioned. It was a nerve-racking game to watch, for though God wanted white to win, He had given the pieces free will; and while every move was His, He was sometimes forced to concede a piece to black. Having established the divine origin of the game, the chronicler described its progress, to show his readers how they could best collaborate with God's strategy, and as he wrote in

terms of kings, bishops, knights (and their castles) the lessons were all the more dramatic.

That the main function of history was to teach was a commonplace reaching from the preface to Bede's *Ecclesiastical History* to North's preface to his translation (1579) of Plutarch's *Lives;* history "is a certain rule and instruction," as North said, "which, by examples past, teacheth us to judge of things present and to foresee things to come, so as we may know what to like of and what to follow, what to mislike and what to eschew." But during the sixteenth century the emphasis on what history taught shifted from morals to wisdom, and in particular, political wisdom. From being a repertory of sins punished, it became a storehouse of historical parallels.

This shift of emphasis was of great importance. It was caused in part by the example of Italian historians, notably by Francesco Guicciardini, whose *History of Italy* was translated into English in 1579, and by Niccolò Machiavelli, whose *History of Florence* was translated in 1595. As Bacon himself said, "We are much beholden to Machiavelli and other writers of that class who openly and unfeignedly declare or describe what men do, and not what they ought to do." And though this was a tribute to the author of *The Prince* rather than the frequently tendentious writer on Florentine history, it expressed a desire to see historical characters as true to life as possible, so that lessons could be learned from their actions that were relevant to life rather than to the hereafter.

This led to a changed attitude toward facts and causation; facts should be more copious and more authentic, and while God remained the first cause of human events, more stress should be laid on secondary causes, the freely willed actions of men. To the medieval chronicler, facts were what he saw and heard about, a few documents that were given wide circulation through copies—like Magna Carta, the charters of his monastery or the privileges of his town, and what he found in the writings of his predecessors. In the sixteenth century, even at its close, historians still reported what they heard from influential friends as though it were fact as well as opinion; they still accepted much that they found in chronicles as fact, but there was a steady tendency to play down the irrational, the "marvel" element in their narratives, and, most important of all, increasing use was made of state papers, the records of the law courts and local archives. Access to state papers depended on the favor of a high official—Camden was licensed to use them by Lord Burghley—or the courtesy of a

great record collector like Sir Robert Cotton, whose papers were a basis of Bacon's *Henry VII,* but however big the gaps, however uncritical the assumption that any document in an archive represented the *truth* rather than a means of getting at the truth, the work of the generation of writers from Stow to Selden established once and for all that documents and not secondary authorities are the essential foundation of reliable history.

While the use of documents was conditioned by the growth of libraries and manuscript collections, the improved organization of the public archives, and a tolerant attitude to their being searched by historians as well as by precedent-seeking lawyers, the appetite for consulting them came from changes in the life of the nation itself. The Reformation isolated Britain from Europe in a way that psychologically went much deeper than the previous losses of her wide territories in France; it stimulated a patriotic interest in the past as well as a desire to justify the break from Rome. And while the Reformation led—as had the violent accession of the Tudor dynasty—to much writing of history as propaganda, by the middle of Elizabeth's reign, when both religious settlement and dynasty seemed reasonably assured, men could at last discuss the astonishing succession of events since the Wars of the Roses without inhibition. Censorship remained, and was vigilant to note any incitement to treason based on past analogy, but by and large historians were able to investigate and celebrate the past as truthfully as they could. They were encouraged, as were the dramatists, by the existence of an enthusiastic audience. Many of this audience still wanted history of the old-fashioned See-the-Mighty-Humbled school, but there was also a wide demand for antiquarian surveys like Camden's *Britannia,* for municipal histories, and as the temper of international politics grew, for history that helped men make quick decisions in the light of similar situations in the past. Distinguished from most of Europe by religion, from all of it by its unique common law, and by a parliament which was regarded with a growing self-consciousness, Englishmen were primarily fascinated by themselves, and though important works on other countries appeared, like Richard Knolles's *General History of the Turks* (1603), historians were encouraged to devote themselves to their own country, and to archives.

The answer to the question "What is a fact?" is one test of the maturity of a period's historiography. The answer given by that generation, "Something written in a document or an inscription rather than

reported by a secondary source," was a significant advance, and it was to be long before documents themselves came to be treated with the caution we associate with the word "historicism." Another test is the extent to which historians are interested in causation; how seriously they try to trace the cause of an effect before throwing in their hands and invoking God, Fortune, or the Spirit of the Times.

It is interesting that one of the first works to call for attention to causes was the *Mirror for Magistrates* (1559). This was an extremely popular collection of stories from English history told in verse, each of which described the catastrophe that overcame some great man because of excessive pride, ambition, or downright wickedness. It held a moralist's mirror to the past so that the present could learn from the succession of images revealed in it. Yet it is in this most conservative work that the following comment on the early Tudor chronicler Fabian occurs:

> Unfruitful Fabian followed the face
> Of time and deeds, but let the causes slip . . .
> But seeing causes are the chiefest things
> That should be noted of the story writers
> That men may learn what ends all causes brings
> They be unworthy of the name of Chroniclers
> That leave these clean out of their registers
> Or doubtfully report them.[1]

The same point is made in a more sophisticated manner by Robert Bolton in his *Hypercritica, or a rule of judgement for writing or reading our Historians,* an essay of about 1618 which sums up the attitudes to historical writing of his day. "Christian authors," he noted, "while for their ease they shuffled up the reasons of events, in briefly referring all causes immediately to the Will of God, have generally neglected to inform their readers in the ordinary means of carriage in human affairs, and thereby maimed their narrations."

This passage gives another clue to the relish with which historical studies were pursued in the late Tudor and early Stuart age. Just as the early humanists in Italy were encouraged by scorn for their benighted forefathers, so Elizabethan historians felt impelled to correct the faults of their predecessors, and to show how history really should be written. Bolton goes on to emphasize that histories should not be

[1] Quoted in H. Butterfield, *The Englishman and His History,* 1944, pp. 15–16.

mere rag bags of miscellaneous information, however accurate, but should be methodically planned without the author exploiting his manner of selection in order to force his own point of view on the reader, and that the style should be appropriate to the subject matter, so that "the majesty of handling our history might once equal the majesty of the argument," and he singles out "Sir Francis Bacon's writings, which have the freshest and most savoury form and aptest utterance that (as I suppose) our tongue can bear." It was probably fortunate that English historians were not influenced by Italian humanist history in the fifteenth century, but by the more vigorous and less didactic vernacular historians of the sixteenth. The Italian voice spoke once directly to English ears in Polydore Vergil's *Anglica Historia* (1534–55), but they paid little heed to it; and the native tradition was brought through Hall and Holinshed into the late sixteenth century, where the influence of Italian and French theory and practice could refine without emasculating it.

Raleigh's *History of the World* represents a transitional stage between the old history and the new. He did not have time to carry out his plan of following up the history of the Jews, Greeks, and Romans with that of Britain, but it is not likely that, writing from the Tower and relying on copyists and the loan of materials, he intended to depend on documents. He is intent on displaying God's providence, and therefore begins with the Creation; he is blatantly patriotic ("If it be demanded, whether the Macedonian or the Roman were the best warror, I will answer: the Englishman."); he digresses in terms of his own experience of war or voyaging, interrupting the narrative in defiance of Bolton's rules, and by constantly juxtaposing ancient and modern situations is prevented from feeling the essential distance in time of his Jews and Romans; he follows the See-the-Mighty-Humbled attitude of the *Mirror for Magistrates*. Talking of adversity, in the Preface, he wrote:

> For seeing God, who is the author of all our tragedies, hath written out for us and appointed us all the parts we are to play, and hath not in their distribution been partial to the most mighty princes of the world; that gave unto Darius the part of the greatest emperor and the part of the most miserable beggar, a beggar begging water of an enemy to quench the great drought of death; that appointed Bajazet to play the Grand Signor of the Turks in the morning and in the same day the footstool of Tamerlane . . . why should other

men, who are but as the least worms, complain of wrongs? Certainly there is no other account to be made of this ridiculous world than to resolve that the change of fortune on the great theatre is but as the change of garments on the less. For when on the one and the other every man wears but his own skin, the players are all alike.

The appeal of history to Raleigh was essentially poetic: it raised men from the grave, it enabled men to visualize the earth when it was created, "how it was covered with waters, and again repeopled. How kings and kingdoms have flourished and fallen, and for what virtue and piety God made prosperous, and for what vice and deformity he made wretched, both the one and the other." And besides, "it is not the least debt which we owe unto History that it both made us acquainted with our dead ancestors and out of the depth and darkness of the earth delivered us their memory and fame." The old and the new are both present here, the old in the harping on vice and virtue, the new in the emphasis on bringing men, real men, to life, described with a verve and an interest in character that made them in practice far more than exemplars of wretchedness and prosperity. And though no exact scholar, he compared sources where he could, and took from them what best aided the human credibility of his story. His precepts looked back, his practice looked forward. In precept he stressed the role of God as a cause, but in practice he pursued the secondary causes of accident and motive; on the title page we meet an allegory of history with the eye of *Providentia* watching over all, but we close the book with the feeling that man's destiny is largely in his own hands. Indeed "he contributed," as a modern historian has put it, "perhaps more than has been recognized, to that segregation of the spiritual from the secular which was the achievement of the seventeenth century." [2] It was his ability to express a new mood while retaining traditional formulae that gave the *History* its long hold over the public imagination. It went through ten editions (apart from abridgments) by 1687, it was commended by Oliver Cromwell to his son and was praised by the political philosopher John Locke. It outsold Spenser and Shakespeare; it remains, like the career of its author, one of the most enthralling witnesses to the contradictions, as well as the achievements, of the age.

[2] Christopher Hill, "Sir Walter Raleigh and History," in *The Listener,* June 7, 1962.

longed to bring them together into a rationally planned structure; knowledge, if consciously pursued and properly systematized, would help man understand his world and improve it. It would promote both happiness and utility. The brilliantly imaginative synthesis which Bacon provided in the *Advancement of Learning* provides the best source for his attitude toward history. He surveyed the whole subject, trouncing its inadequacies and inventing new, and useful, categories. He wanted a systematic history of learning, for instance, "without which the history of the world seemeth to me to be as the statue of Polyphemus with his eye out, that part being wanting which doth most show the spirit and life of the person." He wanted a history of mechanical inventions and scientific experiment, a treatment of natural philosophy such "as shall not vanish in the fume of subtle, sublime or delectable speculation [how he knew where to hit the pedant!], but such as shall be operative to the endowment and benefit of man's life." And he continues in a way that represents his attitude toward history as a whole: "for it will not only minister and suggest to the present many ingenious practices in all trades, by a connexion and transferring of the observations of one art to the use of another, when the experiences of several mysteries shall fall under the consideration of one man's mind; but farther, it will give a more true and real illumination concerning causes and axioms than is hitherto attained."

For the majority of men, it was not speculation but history that brought wisdom, "for it is not St Augustine's nor St Ambrose's works that will make so wise a divine as ecclesiastical history, thoroughly read and observed." But if history is to fulfill its proper purpose of showing how actions flow from men's character, and serving as a guide to men's actions in the present, it must obey certain rules. It must be as full as possible, and as true to life as possible, not like those histories that "do rather set forth the pomp of business than the true and inward resorts thereof." An author ought not to deal with too long a period, as he "cannot but meet with many blanks and spaces, which he must be forced to fill up out of his own wit and conjecture," and he ought to select a period which had some logical shape, such as the history of England "from the uniting of the roses to the uniting of the kingdoms."

The dogmatic tone of the *Advancement* conceals some inconsistency in Bacon's attitude toward history. While he wished it to be based on inductive principles, like the natural sciences, he admitted that it

lacked an adequate certainty. While he wished it to teach in terms of what other men had done, he admitted the dependence of men's actions on a providential First Cause. Above all, he wrote, "I wish events to be coupled with their causes," but he had no clear theory of causation, and confused cause with origin, as though to describe the beginning of a course of action, or an event, was in fact to explain it. He insisted on the need for reliable detail, but scorned the business of acquiring it. "I hold it to be somewhat beneath the dignity of an undertaking like mine," he wrote crushingly, "that I should spend my own time in a matter which is open to almost every man's industry." [3] But if the historian relies on the research of others, how can he be sure that he has the facts he needs for his work of explanation? Without personal acquaintance with the materials, how can the historian realize another of Bacon's aims, "to carry the mind in writing back into the past and bring it into sympathy with antiquity"?

The choice of Henry VII's reign as his single excursion into the writing of history suited most of Bacon's criteria for a satisfactory subject. The records were full, Henry was a politician whose career was pregnant with lessons for others, and as Bacon said in his dedication to the young Prince Charles, Henry was "that king to whom both unions may in a sort refer: that of the roses being in him consummate, and that of the kingdoms by him begun."

The book was written when Bacon was out of favor, and indeed excluded, save for a few weeks, from London, so copious original research was out of the question. He relied on chroniclers—Fabian, Hall, and Holinshed among them—on manuscripts loaned by Sir Robert Cotton, and on downright guesswork and invention. He alone gives us, as his severest critic, Wilhelm Busch, pointed out,[4] the names of the 1496 and 1506 commercial treaties with the Netherlands as *Magnus Intercursus* and *Malus Intercursus;* the account of the fortune left by Henry on his death; the anecdotes about Morton's Fork and Henry's ape, who tore up the account book—to mention only the legends most familiar from textbook repetition. But for all the book's errors, Bacon's style and intelligence produced a historical classic. Who will ever forget that Henry VII was the king who "could not endure to have trade sick"? What other historian had written of unimportant men as Bacon wrote of two of the Cornish rebels: "The

[3] Quoted in F. Smith Fussner, *The Historical Revolution,* 1962, p. 259.
[4] In *England under the Tudors,* English trans., 1895, vol. I, pp. 416–23.

one was Michael Joseph, a blacksmith or farrier of Bodmin, a notable talking fellow, and no less desirous to be talked of. The other was Thomas Flammock, a lawyer, who, by telling his neighbours commonly upon any occasion that the law was on their side, had gotten great sway amongst them. This man talked learnedly, and as if he could tell how to make a rebellion and never break the peace." It was the freedom, the intimacy, and the wit of Bacon, rather than the earnest caution of Camden or the fitful splendor of Raleigh, that reappeared in the work of Clarendon, the first great successor to that triumvirate.

Clarendon is an exception in the list of great English historians, because none of the others, except Camden and Namier, wrote contemporary history, and Clarendon not only wrote about his own times, but included the important role he had played in them himself. His *History of the Rebellion and Civil Wars in England Begun in the Year 1641* was a conflation of a historical narrative (written in 1646–48) and an autobiography (written in 1668–70). His determination to be strictly impartial, however, and his desire "that posterity should not be deceived" by party versions justified the decision to write history rather than memoirs, and the importance of his own role was a further justification, for "there was never yet a grand history written but by men conversant with business." Nor did he think it necessary, for history's sake, to go back to a time he himself did not remember. He determined to start with the beginning of Charles I's reign when he himself was a young man: "I am not so sharp-sighted as those, who have discerned this rebellion contriving from (if not before) the death of Queen Elizabeth." He saw the Rebellion not as the product of long-term causes but of the passions of men coming quickly to the boil.

Edward Hyde, later the Earl of Clarendon, while never an out-and-out royalist, was pushed by the parliamentary extremists into a close personal relationship with the King which lasted until Charles's death. The moment that swung Hyde from being a moderate and critical royalist to becoming the spokesman of the crown was the debate over the Grand Remonstrance,[5] when the Long Parliament in 1641 presented its list of grievances against the crown. Thereafter, though Hyde joined the King's council and became responsible for writing his state papers, and continued writing them from Jersey even when

[5] See pp. 130–38, below.

the King was in custody, and though it was he who drew up in 1660 the Declaration of Breda, which enabled Charles II to return to England, he remembered the principles and the friends of his more radical days; he wrote in the tone of his youth, as a supporter of King and Church well on this side of idolatry.

If Clarendon was cool about his own church, he was sickened by enthusiasm in the cause of a rival creed, and the greatest criticism that can be made against his *History* is its lack of sympathy for the puritan temperament. He could not see puritanism as a force which could link men together in steady opposition to church and state any more than he could see any economic common denominator among the rival parties. His offhand gesture toward a theory of causation put the rebellion down to "the same natural causes and means, which have usually attended kingdoms swoln with long plenty," that is, a growing irresponsibility and factiousness among individuals, as though a party had suddenly got out of hand and the gorged guests had become first querulous then violent. No longer-term view was necessary; all could be explained by watching the last hours of that fabled party, the period of Charles I's personal rule without parliament, as the tempers rose. So "by viewing the temper, disposition, and habit of that time, of the court and of the country, we may discern the minds of men prepared, of some to do, and of others to suffer, all that hath since happened; the pride of this man, and the popularity of that; the levity of one, and the morosity of another; the excess of the court in the greatest want, and the parsimony and retention of the country in the greatest plenty; the spirit of craft and subtlety in some, and the rude and unpolished integrity of others, too much despising craft or art; like so many atoms contributing jointly to this mass of confusion now before us." It is the presentation of these atoms in a series of brilliant character sketches that saves Clarendon's narrative from being a mass of inert information. When he looked at puritanism he saw an incomprehensible fanatic blur, but when he looked at individual puritans he saw courage and fixity of purpose and the appeal of a grave simplicity of manner. Without the "characters" his *History* would still be a remarkable achievement. The complex negotiations between court and parliament, and then between the factions among the royalists and the parties into which their opponents divided and subdivided, are described with a lawyerlike clarity and grasp of detail; long as the work is, his intelligence never slumbers while his pen moves on; it is present, as it is with Gibbon, in every paragraph, and he demands the

same close attention in the reader. From time to time he breaks off the narrative to look about and discuss the implications of some constitutional innovation, or some dramatic change of fortune, and shows himself in these digressions to be wiser than Raleigh and subtler than Bacon. But it is his portraits that raise his chronicle-memoir into a great history, by providing for the first time a story that is really credible in terms of its actors.

These "characters" have become literary anthology pieces, but their greatest merit is psychological. Clarendon drew on a tradition of character writing that started with the Elizabethan fascination with the "humours," and brought it to a refinement which has hardly yet been excelled. By the time of Hume the "character" had degenerated into a mechanical balancing of virtues against vices; Clarendon is at once more casual and more inward, and the range of his sympathies is wide. He employs a tone of musing retrospect, a rapid informality that presents the man and explains his actions and his influence with an effect of far greater realism than any measured obituary could achieve. His account of Hampden's debating technique adds life to the long descriptions of discussions in the Commons, his explanation of the power and the limitations of Pym illuminates much of the restlessness among the puritans, as his portrait of Charles explains much about the difficulties of the royalists. The *History* is a supreme example of how far a historian can be saved from bias and externality by an understanding of human nature.

History can be written, and written vigorously, within the experience of a single nation, but to advance in technique and purpose it must look outside, outside in time—as the Italian humanists looked back to the ancients—or in place, as the Jacobean triumvirate looked across to Italy and France. In the middle of the eighteenth century English historians once more looked over the Channel with the curiosity of Bacon and Camden, and the result was the creation of another "new history," and its first exponents formed a new triumvirate: Hume, Robertson, and Gibbon. Like their predecessors, they did not stand alone, and the company that surrounded them can be studied in T. P. Peardon's excellent *The Transition in English Historical Writing* (1933), but they do stand out, with qualities of mind and style that speak to anyone interested in history, and not merely to the collectors of historiographical curiosities.

The continuity with Bacon was not broken. They too believed that history taught, and taught best through a detailed study of men which

avoided the miraculous; they too sighed at the thought of original research and preferred to systematize and generalize; they too equated "fact" with a statement in an approved authority and wished to study advanced societies rather than groping or barbarous ones; they too believed that history should deal with learning and science as well as politics, with the deeds of peace as well as of war, and by contributing to man's knowledge of himself help him to change his environment for the better. . . . But it is, after all, naive to expect revolutionary changes in attitudes toward history once the secular has come to predominate over the spiritual approach; history is not like a science that can transform itself with each new accretion of knowledge; it is tied too closely to human nature for that. The subject matter of history expands, the definition of a fact becomes more sophisticated, the problem of causation becomes complicated by the idea of impersonal forces: climatic, economic, social, but the motives for writing and reading it remain the same: curiosity, a delight in order, the hope of learning something about ourselves. We may discover a genuinely "new history" among the Martians; our own will always remain intelligible to a Bacon or a Camden.

This is not to say that Gibbon is simply Bacon in a peruke, but to suggest that the second triumvirate were nearer to their predecessors than to their immediate successors—to Macaulay, for instance. Between Gibbon and Macaulay lay the influence of Romanticism, not the romanticism that responded to the exotic—Gibbon thrilled to that—but the romanticism that brought with it an emotional sympathy with people in the past in terms of the ages in which they lived. Gibbon felt close to his Romans, as Machiavelli in his Tuscan farmhouse felt that he could converse with the shades of the ancients; but in each case there was an intellectual sympathy, not an imaginative understanding of their different backgrounds or of the crowded timescape that separated them.

The first volume of Hume's *History of England* appeared in 1754, of Robertson's *History of Scotland* in 1759, of Gibbon's *Decline and Fall* in 1776. In France, Montesquieu's *Considérations sur la Grandeur et la Décadence des Romains* appeared in 1734 and his *Esprit des Lois* in 1748; Voltaire's *Siècle de Louis XIV* was published in 1751, his *Essai sur l'histoire générale* in 1756. These were the works that brought the ideals of the French Enlightenment to England with an almost manifesto-like clarity: History should be secular, nonpartisan, instructive, and philosophical. As a secular study it should expose

superstition and treat men as permanent residents of the world, not as passengers in transit to a better one; it should not serve the interest of party—save the "forward" party, to which all reflective men should belong; it should show that man is happiest when he is politically free and spiritually independent. The "philosophical" criterion is the most elusive, but broadly it meant that the historian should arrange the letters of fact into sentences that had a reassuring or illuminating message. He should enter a significant (i.e., civilized) age in the past, and should explain its significance by careful presentation and, where necessary, by comment. Referring to the praise lavished by Dr. Johnson on Knolles's *History of the Turks,* Gibbon remarked, "I much doubt whether a partial and verbose compilation from Latin writers, thirteen hundred folio pages of speeches and battles, can either instruct or amuse an enlightened age which requires from the historian some tincture of philosophy and criticism."

To English historians, brought up in a narrative tradition, however rambling, the philosophical element in enlightenment history presented a problem: Where did you put it? The yearning to expatiate on the facts, to pursue analogies outside the time sequence, and to bring in social and economic facts were already present in Bolingbroke's *Remarks on the History of England* (1730–31), but he was professedly commenting on a very few facts: it was different when you were trying to find room in a crowded political narrative. The problem was put well by Dugald Stewart in his *Life of Robertson* (1801). "It became fashionable," he noted, "after the example of Voltaire, to connect with the view of political transactions, an examination of their effects on the manners and condition of mankind, and to blend the lights of philosophy with the appropriate beauties of historical composition. In consequence of this innovation, while the province of the historian has been enlarged and dignified, the difficulty of his task has increased in the same proportion: reduced, as he must frequently be, to the alternative either of interrupting unseasonably the chain of events, or, by interweaving disquisition and narrative together, of sacrificing clearness to brevity." The fact that this aspect of the French Enlightenment did not come easily to the descendants of Camden can be seen in the rash of introductions and appendices which appeared in their works, and in the raising of footnotes, as in Gibbon, to the level of table talk. And we should not take the word "philosophical," as applied to Hume, Robertson, and Gibbon, too ponderously. Only Hume wrote as a philosopher with a theory about

man's psychology and his relation to society; with the others it seldom implies more than a thoughtful discursiveness, and sometimes less; when Edmund Burke congratulated Robertson by writing, "You have employed philosophy to judge manners, and from manners you have drawn new resources for philosophy," he only meant that Robertson had included more social history than was customary.

The "philosophical" element was both good and bad for the development of historical writing. It led to confidence; eighteenth-century historians looked on facts and authorities as rocks and sprang buoyantly from one to another. Their belief that history helped men to fuller and freer self-consciousness made them take the greatest pains with their style, so that they would be widely read. Their belief that they should write the history of civilization, not simply of politics, enabled the miscellaneous information about food and clothes and prices and social habits that Bolingbroke put in postscripts—and Hume in short appendices and Robertson in long ones—to become an essential ingredient in any general history and even to emerge in our own time as a rather dubious variety of history in its own right. On the other hand, it led to an impatience with exact scholarship, especially the criticism of sources, and with detail ("*ces malheureux détails,*" as Voltaire called them), while the interpretation of the past in the light of modern needs prevented the English Enlightenment historians from remembering how past the past really was.

They were still caught in the Renaissance dilemma: they wanted certainty but they neither cared for detail nor defined the nature of a fact; they wanted, passionately, to *explain*, and they had no adequate theory of causation. So they stuck to a mainly one-thing-after-another political narrative, and there was as wide a divergence between their theory and practice as between the *Advancement of Learning* and *Henry VII*. But their work was instinct with Enlightenment aspiration, even if they did not express it, and the aspiration turned Robertson from a worthy into an adventurous historian, encouraged Gibbon's wit to play through his erudition, and allowed Hume to move from philosophy to history without feeling that he was turning traitor on his first and deepest passion.

David Hume published the earlier part of his *Treatise of Human Nature* in 1739, his *Essays, Moral and Political* in 1741, and continued to write philosophy until the seventeen fifties, when he turned to history and published his *History of England*, between 1754 and 1761. Why did the foremost English philosopher of the eighteenth

century change his subject, and what happened to history in a philosopher's hands? His main interest as a philosopher was in human nature and the psychological laws that lay behind men's actions, but after a decade of reflection he had run out of material. As a none-too-well-off Scot, he found the opportunities for observing exceptional men were limited and, in any case, like many professed students of human nature, preferred to find his material in books. History was a means of extending his field of observation, and he had already used a desultory reading of the classical historians this way. It may have been, too, that ambition supported the change. His philosophical works had not been widely acclaimed and the public's appetite for indifferent histories suggested that they would offer an enthusiastic welcome to a good one. "There is no post of honour in the English Parnassus more vacant than that of history," he wrote to a friend. He was reflecting a common opinion. The partisan bias of Whig-Tory history was notorious. In 1711 a correspondent to the *Spectator* proposed forming a society for men with "a strong passion toward falsehood. . . . We might be called the *historians*, for *liar* is become a very harsh word." The negative qualities of history in England, its bias, its haphazard or mechanical arrangement, its carelessness of style were widely lamented, and in Edinburgh, as nowhere else in the British Isles, there was an awareness of the positive qualities in the history of the French Enlightenment. From 1752 Hume was keeper of the library of the faculty of Advocates there; it was the finest library in Scotland and contained the materials he needed for his design to restore history to the English Parnassus by combining the impartial scholarship of Camden (the last great historian, in his eyes) with the synthesizing energy of Voltaire.

Not, however, with the rationalism of Voltaire. Hume did not believe that man behaved in terms of reason alone. He was dominated by his passions, he was affected by the customs of society. The utility of history did not lie in castigating past errors and providing blueprints for the future, but in establishing psychological laws that would explain men's actions. It was an advantage to Hume as a philosopher, but a disadvantage to his history, that he thought men were at all times the same. "The same motives always produce the same actions," he wrote in *An Enquiry Concerning Human Understanding*; "the same events follow from the same causes. Ambition, avarice, self-love, vanity, friendship, generosity, public spirit: these passions, mixed in various degrees and distributed through society, have been, from the

beginning of the world, and still are, the source of all the actions and enterprises which have ever been observed among mankind. Would you know the sentiments, inclinations and course of life of the Greeks and Romans? Study well the temper and actions of the French and English: you cannot be mistaken in transferring to the former *most* of the observations which you have made with regard to the latter. Mankind is so much the same, in all times and places, that history informs us of nothing new or strange in this particular." And again, of history: "Its chief use is only to discover the constant and universal principles of human nature, by showing men in all varieties of circumstances and situations, and furnishing us with materials from which we may form our observations and become acquainted with the regular springs of human action and behaviour."

This concentration upon human nature led him to neglect periods like the Middle Ages, when human beings seemed two-dimensional and uninteresting, to play down any materialistic element in causation—climate, race, etc.—and to try to explain away, rather than to accept, religious conviction as a motive for men's actions. Luther, for instance, was an exception, and the historian is not interested in freaks. Hume did not collect spiritual phenomena any more than an entomologist chases after rabbits.

"Style, judgement, impartiality, care" were the qualities he aimed at. (The care did not extend to what he called "the dark industry" of original research, but it embraced novel subject matter—in the "social history" appendices—as well as handling printed materials with what was, for that time, a surprising caution and fairness.) They were qualities that brought him, at last, a wide public recognition. The Stuart volumes (1754 and '57) sold slowly, but as he went back to the Tudors (1759) and back further yet, with the volumes from Julius Caesar to Henry VII (1762), the demand grew, bringing him fame and a modest fortune. Edition followed edition; the *History* was continued by Smollett, it was continued again in 1834–35 by Thomas Hughes; it was bowdlerized for religious households and it was published in shortened forms for students. The editor of an edition in 1884 was the tough and erudite Tudor historian J. S. Brewer, and it is interesting to read his comment on the first modern history of England: "wherever there was *fair* evidence for Hume's statements, I have retained them, and still more frequently Hume's estimate of motives and characters, *when he had the facts* before him, because, though not

entirely free from prejudice, he had excellent good sense and sound judgement."

A measure of his freedom from partisan prejudice was the criticism he met from both sides, Whig and Tory. Whig history had been written to praise the constitution of 1688 and to blame the Stuarts for introducing a tyrannous parenthesis between liberty's infancy under the Tudors and its coming of age with the Glorious Revolution. The Tories denied that the Stuarts had perverted any legally consecrated freedoms inherent in the Tudor constitution; they believed that the "constitution" was no more than the way in which the country was governed at any one time under the leadership of a strong and divinely appointed king. This Whig point of view was not what has usefully come to be called "the Whig view of History," a tendency to stress in the past features still felt to be important in the present; it was rather the product of a specific attitude to the constitution. An extreme version was provided by Bolingbroke, who practiced Toryism in politics and Whiggery in his *Remarks on the History of England*. "The principles of the Saxon commonwealth," he asserted there, "were . . . very democratical; and these principles prevailed through all subsequent change." When these principles were changed it was the fault of the monarch and his court, "from whence it will follow that the great calamities which befell our country in the middle of the last century are unjustly charged on the spirit of Liberty, or on the nature of the British constitution of government."

Hume, as a man of the Enlightenment, was anticlerical, and the clerics in Scotland (as opposed to the parsons of England) were associated with Whiggery. This helped sustain his reluctance, as a historian, to accept the Whig thesis that parliament at the accession of James I represented something sacrosanct. For him constitutional "right" was based not on theory, especially not on legal archaeology which jumped from one favorable precedent to another—from Saxon "democracy" to the last parliaments of Elizabeth, via Magna Carta—but on what worked at a particular time and had the sanction of custom and authority. He saw the later Stuarts in an unfavorable light because they misused authority to flout custom, but as the constitution had been less settled in the reign of James I and Charles I they were not to be blamed too severely for trying to manipulate it. His natural skepticism about the probability of progress, and his interest in indi-

viduals rather than causes, led him to be a neutral. "Hume is really of both parties and of neither," as an acute critic has put it. "Toryism is evident in the defense of the Stuarts, the exaltation of tradition, the distrust of popular movements, the attack on the 'social contract.' Whiggism is evident in the reverence for liberty and toleration, the ridicule of the 'divine right of kings' and of 'passive obedience,' the distrust of oligarchy, the praise of the 'Glorious Revolution,' and the approbation of the commercial and industrial classes as the rulers of the state." [6] For all this six of one and half dozen of the other, Hume's history looked like Tory history, and he Toryized English historical attitudes until Macaulay's attempt to rebut his "vast mass of sophistry" nearly a century later.

His friend and fellow Scotsman, William Robertson, was neither a philosopher nor a historian who chose to find fame where controversy was hottest. A minister and the son of a minister, he lived a tranquil life of study and became Principal of Edinburgh University and Moderator of the General Assembly of the Church of Scotland. Yet, partly because he did not share the extrahistorical interests of Hume and was less volatile intellectually, he wrote better history and allowed French Enlightenment ideas to nourish his work more fruitfully. Englishmen, however, read English history, and Hume's work was read and debated long after his friend's histories of Scotland, Charles V, and America had been forgotten.

Robertson's view of history's proper subject matter was stated at the beginning of his *History of Scotland* (1759). Dividing Scottish history up to 1603 into four periods, he wrote:

> The first period is the region of pure fable and conjecture, and ought to be totally neglected, or abandoned to the industry and credulity of antiquarians. Truth begins to dawn in the second period, with a light, feeble at first, but gradually increasing, and the events which then happened may be slightly touched, but with no particular or laborious inquiry. In the third period, the history of Scotland, chiefly by means of records preserved in England, becomes more authentic: not only are events related, but their causes and effects explained; the characters of the actors are displayed; the manners of the age described; the revolution in the constitution pointed out: and here every Scotsman should begin not to read only, but to study

[6] E. C. Mossner. See introductory note, p. 142.

the history of his country. During the fourth period, the affairs of Scotland were so mingled with those of other nations . . . that its history becomes an object of attention to foreigners.

And later in the same work, he wrote that "to relate real occurrences, and to explain their real causes and effects is the historian's peculiar and only province."

When to this dislike of uncharted territory and this apparently unphilosophic aim, is added a shrinking from the "unpleasant task" of original research, one expects a series of pedestrian excursions along well-beaten tracks. But, in fact, Robertson had a thirst for out-of-the-way information akin to Gibbon's, and he is to be found sending to Vienna for copies of Mexican paintings, theorizing about the first settlement of America via the Bering Straits, and writing the first English contribution to the history of civilization in his stout introductory section *Charles V:* "A view of the progress of society in Europe from the subversion of the Roman Empire to the beginning of the sixteenth century." And all this in a prose which, for those who find Hume too colloquial, and Gibbon too exacting, is the supreme expression of eighteenth-century urbanity. "How could I suspect," wrote Horace Walpole to Robertson, on the publication of the *History of Scotland*, "that a man under forty, whose dialect I scarce understood . . . and who, I was told, had passed his life in a small living near Edinburgh—how could I suspect that he had not only written what all the world now allows to be the best modern history, but that he had written it in the purest English and with as much seeming knowledge of men and courts as if he had passed all his life in important embassies?" An even more striking compliment was Gibbon's comment on the same work. "The perfect composition, the nervous language, the well-turned periods of Dr Robertson, inflamed me to the ambitious hope that I might one day tread in his foot-steps."

There were two schools of historical writing in the eighteenth century: one of erudition, the other of interpretation. The *érudits* collected and published source materials and, especially in France, began to develop the art—by means of philology, palaeography, and archaeology—of cross-examining a document in order to check the reliability of its evidence. They were motivated by pure intellectual curiosity, though their choice of materials was influenced by religious controversy; it was, above all, the sources of early Christianity that were

studied. The interpreters, on the other hand, were interested in periods of achievement, not in origins, and were thus isolated from the *érudits* both in method and the periods studied. Only Gibbon, in studying the decline of Rome and the early Middle Ages, brought the two strands together. In his remarks about the relative importance of the various periods of Scottish history, Robertson had been following very closely the argument of the *Letters on the Study and Use of History* (1752), where Bolingbroke had said that it was mere antiquarianism to study a period before the political conditions in Europe were similar enough to contemporary times to be relevant to them. It was this argument that made him choose for his second work the age singled out by Bolingbroke as the beginning of modern times, the age of Charles V, when the politics of Europe were conducted in terms of a balance of power; and it was the consciousness of the utility of his subject that justified the medieval researches necessary for its prelude, the "View of the State of Europe."

The variety of subject matter in the "View," including religion, war, trade, law, customs, and government, and the care with which their interactions were examined, owed much to Voltaire. Referring to Voltaire's *Essai sur l'histoire générale*, Robertson acknowledged in the "Proofs and Illustrations," which supplemented the "View," that "I have often followed him as my guide in these researches; and he has not only pointed out the facts with respect to which it was important to inquire, but the conclusion which it was proper to draw from them." But he deplored Voltaire's failure to give references. Robertson wanted to contribute to literature, and to be easily read, but he combined this aim with a vision of research as a continuing process, and believed that it was his duty to enable others to carry on where he left off. So he became the pioneer of scholarly apparatus, providing bare references to his text and discussing problems of evidence and interpretation in the "Proofs and Illustrations," which equaled the "View" itself in bulk and amounted to the first English treatise on practical historical method.

It is not to be expected that Robertson should show much actual sympathy for his thousand-year prelude to modern times. He gives a remarkably solid and consistent explanation of how Europe groped its way back to respectability from barbarism, but he was Whiggish in the modern sense in his scorn of the blind alleys it explored en route. He deplored the wasted energies of scholars; "instead of cultivating those

arts which embellish human life, and render it comfortable, they were fettered by authority, they were led astray by example, and wasted the whole force of their genius in speculations as unavailing as they were difficult." However, he acknowledged the refining and progressive element in medieval religious life (including the development of canon law) more handsomely than other Enlightenment historians, and when he came to the Reformation he recognized that it was not just a question of more than half the world coming to its senses through a series of happy accidents.

In this way he outdistanced Voltaire and Hume, extending the techniques of synthesis and explanation he had learned in writing the "View" in a close analysis of the consequences of Spanish rule in the American colonies. For the charm and authority of its narrative, for the constant pressure of inquiry, and for its pioneering emphasis on the influence of geography, the *History of America* is the most interesting of all English Enlightenment contributions to modern history. It is not surprising that when Prescott was working on the same subject he noted in his journal: "Beware of Robertson. Never glance at him till after subject moulded in my mind and thrown into language."

At the present time there is a growing nostalgia among historians for the confidence and sense of purpose of Enlightenment history. More and more openly it is asked: "Why shouldn't we write history that is relevant to our age, selecting what time has shown to favor progress, and leaving blind alleys to the blind, with their specialized but restricted senses?" For such an attitude Robertson is the best and most reassuring model, but he also demonstrates one of its dangers. He had planned to include the history of British settlement in America. Then came the war of Independence. "I long flattered myself," he wrote, "that the war might terminate so favourably for Great Britain that I might go on with my work. But alas! America is now lost to the Empire and to me, and what would have been a good introduction to the settlement of British Colonies, will suit very ill the establishment of independent states." If history is planned exclusively to suit the present, it must run the risk of being overtaken by events.

While Robertson's books ranged the periphery of Englishmen's interest in history, Gibbon, like Hume, spoke to its center. The English were insular and patriotic, but they were educated through a classical curriculum. Nor did Gibbon ask for a suspension of disbelief; human nature was the same at all times, and no imaginative effort was re-

quired to understand the behavior of the Romans, no new set of values was needed to estimate the sorry history of Byzantium. And if Gibbon did not share the Enlightenment urge to explain events through the synthesizing of a great variety of subject matter, he gave the illusion that he did. There were enough asides and reflections in the course of his narrative to give it a "philosophic" cast.

The greatness of Gibbon's achievement depends on his choice of a subject that enabled him to deploy every one of his qualities of mind to the top of its bent; he could immerse himself in the past for long years without looking back to the present. He would have had no peace in writing as Hume did, "where every character is a problem, and every reader a friend or an enemy; where a writer is supposed to hang out a badge of party, and is devoted to the destruction of the opposite faction." But his achievement was due, too, to his method, and the way he set to work is a subject of perennial interest to any historian contemplating more than a slice of easy professionalism.

When—after considering and rejecting others—Gibbon had fixed on his subject, he conducted what G. M. Young has called "a reconnaissance in force, through the Imperial centuries and the Dark Ages up to the walls of Renaissance Rome." The whole was in his mind before he started to write, and every chapter, and every paragraph in every chapter, was considered with reference to the grand sweep of his theme. He was careful, however, not to complete his plan "prematurely," or to subordinate his reading too rigidly to it. "We must be careful," he noted, "not to make the order of our thoughts subservient to that of our subjects; this would be to sacrifice the principle to the accessory. The use of our reading is to aid us in thinking. The perusal of a particular work gives birth, perhaps, to ideas unconnected with the subject of which it treats. I wish to pursue these ideas; they withdraw me from my proposed plan of reading, and throw me into a new track, and from thence, perhaps, into a second, and a third. At length I begin to perceive whither my researches tend." Again, he describes in his *Autobiography* how before reading a book he called to mind the state of the subject with which it dealt and, as he went through it, constantly watched how it was supplementing his knowledge of the subject as a whole. In this way he was enabled to judge the value of a book and use it not merely to fill a notebook but to keep his mental horizon steadily expanding.

It was method that strengthened an already tenacious memory, but

he did make notes and, again, he tells to what use he put the cards on which they were written. He reviewed as many as would ballast a paragraph, and then, walking up and down his study (lined, thanks to a modest fortune, with nearly all the books he needed), he blocked the paragraph in his imagination, and only when its factual content had been absorbed in a general euphony would he write it down. It was some time before this method enabled him to compose fluently. He rewrote the first chapter twice, and the second and third once, before he could work steadily from paragraph to paragraph with little revision. As a result, though the *Decline and Fall* contains a staggering amount of factual information, it is expressed in the authentic tone of Gibbon's conversations with himself. In such circumstances, a man sets a high standard for his talk, and Gibbon's periods have an artifice missing from the speech which Robertson and Hume addressed more directly to the audience of their readers.

The *Decline and Fall* follows a straight narrative course for five centuries, then, after the reign of Heraclius, Gibbon turns his attention to Byzantium, Asia, and Africa in a series of long studies before he brings the threads together with the Crusades and the march of events to the fall of Constantinople. Finally, he surveys the fortunes of Rome through the Middle Ages. As far as originality of subject matter is concerned, the post-Heraclian period is the most impressive. This is the part of the work that led Carlyle to describe the work as "a kind of bridge that connects the ancient with the modern ages. And how gorgeously does it swing across the gloomy and tumultuous chasm of these barbarous centuries."

Gibbon, like his Scottish colleagues, had no taste for original research. He used only printed sources, and he did not scrutinize his authorities with the critical spirit of the French *érudits*. But he used *all* the sources and he read *all* the authorities. Where he can be faulted actually, it is for no sin of omission, but because little work had as yet been done by others; this is particularly true of his Asiatic and Byzantine sections. He could, it is true, be unfair. His refusal to see anything of value in the Byzantine Empire has been called "one of the most untrue, and most effective, judgements ever uttered by a thoughtful historian"; he did not appreciate the spiritual ferment that underlay the extension of Christianity; he can be accused of burking an exercise of the imagination for the sake of a good phrase when he writes of the Crusades, "I shall abridge the tedious and uniform narrative of

their blind achievements, which were performed by strength and are described by ignorance." Little touched by the optimistic belief in progress that could help Voltaire and Robertson recognize in the Middle Ages the promise of better things, he chose to see, as had his humanist predecessors, a steady decline from the peak of pre-Christian Rome. It suited neither his theme nor his temperament to end with a note of interrogation.

Though he wrote about the remote past, he did not avoid controversy, especially because of his skeptical treatment of Christianity and the way in which he yielded to the temptation to poke scabrous fun at it. "His ambition was to shine," wrote an anonymous contemporary, "and shine he will—but with a light like that which illumined Hell—with the double splendour of an Apostate and an Assassin." But while bigots continued to sulk, mere waverers were converted by the *Vindication*, in which he trounced those who had tried to convict him of errors or deliberate distortions of fact, and his work became an impressive popular success. He wrote to a friend that the first volume of the *Decline and Fall* "sold, according to the expression of the publisher, like a threepenny pamphlet on the affairs of the day . . . and I confess to you that so far as I am concerned I much like these praises. Those of women of condition, especially of young and pretty ones, without being of the greatest weight, do not fail to amuse me infinitely. I have had the good fortune to please these creatures, and the ancient history of your learned friend has succeeded like the novel of the day." This success grew from volume to volume, till the work had earned him some nine thousand pounds, and a reputation for wit and scholarship throughout Europe.

Gibbon wrote at the last minute in which it was possible to gain such a reputation by using Enlightenment methods. Romanticism was demanding a different sort of sympathetic involvement with the past, more concern with the common man and still wider subject matter. To Coleridge, the *Decline and Fall* was "an effective bar to all real familiarity with the temper of Imperial Rome." Evangelicism wanted a more positive understanding of medieval Christianity; the humanitarianism of Crabbe and Cowper was expressed in the work of antiquarian historians like Joseph Strutt, who wanted more information about how ordinary people had lived; Gothicists wanted to know more of the conditions in which their favorite art grew up; romantic nationalists wanted to know more about their countries' origins; bankers

wanted to know more about the origin of banks. The closed trunks in the Enlightenment attic were thrown open and their dusty contents shaken out: feudalism, chivalry, the friars, the Crusades, medieval literature (not yet medieval painting). Great men were out of favor. ". . . The arrangements and improvements which have taken place in human affairs result not from the efforts of individuals," wrote John Logan in his *Elements of the Philosophy of History* in 1781, "but from a movement of the whole society. . . . All that Legislators, Patriots, Philosophers, Statesmen and Kings can do, is to give a direction to that stream which is forever flowing," and in 1789 the traveler and agricultural economist Arthur Young complained from Florence that "to a mind that has the least turn after philosophical inquiry, reading modern history is generally the most tormenting employment that a man can have: one is plagued with the actions of a detestable set of men called conquerors, heroes, and great generals; and we wade through pages loaded with military details; but when you want to know the progress of agriculture, of commerce, and industry, their effect in different ages and nations on each other—the wealth that resulted—the division of that wealth—its employment—and the manners it produced—all is a blank. Voltaire set an example, but how has it been followed?"

The demand for more information about manners, trade, travel, arts, and sciences outstripped the supply. Once more historical theory and practice were out of step, but at least on this occasion the cry for new information was acted on with increasing method. In 1797 Sir Frederick Eden's *The State of the Poor* essayed a survey of poverty through the ages, and though his statement that he never wasted time looking for another word when he could use it to find another fact explains why he is dreary reading, the work of investigation was begun, and would in time be turned into literate history.

At the end of the eighteenth and at the beginning of the nineteenth centuries historians were still influenced by the laws of supply and demand. Historical studies did not center on the universities until after the middle of the nineteenth century, and only then did history begin to be written for a narrowing circle of professional colleagues. Before that, historians wanted to be popular. They spent great care in perfecting their style, and, as we have seen, Gibbon was not indifferent to his success among the fair sex. In the same spirit, Macaulay wrote to a friend: "I shall not be satisfied unless I produce something which

shall for a few days supersede the last fashionable novel on the tables of young ladies." The success of Hume, Robertson, and Gibbon had increased the demand for historical reading, but the demand had become more various than hitherto. The romantic audience wanted little more than time-traveling, to be transported backward in a historical capsule which would release them at some picturesque period in the past, where they could wander among the cottages of the poor and watch some unfortunate roasting for heresy. On the other hand, the disasters of the Napoleonic war, together with social unrest at home, led to a demand for a more relevant and reassuring history; "each age," as the *Edinburgh Review* put it, "has its appropriate wants, and some problem or other more peculiarly its own."

Amid so many calls for attention, one clue to the best road to follow was especially attractive to historians. This was the enormous success of the novels of Sir Walter Scott. Evidence of his influence on nineteenth-century historiography could be multiplied, but the witness of Carlyle, Macaulay, and Leopold von Ranke is enough to make it clear. "These historical novels," wrote Carlyle, "have taught all men this truth, which looks like a truism, yet was unknown to writers of history and others, till so taught: that the bygone ages of the world were actually filled by living men, not by protocols, state papers, controversies and abstractions of men." In his early essay on history, Macaulay claimed that if historians had read their sources with a true interest in human beings, "we should not then have to look for the wars and votes of the Puritans in Clarendon, and for their phraseology in *Old Mortality*; for one half of King James in Hume and for the other half in *The Fortunes of Nigel*." And Von Ranke acknowledged that "the romantic historical works of Sir Walter Scott, which were well known in all languages and to all nations, played a principal part in awakening my sympathy for the actions and passions of past ages."

Scott wrote some straightforward history, the *Life of Napoleon* (1827) and a *History of Scotland* (1830), but his influence did not come from these routine and hastily compiled works, but from the extraordinary panorama of British history deployed through his novels: the age of Richard I in *The Talisman* and *Ivanhoe,* of Richard III in *The Fair Maid of Perth*, of Mary Stuart in *The Monastery*, of Elizabeth in *Kenilworth,* of James I in *Nigel,* of the Commonwealth in *Woodstock*, of Charles II in *Peveril of the Peak*, of William III in *Old Mortality*, of George I in *Rob Roy*, George II in *Waverley*, and

George III in *Redgauntlet*. They contain mistakes of fact, they blend information from several periods into the portrait of one, but their general fidelity to the spirit and manner of the times they represent was backed by a formidable mass of miscellaneous learning and some downright scholarship. Scott had begun life with strong antiquarian interests, and a knowledge of Italian, Spanish, French, and German, with some Old Norse and Old English, enabled him to pursue them in a scholarly way. From the beginning he was fascinated by the information about the habits and attitudes of the past contained in early literature, especially ballad literature. His review of Ellis's *Specimens of Early English Metrical Romances* can be read as an introduction to his future career as a novelist.

> Since the attention of our antiquaries has been turned towards the metrical romances of England and Normandy, we have gained more insight into the domestic habits, language and character of our ancestors during the dark, warlike and romantic period of the middle ages, than Leland and Hearne were able to attain from all the dull and dreary monastic annals, which their industry collected, and their patience perused. In fact, to form a just idea of our ancient history, we cannot help thinking that these works of fancy should be read along with the labours of the professed historian. The one teaches what our ancestors thought; how they lived; upon what motives they acted, and what language they spoke; and having attained this intimate knowledge of their sentiments, manners and habits, we are certainly better prepared to learn from the other the actual particulars of their annals. From the romance, we learn what they were; from the history what they did; and were we to be deprived of one of these two kinds of information, it might well be made a question, which is most useful or interesting?

The process of putting these sentiments into action came when he was asked to complete a historical novel, *Queenhoo-Hall*. Two extracts will show from what bonds Scott was to liberate the seriously intended historical novel:

" 'By the soul of Saint Dunstan, I am not awaped, though the moor-cock crow so loudly!' " remarks one of his characters. " 'An' you take not good heed, goodman bell-swaggerer, I will crack a fool's costard before May-day be done.' "

" 'Certes,' quoth the damsel, courteseying as she received the money,

'this guerdon exceeds our poor deservings; the work, so please your ladyships, you deem so quaintly wrought, is purfled by one more couthful at the needle than we be.' "

Queenhoo-Hall was published in 1808. Commenting in 1829 on its lack of success, Scott observed that "when an author addresses himself exclusively to the Antiquary, he must be content to be dismissed by the general reader with the criticism of Mungo, in the *Padlock*, on the Mauritanian music, 'What signify me hear, if me no understand?' "

In general, Scott's attitude toward history follows that of the Enlightenment. He scorned "the repulsive dryness of mere antiquity," unanimated collections of obscure facts; he believed, with Hume, that "the passions . . . are generally the same in all ranks and conditions, all countries and ages"; and, though the manner is fictional, his description of a declining feudal economy in *The Bride of Lammermoor* and of the social background of the Jacobite-Hanoverian conflict in *Rob Roy* are composed according to the synthesizing methods of Robertson. What was new was the lesson that any age, even the Middle Ages, was interesting for its own sake, however little it had to offer the future, and more important still, the lesson that history involves an imaginative, as well as an intellectual, commitment to the past.

The color, the passion, the pathos with which Scott invested the past needed a corrective before a careful historian could accept it with an easy conscience. The corrective was provided by his contemporary Henry Hallam, and it was a combination of the shot silk of Scott and the linsey-woolsey of Hallam that produced the historical outlook of Macaulay. While accepting the prestige of Hallam among his contemporaries, and the extent to which he stood out among such admirable scholars as Sharon Turner, Palgrave, and Lingard, it must be admitted that his fame is usually taken on trust: he is not a historian who is willingly read. Robertson strove to attract his readers by exalting the dignity of history in style and subject matter, but Hallam achieved, without trying, a dignity that disgusts. Here—to dispose of this topic as quickly as possible—is Hallam on Chaucer: "As the first original English poet, if we except Langland, as the inventor of our most approved measure, as an improver, though with too much innovation of our language, and as a faithful witness to the manners of his age, Chaucer would deserve our reverence, if he had not also intrinsic claims for excellencies, which do not depend upon any collateral considerations." There is an occasional light relief as when, in a

footnote, he compares an antiquary's estimate of Roger Bacon to "an oyster judging of a line-of-battle ship," but all too often Hallam's prose verges on the intimidating.

Hallam was a precociously intelligent child, born in easy circumstances, and the course of his career as lawyer and private scholar is as much in contrast with the heroic and pathetic struggles of Scott as is his prose. He produced three works, each of which cost him some ten years of steady preparation: *A View of the State of Europe during the Middle Ages* (1818), *The Constitutional History of England from the Accession of Henry VII to the Death of George II* (1827), and *An Introduction to the Literature of Europe during the Fifteenth, Sixteenth and Seventeenth Centuries* (1837–39). Of these the first two deserve to be called great historical works: great in conception, great in execution, great in influence. The *View* covered a thousand years, from Clovis to the Italian wars of Charles VIII, and in describing the political development, one by one, of the European states, Hallam indicated the possibility of comparative institutional history without actually attempting it himself, and in the lengthy concluding section—"On the state of society in Europe during the Middle Ages"—he moved considerably further than had Robertson in the direction of the matured *Kulturgeschichte* of Burckhardt. Hallam is the first great English medieval historian, yet he had no affection for the Middle Ages; they represented little more than a corpse whose dissection was a necessary stage in understanding the functions of a living body. His approach was still that of the Enlightenment; he judged the Middle Ages by the standards of his own day, and made no attempt to involve himself in the thought processes of the past. Here is Robertson: "The Spaniards had hardly taken possession of America, when, with a most preposterous policy, they began to erect convents, where persons of both sexes were shut up, under a vow to defeat the purpose of nature, and to counteract the first of her laws." Here is Hallam: "Usury, or lending money for profit, was treated as a crime by the theologians of the middle ages; and though the superstition has been eradicated, some part of the prejudice remains in our legislation." The tone is the same: external and patronizing. Yet Hallam's curiosity is insatiable, and it is never merely descriptive: his facts are always subordinated to a desire to show his reader what the past was like as a whole. He does not amputate a particular limb and show it to his students in an access of professional glee; he methodically flays the entire body. He

deplores the lack of teaching aids and does his best to provide them. "No chapter in the history of national manners"—he writes in the "State of Society"—"would illustrate so well, if duly executed, the progress of social life, as that dedicated to domestic architecture. The fashions of dress and of amusements are generally capricious and irreducible to rule; but every change in the dwellings of mankind, from the rudest wooden cabin to the stately mansion, has been dictated by some principle of convenience, neatness, comfort, or magnificence. Yet this most interesting field of research has been less beaten by our antiquaries than others comparatively barren." He then provides a connected account of the development of domestic, including farmhouse, architecture, which has considerable pioneering importance. He has no more interest in the question "What is a fact?" than his predecessors had; he is as indifferent to the development of source criticism on the continent as they had been; but he develops their search for cause and effect to such an extent that his acceptance of certain events, like the development of the mariner's compass, or the invention of printing, as historical "accidents" comes as something of a shock.

If the *View* provided the first detailed survey of the Middle Ages, his *Constitutional History* set for his readers a new standard of impartiality in the writing of modern history; Macaulay called it the most impartial book he had ever read. It extended the survey of the medieval constitution which had formed a long section of the *View*, and though it can be labeled "Whig," this tone emerges from the most thoughtful and well-informed survey to which any period of English history had been subjected. It came near to freeing constitutional history from party history, and set a new standard of scholarship and objectivity for English history as a whole.

Before objectivity could become a habit, there erupted on to the historiographical scene the most passionately subjective of all English historians, Thomas Carlyle. The needs of Carlyle's personality took him far beyond a mere extension of prevailing rationalist or romantic attitudes toward history. The list of the influences which shaped his historical approach are many. He acknowledged his debt to Scott and the doubts he threw on the Enlightenment formula that history was "philosophy teaching through examples." After Scott, he wrote, historians must search for "direct inspection and embodiment: this, and this only, will be counted experience; and till once experience have got in, philosophy will reconcile herself to wait at the door." He inherited Hume's

skeptical attitude toward the idea of progress and his emphasis on men's passions rather than on their reason; his attention was drawn to the cautious and critical use of evidence by Von Ranke and the great German classical historian Niebuhr. On the other hand, he followed the Enlightenment's stress on a wider subject matter and on studying phenomena that were important to the present. But lessons that might simply have added layers of sophistication to the historical instincts of a less volatile man transformed the very core of Carlyle's. He wished history to reveal *all,* to show man what he was and what God wanted of him. He rejoiced at each lesson that showed how history's domain could be extended; each warning of its limitations fell on raw nerves. How he hated the commonplace assumption that men read history to find out about human nature! When men don't know themselves, don't really know their most intimate friends, what cant to think that they can discover truth in the maimed records of the past! "History is the essence of innumerable biographies," he wrote—but this was not a manifesto for the historical work that lay ahead of him, it was a cry of disgust at the subject's limitations. "But if one Biography," he went on, "nay our own Biography, study and recapitulate it as we may, remain in so many points unintelligible to us; how much more must those millions, the very fact of which, to say nothing of the purport of them, we know not, and cannot know!"

Carlyle's feeling for history was like that of a miser stumbling on a mass of coin but with only two hands to grasp, two pockets to carry; or like a dying man's sudden vision of a project that will take fifty years to put into effect. The pity of it! And the stupid pride of those who will not recognize it. The past is in ruins, a wilderness of stumps and fragments. We hear a call or a scream, but we lose a thousand murmurs. "When the oak-tree is felled, the whole forest echoes with it: but a hundred acorns are planted silently by the same unnoticed breeze." And when a fact survives, what does it mean? Three men described a brawl beneath Sir Walter Raleigh's prison window; all three described it differently, and his own version was different from theirs. Most is lost, what remains is dark. He damns the Enlightenment in a single sneer: "So imperfect is that same experience, by which Philosophy is to teach."

And if we venture into that landscape and try to reconstruct its original form—as we must, for the past is "the true fountain of knowledge; by whose light alone [no Macaulayan sensitivity to meta-

phors about Carlyle], consciously or unconciously employed, can the Present and the Future be interpreted or guessed at"—how do we write it down? Facts have three dimensions, the act of writing only one. "Narrative is *linear,* Action is *solid.* Alas for our 'chains' or chainlets, of 'causes and effects,' which we so assiduously track through certain handsbreadths of years and square miles, when the whole is a broad, deep Immensity, and each atom is 'chained' and complected with all!"

No major historian had looked so long or with such anguish at the nature of history or the problem of writing it. But what he saw was not entirely without hope. Though much had gone, something remained, and imagination could quicken it. And some clue as to how this could be done was offered by two Germans whose works he knew well: Schiller and Herder. The dramatic intensity of Schiller, and his bold handling of the masses as literally masses in the pictorial sense, showed the effectiveness of an emotional approach which generalized from the facts available, as an ancient chariot can be reconstructed from a hub and a shaft and driven with something like its original swiftness. From Herder's *Ideen zur Philosophie der Geschichte der Menschheit* (1784–91) he took the notion of a people being formed of all the influences playing on them, a notion which allowed a national psyche, or the *Zeitgeist,* to be invoked to give the historian a sense of direction when the evidence failed him. But most essential was his development of what he admired in Scott; the historian must see, and feel, before he can portray; see everything and feel for all men, and sense too, that spirit of the times his characters themselves could not see, and did not know they felt. History, he wrote to John Stuart Mill, "is an address (literally out of Heaven, for did not God order it all?) to our *whole* inner man; to every faculty of Head and Heart, from the deepest to the slightest; there is no end to such purposes; none to one's amazement and contemplation over it. Now for *all* such purposes, high, low, ephemeral, eternal, the first indispensable condition, is that we *see* the things transacted, picture them wholly as if they stand before our eyes."

He saw history as a miraculous icon. It taught no cut-and-dried lesson, but it was created by God, and its contemplation deepened an awareness of God. And the image that best stirred a sense of awe and wonder was of a moment when a society was at the point of deepest ferment, when its spokesmen were no longer isolated warriors or prophets, but the people as a whole.

This feeling that the spirit of a people could best be apprehended

at a moment of crisis, of *ad hoc* decisions, of impulse rather than reflection, freed Carlyle from the cause-and-effect narration which he distrusted; and because a mob, a whole people, acts, as he thought, with a shared divine possession, the poverty of the facts mattered less; a little information here, a little there, could be used as representative of the whole. This is what gave him confidence to begin *The French Revolution*. There are plenty of footnotes in the work, but the number of books he read would have served only as a preliminary investigation for Robertson or Hallam. In the Appendix to his *Lectures on the French Revolution* Lord Acton remarked of Carlyle that "the mystery of investigation had not been revealed to him when he began his most famous book. He was scared from the Museum by an offender who sneezed in the Reading Room . . . the usual modest resources of a private collection satisfied his requirements." And as a result, he concludes, Carlyle's volumes "remain one of those disappointing storm-clouds that give out more thunder than lighting."

Carlyle used his reading to support him as, by a violent effort of the will and imagination, he identified himself with the past. As with Gibbon—but with what a startling difference of effect—he kept his knowledge not only in notebooks but in his head. His aim, he said, was "to keep the whole matter simmering in the living mind and memory rather than laid up in paper bundles or otherwise laid up in an inert way. . . . Only what you *have living* in your own memory and heart is worth putting down to be printed; this alone has much chance to get into the living heart and memory of other men." This was his aim: to create the whirlwind, force men's attention to it, and then speak to them from its midst. "As an actually existing Son of Time," he said on one such occasion, "look, with unspeakable manifold interest, oftenest in silence, at what the Time did bring." And having lived each several part of the events he describes, having watched at the guillotine, waited on street corners, screamed with the mob, sat trembling with the court at Versailles, and all this without real knowledge of the background, the why and wherefore of these events, improvising and striving to be true to the brief scenario of his reading, like a *commedia dell' arte* actor to his plot, when it was over, he told his wife, in anger at the toll this wretched, sacred craft had taken of him, "I know not whether this book is worth anything, nor what the world will do with it; but there has been nothing for a hundred years that comes more direct and flamingly from the heart of a living man."

In later years, his love-hate relationship with history became less tense. In the *Life and Letters of Oliver Cromwell* (1845) and *Frederick the Great* (1857–65) a wider reading left less space for improvisation, as did his growing confidence that great, well-documented men can be used as representative of the spirit of their age. But it is for his early, most emotional book that he will be remembered; it was with the *French Revolution* that he rose to share with Macaulay the admiration of the history-reading public until the shades of the university began to fall around a history that was poignantly felt and idiosyncratically written.

If no English historian has depended so much on instinct as did Carlyle in writing the *French Revolution*, none has so depended on calculated literary effect than did Macaulay in writing his *History of England from the Accession of James II.* Not even Gibbon. Gibbon lavished much care on making his style true to himself, to his own highly refined version of a manner accepted in a small cultivated circle. Macaulay took pains to appeal to the reading public as a whole; his criterion was not, What will satisfy me? but, What will please them?

Macaulay

This preoccupation with presentation dates from his youthful essay on History (1828). He surveys the course of English historiography from Hume to the present and finds little to praise, nothing unreservedly to admire: "We are acquainted with no history which approaches to our notion of what a history ought to be." Hume, Gibbon, and the rest had all been "seduced from truth, not by their imagination, but by their reason." They had taken sides, they had omitted aspects of the past which would have qualified the implications of the subject matter which they did exploit. "A history in which every particular incident may be true may on the whole be false. The circumstances which have the most influence on the happiness of mankind, the changes of manners and morals, the transition of communities from poverty to wealth, from knowledge to ignorance, from ferocity to humanity—these are, for the most part, noiseless revolutions." Yet without their presence, the history of statecraft and war cannot be true to the past. "The perfect historian is he in whose work the character and spirit of an age is exhibited in miniature. . . . He shows us the court, the camp, and the senate. But he shows us also the nation. He considers no anecdote, no peculiarity of manner, no familiar saying, as too insignificant for his notice which is not too insignificant to illustrate the operation of laws, of religion, and of education, and to mark the

progress of the human mind. Men will not merely be described, but will be made ultimately known to us." He concludes: "A historian, such as we have been attempting to describe, would indeed be an intellectual prodigy." It is not impossible that Macaulay, whose early precocity had made him something of an infant prodigy, already thought he had it in him to be such a historian.

Certainly this ideal picture of the historian's subject matter was one he tried to realize in his long essays for the *Edinburgh Review* and later in his *History*. He developed the theme in his essay on Hallam a few months later, repeating that "good historians, in the proper sense of the word, we have not. But we have good historical romances and good historical essays." The ideal would be a blend of Scott and Hallam, of Scott so that the reader could see the past, of Hallam so that he could think about it. Both Carlyle and Macaulay drew, then, the same moral from Scott, but while Carlyle was led to ask, What is the past? How do you leap back there? Macaulay, keeping the Scott-Hallam balance more firmly poised, and untroubled by the void spaces that so distressed Carlyle, asked, "How do I bring forward the past for the inspection of the present, so that men can be amused by the picture and thoughtfully compare it with the features of their own age?" Macaulay did visit the past mentally, but as the ideal traveler he describes in his essay on History, who does not only go to court but to the coffeehouses, who listens to the accent of the butcher and baker as well as to philosophers and statesmen; he wished to understand it, but not to identify himself with it with the almost trance-like intensity of Carlyle.

He began work on the *History* in 1841, and his letters and journals show him at work. He must write so that he will be read. "How little the all-important art of making meaning pellucid is studied now! Hardly any popular writer, except myself, thinks of it." He aimed to combine color with clarity, to combine a mass of allusion and imagery with rapid comprehensibility. "My account of the Highlands," he wrote in July, 1850, "is getting tolerable shape. Tomorrow I shall begin to transcribe again, and to polish. What trouble these few pages will have cost me! The great object is that, after all this trouble, they may read as if they had been spoken off, and may seem to flow as easily as table-talk." He thought that every aspect of historical writing needed improving: narrative, transition from one scene, or one topic, to another, analysis; he labored to correct them all. And every effort was successful;

his narrative combines pace with a glamorous freight of literary device, it turns from scene to scene without any preliminary clearing of the throat or shuffling of notes; his analysis of the state of parties, or of public opinion, combines an impression of thoughtful completeness with immediacy. The problem of summing up attitudes had been approached in antiquity and in the Renaissance through the device of the imaginary speech, which drew together various points of view. Macaulay adopted a halfway measure: a synopsis of views, which he termed the declamatory disquisition. "The declamatory disquisition which I have substituted for the orations of the ancient historians," he noted in his journal, "seems to me likely to answer. It is a sort of composition which suits my style, and will probably take with the public." The extent to which his pains did take was shown by sales which soared above those of the works of any previous historian and made him a rich man. Nor did he spare pains in collecting material. He describes his approach to the reign of William III:

> I will first set myself to know the whole subject; to get, by reading and travelling, a full acquaintance with William's reign; I reckon that it will take me eighteen months to do this. I must visit Holland, Belgium, Scotland, Ireland, France. The Dutch archives and French archives must be ransacked. I will see whether anything is to be got from other diplomatic collections. I must see Londonderry, the Boyne, Aghrim, Limerick, Kinsale, Namur again, Landen, Steinkirk. I must turn over hundreds, thousands, of pamphlets. Lambeth, the Bodleian and the other Oxford libraries, the Devonshire Papers, the British Museum, must be explored, and notes made: and then I shall go to work. When the materials are ready, and the History mapped out in my mind, I ought easily to write on an average two of my pages daily. In two years from the time I begin writing I shall have more than finished my second part. Then I reckon a year for polishing, retouching, and printing.

No historian had used so much miscellaneous information from plays, pamphlets, broadsheets, songs, or memoirs before, but if Macaulay was cautious about the reliability of some of his sources, he was not touched by the spirit of painstaking source criticism that was rising like a dye through historical work on the continent, and through the books of English historians of antiquity like Thomas Arnold and George Grote, his contemporaries. Macaulay's salient characteristic

was confidence; he knew that if he appeared to distrust his sources his audience would distrust him. He had not been twice a Member of Parliament for nothing. The same confidence marked the judgments he passed on the characters in his *History*. While not crudely black and white, they extinguish the possibility of appeal. It is for faults of interpretation that Macaulay has been most severely castigated, not for factual errors, and the explanation lies in the precocity with which he judged men when he had first read about them, and the extent to which his opinion hardened while dealing with them in the sometimes slapdash course of his journalistic career. It has been said that Macaulay found the historical essay brick, and left it marble; certainly his work for the *Edinburgh Review* petrified many of his opinions. His amazing memory, on which he greatly relied, brought into his *History* not only information gleaned in his youth, but judgments passed there. Nor was Macaulay made cautious, as Robertson had been, by any vision of history as a subject which was constantly developing. He transformed it from brick into marble and thought it would keep its shape; he did not see his judgments as interim judgments, or his evidence as capable of extension.

The aspect of his confidence which has caused most offense is the assumption that Britain in the mid-nineteenth century was in every sense a better place than it had been at any time in the past. After warning his readers at the beginning of the *History* that he would have to recount disasters and follies, as well as triumphs, he reassured them, for "unless I greatly deceive myself, the general effect of this chequered narrative will be to excite thankfulness in all religious minds, and hope in the breasts of all patriots. For the history of our country during the last hundred and sixty years is eminently the history of physical, of moral, and of intellectual improvement." And he continued, at regular intervals, to jog his reader into a flutter of pride at his own good fortune. Speaking of Manchester, in the celebrated survey of England in the third chapter, he remarks, "That wonderful emporium, which in population and wealth far surpasses capitals so much renowned as Berlin, Madrid, and Lisbon, was then a mean and ill built market town, containing under six thousand people. It then had not a single press. It now supports a hundred printing establishments. It then had not a single coach. It now supports twenty coachmakers." It may be that there is vulgarity here, a tendency to crow over the past rather than to illuminate it by contrast, but in general, Macaulay's manner

was a perfectly legitimate blend of cajolery and shock. Without confidence in our own society, we may find the "look here upon this picture, and on this" technique crude, but it did involve his readers in history, and it did sharpen their mental picture of the past. Even Tory Hume, skeptical of progress as he was, wrote that the English people ought to cherish "that noble liberty, that sweet equality, and that happy security, by which they are at present distinguished above all nations in the universe." Even dour and impartial Hallam looked on "the long and uninterruptedly increasing prosperity of England as the most beautiful phenomenon in the history of mankind." When he was working on the second volume of the *History* at the end of 1848, the year of revolutions in the rest of Europe, Macaulay reminded his readers of their own comparative tranquillity: "And, if it be asked, what has made us to differ from others, the answer is that we never lost what others are wildly and blindly seeking to regain. It is because we had a preserving revolution in the seventeenth century that we have not had a destroying revolution in the nineteenth." We may censure this confidence on personal grounds, because we don't like its tone—too brash, too intolerant—but it can only be censured on historical grounds if it perverted his judgment of the past and made him unduly selective in his treatment of affairs. Neither of these objections can be sustained to a really damaging degree. His acts of injustice to some of his characters were based on their behavior as individuals rather than as supporters or opponents of the principles of 1688, and while he neglected certain aspects of the national life, he greatly increased the wealth of detail with which it was henceforward to be described. The most pertinent criticism of his constant reference to the present would be this: that it obscured the extent to which development was taking place throughout the period with which he dealt. It is possible to shrink from Macaulay the Whig while admiring the Whiggery of his historical method. "He remains to me," Lord Acton said, "one of the greatest of all writers and masters, although I think him utterly base, contemptible and odious for certain reasons."

While Hallam, Carlyle, and Macaulay were in the heyday of their reputation and Englishmen were congratulating themselves on being a historical nation, there appeared an iconoclast of what seemed a particularly shocking sort. Historians, he claimed, had enlarged their subject matter, but to a pitifully small degree; they had generalized a little more than in the past, but with what timidity!

> In all the other great fields of inquiry, the necessity of generalization is universally admitted, and noble efforts are being made to rise from particular facts in order to discover the laws by which those facts are governed. So far, however, is this from being the usual course of historians, that among them a strange idea prevails, that their business is merely to relate events, which they may occasionally enliven by such moral and political reflections as seem likely to be useful. According to this scheme, any author who from indolence of thought, or from natural incapacity, is unfit to deal with the highest branches of knowledge, has only to pass some years in reading a certain number of books, and then he is qualified to be an historian.

And again, "The most celebrated historians are manifestly inferior to the most successful cultivators of physical science." The iconoclast was Henry Thomas Buckle, and this challenge to the panjandrums of his subject was made in volume one of his *History of Civilization in England* (1857).

Buckle is a sport in the development of English historiography. He had no native predecessor, and no disciple. A gifted linguist, an omnivorous reader, he had been forcibly impressed by the positivist philosophy of Auguste Comte, and resolved to write the first history of English civilization that would really discover the principles that underlay its development. It would not be based on great political or military leaders—they and their deeds did little more than ruffle the surface of events; it would not give weight to religious leaders, for morals remained static: only intellect advanced; it would deal with men in the mass, how they were shaped by climate, geography, and diet into becoming intelligent beings, and how they in turn, by the use of intelligence, gradually came to exploit the world about them. It would, then, by deducing the fixed laws that determine human actions, help men to progress still further. Unfortunately, because of the stupidity of historians, the materials from which the science of man was to be constructed had been so neglected "that whoever now attempts to generalize historical phenomena must collect the facts, as well as conduct the generalization." In consequence of his labor, however, he hoped "to accomplish for the history of man something equivalent, or at all events analogous, to what has been effected by other inquiries for the different branches of natural science."

From his study in mid-nineteenth-century London, Buckle not only poured scorn on his fellow historians but he reached toward a materialism that found little echo in England until the present century, and a sociological technique that historians have not adopted even today. And he did it with a clumsy eagerness that enabled those who recoiled in horror from his attempt to explain men by statistics to cover themselves by poking fun at him. "Rejecting the metaphysical dogma of free will," he wrote, "and the theological dogma of predestined events, we are driven to the conclusion that the actions of men, being determined solely by their antecedents, must have a character of uniformity." And as evidence he quoted—amongst much else—statistics that showed in any year there were roughly the same number of suicides, marriages, and letters sent undirected: "so that for each successive period we can actually fortell the number of persons whose memory will fail them in regard to this trifling and, as it might appear, accidental occurrence." It was bad enough for a man to be told that his inclination to marry was influenced by the price of corn, but when he was told that he would learn more about morals from the law of averages than from Shakespeare and Homer, and that his religious sense was determined by the number of earthquakes and volcanoes in his vicinity, he was not surprised to hear Buckle denounced from the pulpit and hounded by university historians in holy orders. What of conscience? Of free will? Of the subjective elements in choice? All, according to Buckle, could be explained if all were known. And much could be known, if only historians and moralists had spent more time collecting statistics and less in parroting the truisms of their trades.

The young Acton concluded a savage review of Buckle in *The Rambler* (1858) by saying that "in his laborious endeavour to degrade the history of mankind, and of the dealings of God with man, to the level of the natural sciences, he has stripped it of its philosophical, of its divine, and even of its human character and interest." Buckle was lampooned by John Phillimore:

> This is the creed, let no man chuckle,
> Of the great thinker, Henry Buckle:
> I believe in fire and water,
> And in fate, dame Nature's daughter;
> I believe in steam and rice.
> Not in virtue or in vice (*and so on*).

Macaulay was against him; so was Carlyle, so was Froude, so was Stubbs.

Buckle was certainly vulnerable. Amidst the horror and the mockery that greeted his work there were calmer and graver criticisms. While in theory *against* the special contributions which great men could make to the development of society, Buckle devoted much attention to them. While preaching an all-inclusive mechanical causality, he admitted the role of the accidental. His claim that history demonstrated "one glorious principle of undeviating regularity" was blindly sweeping, and he invited the sort of answer given in 1859 by the shrewdest of his critics, the Oxford professor Goldwin Smith: "History cannot furnish its own inductive laws: an induction to be sound must take in, actually, or virtually, all the facts. But history is unlike all other studies in this, that she never can have, actually or virtually, all the facts before her. Moreover history, unlike the sciences, dare not predict."

It was not the least of the services of Buckle's *History* to force historians to prepare their armory for the question that was later to be asked with increasing insistence: Is history a science? Buckle's plea that historians should look to neighbor fields of study, especially what came to be called the social sciences, went unheeded, but he forced them to take stock of the possibilities and limits of their subject, as Goldwin Smith did, in a way which anticipates with curious closeness some of the arguments in recent discussions. Much that long seemed dead in Buckle now leaps to the eye with an odd sense of familiarity. Speaking of science on the one hand, and the humanities on the other, he wrote:

> There has arisen an unnatural separation of the two great departments of inquiry; the study of the internal and of the external: and although, in the present state of European literature, there are some unmistakable symptoms of a desire to break down this artificial barrier, still it must be admitted that as yet nothing has been actually accomplished towards effecting so great an end. The moralists, the theologians, and the metaphysicians continue to prosecute their studies without much respect for what they deem the inferior labours of scientific men; whose inquiries, indeed, they frequently attack, as dangerous to the interests of religion, and as inspiring us with an undue confidence in the resources of the human understand-

ing. On the other hand, the cultivators of physical science, conscious that they are an advancing body, are naturally proud of their own success; and, contrasting their discoveries with the more stationary position of their opponents, are led to despise pursuits the barrenness of which has now become notorious."

It is to be hoped that the future historian of the Two Cultures controversy will pay some tribute to its founding father.

Two years after Buckle's death, James Anthony Froude, then the most popular historian in England, lectured at the Royal Institution on "The Science of History," and paid a tribute to "the eminent person whose name is connected with this way of looking at History" before settling down to the task of demolishing his theories. Froude's own attitude toward history was influenced by three men—they make a beguiling juxtaposition—Carlyle, Buckle, and Shakespeare. His relation with Carlyle was close. Carlyle read the proofs of the first volumes of his *History of England from the Fall of Wolsey to the Defeat of the Spanish Armada,* and Froude remained a constant disciple and became his literary executor and biographer. From Carlyle he learned to resent the fragmentary, disconnected nature of the past, which made history "like a child's box of letters, with which we can spell any word we please," and the little trust that could be put in historians: "Read Macaulay on the condition of the English poor before the last century or two, and you wonder how they lived at all. Read Cobbett, and I may say Hallam, and you wonder how they endure the contrast between their past prosperity and their present misery." Buckle's influence was also a negative one. Froude revolted against a mechanistic interpretation which would rob men of their own volition. There must be free choice, or it would make nonsense of the standards by which we praise men or blame them. Men are not masses, analyzable in terms of statistical norms; they are an aggregation of individuals, and history is the record of individual actions. Philosophers of history became anathema to him. "Hegel falls out of date, Schlegel falls out of date, and Comte in good time will fall out of date." In a later lecture he declared, "I object to all historical theories. I object to them as calculated to vitiate the observation of facts."

If a man wants to write history, but distrusts the historical record, and cannot accept any "philosophical" aid in arranging the facts and bridging the lacunae between them (for "a history is durable or perish-

able as it contains less or more of the writer's own speculations"), what is he to do? Froude found encouragement in Shakespeare's history plays, where, he claimed, "the most perfect English history which exists is to be found." By this he meant that Shakespeare kept near to the facts as he found them, letting the characters speak as the chronicles said they had spoken, and did not try to moralize or philosophize about the deeds he was narrating. He invented, of course. Eastcheap was introduced to give body to the statement that Henry V had lived among loose companions in his youth, but his invention took the form of ornament, not commentary. "The greatness of the poet," he told his audience at the Royal Institution, "depends on his being true to nature, without insisting that nature shall theorise with him, without making her more just, more philosophical, more moral than reality; and, in difficult matters, leaving much to reflection which cannot be explained. . . . May we not thus learn something of what history should be, and in what sense it should aspire to teach?"

What it taught was that men's lives were a battlefield of right and wrong, and that eventually right triumphed; from history men learned to love the noble and hate the base. If a subject could be found, then, that would show right battling with, and in a conquest of Titans overcoming, wrong, and also be rich in the verbatim accents of its protagonists, then the criteria of great drama and high purpose would be fulfilled. Such a subject Froude found in the history of England from the destruction of Romish error to the scattering of a Romish fleet and the death of a triumphant Protestant Queen. So began a work that held its own in sales even with the later volumes of Macaulay's *History*, and from the Reformation volumes of 1856 proceeded with two volumes each in 1858, 1860, 1863, and 1866 to 1870, when, overwhelmed by his material, he ended with the Armada.

It is very rare, as we have seen, for a historian to write a book which actually conforms to his statements about what a history should be. Froude is no exception. In a lecture "On the Means of teaching English History" he used Hume as a whipping boy for the theme that a historian should not write about what he cannot intuitively sympathize with; yet the Catholics in his *History* got as short shrift as Hume gave John Knox, and his growing dislike for Elizabeth led to his bringing Burghley forward as the true architect of Elizabethan greatness. He protested against the way historians had concentrated on major figures, giving the impression that the history of a country

was the history of its kings, and that the people themselves had no existence worth recording; yet in J. R. Green's view, Froude's great fault was that "in a history of England he had omitted the English people." He repeated his view that "the better people know things the less they have views about them. The thing itself was the true object of knowledge, and the mind rests in that." Yet his mind rested on Henry VIII and subjected him to such a whitewashing that even the Protestants, as Leslie Stephen recorded, "refused to accept such a champion, and the burly figure looked awkward in wings and a white robe." Carlyle had written on an early draft of the *History:* "The rule throughout is, that *events* should speak. Commentary ought to be sparing: clear insight, definite conviction, brought about with a *minimum* of Commentary: that is always the *Art* of history." Both he and Froude believed that events might be put in an ornamental frame, in the Shakespearean sense, but this advice, echoed and echoed again by Froude, did imply a strict impartiality. Yet Froude came to tug the "definite conviction" so far out of context that by 1891, when he published *The Divorce of Catherine of Aragon,* he could state, "I do not pretend to impartiality. I believe the Reformation to have been the greatest incident in English history; the root and source of the expansive force which has spread the Anglo-Saxon race over the globe, and imprinted the English genius and character on the constitution of mankind," and admit that "something of ourselves must always be intermixed before knowledge can reach us."

The admission is perfectly consistent with his earlier revulsion from a science of history. It would be universally endorsed today; the interest lies in his tardy recognition that not only is history not a science, but the use of historical evidence cannot be scientific. In the post-Buckle period there was much discussion of these two concepts, and much confusion between them. German scholarship and the work of Stubbs and the record editors seemed to suggest that historians could hate Buckle and still catch a little glamour from the sciences through their use of evidence, but well before Acton's successor J. A. Bury pronounced in his Cambridge inaugural lecture in 1903 that history was "a science, no more and no less," the issue had been decided against him in the hearts of thoughtful historians, and its repeated proppings up and knockings down up to the present day have become the dreariest, and the most mechanical, item of historical apologetics.

Ironically, Froude's use of evidence did in a sense become more

scientific as his narrative proceeded. He relied increasingly on source materials and on growing supplies of them. He worked prodigiously in the public records (then in the Rolls House) and the British Museum, and among the Spanish archives in Simancas. It has been said that probably no previous historical work incorporated so much new material. Unfortunately he printed some of it inaccurately. H. A. L. Fisher, a wiser and wittier man than Froude, though his inferior as a historian, went so far as to accuse him of being constitutionally inaccurate. "Writing, for instance, of Adelaide, in Australia, he says:—'Seven miles away we saw below us, in a basin with a river winding through it, a city of 150,000 inhabitants, not one of whom has known, or will ever know, one moment's anxiety as to the recurring regularity of his three meals a day.' Adelaide is on high ground, not in a valley: there is no river running through it; its population was not more than 75,000: and at the very moment when Mr. Froude visited it, a large portion of that population was on the verge of starvation." Yet neither Fisher's urbanely malicious comments on his travel book, nor Freeman's far from urbane attacks on the *History* ("One can belabour Froude on a very small amount of knowledge," he confessed to a friend. "I am profoundly ignorant of the sixteenth century.") have damaged the authority of his picture of Elizabeth's reign. His reading of character, especially that of Henry VIII, has been rebutted, but the essential authoritativeness of the Elizabethan volumes remains, and his slips and carelessnesses in transcription have never been shown to spring from a desire to distort the evidence. It was not just the excellence of his style—easy, supple, colorful without ever becoming turgid—but the range of his story and the directness with which he brought it home to the reader which prompted so critical a man as Leslie Stephen to say, ". . . if I want to know something of the Elizabethan period, I can nowhere find so vivid and interesting a narrative." Froude remained true to his aims in this respect at least; he is the most Shakespearean of our historians.

Even as Froude was working, the manner of writing history was turning from the literary to the academic. The growing documentation of his last volumes reflects it, and his reception in Oxford when he returned there as professor in 1892 symbolizes it. The young don who had been rejected because of his ideas was brought back because of his facts, but his welcome had a certain chill politeness about it.

The study of history was becoming more exact, more preoccupied

with sources, less philosophical. When Buckle's work appeared, William Stubbs, the greatest English medievalist of any age, said, "I don't believe in the philosophy of history, so I don't believe in Buckle." Stubbs was Regius Professor of Modern History at Oxford from 1866 to 1884, the first properly trained historian to hold the post, and an acquaintance recorded how he came upon him reading a review by Froude of G. O. Trevelyan's *Life of Macaulay* and heard him say, as he abruptly got up, "When rhetoricians fall out, historians may come by their own."

The third quarter of the nineteenth century saw the foundations of modern research laid, and a series of massive blocks of scholarship raised on them. The Rolls series of medieval sources commenced in 1857, and in the same year began the great series of printed calendars of state papers. In 1869 the Historic Manuscripts Commission began its work of cataloguing documents in private collections. The first British periodical devoted to scholarly historical studies, the *English Historical Review,* was founded in 1886. In 1871 the Oxford "School of Modern History" permitted undergraduates to study history, and history alone, for the first time, and Cambridge followed suit with a separate History Tripos in 1873. The study of history became increasingly identified with the universities as its scholarly standards became more exacting. Stubbs's *Constitutional History of Medieval England* appeared in 1874–78; E. A. Freeman's *History of the Norman Conquest,* in 1867–79; the first volume of Samuel Gardiner's history of seventeenth-century England in 1863. All were based on the newly published record collections, and each author was at the time of writing, or later became, a university professor. Froude's *History,* which filled the chronological gap between Stubbs's work and Gardiner's, was easily the most vulnerable to scholarly criticism among these works.

It is tempting to see history itself becoming divided into Two Cultures in this period: on the one side, the professional academics, austere and unreadable; on the other, the popular but unreliable amateur. Such a baleful division did occur but its establishment depended on factors that did not begin to operate seriously until the twentieth century—the loss of faith by historians in their own subject save as a training for the mind; the cult of research work on narrow subjects at the universities; and the isolation of a small group of "serious" readers of history from the reading public at large. Perhaps another factor

was the extension of women's higher education, with its intemperate admiration for accuracy at the expense of imagination; there has been no great woman historian, though the names of Eileen Power, Beatrice Webb, and Barbara Hammond will be remembered both for scholarship and humanity.

The day of the private scholar was waning. It was no longer easy for bankers like William Roscoe, the historian of the Medici, or Grote, the historian of Greece, or lawyers like Hallam and Buckle, or politicians like Macaulay, or parsons like Robertson, to gain an international reputation for historical scholarship. But Stubbs prepared for his publications as a professor by his research as a country parson. Freeman wrote as a private scholar of independent means before he took his chair; William Lecky, whose *History of England in the Eighteenth Century* (1878–90) continued chronologically the basic surveys of Freeman, Stubbs, Froude, and Gardiner, never held a university post; and John Richard Green, whose *Short History of the English People* (1874) was second as a best seller only to Macaulay's *History,* while a confidant of Freeman, and a friend of Stubbs, lived and worked as a vicar in the East End of London. But the influence of the universities was, nevertheless, a pervasive one. They could tempt the private scholar with a chair, they could reward work of which they approved—as they did Lecky's—with honorary degrees. It was largely their influence that prompted Frederick Harrison, himself a private scholar and a historian, to express in 1898 his nostalgia for the days of Carlyle and Macaulay:

> The historians of the present century, under the influence originally of Ranke in Germany, of Guizot in France and Sir Henry Ellis and other editors of the Museum and Rolls records in England, have devoted themselves rather to original research than to eloquent narrative, to the study of special institutions and limited epochs, to the scientific probing of contemporary witness and punctilious precision of minute detail. The school of Freeman, Stubbs, Gardiner, and Bryce [Professor of Civil Law at Oxford and author of the *Holy Roman Empire*] has quite displaced the taste of our grandfathers for artistic narration and a glowing style. Where the older men thought of permanent literature, the new school is content with scientific records. Would that J. R. Green had lived out his life!

But Harrison's nostalgia need not be ours. England had been cut

off by her insularity from the refinements in scholarship that had become commonplace in France and Germany, but could not stand on her tradition of spacious thought, fine writing, and indiscriminate reading forever. And this first generation of exact historians, convinced, as great historians must be, that the work of their predecessors must be done all over again, produced a body of work that if taken as a whole is still unsurpassed. All the four men Harrison refers to wrote well; none was as plodding as Hallam, none so stood on his dignity as did Robertson, none was so fretful as Buckle, none so unfair as Gibbon or Macaulay. There was a growing wariness, and a tap on the knuckles in the *English Historical Review* came to be feared more than a cudgel blow on the head in the *Edinburgh* or the *Quarterly,* but the vice of timidity had not yet taken a firm hold, and Stubbs, Freeman, and Gardiner treated their great themes and long periods with as much confidence as scholarship. An age of glamour it may not be, but it is an age of grandeur.

And amid so many other names, it is pre-eminently the age of Stubbs. That this monosyllable should still so haunt the study of medieval English constitutional history is the measure of the authority with which he presided over every state of what—in spite of Hallam's chapter on England in the *Sketch of Europe in the Middle Ages*—was still its infancy. He deciphered manuscripts, he edited fundamental texts—nineteen of the volumes in the Rolls series were his; his *Select Charters* (1870) still retains its value as an anthology of sources, his *Constitutional History* surveyed the whole scene from Julius Caesar to the accession of the Tudors with a richness of detail, a firmness of plan, and an awareness of the main currents of national life that have never been matched. And his concern for his subject went well beyond his writings. He was abreast of continental scholarship as none of his predecessors had been, his lectures were designed to provoke thought as well as to fill notebooks, and he had the true academician's realism about the impossibility of being definitive. "History," he said, "knows that it can wait for more evidence and review its older verdicts; it offers an endless series of courts of appeal, and is ever ready to re-open closed cases." The publication of records on a large scale, and the concentration of historical studies in the universities, with their continuing routine of teaching and research, added a new dimension to men's thinking about history. The private scholar had looked on history as a record of man's activities reaching to the present, a record

which could be plundered to produce a book which would portray, definitively, some aspect of the past. Now to this concept was added a notion of history as a subject with laws of development of its own. The notion implied a built-in obsolescence, the impossibility of the definitive, and historians increasingly tried to save themselves from being swept out of sight by throwing overboard what they thought most perishable in their work: their own opinions and judgments, connections between their subjects and their own day. Then they became aware that even facts, by the mere acts of selection and arrangement, become mortal and have to be selected and arranged again and again. Carlyle rebelled against the gaps in the past and the pain it cost to bring it to life. Buckle abused the misdirected energies of his fellow historians, but did not shake their conviction that something could be done and that their efforts would bring a lasting reward. It was left for their successors to feel that history offered no hard surface where a man could chisel his name for posterity, and to suffer a failure of nerve much more debilitating than that produced by academic jealousy or a lack of faith in the progress of society.

The consequences of academized history still lay in the future when Stubbs wrote. The spate of record publications was impressive, but his generation saw them as making it possible to write history that was truer to the past, and embarked on them with excitement; they had not yet become an uncontrollable flood, and work in the archives was not yet a necessary badge of academic respectability. Stubbs's *Constitutional History* was written from printed sources; so were Green's work and Freeman's. Gardiner worked in Brussels and Venice and Simancas, not to add prestige to his work but to get information that had not been printed. The "dark industry" which Hume had groaned over was not yet something to brag about, nor did historians yet choose to work by preference where the industry would be darkest. Stubbs was a painstaking editor of texts, yet the introductions to his volumes in the Rolls series show how eager he was to see the period dealt with by the text as broadly as possible, and they contain striking and energetic portraits of the main characters concerned—Dunstan, or Henry II, or Richard I, or John. His *Constitutional History* created this subject as a branch of specialized inquiry at a blow, but it was also, because of his insistence on seeing the dependence of constitutional changes on specific political, or military, or economic needs, the best available general history of medieval England. It is

massively impartial. Stubbs declared in a lecture that he was not interested in making men into Whigs or Tories but in making the Whigs good, sensible Whigs, and Tories good, sensible Tories, and the biases that have been read into the work have appeared in retrospect, not because Stubbs put them there—save in the one instance that this parsonical professor, and future bishop, respectively, of Chester and Oxford, could not feel that any good had come from Rome and adjusted his account of the post-conquest church to prove it. The main criticism leveled against Stubbs is that he anticipated the maturity of the medieval parliament, and wrote too much in terms of its development. But to Stubbs, the twice-reformed parliament, with Disraeli and Gladstone at the height of their powers, really did seem to dominate the constitution, and the printed sources revealed its working in the Middle Ages as they did the functions of no other device of government. He anticipated his critics in a warning he delivered against "the danger of generalising from results, and attributing to men of the past the historian's own formulated conclusions," and where he exaggerated the development of early parliaments, and saw the nation speaking where only a faction bargained—as in Magna Carta—he was heeding the old Adam of the Enlightenment far less than the message of the sources, and the opinions of his colleagues on the continent. For Maitland, the greatest of English legal historians, to read Stubbs "is a training in justice."

If Stubbs tackled the most neglected period of English history, Samuel Gardiner accepted the challenge of the most written about, the most controversial, period of all. The attraction of the seventeenth century is easy to understand. It saw the first fully articulate conflict between large sections of the nation in both politics and religion, and a settlement of these issues in 1688 which loomed as large in the eyes of Englishmen as did the Declaration of Independence to Americans. The personalities of the Stuarts, and of Cromwell, were not only vividly interesting but they could be studied, through state papers, pamphlets, and memoirs, as no earlier historical characters could; the sixteenth century had no Clarendon. For Gardiner the truth had been obscured by the Whig or Tory bias of earlier historians. No partisan himself, he resolved to guard against contemporary partisanship by basing his work on primary sources, state papers and the like, wherever possible, and using pamphlets and memoirs sparingly and with the utmost caution. To resist any temptation that might develop in himself to stress

certain aspects in his story at the expense of others, he decided to work through the material year by year, publishing as he went, so that his work should demonstrate what actually happened, and not his hindsight of what had happened. This reversal of the methods of Hume, Hallam, and Macaulay might have led to his producing a set of annals, a mere reference book; but his constant linking of cause and effect, his belief that history was "the record of change, of the new circumstances into which communities of men are brought, and of the new ideas called forth by the circumstances, and by which circumstances in turn are moulded," enabled him to give a credibility and sense of growth even to a brief span of years.

He thought the subjective element in a historian's work emerged most dangerously in the thematic treatment of the past, and in large-scale portraiture, so he avoided both. To have a clear picture of James I or Cromwell before writing about their times was to see their actions in terms of the behavior of a literary concoction. "Historians," he wrote, "coolly dissect a man's thoughts as they please, and label them like specimens in a naturalist's cabinet. Such a thing, they argue, was done for mere personal aggrandisement; such a thing for national objects; such a thing from high religious motives. In real life we may be sure it was not so." Gardiner was much humbler than Stubbs, and his sacrifice of nearly every device whereby a historian writes himself into his history makes him the first English historian to write in the modern manner.

He was as aware as Stubbs of the need to keep European history as a whole constantly in view when writing about England, he was as critical in his use of authorities, and circumstances forced him to work far more in archives than did Stubbs. He was careful not to rely on the horizontal, the contemporary, dimension. "No one can really study any particular period of history," as he said, "unless he knows a great deal about what preceded it. . . . He has to bear in mind that it is a portion of a living whole." He accordingly began his first volume with a summary of previous events, which in the expanded form of *An Introduction to English History* (1881), became (after Green's *Short History*) the most influential textbook of its day. And Gardiner's impersonal attitude, and his refusal to draw morals or point lessons, did not mean that he thought the writing of history to be merely an end in itself, of no more use to society than a meticulously arranged collection of tram tickets. "It has always been my wish," he wrote,

"that I might so be able to write the history of the period as to convey something better than information. It seems to me that, without any attempt at preaching, merely to explain how men acted towards one another, and the reason for their misunderstandings, ought to teach us something for the conduct of our own lives."

Widely as Stubbs and Gardiner were esteemed, they were not popular, and their influence was largely restricted to the universities. Of John Richard Green, however, it could be said, as it was said of Gibbon and Macaulay (and with the same degree of exaggeration), that here was a serious and scholarly historian who was read as popular novels are read. Green's *Short History of the English People* was a work of the greatest independence of mind. Stubbs and Freeman were his friends and he had a respectful admiration for the work of Gardiner, yet while he sympathized with their aims, he could not follow them. They were all primarily interested in public events, and if Freeman's dictum: "history is past politics" was an unfair comment even on his own work, there was enough truth in it to justify Green's resolution to have no truck with "trumpet and drum" history, as he called it in a phrase that was to become famous. For Green, history should deal with the progress of the nation as a whole. It was not, as we have seen, a particularly original idea, but he alone kept it steadily in view throughout a major work, and this at a time when the idea had practically the whole force of responsible opinion against it. He felt this; he regretted that he could not win the good opinion of Gardiner, that Freeman would have to belabor him in the press and Stubbs wince in public for his views. When Stubbs and Green were conducting a viva voce examination together in Oxford on one occasion, Stubbs said to a candidate, "You say that George III had an inveterate hatred of men of genius. Where did you get that extraordinary statement from?" The man looked very uncomfortable but said nothing. Green wrote on a piece of paper and passed it to Stubbs: "Verbatim from my *Short History*." The editor of Stubbs's letters adds, *"solventur risu tabulae,"* but Green was sensitive about the extent to which his emphasis on the common man, his playing down of court and camp and law court, his graphic character sketches, and his use of men like Chaucer, Bacon, and Milton as the representatives of their times would disappoint the men he most revered.

He was unrepentant, however. When he wrote the book, he recorded, "I felt as if I were a young knight challenging the world with

my new material," and when Freeman sent him a copy of a sharply critical review, he admitted that the style might have been on the periphrastic side, but, he went on:

> . . . there are other "faults"—if faults they are—which I can hardly correct unless I wholly alter my conception of the book, and indeed of history. One is the suppression or omission of facts which appear to me to have no historic value. . . . In the same way the "putting things out of their place" means, I suppose, putting things out of the place they have hitherto occupied in common histories. But then my *plan* is in many ways different from that of common histories. . . . I give English History in the only way it is intelligible or interesting to *me,* but it does not follow that others will find my rendering of it intelligible or interesting. Then again, there is such a just aversion to "philosophies of history" on account of the nonsense which has passed under that name, that it is quite likely people may turn away from a story which strives to put facts on a philosophical basis, and to make events the outcome of social or religious currents of thought.

His hope had been to supersede Hume, not by rivaling his style but, he said, "because I have a larger and grander conception than he had of the organic life of a nation as a whole."

Today the idea of a one-volume account of a national civilization is a commonplace, but in Green's day there was no such thing. There was not even a convenient political outline; he had to invent the form and bring it to life in the same work. And his plan involved, not only turning the usual proportions of political, religious, social, and intellectual history upside down, but introducing a different periodization, following not dynasties but changes in the mood of society. It was high praise when in spite of Green's iconoclasm, Stubbs could describe the book as the best general history of England, and add, "when it comes to be superseded, it will be by a history on the lines of Green rather than on the lines of his critics." And when in fact it was superseded, it was by G. M. Trevelyan's *History of England,* a work which was at once recognized as being on the lines of Green, and this was not until fifty years later, in 1926.

Green's favorite period was the Middle Ages, and after publishing an expanded version of the *Short History* he took up the notes he had started making on the Anglo-Saxon conquests, and published, shortly

before his premature death from tuberculosis, *The Making of England* and *The Conquest of England.* Again he was plunging in against the advice of his friends. "In doing so, however," he said in the Preface to *The Making of England,* "I have largely availed myself of some resources which have been hitherto, I think, unduly neglected." The most important of these was the character of the land itself, "the fullest and the most certain of documents. Physical geography has still its part to play in the written record of that human history to which it gives so much of its shape and form; and in the present work I have striven, however imperfectly, to avail myself of its aid." This emphasis on a close study of geography was another of Green's contributions to historiography. In the eighteenth century it did not occur to historians to wish to visit the places they were writing about. Even when the Romantic doctrine of the influence of landscape on character was burgeoning, Roscoe did not leave Liverpool for Italy, and Grote did not quit London for Greece. By the middle of the century, Macaulay made a point of visiting fortified towns and battlefields, and Gardiner did the same for his Civil War volumes as a matter of course, and historians like Freeman, John Addington Symonds—author of *Renaissance in Italy*—and Green himself traveled on the continent and wrote sketches and essays on the towns which moved their historical sense. But this interest went no further than a liking for the picturesque, on the one hand, and a desire to see if such and such an authority was right in saying that the cavalry fell into a ditch. Green was the first to try to re-create the original features of the countryside as a whole and, by watching his Angles, Saxons, and Jutes grope their way through it, was able to chart settlements and movements that the documents left unexplained. His interest in the effect of geography on history led to his writing, with his wife, a *Short Geography of the British Isles* (1879), and the detailed regional maps in his Anglo-Saxon volumes are an essential commentary on the text, just as the walks he took through the countryside were an essential preparation for it. Mr. E. H. Carr has recently, in his *What Is History?*, referred to J. R. Green as "a rather pedestrian historian." This is unfair. Green was the most pedestrian of all our historians. It is the combination of his close knowledge of the countryside and sympathy for its people, together with a clear and lively style and scholarly zeal to reform the Englishman's attitude toward the past, that has put him among our great ones.

Partly because of German scholars, who were interested in the Teutonic origins of Anglo-Saxon England, early medieval history attracted greater attention among professional historians at the end of the nineteenth century than any other period. Green had shown what could be learned from topography; Frederic Seebohm's *English Village Community* (1883), how far a study of medieval husbandry and land tenure could supplement the picture of early society given by the charters, chronicles, and governmental records used by Stubbs. The greatest desideratum, however, was a study of early English law, for "legal documents are the best, often the only evidence we have for social and economic history, for the history of morality, for the history of practical religion. There are large and fertile tracts of history which the historian has to avoid because they are too legal for him." This was the opinion of Frederic Maitland, who not only revealed the wealth of the material in volume after volume which he edited for the Selden Society, but showed how it could be interpreted in the massive *History of English Law* (1895) which he wrote—and to which he contributed the greater part—in collaboration with Sir Frederick Pollock.

While not the greatest, Maitland is perhaps the most perfect of English historians. He was nobly and affectionately praised in his own day. Lord Acton called him "the ablest historian in England" at a time when Stubbs and Gardiner were still living and, after comparing his gift of analogy and the concreteness of his vision with Macaulay's, A. L. Smith asked, ". . . can we name anyone since Gibbon who has so combined the two sides . . . the scientific and the literary, the analyst and the artist, the Stubbs and the Froude?" And his reputation has remained serenely consistent. He is the only significant English historian who has never been adversely criticized.

He possessed all the historical talents. He was formidably industrious. He died at the age of fifty-six, but it is doubtful if any other historian has produced so much solid and original work. He was passionately careful. In spite of the rapidity with which he worked, he did not put pen to paper until he had thoroughly mastered the intricacies of his material. This habit led him, when toward the end of his life he was eager to write a continuation of his *History of English Law,* to carry out a pioneer study of legal Anglo-French which was hailed by a distinguished French philologist as of fundamental importance. He was determined that his work should not only be

technically accurate, but should really illuminate the life of the past; he tied every abstraction to concrete examples, and by a wonderfully deft use of modern analogy made the early Middle Ages not only more real but more distant than other historians had managed to do. One of the pleasures of reading Maitland is to be aware simultaneously of the intelligence which is shaping the material and feeling its way among its obscurities, and of the charm of his personality. In comparison, the other institutional historians of his day, including his younger contemporary T. F. Tout, are very dull dogs indeed. Throughout a range of studies so wide that a legal historian has remarked recently that it would take a committee or an academy to pass an adequate judgment on them, he retained an incomparable lightness of touch, and never had to have recourse to the forced geniality with which so many of his colleagues sought to persuade their readers that they too saw with the eyes and shared the interests of other men.

In the year the *History of English Law* was published, Maitland was joined at Cambridge by a man who makes him appear an amiable lightweight. John Emerich Edward Dalberg, First Baron Acton, was as formidable as he sounds. Descended from an illustrious German family and from a Prime Minister of the Kingdom of Naples, Acton, before he was made Regius Professor, had seen more of the world and its great men than the rest of his colleagues put together. With his stepfather, Lord Granville, he had been on a mission to Moscow; he had toured (and not as a lecturer, as had Froude) the United States with a relative, the Earl of Ellesmere; he had sat both in the Commons and in the Lords, had been an intimate friend of Gladstone and a lord in waiting to Queen Victoria. He was a member of exclusive clubs, the frequenter of exclusive society. Almost as unusual in the holder of a Regius Chair, he was a Catholic. Less unusual, perhaps, was the fact that he had never written a book. But for all his title, his international acquaintance, and his wealth, the choice of Acton was unimpeachable. He may have had a library of 59,000 books, but it had been more thoroughly read than many a library of 2,000. Acton's claim to be the most omnivorous reader of the nineteenth century would be difficult to refute, and so would his claim to be among its most scrupulous scholars and its most tenacious thinkers. And if he had written no book, he had written copiously on church matters—for the *Rambler* and then the *Home and Foreign Review,* both of which were suppressed for the polemical use to which

he put his scholarship—and had contributed to the *English Historical Review*, from its first number, articles and reviews which displayed a redoubtable learning and force of character. It was only fitting that a man who had spoken ex cathedra from his youth should be appointed to a chair.

The Cambridge chair was especially appropriate, for his inability to go there as an undergraduate, on religious grounds, was responsible for much of his background as a historian. At the age of sixteen he went to live in Munich with Döllinger, the most renowned of Catholic scholars. Precocious and serious-minded, the young Acton set out to read the best books and meet the most important people, and while he quickly hauled himself abreast of the pragmatic and critical scholarship associated with Von Ranke, he was attracted to the philosophy of history, which he saw as "the most sublime of all subjects of study." His ideas matured at a speed which would hardly have been possible at home. "Being refused at Cambridge," he wrote later in life, "and driven to foreign universities, I never had any contemporaries, but spent years in looking for men wise enough to solve the problems that puzzled me, not in religion or politics so much as along the wavy line between the two. So I was always associated with men a generation older than myself." The habit, which he shared with Gibbon, of constantly reviewing the contents of his memory and of fitting the books he read into the proper niche in the historiographical descent of the subject they dealt with, made his writings tend to the opaque: it is easier to feel their significance than to see it; a dozen paragraphs of Acton sometimes read like the concluding passages, and rather gnomic ones at that, of as many articles. His Cambridge lectures helped to loosen his style, but his inaugural must have seemed as strange in manner as in matter. From this dense meditation on the meaning and nature of history rang out epigrams extolling the moral purpose of history as the true demonstration of religion and warning his audience of "scientific" fact collectors that the historian should study problems, not periods, and must judge, and judge fiercely. "The weight of opinion is against me when I exhort you never to debase the moral currency or lower the standard of rectitude, but to try others by the final maxim that governs your own lives, and to suffer no man and no cause to escape the undying penalty which history has the power to inflict on wrong." His predecessor, Seeley, had praised history as above all a school of statesmanship: "Our university is and must be a

great seminary of politicians." But for Acton, ". . . ours is a domain that reaches farther than affairs of state, and is not subject to the jurisdiction of governments. It is our function to keep in view and to command the movement of ideas, which are not the effect but the cause of public events." And of all ideas, the most important was the idea of liberty, for "progress in the direction of organised and assured freedom, is the characteristic fact of Modern History, and its tribute to the theory of Providence." He went on to admit that "Ranke, who was my own master, rejected the view that I have stated . . . and many of our recent classics—Carlyle, Newman, Froude—were persuaded that there is no progress justifying the ways of God to man," but progress there was, and it was the sacred duty of history to reveal it and, by revealing it, to promote its growth, but reveal it always with ardent critical honesty.

He had no consolation to offer those who studied history mainly in order to write books. His own youthful project of a vast *History of Liberty* had ceased to appear a possibility—the more one knew the more one needed to know—but this did not matter, for more important than information was wisdom. Archive after archive was being opened all over Europe. "We are still at the beginning of the documentary age, which will tend to make history independent of historians, to develop learning at the expense of writing." What did this mean? That the serious historian would no longer have to spend nine tenths of his time groping past secondary authorities toward the truth, and could devote himself to contemplation, while written history was left to mere popularizers? It is difficult to imagine that so combative a man, one who believed so much in the educative force of history, could think that. There is something of this, however, in what he told his audience later: The study of history "fulfils its purpose even if it only makes us wiser, without producing books, and gives us the gift of historical thinking, which is better than historical learning." Yet three years later Acton was writing instructions for the guidance of the men he had chosen to write for that mammoth work the *Cambridge Modern History,* to which he intended to contribute five chapters himself.

Acton cannot be finally assessed. His published writings only represent a series of massy fragments of the unwritten work that lurked in his mind, his books, and his notes. The notes have been in part studied, but they are often cryptic and their relation to the whole remains

obscure. That at certain points they contradict his written thoughts is a warning to be cautious. One anomaly is so glaring, however, that it tempts an explanation. Acton believed that history was a search after truth. The historian must investigate a document till he knows what it means and it can speak for itself—"there is virtue in the saying that a historian is seen at his best when he does not appear." In the instructions to contributors to the *C.M.H.* he insisted that "nothing shall reveal the country, the religion, or the party to which the writers belong," for "impartiality is the character of legitimate history." On the other hand he believed that the historian had an imperative duty to judge. To a letter written in 1887 to Bishop Creighton he added a series of "canons" on this theme. They are cruelly extreme. "In Christendom, time and place do not excuse—if the Apostle's Code sufficed for Salvation; the Reign of Sin is more universal, the influence of unconscious error is less, than historians tell us. . . . A good cause proves less in a man's favour than a bad cause against him. . . . The final judgement depends on the worst action." And there is more in the same vein. The historian is exhorted not only to judge but to seek opportunities for judging. Taking this attitude in conjunction with his Whig emphasis on selectivity—"only those facts and elements in the people's life which bear on the actual progress of events can be admitted into an historical work"—and the contradiction is complete. There appear to be two Actons.

One Acton gloried in a task for which a strong intellect made him superbly efficient: mastering the most advanced forms of historical criticism and analysis. The other saw history in terms of conscience; the jerky progress from the absolute intolerance of the early Dark Ages toward a condition in which man can obey conscience without fear of reprisal. For a man of strong faith, but at odds with certain aspects of its authority as he was (his periodicals suppressed, his hopes for a tolerant Catholicism blighted by the Vatican decrees of 1870, which included the dogma of Infallibility), there was a strong temptation to show that Providence wrote "freedom of conscience for *all*" into history. But progress toward the organization of protection for conscience, both in church and state, is brought about by great men, and "great men are almost always bad men," for "power tends to corrupt and absolute power corrupts absolutely"—the phrases are in his letter to Creighton—so the historian should not only extract from history the story of liberty of conscience, but scourge the men who

slowed its progress, and thus alert living men to the fact that they are judged (though not by the law) on earth as well as hereafter.

No historian has followed Acton in the question of moral judgments, and the current flowed against his emphasis on selecting from the past what was relevant to the present. He left no book as a model, and it is doubtful that, even had he lived, the *Cambridge Modern History* would have provided, as he hoped, "an illumination of the soul." What remains is the force of the impassioned claims he made for the dignity of his subject, his emphasis on universal and on problematic history at the expense of the parish pump or the easy isolation of a few years; and the record, in a few articles and lectures, of the most disturbingly thoughtful mind in English historical literature.

In one other respect Acton failed to sound a note congenial to his young contemporaries. When he rejoiced in the opening of archives all over Europe it was not because they would illuminate the social life, or voting habits, or economic activities of men in the past, but because great men would be stripped bare and could at last receive a minutely calculated sentence for their crimes. Discussing the materials on which his lectures on the French Revolution were based, he commented that in a few years "all will be known that ever can be known. . . . In that golden age our historians will be sincere, and our history certain. The worst will be known, and then sentence need not be deferred." All that will be needed is a historian with the courage to be honest with friend and foe—"assuming that it would be possible for an honest historian to have a friend." And on this gloomily obsessive note his last published lecture course ends. English historians were not to use new documentary evidence in this sense. With Tawney they were to bring charity, and with Namier clarity, into vital sections of the past through which Acton hurried, with his mind muscling world history into patterns and his nose twitching to find a taint in the backstairs cupboard of some canonized archbishop.

In his lecture audiences was a young man on whom a much softer version of his mantle fell. George Macaulay Trevelyan was named after his great-uncle and spent much of his life continuing what he felt to be good in Macaulay's work and atoning for what was bad—as when, in his *England under Queen Anne,* he made brilliant reparation for Macaulay's savage caricature of Marlborough. He maintained his concern for readability, his combination of Scott and Hallam, his special emphasis on social history, his Whiggish belief

that the lessons of the past are reassuring to the present. He felt the same romantic excitement about repeopling places he had visited with their former inhabitants. "The poetry of history," he wrote, "lies in the quasi-miraculous fact that once, on this familiar spot of ground, walked other men and women, as actual as we are today, thinking their own thoughts, swayed by their own passion, but now all gone, one generation vanishing after another, gone as utterly as we ourselves shall shortly be gone like ghosts at cock-crow."

With his *England under the Stuarts* (1904), *Garibaldi's Defence of the Roman Republic* (1907) and its successors, *History of England* (1926), and his *English Social History: A Survey of Six Centuries* (1942), he became the most widely read of all English historians; like Macaulay and Green he brought an interest in the past to thousands who had read no history before. And he achieved this while staying within the liberal, literary tradition of the nineteenth century, the tradition of Macaulay and Carlyle rather than of Buckle, of Green rather than of Seeley. His reaction from German methods ("an attempt has been made to drill us all into so many Potsdam Guards of learning") and their adoption in England made him give up a fellowship at Trinity and withdraw from the critical and scientific-historical atmosphere of Cambridge to a life of country-house scholarship. Insulated from the inner life of his subject's growth, he was able to provide a public which was increasingly isolated from its professionalism with a marvelously refined version of the old history, a Macaulay purged of rhetoric and party passion, a Carlyle without fanaticism, a Green tranquilly unaware of the displeasure of Stubbs.

His greatest gift was for narrative, and his narrative flowed best when he could see his subject as a drama, either of the whole English people or of a grandly simple individual, like Garibaldi. He wrote lives of John Bright, the Manchester Free trader, and of Lord Grey, but these studies of early nineteenth-century finance and politics were not successful; unlike Acton, he had no taste for intrigue and the subtle manipulation of public opinion, he was as much a countryman as Acton was a frequenter of salons, and the firm continuity of his own upper-middle-class family led him to confront the past with the genial instincts of a rural magistrate.

The quality of his imagination has brought him the title of the poet of English history. In an early essay, "Clio" (written 1904, revised 1913), Trevelyan wrote that "he will give the best interpretation who,

having discovered and weighed all the important evidence available, has the largest grasp of intellect, the warmest human sympathy, the highest imaginative powers." This is well said, and true. Trevelyan's imagination was, however, the servant of his sympathies and, warm as these were, his very longing to grasp the hands of the dead and warm them by his understanding narrowed the scope of their operation. His imagination was only fired by what he could see and hear, and the majority of men perish without a portrait or a book to speak for them. "Those who write or read the history of a period should be soaked in its literature"—yes: but literature only reveals the literate, and what the literate chose to think of the illiterate. While his contemporaries were using records, above all economic records, to extend the view of social history, Trevelyan, shrinking from techniques that ended in "-ology," and smacked of science, wrote social history in terms of the sorts of materials that Macaulay had used. It was in this field that he achieved his greatest popular success. The social history chapters from his *England under the Stuarts* and *England under Queen Anne* were reprinted separately, and the *Social History* outsold all his other books. Trevelyan was a great writer, a wise and generous and scrupulously fair man; if only his imagination had embraced history as a subject, as well as the past, if only his sympathy had included the impersonal poorhouse as warmly as the visible beggar in the street, he might have humanized the abstractions of the Marxists and the sociologists in a social history that was a poet's homage to the aspirations of history as a whole, not to the special emotions and nostalgias of one man. Trevelyan will remain a great name in the history of English historiography for his personality, his craftsmanship, and his success, but probably no famous historian has made a smaller contribution to the inner history of his subject.

Trevelyan's personal concern for the past, and his need to extend his own personality by linking it in partnership with the dead, was shared by his more ebullient contemporary R. H. Tawney. "Whatever else the world may contain," Tawney wrote in a lecture on "Social History and Literature," "man's relations with nature, his commerce with his fellows, and the convictions, aspirations and emotions composing his inner life, are for us, as for the poet, its capital constituents." But the ardent nature of Tawney's sympathy with the men, and especially with the poor, of his chosen period—the sixteenth and seventeenth centuries—and the fact that he expressed it in terms

(though in very personal terms) of the modish sociological methods of German economic historians, made an impact on his professional colleagues out of all proportion to the noncommittal politeness with which they received the works of Trevelyan. Seen as a stimulus to other historians, and for the direction it gave to further research, his *The Agrarian Problem in the Sixteenth Century* (1912) was the most significant work an English historian had yet produced. His *Religion and the Rise of Capitalism* (1926) is the foundation stone of the vast and still rising fabric of religious sociology in England. His essay of 1941 on "The Rise of the Gentry" in the *Economic History Review,* together with its companion lecture in the same year on "Harrington's Interpretation of his Age," started the most publicized historical controversy of the present generation. Four years before his death he produced a work, *Business and Politics under James I: Lionel Cranfield as Merchant and Minister* (1958), which promises to have something like the fertilizing effect of his *Agrarian Revolution.* His sharpest critic, Professor Hugh Trevor-Roper, and his successor in his London chair, Professor F. J. Fisher, have both recently dubbed the years 1540–1640 "Tawney's century."

As that period saw the most crucial and puzzling changes in English religious, economic, and political life before the Industrial Revolution, this is no mean compliment. And it is not due merely to Tawney's having indicated the problems, and provided in the three volumes of *Tudor Economic Documents* (1924), which he edited with Eileen Power, a basic research tool for their elucidation. It is a tribute to the most warmly generous personality to concern itself with serious historical writing since J. R. Green, and to the infectious vigor of his style as a writer.

Tawney grew up as English socialism was becoming self-conscious and working out its programs. It was a period when publishers' lists were crammed with books on wage strictures and labor conditions and on the reform of poor law, prisons, and education. Though there was much utopianism in the air, much of this literature turned to history as its chief support. The Webbs were making their massive contributions to the history of local government and of the poor law, the Hammonds were painting their sobering picture of labor in town and country during the Industrial Revolution. Tawney found both inspiration and refreshment in the work he did for the adult education movement. "The friendly smitings of weavers, potters, miners, and

engineers," he acknowledged, "have taught me much about problems of political and economic science which cannot easily be learned from books." His political convictions were stated in two nonhistorical works, *The Acquisitive Society* and *Equality;* what sounded through his historical books was not the surf of polemic but the ground swell of a passionate sympathy for the underprivileged, and his search for the origin of the relations between class and class, government and people, which stood in need of such urgent reform of his own day. "The supreme interest of economic history," he wrote in the Preface to *The Agrarian Revolution,* "lies, it seems to me, in the clue which it offers to the development of those dimly conceived presuppositions as to social expediency which influence the actions not only of statesmen, but of humble individuals and classes, and influence, perhaps, most decisively, those who are least conscious of any theoretical bias." His belief that history, not abstract theories of social justice ("since even quite common men have souls"), was the political reformer's best teacher did not lead him to see the past simply in terms of oppressors and oppressed; whether he was discussing the medieval church or Elizabethan justices, he always gave the devil picturesquely his due. Where he has been faulted by later research, it is for an underdisciplined deployment of statistics, not for distorting "Tawney's century" to make a point about Queen Victoria's. A glance at his superb reconstruction of the Puritan temperament in *Religion and the Rise of Capitalism* (especially the opening pages of "The Puritan Movement") will show that he was as quick to understand its narrow fanaticism as the demands it made for individual freedom.

Tawney was a rhetorical writer, and some fastidious critics have withdrawn their academic gowns from contact with him on this account. It is worth looking for a few moments at the purplest of his patches to see if this disdain is merited. "On a world heaving with expanding energies," he wrote near the beginning of "The Puritan Movement,"

> and on a church uncertain of itself, rose, after two generations of premonitory mutterings, the tremendous storm of the Puritan movement. The forest bent; the oaks snapped; the dry leaves were driven before a gale, neither all of winter nor all of spring, but violent and life-giving, pitiless and tender, sounding strange notes of yearning and contrition, as of voices wrung from a people dwelling in

> Meshech, which signifies Prolonging, in Kedar, which signifies Blackness; while amid the blare of trumpets, and the clash of arms, and the rending of the carved work of the Temple, humble to God and haughty to man, the soldier-saints swept over battlefield and scaffold, their garments rolled in blood.
>
> In the great silence which fell when the Titans had turned to dust, in the Augustan calm of the eighteenth century, a voice was heard to observe that religious liberty was a considerable advantage, regarded "merely in a commercial view." A new world, it was evident, had arisen.

Rhetoric indeed; but with what deliberation its gusto is used, how excitingly—and how fairly—the contrast is achieved! Often serious, never solemn, often fiercely ironical, never unjust: Tawney lives in every line he wrote, and he lures the reader on through the stiffest canebrakes of analysis with paradoxes and with images, startling or humorous, that contrive to pass on both the depth of concern he felt for his subject and the zest he felt in thinking and writing about it. Of Europe's medieval economy: "tapping the wealth of the East by way of the narrow apertures of the Levant, it resembled, in the rigidity of the limits imposed on its commercial strategy, a giant fed through the chinks of a wall"; "the correspondence of Burleigh, in the last decade of Elizabeth, reads like the report of a receiver in bankruptcy to the nobility and gentry"; ". . . the Age of Reason, which, as far as its theory of the conduct of men in society is concerned, deserves much more than the thirteenth century to be described as the Age of Faith." Even where his prejudices are most deeply involved, there remains a lightness of touch that recalls Lytton Strachey, as in his famous reference to

> that blind, selfish, indomitable aristocracy of country families, which made the British Empire and ruined a considerable proportion of the English nation. From the galleries of their great mansions and the walls of their old inns their calm, proud faces, set off with an occasional drunkard, stare down on us with the unshakable assurance of men who are untroubled by regrets or perplexities, men who have deserved well of their order and their descendants, and await with confidence an eternity where preserves will be closer, family settlements stricter, dependents more respectful, cards more reliable, than in this imperfect world they well can be. Let them

> have their due. They opened a door which later even they could not close. They fostered a tree which even they could not cut down.

Few historians are more quotable, and it is an indication of the tact which ruled his splendid command of language that when he came to deal with Luther, the most rhetorical of the protagonists in *Religion and the Rise of Capitalism,* Tawney's own language became the chastest foil for the German reformer's glowing prose. Resolutely original in statement, Tawney was unfailingly courteous in controversy; while attracting critics, he made no enemies. He was heavily indebted to German scholarship, but his writings convey, even more clearly than Trevelyan's, a quintessential Englishness.

With Namier we are back in the atmosphere that Acton breathed; the same cosmopolitan background and cosmopolitan outlook, the same burly intellect, the same distaste for revolutions and the intellectuals who try to guide them, a similar arrogance, a similar preoccupation with political rather than social or economic man, a similar combination of interest in the widest survey and the minutely detailed study. What was said of Namier—that he used nothing between the telescope and the microscope—can be said with an equal degree of fairness of Acton. His pronouncements on history echo, time after time, the phrases of Acton's Inaugural: "the crowning attainment of historical study is a historical sense," for instance, or his statement that "the past is on top of us and with us all the time; and there is only one way of mastering it even remotely in any one sector: by knowing how these things have come to be, which helps to understand their nature, character, and their correlation, or lack of correlation, to the present realities of life," which is not far from Acton's "if the Past has been an obstacle and a burden, knowledge of the Past is the safest and surest emancipation." Unlike Acton, however, who left Commandments but no disciples, Namier was surrounded by Namierites, and was the first English historian to see group scholarship in terms of an *équipe* of mature scholars sharing between them material no one man could master.

Namier's attitude toward past politics was so original that the techniques he worked out to express it have been named after him: he Namierized the study of political history. Tired of the way in which eighteenth-century parliamentary history had been written and re-written in terms of Party and Principle, he determined to see past these

abstractions to the real motives of individuals and, as soon as he did, eighteenth-century history had to be written. His manifesto was written as the first part of the most influential book (among professionals) ever produced by an English historian, *The Structure of Politics at the Accession of George III* (1929). It was headed "Why men went into Parliament," and instead of such subheadings as Whig, Tory, Crown Corruption, etc., there were these: "Predestination: the Inevitable Parliament Man; Honour with Ease: The Country Gentleman; The Treasury Bench: The Politicians; Private and Pecuniary: Place Men and Purveyors of Favours; Professional Advancement: The Services and the Law; Contracts, Remittances and Loans: The Merchants and Bankers"; and lastly, "Immunity: Robbers, Muddlers, Bastards and Bankrupts." The blend of aggressive common sense and humor used to shock and goad rather than (as with Maitland) to explain, was a deliberate consequence of his contention that "Parliamentary politics not based on parties are to us a non-Euclidian system, and similarly require a fundamental readjustment of ideas and, what is more, of mental habits."

Like Trevelyan, Namier gave up a Fellowship (at Balliol) in order to have more time for research and writing. Unlike Trevelyan, he kept in touch with what other historians were doing, and worked in terms of reforming, not refining, the craft of history, and when he went to a chair at Manchester he was greeted not as a revered anachronism but as the head of a bustling industry.

"Namierization" arose from the need to explore the grammar of political behavior before writing the text he had originally planned: *England on the Eve of the American Revolution* (1931), but Namier was interested in two other periods: the diplomacy of the 1930's and nineteenth-century Europe. In all three fields he wrote as a master, with a breadth of vision and a confidence of interpretation which enabled him to multiply the sarcasms, rough jokes, and deflating analogies that make reading him such an exhilarating and jolting experience.

In all three his special interest was in biography, but never in biography for its own sake. "Far too much of modern British history is ensconced in biographies which dribble away their material without coming to grips with basic problems." As Acton had scorned the period and recommended the problem, so Namier thought that men who chose biography did so because it simplified the business of selection and isolated them from a responsibility to look outward. Namier-

ization involved not one big "representative" biography but as many little biographies as would illuminate the working of an important group, hence his eventual emphasis on concerted research. There is little doubt that intellectual conviction made him put aside a personal inclination toward detailed biography. Namier was fascinated by psychology. He was psychoanalyzed himself, he criticized Toynbee's neglect of it, he spoke of mass psychology as "the most basic factor in history" and regretted how little attention had been paid to it. Certainly it has not been taken so seriously by any other academic historian. He saw history itself as having a psychoanalytic function, healing by explaining, and remarked that "it further resembles psychoanalysis in being better able to diagnose than to cure." This interest in psychology added a strain of delicacy to the otherwise rather brassy surface of his estimates of men and his discussion of events. Writing on human nature in politics, he said that

> a sentence in Talleyrand's *Memoirs* seemingly unrelated to politics in a flash illuminates one aspect of his political conduct. He writes: "I say in order to have said it once, and hoping never to think of it again: that I am perhaps the only man of distinguished birth . . . who has not for a single week of his life known the joy of staying under his parental roof." Here was bitterness which he, writing at the age of 60, wished he could overcome. Neglected by his parents and brought up by dependents who extolled to him the greatness of his family, he went through life a very conscious *grand seigneur* who associated by preference with inferiors and, devoid of any feeling for his own class—its primary representatives were to him his parents—contributed with cold indifference to its downfall.

And in his character sketch, printed here, of George III, and his account in "Une Amitié Amoureuse" (*Vanished Supremacies*) of the relationship between the Emperor Francis Joseph and the actress Frau Schratt, he shows a special, and possibly revealing, interest in immature, unloved hearts doomed to pompous responsibility, self-distrustful behind their impressive façades.

Namier was above all a conservative and a realist. But his realism took account of the extent to which men's actions are irrational, and he saw in psychology a science of which historians would have to make increasing use. In this way he speaks not only to the disciples who are Namierizing other tracts of English parliamentary history,

and have their eyes on German diets and Roman conclaves, but to all students of history. Not only the generation which closed with his death in 1960, but the one which is beginning now, may well be called by historiographers of the nineties "The Age of Namier."

BIBLIOGRAPHY

This is a selective list of the *general* books and articles I have found most directly useful. Works dealing with individual historians are given in the introductory note to each series of extracts; again, I only refer to those I have drawn on directly. Toward the authors of all these books, essays, and articles I have a sense of lively and admiring obligation.

FRITZ STERN, ED. *Varieties of History*, New York, 1956; London, 1957.

H. BUTTERFIELD *The Englishman and His History*, Cambridge, England, 1944.

W. R. TRIMBLE "Early Tudor Historiography 1485–1548," *Journal of the History of Ideas*, 1950.

LILY B. CAMPBELL, ED. Tudor Conceptions of History and Tragedy in *A Mirror for Magistrates*, University of California, 1936.

L. F. DEAN *Tudor Theories of History Writing*, "Contributions in Modern Philology" Series, University of Michigan, 1947.

F. SMITH FUSSNER *The Historical Revolution—English Historical Writing and Thought 1580–1640*, New York, 1962; London, 1962.

LEVI FOX, ED. *English Historical Scholarship in the 16th and 17th Centuries*, London, 1956.

D. C. DOUGLAS — *English Scholars 1660–1730*, 2nd ed., London, 1951.

J. B. BLACK — *The Art of History: a study of four great historians of the 18th century*, London, 1926.

R. N. STROMBERG — "History in the 18th Century," *Journal of the History of Ideas*, 1951.

T. P. PEARDON — *The Transition in English Historical Writing, Harvard, 1760–1830*, 1933.

E. NEFF — *The Poetry of History*, New York, 1947; reprinted 1961.

G. P. GOOCH — *History and Historians in the Nineteenth Century*, London, 1913; new ed., 1952; Boston, 1959.

D. FORBES — *The Liberal Anglican Idea of History*, New York and Cambridge, England, 1952.

HERBERT FISHER — *Pages from the Past*, London, 1939.

H. BUTTERFIELD — *Man on His Past*, New York, 1954; Cambridge, England, 1955; reprinted, Boston, 1960.

E. H. CARR — *What Is History?*, London, 1961.

THE EVOLUTION OF BRITISH HISTORIOGRAPHY

From Bacon to Namier

SIR WALTER RALEIGH

1552–1618

This passage includes parts 2–4 of chapter 2 in the fourth book of The History of the World. *I have modernized spelling and punctuation from the first edition of 1614, and omitted some forty lines which deal with the measures taken by Alexander to consolidate the regions he had conquered. The passage is characteristic of Raleigh's narrative style, his intermingling of First and Second Causes, his critical attitude toward some of his sources, his harping on the usefulness of history, and his use of generalizing asides ("We find it in daily experience, that all discourse of magnanimity [appeals to patriotism, justice, etc.] of national virtue, of religion, of liberty, and whatsoever else hath been wont to move and encourage virtuous men, hath no force at all with the common soldier in comparison of spoils and riches"). His remark that military men "seldom live to obtain great empires" is expanded on p. 617 of part two, in a passage that draws, as he does so often, on the lessons of his own career. The present passage begins Raleigh's account of Alexander's invasion of Persia.*

The most useful article on Raleigh as a historian is C. A. Firth's "Raleigh's History of the World," *in* Proceedings of the British Academy, *1918. There is a full bibliography in W. M. Wallace's excellent life,* Sir Walter Raleigh, *Princeton, 1959.*

WHEN all was now quieted at home, Alexander, committing to the trust of Antipater both Greece and Macedon, in the first of the Spring

did pass the Hellespont, and being ready to disembark, he threw a dart towards the Asian shore as a token of defiance, commanding his soldiers not to make any waste in their own territory, or to burn or deface those buildings which themselves were presently and in the future to possess. He landed his army, consisting of two and thirty thousand foot, and five thousand horse, all old soldiers, near unto Troy, where he offered a solemn sacrifice upon Achilles' tomb, his maternal ancestor.

But before he left his own coast, he put to death without any offence given him, all his mother-in-law's kinsmen, whom Philip his father had greatly advanced, not sparing such of his own as he suspected. He also took with him many of his tributary princes, of whose fidelity he doubted; thinking by unjust cruelty to assure all things, both in the present and future. Yet the end of all fell out contrary to the policy which his ambition had commended unto him, though agreeing very well with the justice of God; for all that he had planted was soon after withered and rooted up; those whom he most trusted were the most traitorous; his mother, friends, and children fell by such another merciless sword as his own, and all manner of confusion followed his dead body to the grave and left him there.

When the knowledge of Alexander's landing on Asia side was brought to Darius, he so much scorned the army of Macedon, and had so contemptible an opinion of Alexander himself, as having stiled him his servant on a letter which he wrote unto him, reprehending his disloyalty and audacity (for Darius entitled himself King of Kings, and the kinsman of the gods), he gave order withal to his lieutenants of the lesser Asia that they should take Alexander alive, whip him with rods, and then convey him to presence: that they should sink his ships, and send the Macedonians taken prisoners beyond the Red Sea, belike into Ethiopia, or some unhealthful part of Africa.

In this sort did this glorious king, confident in the glittering but heartless multitude which he commanded, dispose of the already vanquished Macedonians. But the ill destinies of men bear them to the ground, by what strong confidence soever armed. The great numbers which he gathered together and brought in one heap into the field gave rather an exceeding advantage to his enemies than any discouragement at all. For besides that they were men utterly unacquainted with dangers, men who by the name and countenance of their king were wont to prevail against those of less courage than themselves, men that

took more care how to embroider with gold and silver their upper garments, as if they attended the invasion but of the sun-beams, than they did to arm themselves with iron and steel against the sharp pikes, swords, and darts of the hardy Macedonians: I say, besides all these, even the opinion they had of their own numbers, of which every one in particular hoped that it would not fall to his turn to fight, filled every of them with the care of their own safety, without any intent at all to hazard anything but their own breath, and that of their horses, in running away. The Macedonians, as they came to fight, and thereby to enrich themselves with the gold and jewels of Persia, both which they needed; so the Persians, who expected nothing in that war but blows and wounds, which they needed not, obeyed the king who had power to constrain them in assembling themselves for his service; but their own fears and cowardice, which in time of danger had most power over them, they only then obeyed when their rebellion against so servile a passion did justly and violently require it. For, saith Vegetius: *Quemadmodum bene exercitatus miles prœlium cupit, ita formidat indoctus; nam sciendum est impugna usum amplius prodesse quam vires:* As the well-practised soldier desires to come to battle, so the raw one fears it: for we must understand that in fight it more avails to have been accustomed unto the like than only to have rude strength. What manner of men the Persians were, Alexander discovered in the first encounter, before which time it is said, by those that write his story, that it was hard to judge whether his daring to undertake the conquest of an empire so well peopled with a handfull of men, or the success he had, were more to be wondered at. For at the river of Granick, which severeth the territory of Troy from Propontis, the Persians sought to stop his passage, taking the higher ground and bank of the river to defend, which Alexander was forced as it were to climb up unto, and scale from the level of the water. Great resistance, saith Curtius, was made by the Persians, yet in the end Alexander prevailed. But it seems to me, that the victory then gotten was exceeding easy, and that the twenty thousand Persian footmen said to be slain were rather killed in the back, in running away, than hurt in the bosoms by resisting. For had those twenty thousand foot and two hundred and fifty horsemen, or, after Plutarch, two thousand and five hundred horsemen, died with their faces towards the Macedonians, Alexander could not have bought their lives at so small a rate, as with the loss of four and thirty of all sorts of his own. And if it were also true, that

Plutarch doth report, how Alexander encountered two of the Persian commanders, Spithridates and Rhoesaces, and that the Persian horsemen fought with great fury though in the end scattered; and lastly, how those Grecians in Darius his pay, holding themselves in one body upon a piece of ground of advantage, did, after mercy was refused them, fight it out to the last: how doth it then resemble truth, that such resistance having been made, yet of Alexander's army there fell but twelve footmen, and two and twenty horsemen?

The winning of this passage did greatly encourage the Macedonians, and brought such terror upon all those of the lesser Asia, as he obtained all the kingdoms thereof without a blow, some one or two towns excepted. For in all invasions, where the nations invaded have once been beaten upon a great advantage of the place, as in defence of rivers, straits, and mountains, they will soon have persuaded themselves that such an enemy upon equal terms and even ground can hardly be resisted. It was therefore Machiavel's counsel, that he which resolveth to defend a passage, should with his ablest force oppose the assailant. And to say truth, few regions of any great circuit are so well fenced that armies of such force as may be thought sufficient to conquer them, can be debarred all entrance by the natural difficulty of the ways. One passage or other is commonly left unguarded. If all be defended, then must the forces of the country be distracted; and yet lightly some one place will be found that is defended very weakly. How often have the Alps given way to armies breaking into Italy? Yea, where shall we find that ever they kept out an invader? Yet are they such as, to speak briefly, afflict with all difficulties those that travel over them; but they give no security to those that lie behind them, for they are of too large extent. The towns of Lombardy persuaded themselves that they might enjoy their quiet, when the warlike nation of the Switzers had undertaken to hinder Francis the French king from descending into the Duchy of Milan; but whilst these Patrons of Milan, whom their own dwelling in those mountains had made fittest of all other for such a service, were busied in custody of the Alps, Francis appeared in Lombardy, to so much the greater terror of the inhabitants by how much the less they had expected his arrival. What shall we say of those mountains which lock up whole regions in such sort as they leave but one gate open? The straits, or, as they were called, the Gates of Taurus in Cilicia, and those of Thermopylae, have seldom

been attempted, perhaps because they were thought impregnable; but how seldom, if ever, have they been attempted in vain. Xerxes, and long after him, the Romans, forced the entrance of Thermopylae; Cyrus the younger, and after him Alexander, found the Gates of Cilicia wide open. How strongly soever they had been locked and barred, yet were those countries open enough to a fleet that should enter on the back side. The defence of rivers, how hard a thing it is, we find examples in all histories that bear good witness. The deepest have many fords, the swiftest and broadest may be passed by boats, in case it be found a matter of difficulty to make a bridge. He that hath men enow to defend all the length of his own bank, hath also enow to bear his enemy; and may therefore do better to let him come over, to his loss, than by striving in vain to hinder the passage as a matter tending to his own disadvantage, fill the heads of his soldiers with an opinion that they are in ill case, having their means of safeguard taken from them by the skill or valour of such as are too good for them. Certainly, if a river were sufficient defence against an army, the Isle of Mona, now called Anglesey, which is divided from North Wales by an arm of the sea, had been safe enough against the Romans, invading it under conduct of Julius Agricola. But he wanting, and not meaning to spend the time in making, vessels to transport his forces, did essay the fords. Whereby he so amazed the enemies attending for ships and suchlike provision by sea, that surely believing nothing could be hard or invincible to men which came so minded to war, they humbly entreated for peace, and yielded the Island. Yet the Britains were men stout enough, the Persians were very dastards. . . .

Here he understood of the death of Memnon, Darius' lieutenant, which heartened him greatly to pass on towards him; for of this only captain he had more respect than of all the multitude by Darius assembled, and of all the commanders he had besides. For so much hath the spirit of some one man excelled, as it hath undertaken and effected the alteration of the greatest states and commonwealths, the erection of monarchies, the conquest of kingdoms and empires, guided handfuls of men against multitudes of equal bodily strength, contrived victories beyond all hope and discourse of reason, converted the fearful passions of his own followers into magnanimity, and the valour of his enemies into cowardice; such spirits have been stirred up in sundry ages of the world and in divers parts thereof, to erect and cast down again, to establish and to destroy, and to bring all things, persons and

states, to the same certain ends which the infinite spirit of the Universal, piercing, moving, and governing all things, hath ordained. Certainly the things that this king did were marvellous, and would hardly have been undertaken by any man else; and though his father had determined to have invaded the lesser Asia, it is likely enough that he would have contented himself with some part thereof, and not have discovered the river of Indus as this man did. The swift course of victory, wherewith he ran over so large a portion of the world in so short a space, may justly be imputed unto this, that he was never encountered by an equal spirit concurring with equal power against him. Hereby it came to pass that his actions, being limited by no greater opposition than desert places, and the mere length of tedious journeys could make, were like the colossus of Rhodes, not so much to be admired for the workmanship, though therein also praiseworthy, as for the huge bulk. For certainly, the things performed by Xenophon discover as brave a spirit as Alexander's, and working no less exquisitely, though the effects were less material, as were also the forces and power of command by which it was wrought. But he that would find the exact pattern of a noble commander must look upon such as Epaminondas, that encountering worthy captains and those better followed than themselves, have by their singular virtue overtopped their valiant enemies and still prevailed over those that would not have yielded one foot to any other. Such as these are do seldom live to obtain great empires. For it is a work of more labour and longer time to master the equal forces of one hardy and well-ordered state, than to tread down and utterly subdue a multitude of servile nations, compounding the body of a gross unwieldy empire. Wherefore these *Parvo Potentes,* men that with little have done much upon enemies of like ability, are to be regarded as choice examples of worth; but great conquerors, to be rather admired for the substance of their actions than the exquisite managing; exactness and greatness concurring so seldom that I can find no instance of both in one, save only that brave Roman, Caesar.

Having this far digressed, it is now time that we return unto our Eastern conqueror, who is travelling hastily towards Cilicia, with a desire to recover the straits thereof before Darius should arrive there. But first making a despatch into Greece, he sent to those cities in which he reposed most trust some of the Persian targets which he had recovered in his first battle; upon which, by certain inscriptions, he made them partakers of his victory. Herein he well advised himself;

for he that doth not as well impart of the honour which he gains in the wars, as he doth of the spoils, shall never be long followed of those of the better sort. For men which are either well born or well bred, and have more of wealth than of reputation, do as often satisfy themselves with the purchase of glory, as the weak in fortune and strong in courage do with the gain of gold and silver.

The governor of Cilicia, hearing of Alexander coming on, left some companies to keep the straits, which were indeed very defencible; and withal, as Curtius noteth, he began over-late to prize and put in execution the counsel of Memnon, who in the beginning of the wars advised him to waste all the provisions for men and horse that could not be lodged in strong places, and always to give ground to the invader till he found some such notable advantage, as might assuredly promise him the obtaining of victory. For the fury of an invading army is best broken by delays, change of diet, and want, eating sometimes too little and sometimes too much, sometimes reposing themselves in beds and more oftener on the cold ground. These and the like sudden alterations bring many defeats upon all nations out of their own countries. Therefore, if Darius had kept the Macedonians but a while from meat and sleep, and refusing to give or take battle, had wearied them with his light horse, as the Parthians afterward did the Romans, he might perchance have saved his own life and his estate. For it was one of the greatest encouragements given by Alexander to the Macedonians, in the third and last fatal battle, that they were to fight with all the strength of Persia at once.

Xerxes, when he invaded Greece and fought abroad, in being beaten lost only his men, but Darius being invaded by the Greeks and fighting at home, by being beaten, lost his kingdom. Pericles, though the Lacedaemonians burnt all in Attica to the gates of Athens, yet could not be drawn to hazard a battle; for the invaded ought evermore to fight upon the advantage of time and place. Because we read histories to inform our understanding by the examples therein found, we will give some instances of those that have perished by adventuring in their own countries to charge an invading army.

The Romans, by fighting with Hannibal, were brought to the brink of their destruction. Pompey was well advised for a while, when he gave Caesar ground, but when by the importunity of his captains he adventured to fight at Pharsalia, he lost the battle, lost the freedom of Rome, and his own life. Ferdinand, in the conquest of Naples, would

needs fight a battle with the French to his confusion, though it was told him by a man of sound judgement that those counsels which promise surety in all things are honourable enough. The Constable of France made frustrate the mighty preparation of Charles the Fifth, when he invaded Provence, by wasting the country and forbearing to fight; so did the Duke of Alva weary the French in Naples, and dissolve the boisterous army of the Prince of Orange in the Low Countries. The Leigers, contrary to the advice of their general, would needs fight a battle with the Bourgonians invading their country, and could not be persuaded to linger the time and stay their advantage; but they lost eight and twenty thousand upon the place. Philip of Valois set upon King Edward at Crecy; and King John, when the English were well near tired out, and would in short time by an orderly pursuit have been wasted to nothing, constrained the Black Prince with great fury, near Poitiers, to join battle with him. But all men know what lamentable success these two French Kings found. Charles the Fifth of France made another kind of Fabian-Warfare, and though the English burnt and wasted many places, yet this King held his resolution to forbear blows, and followed his advice, which told him that the English could never get his inheritance by smoke; and it is reported, by Belloy and Herrault, that King Edward was wont to say of this Charles that he won from him the Duchy of Guienne without ever putting on his armour.

But where God hath a purpose to destroy, wise men grow short-lived, and the charge of things is committed unto such as either cannot see what is for their good, or know not how to put in execution any sound advice. The course which Memnon had propounded must in all appearance of reason have brought the Macedonians to a great perplexity, and made him stand still a while at the straits of Cilicia, doubting whether it were more shameful to return, or dangerous to proceed. For had Cappadocia and Paphlagonia been wasted whilst Alexander was far off, and the straits of Cilicia been defended by Arsenes, governor of that province, with the best of his forces, hunger would not have suffered the enemy to stay the trial of all means that might be thought upon, of forcing that passage; or if the place could not have been maintained, yet might Cilicia at better leisure have been so thoroughly spoiled that the heart of his army should have been broken by seeking out miseries by painful travel.

But Arsenes, leaving a small number to defend the straits, took the

best of his army with him, to waste and spoil the country, or rather, as may seem, to find himself some work by pretence of which he might honestly run further away from Alexander. He should rather have adventured his person in custody of the straits, whereby he might perhaps have saved the province, and in the mean time all that was in the fields would have been conveyed into strong towns. So should his army if it were driven from the place of advantage, have found good entertainment within walled cities, and himself, with his horsemen, have had the less work in destroying that little which was left abroad. Handling the matter as he did, he gave the Cilicians cause to wish for Alexander's coming, and as great cause to the keepers of the passage not to hinder it. For cowards are wise in apprehending all forms of danger. These guardians of the straits, hearing that Arsenes made all haste to join himself with Darius, burning down all as he went like one despairing of the defence, began to grow circumspect and to think that surely their general, who gave as lost the country behind their backs, had exposed themselves unto certain death, as men that were good for nothing else but to dull the Macedonian swords. Wherefore, not affecting to die for their Prince and country, which honour they saw that Arsenes himself could well forbear, they speedily followed the footsteps of their general, gleaning after his harvest. Thus Alexander, without labour, got both the entrance of Cilicia, abandoned by the cowardice of his enemies, and the whole province that had been alienated from the Persian side by their indiscretion.

In the mean season, Darius approached, who, as Curtius reports, had compounded an army of more than two hundred and ninety thousand soldiers out of divers nations. Justine musters them at three hundred thousand foot and a hundred thousand horse, Plutarch at six hundred thousand.

The manner of his coming on, as Curtius describes it, was rather like a masker than a man of war, and like one that took more care to set out his glory and riches than to provide for his own safety, persuading himself, as it seemed, to beat Alexander with pomp and sumptuous pageants. For before the army there was carried the holy fire which the Persians worshipped, attended by their priests, and after them three hundred and threescore and five young men, answering the number of the days of the year, covered with scarlet; then the chariot of Jupiter drawn with white horses, with their riders clothed in the same colour

with rods of gold in their hands; and after it, the horse of the Sun. Next after these follow ten sumptuous chariots, inlaid and garnished with silver and gold, and then the vanguard of their horse, compounded of twelve several nations, which, the better to avoid confusion, did hardly understand each other's language, and these marshalled in the head of the rest, being beaten, might serve very fitly to disorder all that followed them. In the tail of these horses, the regiment of foot marched, with the Persians called immortal, because if any died, the number was presently supplied; and these were armed with chains of gold, and their coats with the same metal embroidered, whereof the sleeves were garnished with pearl: baits either to catch the hungry Macedonians withal, or to persuade them that it were great incivility to cut and to deface such glorious garments. But it was well said: *Sumptuose inductus miles, se virtute superiorem aliis non existimet, cum in prœliis oporteat fortitudine animi, et non vestimentus muniri, quoniam hostes vestibus non debellantur*; Let no man think that he exceedeth those in valour whom he exceedeth in gay garments; for it is by men armed with fortitude of mind, and not by the apparel they put on, that enemies are beaten. And it was perchance from the Roman Papyrius that this advice was borrowed, who, when he fought against the Samnites in that fatal battle wherein they all swear either to prevail or die, thirty thousand of them having apparelled themselves in white garments with high crests and great plumes of feathers, bade the Roman soldiers to lay aside all fear: *Non enim cristas vulnera facere, et per picta atque aurata scuta transire Romanum pilum*; For these plumed crests would wound nobody, and the Roman *pilum* would bore holes in painted and gilded shields.

To second this court-like company, fifteen thousand were appointed more rich and glittering than the former, but apparelled like women (belike to breed the more terror) and these were honoured with the title of the King's kinsmen. Then came Darius himself, the gentlemen of his guard-robe riding before his chariot, which was supported with the gods of his nation, cast and cut in pure gold; these the Macedonians did not serve, but they served their turns of these by changing their massy bodies into thin portable and current coin. The head of this chariot was set with precious stones, with two little golden idols, covered with an open-winged eagle of the same metal. The hinder part, being raised high whereon Darius sat, had a covering of inestimable value. This chariot of the King was followed with ten thousand horse-

men, their lances plated with silver and their heads gilt; which they meant not to imbrue in the Macedonian blood for fear of marring their beauty. He had for the proper guard of his own person two hundred of the blood royal, blood too royal and precious to be spilt by any valourous adventure (I am of opinion that two hundred sturdy fellows, like the Switzers, would have done him more service), and these were backed with thirty thousand footmen, after whom again were led four hundred spare horses for the King, which if he had meant to have used, he would have marshalled somewhat nearer him.

Now followed the rearward, the same being led by Sisygambis, the King's mother, and by his wife, drawn in glorious chariots, followed by a great train of ladies, their attendants on horseback, with fifteen wagons of the King's children, and the wives of the nobility, waited on by two hundred and fifty concubines, and a world of nurses and eunuchs, most sumptuously apparelled. By which it should seem that Darius thought that the Macedonians had been comedians or tumblers, for this troop was far fitter to behold those sports than to be present at battles. Between these and a company of slight-armed slaves, with a world of valets, was the King's treasure, charged on six hundred mules, and three hundred camels, brought, as it proved, to pay the Macedonians. In this sort came the May-game King into the field, encumbered with a most unnecessary train of strumpets, attended with troups of divers nations, speaking divers languages, and for their numbers impossible to be marshalled, and for the most part so effeminate, and so rich in gold and in garments, as the same could not but have encouraged the nakedest nation of the world against them. We find it in daily experience, that all discourse of magnanimity, of national virtue, of religion, of liberty, and whatsoever else hath been wont to move and encourage virtuous men, hath no force at all with the common soldier in comparison of spoils and riches. The rich ships are boarded upon all disadvantages, the rich towns are furiously assaulted, and the plentiful countries willingly invaded. Our English nation have attempted many places in the Indies, and run upon the Spaniards headlong, in hope of the royals of plate and pistolets; which, had they been put to it upon the like disadvantages in Ireland, or in any poor country, they would have turned their pieces and pikes against their commanders, contesting that they had been brought without reason to the butchery and slaughter. It is true that the war is made willingly, and for the most part with good success, that is ordained against the

richest nations; for as the needy are always adventurous, so plenty is wont to shun peril, and men that have well to live, do rather study how to live well, I mean wealthily, than care to die, as they call it honourably. *Car où il n'y a rien a gaigner que des coups, volontiers il n'y va pas.* No man makes haste to the market, where there is nothing to be bought but blows.

Now, if Alexander had beheld this preparation before his consultation with his soothsayers, he would have satisfied himself by the outsides of the Persians, and never have looked into the entrails of beasts for success. For leaving the description of this second battle (which is indeed nowhere well described, neither for the confusion and hasty running away of the Asians could it be), we have enough by the slaughter that was made of them, and by the few that fell of the Macedonians, to inform us what manner of resistance was made. For, if it be true that threescore thousand Persian footmen were slain in this battle, with ten thousand of their horsemen, or, as Curtius saith, an hundred thousand footmen, with the same number of horsemen, and besides this slaughter, forty thousand taken prisoners, while of Alexander's army there miscarried but two hundred and fourscore of all sorts, of which numbers Arianus and other historians cut off almost the one half: I do verily believe, that this small number rather died with the over-travail and painstaking in killing their enemies, than by any strokes received from them. And surely, if the Persian nation (at this time degenerate and the basest of the world) had had any savour remaining of the ancient valour of their forefathers, they would never have sold so good cheap, and at so vile a price, the mother, the wife, the daughters, and other the King's children, had their own honour been valued by them at nothing, and the King's safety and his estate at less. Darius by this time found it true, that Charidemus, a banished Greecian of Athens, had told him, when he made a view of his army about Babylon, to wit, that the multitude which he had assembled of divers nations, richly attired but poorly armed, would be found more terrible to the inhabitants of the country, whom in passing they would devour, than to the Macedonians, whom they meant to assail; who, being all old and obedient soldiers, embattled in gross squadrons which they call their phalanx, well covered with armour for defence and furnished with weapons for offence of great advantage, would make so little account of his delicate Persians, loving their ease and their palate, being withal ill armed and worse disciplined, as except it would please

him to entertain (having so great abundance of treasure to do it withal) a sufficient number of the same Greecians, and so to encounter the Macedonians with men of equal courage, he would repent him overlate, as taught by the miserable success like to follow.

But this discourse was so unpleasing to Darius, who had been accustomed to nothing so much as to his own praises, and to nothing so little as to hear truth, as he commanded that this poor Greecian should be presently slain; who, while he was asundering in the tormentor's hand, used this speech to the King: that Alexander, against whom he had given this good counsel, should assuredly revenge his death, and lay deserved punishment upon Darius for despising his advice.

It was the saying of a wise man: *Desperata eius Principis salus est, cuius aures ita formatae sunt, ut aspera quae utilia, nec quicquam nisi iucundum accipiat*; That princes' safety is in a desperate case whose ears judge all that is profitable to be too sharp, and will entertain nothing that is unpleasant. For liberty in counsel is the life and essence of counsel; *Libertas consilii est eius vita, et essentia, qua erepta consilium evanescit.*

Darius did likewise value at nothing the advice given him by the Grecian soldiers that served him, who entreated him not to fight in the straits. But had they been counsellers and directors in that war, as they were underlings and commanded by others, they had with the help of a good troup of horsemen been able to have opposed the fury of Alexander without any assistance of the Persian footmen. For when Darius was overthrown with all his cowardly and confused rabble, those Grecians under their captain Amyntas held firm and marched away in order, in despite of the vanquishers. Old soldiers are not easily dismayed; we read in histories ancient and modern what brave retreats have been made by them, though the rest of the army in which they have served hath been broken.

At the battle of Ravenna, where the Imperials were beaten by the French, a squadron of Spaniards, old soldiers, came off unbroken and undismayed, whom, when Gaston de Foix, Duke of Nemures and nephew to Louis the Twelfth, charged, as holding the victory not entire by their escape, he was overturned and slain in the place. For it is truly said of those men, who, by being acquainted with dangers fear them not, that *Neglecto periculo imminentis mali opus ipsum quantumuis difficile aggrediuntur*; They go about the business itself, how hard soever it be, notwithstanding to consider of the danger which the

mischief hanging over their heads may bring, and as truly of those that know the wars but by hearsay: *Quod valentes sunt et praevalentes ante pericula, in ipsis tamen periculis discedunt*; They have ability enough and to spare till dangers appear, but when peril indeed comes, they get them gone.

These Grecians also, that made the retreat, advised Darius to retire his army into the plain of Mesopotamia, to the end that Alexander, being entered into those large fields and great champaigns, he might have environed the Macedonians on all sides with his multitude; and withal, they counselled him to divide that his huge army into parts, not committing the whole to one stroke of Fortune, whereby he might have fought many battles, and have brought no greater numbers at once than might have been well marshalled and conducted. But this counsel was so contrary to the cowardly affections of the Persians, as they persuaded Darius to environ the Grecians which gave the advice, and to cut them in pieces as traitors. The infinite wisdom of God doth not work always by one and the same way, but very often, in the alteration of kingdoms and estates, by taking understanding from the governors, so as they can neither give nor discern of counsels. For Darius that would needs fight with Alexander upon a straitened piece of ground near unto the city of Issus, where he could bring no more hands to fight than Alexander could, who, by the advice of Parmenio stayed there as in a place of best advantage, was utterly overthrown, his treasure lost, his wife, mother, and children (whom the Greecians his followers had persuaded him to leave in Babylon, or elsewhere) taken prisoners, and all their train of ladies spoiled of their rich garments, jewels, and honour. It is true, that both the Queen, with her daughters, who had the good hap to be brought to Alexander's presence, were entertained with all respect due unto their birth, their honours preserved, and their jewels and rich garments restored unto them; and though Darius' wife was a most beautiful lady, and his daughters of excellent form, yet Alexander mastered his affections towards them all. Only it is reported out of Aristobulus the historian that he embraced the wife of the valiant Memnon, her husband lately dead, who was taken flying from Damascus by Parmenio, at which time the daughters of Ochus, who reigned before Darius, and the wives and children of all the nobility of Persia, in effect, fell into a captivity; at which time also Darius' treasure not lost at Issus was seized, amounting

to six thousand and two hundred talents of coin, and of bullion five hundred talents, with a world of riches besides.

Darius himself leaving his brother dead, with divers others of his chief captains—casting the crown from his head—hardly escaped.

After this overthrow given unto Darius, all Phoenicia, the city of Tyre excepted, was yielded to Alexander, of which Parmenio was made governor.

WILLIAM CAMDEN

1551–1623

Modernized from pages 128–33, 136–44, and 146–47 of the English edition of 1630. I have omitted details of peace negotiations and some domestic events. Camden gives no references, for he wanted The History of the most renowned and virtuous princess Elizabeth, late Queen of England . . . composed by way of Annals *to be a popular book, and it is worth comparing his account with that given in Garrett Mattingly's superb* The Spanish Armada *(1959). Camden's careful handling of the religious issue is partly due to fear of the censorship, but his decision to leave details "to the ecclesiastical historiographer" had a theoretical justification; Bacon sharply distinguishes between civil and ecclesiastical history, and permits each to carry out only intermittent raids into the other's territory. The reference to the astronomer of Konigsberg should not be taken to show that Camden believed that human events were determined by supernatural phenomena. He describes a series of earthquakes in 1580 followed by Catholic infiltration into the state, but quickly adds that the papists were responsible themselves for the troubles that resulted.*

For the Britannia, *see Stuart Piggott, "William Camden and the* Britannia," *in* Proceedings of the British Academy, *1951; for the* Annals, *F. Smith Fussner,* The Historical Revolution, *1962, chapter 9; for a sympathetic general picture, F. M. Powicke, "Camden," in* Essays and Studies, *1948.*

Now are we come to the year of Christ one thousand, five hundred, eighty and eight, which an astronomer of Kongisberg above an hundred years before, foretold would be an admirable year, and the German chronologers presaged would be the climaterical year of the world. The rumours of wars, which before were but slight, began now to increase every day more and more; and now not by uncertain fame, but by loud and joint voice of all men, it was noised abroad that a most invincible Armado was rigged and prepared in Spain against England, and that the famousest captains and expertest leaders and old soldiers were sent for out of Italy, Sicily, yea and out of America, into Spain.

For of late the Bishop of Rome, certain religious men of Spain, and some English fugitives out of their country, had revoked the Spaniard to his design for conquering of England, which was interrupted ten years before by the Portugal wars; earnestly exhorting him, that seeing God has blessed him with immeasurable blessings and benefits: Portugal, with East India, and very many most rich islands being laid to his dominions, he in like manner would perform somewhat which might be acceptable to God the giver of so great good things, and most worthy the majesty of the Catholic King. But nothing was more acceptable to God, or more worthy of him, than to propagate the Church of God. That the Church of God could not be more gloriously, nor with greater merit propagated, than by conquering of England, and replanting the Catholic Roman religion, abolishing heresy. This war, said they, would be most just, not only because it was necessary, but also for that it was for maintenance of Christ's religion; considering that the Queen of England being excommunicate, persisted contumacious against the Church of Rome, supported his rebels in the Netherlands, annoyed the Spaniards with continual depredations, surprised and sacked his towns in Spain and America, and had very lately put the Queen of Scots to death, violating the majesty of all kings. And no less profitable would this war be, than it was just. For so should he lay unto his empire most flourishing kingdoms, extinguish the rebellion in the Low Countries which was cheered as it were with an English gale, secure his voyages from both Indies, and abate his yearly expenses in convoying his Indian fleets forward and backward. And for easy proof hereof they suggested that the English navy was neither for number, nor greatness, nor strength, comparable to that of Spain, the

Portugal fleet being now joined unto it; that England was not fortified, that it was unprovided of leaders, soldiers, horsemen, and munition, bare of wealth and friends; that there were many in all parts of the realm addicted to the Romish religion, which would presently join their forces with his. In brief, that so great was the strength of the Spaniard both by sea and land, and so unmatchable the valour of the Spaniards that no man durst oppose against him, and they might most confidently assure themselves of the victory. Moreover, that now an opportunity was offered him as it were by God, when he had no cause to fear any thing neither from the Turk, having lately concluded a truce with him, nor from the French, who were now embroiled in civil war. They made him believe also that England was easier to be conquered than the Netherlands; for that it was a shorter cut by sea, and more opportune out of Spain into England, namely by an open sea, but into the Netherlands longer and more difficult, by a sea for a great part shut up and lying over against England. Also, that the Low Countries were as it were a continued bulwark, fortified everywhere with so many cities and castles, but England with none; so as it was an easy matter for them to pierce presently into the very bowels of the land, as well as they had done of late into Portugal. And lastly, out of that military axiom: that it is not good leaving an enemy at our back, that the English therefore being most bitter enemies to the Spaniards, must before all things needs be vanquished, upon whose aid the Netherlanders relying, had so long time sustained the burden of the war, and without whom they could not subsist. So as England being once conquered, the Low Countries must of necessity be subdued.

These things being thus disposed, they enter into serious consultation about the manner of invading England. Don Alvares Bassano, Marquess of Santa Cruce, to whom was committed the principal charge and conduct of the Armado, was of opinion that first and foremost some port town in Holland or Zealand was at unawares to be surprised by the Prince of Parma's land forces, and by some Spanish ships sent before, where the Spanish fleet might have harbour, and from whence it might commodiously begin the invasion, considering that in the troublous British sea, the winds often changing, and wherein the tides were especially to be observed, the fleet could not ride in safety. With him agreed in opinion the Prince of Parma, who urged this expedition tooth and nail. Yet others liked not this project, as being a matter difficult, full of danger, of long time, much labour, great expense, and

doubtful success; and that it could neither be done privily, nor at unawares, but would easily be prevented by the English. These men were of opinion, that with the same charge England might easilier be won, and that the victory would be certain and assured, if a well appointed army out of Spain and the Low Countries, might be landed with a strong fleet at the Thames mouth, and London, the chief city, surprised by a sudden assault. This seemed to them most easy to be effected, and therefore all concurred in opinion that it was forthwith to be put in execution. Amongst these, notwithstanding, some thought it meet, that war should be first denounced by an herald, and that, in a subtle purpose as they thought, both to remove suspicion out of the neighbour princes' minds, and also to drive the Queen to call foreign forces to her aid, hoping that they (according to the insolent manner of mercenaries) would mutiny and spoil the country; and that thereby she would procure the ill will of her subjects, all things would grow most confused in England. But these were not harkened unto amongst men grown fierce with confidence of their own strength, and they held it sufficient to commend the cause, Armado, and army to the Bishop of Rome, and the prayers of the Catholics to God and the Saints, and to set forth a book in print with maps for a terror, wherein the whole preparation was particularly set down; which certainly was so great throughout all Spain, Italy, and Sicily that the Spaniards themselves were abashed at it, and named it The Invincible Armado.

The Prince of Parma also in the Netherlands, by the King of Spain's commandment, built ships and very many flat-bottomed boats, each of them big enough to carry 30 horse, with bridges fitted to them; hired mariners from East Germany, prepared piles sharpened at the nether end, headed with iron and hooked on the sides; made ready twenty thousand barrels and an infinite number of faggots; and in the coast towns of Flanders he had an army in readiness of 103 companies of foot, and 4,000 horse, amongst which were 700 English fugitives who of all others were held in greatest contempt; neither was Stanley, who had the command of them, nor Westmorland, nor others which offered their service and counsel, once heard, but for their impiety to their country barred from all access, and as most inauspicious conductors, worthily with detestation rejected. Sixtus Quintus also, Bishop of Rome, that he might not seem to fail the cause, sent Cardinal Allen, an Englishman, into the Low Countries, renewed the Bulls declaratory of Pius Quintus and Gregory the 13th, excommunicated the Queen, un-

throned her, absolved her subjects from all allegiance, and published his Croisado in print, as against Turks and infidels, wherein out of the treasure of the Church he gave plenary indulgences to all that gave their assistance. Whereupon the Marquess of Burgawe of the house of Austria, the Duke of Pastrana, Amadeus of Savoy, Vespasian Gonzaga, John de Medici, and very many noblemen from all parts gave their names voluntarily to this enterprise.

Queen Elizabeth on the other side, that she might not be taken unprovided, prepared with all diligence as strong a fleet as she could, and all thing necessary for war. And she herself, who in discerning of men's dispositions was of most sharp judgement, and ever most happy, having the free choice in her self, and not by the commendations of others, assigned to every office by name the best men. The charge of the whole fleet she committed to Charles Howard of Effingham, Lord Admiral of England, of whose happiness she had a very good persuasion, and whom she knew both by his moderation and nobility to be skilfull in sea matters, wary in providence, valiant in courage, industrious in action, and of great authority amongst the sailors of her navy. Him she sent betimes to the west parts of England, where Drake, whom she made Vice Admiral, joined with him. The lord Henry Seymour, second son to the Duke of Somerset, she commanded to lie upon the coast of the Low Countries with 40 ships, English and Netherlandish, and to watch that the Prince of Parma might not come forth with his forces; though some there were which earnestly persuaded her to attend the enemy's coming, and to welcome him with a land battle, according as had been deliberated in the reign of Henry VIII when the French with a strong fleet threatened England.

For land fight there were disposed along the south coasts 20,000 men: and two armies besides of most choice and expert men were levied, the one under the command of the Earl of Leicester, consisting of 1,000 horse and 22,000 foot: which encamped at Tilbury, not far from the Thames mouth (for the enemy was fully resolved to set first upon London); the other under the leading of the Lord of Hunsdon, consisting of 34,000 foot and 2,000 horse, to guard the Queen's person.

Arthur Lord Grey, Sir Francis Knolles, Sir John Norreys, Sir Richard Bingham, and Sir Roger Williams, knights and worthy warriors, were selected to consult about the manner of the land war. These men thought good that the commodious landing places for the enemy, as well out of Spain as out of the Low Countries, should be manned

and fortified: namely, Milford Haven, Falmouth, Plymouth, Portland, the Isle of Wight, Portsmouth, that open coast of Kent which we call The Downs, the Thames mouth, Harwich, Yarmouth, Hull, etc., and that the trained soldiers throughout the coast shires should meet upon a signal given to defend the said places, and do their best to prohibit the enemy's landing. And if the enemy did land, to leave all the country waste round about, to taint all things that might be of use unto them, that they might find nothing for food but what they should carry on their shoulders; and to hold the enemy busied night and day with continual alarums in such sort as they should give them no rest: but not to attempt the hazard of a battle till more leaders with their companies were come together. Of which leaders they named one in every shire to have the principal command. I list not to relate particularly what midland shires they assigned to aid this and that coast, what number, what arms, and what manner of fight they prescribed.

In this troublesome season, when some beat many times into the Queen's ears that the Spaniards abroad were not so much to be feared as the Papists at home, for that the Spaniards would not attempt any hostility against England, but upon confidence of aid from them; and that therefore for the more security the Papist's heads were for some cause or other to be cut off; alleging the example of King Henry VIII, when the Emperor and the French King, by the instigation of the Pope, were ready to invade England. For as soon as he had put to death the Marquess of Exeter, the Baron of Montacute, Edward Neville, and others whom he suspected would favour their enterprise, their expedition presently was dashed. But the Queen, disliking this as cruel counsel, thought it sufficient to commit some of the Papists, and those not of the chief, to custody at Wisbeach in the Fens. And casting her eyes and mind on all sides, she by often letters excited the estates, who slept not all this while. Sir William FitzWilliams, Lord Deputy of Ireland, she instructed what she should do; the King of Scots she put in mind by her favourers in Scotland and by messengers to be most wary of Papists and the Spanish faction. But he, not ignorant how great a tempest and destruction threatened, was of his own accord incited, and, according to his continual affection to the true religion and the Queen, had before already refused to give audience to the Bishop of Dumblane that was sent from the Bishop of Rome, and had procured a confederacy to be made betwixt the Protestants of Scotland for resisting the Spaniards. And he himself marching in person with an

army into Annandale, forced Maxwell out of his trenches, who, contrary to his faith given, was returned out of Spain into Scotland favouring the Spaniard, and cast him in prison, proclaimed the Spaniards to be holden for enemies, and prepared against them with great alacrity.

Amongst these no small preparations for war on both sides, projects of peace were not quite laid aside. . . .

* * *

[These, however, came] to nothing; undertaken by the Queen, as the wiser sort have judged, to divert the Spanish fleet, and continued by the Spaniard to the end to surprise England unawares and unprovided, so as they seemed on both sides to sew the fox's skin to the lion's.

The said Spanish fleet, being the best appointed of men, munition and all manner of provision, of all that ever the ocean saw, and called by the arrogant name of Invincible, consisted of 130 ships, in which were.

Soldiers	19,290
Sailors	8,350
Galley-slaves	2,080
Great ordinance	2,630

Don Alphonso Perez de Guzman, Duke of Medina Sidonia, had the principal command thereof (for Don Antonio Columna, Duke of Paliano, and the Marquess of Santa Croce, to whom this command was appointed, died both of them while the fleet was in rigging), and under him John Martinez de Recalde, a most skilful seaman.

The 29th of May the fleet set sail out of the river Tajo, and while it bent the course towards the Groin in Galicia, it was wholly scattered asunder by a hideous tempest, and hardly met again some few days after at the Groin and other harbours near thereabouts, three galleys being conveyed into France by the help of David Gwynne, an English slave, and treachery of the Turkish owners. It was reported to be so weatherbeaten and distressed that the Queen was certainly persuaded that this fleet was not to be looked for this year; and Secretary Walsingham wrote to the Lord Admiral to send back four of the greatest ships, as if the war were now at an end. The Lord Admiral did not lightly believe it, and therefore by a gentle answer prayed that nothing might be rashly credited in so weighty a matter, and that he might

retain them, though it were at his own charges. And taking the benefit of a favourable wind, he set sail toward Spain to surprise the enemy's weatherbeaten ships in the harbours. When he was not far from the coast of Spain, the wind turned into the south, and he, who was commanded to defend the coast of England, fearing lest with the same wind they might arrive in England undescried, returned to Plymouth.

With the same wind the Duke of Medina set sail with the whole fleet from the Groin the 12th day of July, according to the account of the Julian year; and after a day or two he sent Roderico Tely before into the Low Countries, to advertise the Prince of Parma of the coming of the fleet, and to put him in mind what was best to be done. For he had in charge to join with the Prince of Parma's forces and shipping, and to conduct them under the favour of his fleet into England, and withal to set the land forces on shore at the Thames mouth. And now will I briefly relate out of the most credible reports as well of the Spaniards, as of our own countrymen, what was done every day in this voyage, that the truth may the more plainly appear.

The 16th day there was a great calm, and a thick fog till noon; then the northeast wind blew very strongly, and soon after the west wind till midnight, and then the east-south-east wind, insomuch as the Spanish fleet being dispersed was hardly gathered together again till it came within kenning of England the 19th day. Upon which day the Lord Admiral of England, being certainly advertised by Fleming, a captain of a pinnace, that the Spanish fleet was entered into the British sea (which the common sort of soldiers call the Channel) and was seen near the point called the Lizard, towed the English fleet forth into the deep sea, not without great difficulty, certainly with singular diligence and admirable alacrity of the sailors, cheering them with his own presence amongst them at their hawser work, the wind blowing sore into the haven.

The next day the English descried the Spanish fleet with lofty towers castle-like, in front like a half-moon, the horns stretching forth about the breadth of seven miles, sailing as it were with labour of the winds, and groaning of the ocean, slowly though with full sails; and willingly they suffer it to pass by, that they might chase them in the rear with a foreright wind.

The 21st of July the Lord Admiral of England, sending a pinnace before called the Defiance, denounced war by discharging her ordinance, and presently with much thundering out of his own ship,

called the Arkroyal, he first set upon the Admiral (as he thought) of the Spaniards (but it was Alphonso de Leva's ship). Soon after, Drake, Hawkins and Forbisher played with their ordinance upon the hindmost squadron, which was commanded by Recalde, who laboured all he could to stay his men that fled to the fleet till his own ship being much battered with shot, and now grown unserviceable, hardly withdrew itself to the main fleet. At which time the Duke of Medina gathered together his fleet scattered here and there, and hoisting more sail, held on his intended course. Neither could he do any other, seeing both the wind favoured the English, and their ships would turn about with incredible celerity which way soever they would to charge, wind, and tack about again. And now had they maintained an hot fight the space of two hours, when the Lord Admiral thought no good to continue the fight any longer, for that 40 of his ships were not yet come in, being scarce yet gotten out of the haven.

The next night following, the Saint Catherine, a Spanish ship, having been much torn and battered in this fight, was taken into the middest of the fleet to be repaired. And an huge ship of Biscay, of Oquendo's, in which was the King's treasurer, began to flame of a light fire by force of gunpowder, which was fired of purpose by a Netherland gunner which was misused. Yet was the fire soon quenched by ships sent in to help her; amongst which the galleon of Don Pedro de Valdes, falling foul of another ship, broke her foremast or bowsprit, and being left behind, for that no man (the sea being troublous and the night dark) could come to rescue her, fell into Drake's hands as good prize, who sent Valdes to Dartmouth, and left the money to be rifled by his men. He being commanded to carry a lantern that night, neglected it, having five great hulks in chase belonging to merchants of Germany, supposing them to be enemies: whereby he caused almost the whole English fleet to lie still, for that the night light was nowhere to be seen. Neither did he and the rest of the fleet till towards night the next day, recover sight of the Lord Admiral, who all the night before, with two ships, the Bear and the Maryrose, followed the Spanish lantern. All this day the Duke laboured securely in setting his fleet in order. To Alphonso de Leva he gave in charge to join the first and the last squadron together: to every ship he assigned his quarter to ride in, according to the form prescribed in Spain, upon pain of death to those that should abandon their quarter; Glich, an ensign-bearer, he sent to the Prince of Parma, to show him in what state he was; and the aforesaid Biscayne ship of Oquendo's he committed to the waves,

having shipped the King's money and the men into other ships. Which ship fell the same day into the Englishmen's hands, with about 50 sailors and soldiers, most pitifully maimed and half burnt, and was brought into the haven of Weymouth.

The 23rd day of the month, betimes in the morning, the Spaniards, taking the benefit of a northerly wind, turned about against the English, who for their advantage soon turned aside towards the west: and after they had strived to get the wind one of another, they prepared themselves on both sides to fight; and fight they did confusedly and with variable fortune, whilst on the one side the English manfully rescued the ships of London that were hemmed in by the Spaniards, and on the other side the Spaniards as stoutly delivered Recalde, being in danger. Never was heard greater thundering of ordinance on both sides; which notwithstanding from the Spaniards flew for the most part over the English without harm: only Cock, an Englishman, died with honour in the midst of the enemies in a small ship of his. For the English ships, being far the lesser, charged the enemy with marvellous agility, and having discharged their broadsides, flew forth presently into the deep, and levelled their shot directly without missing at those great ships of the Spaniards, which were heavy and altogether unwieldy. And the Lord Admiral thought not good to hazard fight by grappling with them, as some unadvised people persuaded him. For the enemy had a strong army in the fleet; he had none. Their ships were far more in number, of bigger burthen, stronger, and higher built: so as from those which defended aloft from the hatches nothing but certain death would hang over the heads of those which would charge from beneath. And he foresaw that the overthrow would endamage him much more than the victory would avail him. For being vanquished he should have brought England into extreme hazard; and being conqueror he should only have gained a little glory for overthrowing the fleet and beating the enemy.

The 24th day of the month they ceased on both sides from fighting. The Lord Admiral sent some of the smaller ships to the next coasts of England, to fetch powder and other provision for fight: and divided the whole fleet into four squadrons, whereof the first he commanded himself, the second he committed to Drake, the third to Hawkins, and the fourth to Frobisher; and appointed out of every squadron certain small vessels to give the charge from divers parts in the dead of the night; but being becalmed, his design failed of the effect.

The 25th, which was Saint James his day, the Saint Anne, a galleon

of Portugal which could not hold course with the rest, was set upon by certain small English ships: to whose rescue came Leva and Don Diego Telles Enriques with three galleases: which the Lord Admiral himself, and the Lord Thomas Howard in the Golden Lion, towing three ships with their boats (so great was the calm), charged in such sort with force of their ordinance that much ado they had, and not without loss, to free the galleon; and from that time no galleases would undertake to fight. The Spaniards' report that the English the same day beat the Spanish Admiral in the outer squadron with their great ordinance nearer than before, and having slain many men shot down her main mast, but Mexia and Recalde in good time repulsed the English; that the Spanish Admiral, assisted by Recalde and others, set upon the English Admiral, and that the English Admiral escaped by means of the wind turning; that the Spaniards from that time gave over the pursuit, and holding on their course, dispatched a messenger again to Parma to join his fleet with all speed with the King's Armado, and withal to send great shot. These things were unknown to the English, who write that from one of the Spanish ships they rent the lantern, and from another the beak head, and did much hurt to the third; that the Nonpareil and the Maryrose fought awhile with the Spaniards; and that other ships rescued the Triumph which was in danger. Thus in the manner of the fights, they which were present thereat do not report the same things of the same, whilst every one on both sides mentioned what he himself observed.

The next day the Lord Admiral knighted the Lord Thomas Howard, the Lord Sheffield, Roger Townsend, John Hawkins and Martin Frobisher for their valour. And it was resolved from thenceforth to assail the enemy no more till they came to the British firth or Straight of Calais, where the Lord Henry Seymour and Sir William Winter awaited their coming. So with a fair Etesian gale (which in our sky bloweth for the most part from the south-west and by south clear and fair), the Spanish fleet sailed forward, the English fleet following it close at the heels. But so far was it from terrifying the sea coast with the name of Invincible, or with the terrible spectacle, that the youth of England with a certain incredible alacrity (leaving their parents, wives, children, cousins and friends out of their entire love to their country) hired ships from all parts at their own private charges and joined with the fleet in great number: and amongst others the earls of Oxford, Northumberland, Cumberland, Thomas and Robert Cecil, Henry Brooke, Charles Blunt, Walter Raleigh, William Hatton, Robert Cary,

Ambrose Willoughby, Thomas Gerard, Arthur Gorges, and others of good note.

The twenty seventh day of this month, towards night, the Spaniards came to an anchor before Calais, being warned by the pilots that if they proceeded any farther it was to be feared lest they should be driven by force of the tide into the North Ocean. And near unto them also rode at anchor the Lord Admiral with his ships within cannon shot of them: with whom Seymour and Winter joined their ships. And now were there in the English fleet 140 sail, all able ships to fight, sail, and wind about which way they would: yet were there not above fifteen which in a manner sustained and repulsed the whole weight of the fight. The Spaniards forthwith, as they had done many times before, urged the Duke of Parma by messengers dispatched one after another, to send 40 flyboats, that is, light vessels, without which he could not well fight with the English by reason of the over-greatness and slowness of the Spanish ships and the singular agility of the English; and they most earnestly prayed him to put to sea with his army, which the Spanish fleet would protect as it were under her wings (for so it was resolved) till it were landed in England. But he being unready could not be present at their call, his flat-bottomed boats for the shallow channels leaked, his provision of victuals was not ready, and his sailors, having been stayed hitherto against their wills, had withdrawn themselves. There lay watching also at the entrance of the havens of Dunkirk and Newport, whence he was to put forth to sea, the ships of war of the Hollanders and Zealanders, so strangely provided of great ordinance and musketeers that he could not put from shore unless he would wilfully thrust himself and his upon present death. And yet he, a skilful and industrious warrior, seemed to omit nothing, being inflamed with desire of the conquest of England.

But Queen Elizabeth's foresight prevented both his diligence and the credulous hope of the Spaniards; for by her commandment, the next day after the Spaniards had cast anchor, the Lord Admiral made ready eight of his worst ships, besmeared with wild-fire, pitch, and rosin, and filled with brimstone and other combustible matter, and sent them down the wind in the dead of the night under the guiding of Young and Prouse, into the Spanish fleet. Which when the Spaniards espied approaching towards them, the whole sea being light with the flame thereof, supposing that those incendiary ships, besides the danger of the fire, were also provided of deadly engines and murdering inventions, they raised a pitiful cry, weighed anchor, cut their cables,

and in a terrible panic fear, with great haste and confusion, put to sea. Amongst which the great galleas, having broken her rudder, floated up and down, and the next day, fearfully making towards Calais, ran aground upon the sands and was fought withal with variable fortune by Amyas Preston, Thomas Gerard, and Harvey; Don Hugo de Moncada the captain being slain, and the soldiers and rowers either drowned or put to the sword, and a great quantity of gold being pillaged. The ship and ordinance fell to the Governor of Calais.

The Spaniards report that the Duke, when those incendiary ships approached, commanded the whole fleet to weigh anchor, yet so as, having avoided the danger, every ship should return to his quarter. And certainly he returned himself, giving a sign to the rest to do the like by discharging a great piece, which notwithstanding was heard but of a few, for that they being scattered all about, were driven for fear, some of them into the wide ocean, and some upon the shallows of Flanders.

In the mean time Drake and Fenner played hotly with their ordinance upon the Spanish Fleet that was gathering together again, over, against, Gravelines; with whom presently after joined Fenton, Southwell, Beeston, Cross, Riman, and, soon after, the Lord Admiral himself, the Lord Thomas Howard, and the Lord Sheffield. The Duke, Leva, Oquendo, Recalde, and the rest, with much ado got clear of the shallows and sustained the charge all they could, insomuch as most of their ships were very much torn and shot through. The galleon Saint Matthew, under the command of Don Diego Pimentelli, coming to rescue Don Francisco de Toledo in the Saint Philip (which was sore battered with many great shot by Seymour and Winter, driven near Ostend and again shot through and through by the Zealanders, and taken by the Flushingers) was likewise taken, and the whole Spanish fleet most grievously distressed all the day long.

The last day of the month betimes in the morning the west-north-west wind blew hard, and the Spanish fleet, labouring to return to the narrow strait, was driven toward Zealand. The English gave over the chase because (as the Spaniards think) they saw them almost carried to their ruin: for, the west-north-west wind blowing, they could not but run aground upon the sands and shallows near Zealand. But the wind turning presently into the south-west and by west, they sailed before the wind, and being clear of the shallows, in the evening they consulted what to do, and by common consent it was resolved to return into

Spain by the North Ocean, for that they wanted many necessaries, especially great shot, their ships were torn, and no hope there was that the Prince of Parma could bring forth his fleet.

Wherefore being now carried forth into the deep, they directed their course northward, the English fleet having them in chase; against which now and then they turned head. And whereas most men thought they would return, the Queen with a manly courage took view of her army and camp at Tilbury, and walking through the ranks of armed men placed on both sides, with a leader's truncheon in her hand, sometimes with a martial pace, and sometimes like a woman, incredible it is how much she strengthened the hearts of her captains and soldiers by her presence and speech.

The same day that the last fight was, the Prince of Parma, after he had made his prayers to our Lady of Hall, came somewhat late to Dunkirk, where he was received with opprobrious speeches of the Spaniards, as if in favour of Queen Elizabeth he had overthrown a goodly opportunity to work some noble exploit. The Duke, to give them some kind of satisfaction, punished the purveyors of victuals, laughing in his sleeve at the insolency of the Spaniards, for that he had heard them boasting that whithersoever they went they carried assured victory along with them; and that the English would not once abide to look them in the face. And surely Don Bernardin de Mendoza vainly and falsely printed a poem in France of a triumph before the victory. Howbeit, that Parma might not come forth from Dunkirk, the Lord Admiral commanded the Lord Henry Seymour and the Hollanders to keep watch upon the coast of Flanders while he himself chased the Spaniards till they were gone past Edinburgh Firth in Scotland, anciently called Bodotria. For some there were which feared lest they would have recourse to the King of Scots, who was already exasperated for his mother's death. Certainly Ashby, the Queen's Ambassador in Scotland, to pacify his mind, offered him this month large conditions; to wit, the title of a dukedom in England, a yearly pension of £5000, a guard to be maintained at the Queen's charge, and other matters, whether out of his own head or by commandment of others I cannot well say, nor do I list to be curious in searching: but upon him the blame fell, and the conditions were never performed.

But the Spaniards now casting away all hope of returning, and seeking to save themselves by no other means but by flight, stayed in no place. And thus the Armado, which had been full three years in rigging and preparing, with infinite expense, was within one month many times

assailed, and at the length defeated with the slaughter of many men, not an hundred of the English being lacking, nor one small ship lost, save only that of Cock's: for all the shot out of the tall Spanish ships flew quite over the English ships. And after it had been driven round about all Britain, by Scotland, the Orcades, and Ireland, most grievously tossed, and very much distressed and wasted by storm, wracks, and all kind of miseries, at length returned home with dishonour. Whereupon moneys were stamped, some in memory thereof with a fleet flying with full sails, and this inscription, *Venit, vidit, fugit;* that is: It came, it saw, it fled; others in honour of the Queen, with incendiary ships and a fleet confused, and inscribed, *Dux foemina facti;* that is: A woman was conductor of the fact. In their flight certain it is that many ships were cast away upon the coasts of Scotland and Ireland, and above 700 soldiers and sailors cast on land in Scotland, which at the intercession of the Prince of Parma to the King of Scots, and by permission of Queen Elizabeth, were after a year sent over into the Low Countries. But more unmercifully were those miserable wretches dealt withal whose hap was to be driven by tempests into Ireland, for they were slain some of them by the wild Irish, and some put to the sword by commandment of the Lord Deputy. For he fearing lest they would join with the Irish rebels, and seeing that Bingham, Governor of Connaught, having been once or twice commanded to show rigour upon them which had yielded themselves had refused to do it, sent Fowl, Deputy Marshall, who drew them out of their lurking holes and beheaded about 200 of them; which the Queen from her heart condemned as a matter full of cruelty. Herewith the rest being terrified, sick and starven as they were, they committed themselves to the sea in their broken vessels, and were many of them swallowed of the waves.

The Spaniards that returned imputed this misfortune to the Prince of Parma's negligence, and their own obsequious wisdom who thought it a foul fault to break the religious observance of their instructions; for by their instructions they were most strictly commanded not to attempt anything before such time as the Prince of Parma had joined his forces with theirs, and nothing was left to their own judgement and discretion as occasion should serve. Otherwise they bragged that they could very easily have surprised the English fleet in the haven. And martial men sharply disputed whether instructions were religiously to be observed whatsoever should befall, lest through neglect of obedience, the royal authority and command should be violated;

or whether they might upon necessity correct their instructions, and apply them to the present use according as new matter should arise, lest weighty importances and opportunities to work great matters should be lost.

The Spanish King himself bore the overthrow patiently, as received from God, and gave and commanded to be given all over Spain thanks to God and the Saints that it was no more grievous; and used singular mercy in relieving the distressed soldiers and sailors.

Queen Elizabeth in like manner commanded public rejoicing and prayers and thanksgiving to be used throughout all the churches of England: and she herself, going as it were in triumph, went with a very gallant train of noblemen through the streets of London, which were hung with blue cloth, and the companies of the City standing on both sides with their banners in goodly order, being carried in a chariot drawn with two horses (for coaches were not then so much in use amongst princes as now they are amongst private men) to Paul's Church (where the banners taken from the enemy were hung forth to be seen), gave most humble thanks to God, and was present at a sermon wherein the glory was given to God only. To the Lord Admiral she assigned certain rents for his service, and many times commended him and the captains of her ships as born for the preservation of their country. The rest she graciously saluted by name as oft as she saw them, as men of passing good desert (wherewith they held themselves well rewarded), and those that were hurt and poor she rewarded with reasonable pensions. The learned both at home and abroad, congratulating the victory with hearts leaping for joy, wrote triumphall poems in all languages. . . .

* * *

As England was troubled with outward war, so did it travail this year of an inward schism also (for schism evermore springeth up most rankly in the heat of war). And certainly never did contumacious impudency, and contumelious malapertness against ecclesiastical magistrates advance itself more insolently. For when the Queen (who was *Always the Same*) would not harken to innovators in religion who would, as she thought, cut the sinews of the ecclesiastical government and her royal prerogative, some of those which only esteemed the discipline of the church of Geneva thought there could not be any other means devised to establish the same in England than by inveighing against the English hierarchy, and raising ill-will among the

people against the bishops and prelates. These men therefore set forth scandalous books against both the Church government and prelates, the titles whereof were *Martin Marr-Prelate, Mineralls, Diotrephes, Demonstration of discipline,* etc. Wherein they belched forth most virulent calumniations and opprobrities in such scurrilous manner that the authors might seem rather scullions out of the kitchen then followers of piety. Yet the authors thereof were Penry and Udall, ministers of the word, and Job Throckmorton, a learned man and a pleasant talker. Their favourers were Sir Richard Knightley and Wigston, knights, men otherwise good, grave, and wise (but circumvented by certain ministers which aimed at some private respect of their own). For which the said Knights had smarted by a grievous fine laid upon them in the Star Chamber, had not the Archbishop of Canterbury (such was his mildness) with much ado entreated and obtained a release thereof from the Queen.

Whilst these men, I say, by calumniations made way for their said discipline, others that had a hand in their counsels began to exercise the same in corners, contemning the authority of the laws, holding synods and conventicles in certain places, and instituting presbyteries. And for this cause were called into question Thomas Cartwright, Edmund Snape, Andrew King, Proudlow, Payne, and other ministers of the word: whom some over-hot people conspired to deliver out of the magistrates' hands. But how great the petulancy of these ministers was, which the Archbishop by his prudence and patience overcame, I leave to the ecclesiastical historiographer, to whom it belongeth.

SIR FRANCIS BACON

1561–1626

Of the two sections given here from The History of the Reign of King Henry the Seventh, *the first shows Bacon's interest in laws, "the principle acts of peace," as opposed to the more popular interest in battles and the principle acts of war. The second, which describes the origins of the Perkin Warbeck conspiracy and its conclusion with the King's decision to execute the ringleader (note the appeal of "the glimmering of a confiscation" to Henry's money mania), demonstrates how Bacon took advantage of his freedom from a strict annalistic chronology.*

A modern version of the events of Henry's reign will be found in J. B. Mackie, The Early Tudors, *revised edition 1952; and the best discussion of Bacon's attitude toward history in L. F. Dean, "Francis Bacon's theory of civil history-writing," in* English Literary History, *1941. For a biography and Bacon's correspondence, see J. Spedding, R. C. Ellis, and D. D. Heath,* Collected Works of Francis Bacon, *14 vols., 1857–74.*

I

IN THE END of the fourth year the king had called again his parliament, not, as it seemeth, for any particular occasion of state: but the former parliament being ended somewhat suddenly, in regard of the preparation for Britain, the king thought he had not remunerated his people sufficiently with good laws, which evermore was his retribution for treasure. And finding by the insurrection in the north, there was discontentment abroad, in respect of the subsidy, he thought it good

to give his subjects yet farther contentment and comfort in that kind. Certainly his times for good commonwealth's laws did excel. So as he may justly be celebrated for the best lawgiver to this nation, after king Edward the First: for his laws, whoso marks them well, are deep, and not vulgar; not made upon the spur of a particular occasion for the present, but out of providence of the future, to make the estate of his people still more and more happy; after the manner of the legislators in ancient and heroical times.

First therefore he made a law, suitable to his own acts and times: for as himself had in his person and marriage made a final concord, in the great suit and title for the crown; so by this law he settled the like peace and quiet in the private possessions of the subjects: ordaining, "That fines thenceforth should be final, to conclude all strangers' rights;" and that upon fines levied and solemnly proclaimed, the subject should have his time of watch for five years after his title accrued; which if he forepassed, his right should be bound for ever after; with some exception nevertheless of minors, married women, and such incompetent persons.

This statute did in effect but restore an ancient statute of the realm, which was itself also made but in affirmance of the common law. The alteration had been by a statute, commonly called the statute of *non-claim,* made in the time of Edward the Third. And surely this law was a kind of prognostic of the good peace, which since his time hath, for the most part, continued in this kingdom until this day: for statutes of *non-claim* are fit for times of war, when men's heads are troubled, that they cannot intend their estate; but statutes that quiet possessions, are fittest for times of peace, to extinguish suits and contentions, which is one of the banes of peace.

Another statute was made, of singular policy, for the population apparently, and, if it be thoroughly considered, for the soldiery and military forces of the realm.

Enclosures at that time began to be more frequent, whereby arable land, which could not be manured without people and families, was turned into pasture, which was easily rid by a few herdsmen; and tenances for years, lives, and at will, whereupon much of the yeomanry lived, were turned into demesnes. This bred a decay of people, and, by consequence, a decay of towns, churches, tithes, and the like. The king likewise knew full well, and in no wise forgot, that there ensued withal upon this a decay and diminution of subsidies and taxes; for the more gentlemen, ever the lower books of subsidies. In

remedying of this inconvenience the king's wisdom was admirable, and the parliament's at that time. Enclosures they would not forbid, for that had been to forbid the improvement of the patrimony of the kingdom; nor tillage they would not compel, for that was to strive with nature and utility; but they took a course to take away depopulating enclosures and depopulating pasturage, and yet not by that name, or by any imperious express prohibition, but by consequence. The ordinance was, "That all houses of husbandry, that were used with twenty acres of ground and upwards, should be maintained and kept up for ever; together with a competent proportion of land to be used and occupied with them;" and in no wise to be severed from them, as by another statute, made afterwards in his successor's time, was more fully declared: this upon forfeiture to be taken, not by way of popular action, but by seizure of the land itself by the king and lords of the fee, as to half the profits, till the houses and lands were restored. By this means the houses being kept up, did of necessity enforce a dweller; and the proportion of land for occupation being kept up, did of necessity enforce that dweller not to be a beggar or cottager, but a man of some substance, that might keep hinds and servants, and set the plough on going. This did wonderfully concern the might and mannerhood of the kingdom, to have farms as it were of a standard, sufficient to maintain an able body out of penury, and did in effect amortise a great part of the lands of the kingdom unto the hold and occupation of the yeomanry or middle people, of a condition between gentlemen and cottagers or peasants. Now, how much this did advance the military power of the kingdom, is apparent by the true principles of war and the examples of other kingdoms. For it hath been held by the general opinion of men of best judgment in the wars, howsoever some few have varied, and that it may receive some distinction of case, that the principal strength of an army consisteth in the infantry or foot. And to make good infantry, it requireth men bred, not in a servile or indigent fashion, but in some free and plentiful manner. Therefore if a state run most to noblemen and gentlemen, and that the husbandmen and ploughmen be but as their workfolks and labourers, or else mere cottagers, which are but housed beggars, you may have a good cavalry, but never good stable bands of foot; like to coppice woods, that if you leave in them staddles too thick, they will run to bushes and briers, and have little clean underwood. And this is to be seen in France and Italy, and some other parts abroad, where in effect all is nobless or peasantry, I speak

of people out of towns, and no middle people; and therefore no good forces of foot: insomuch as they are forced to employ mercenary bands of Switzers, and the like, for their battalions of foot. Whereby also it comes to pass, that those nations have much people, and few soldiers. Whereas the king saw, that contrariwise it would follow, that England, though much less in territory, yet should have infinitely more soldiers of their native forces than those other nations have. Thus did the king secretly sow Hydra's teeth; whereupon, according to the poet's fiction, should rise up armed men for the service of the kingdom.

The king also, having care to make his realm potent, as well by sea as by land, for the better maintenance of the navy, ordained; "That wines and woads from the parts of Gascoign and Languedoc, should not be brought but in English bottoms"; bowing the ancient policy of this estate, from consideration of plenty to consideration of power. For that almost all the ancient statutes incite by all means merchant-strangers, to bring in all sorts of commodities; having for end cheapness, and not looking to the point of state concerning the naval power.

The king also made a statute in that parliament, monitory and minatory towards justices of peace, that they should duly execute their office, inviting complaints against them, first to their fellow-justices, then to the justices of assize, then to the king or chancellor: and that a proclamation which he had published of that tenor, should be read in open sessions four times a year, to keep them awake. Meaning also to have his laws executed, and thereby to reap either obedience or forfeitures, wherein towards his latter times he did decline too much to the left hand, he did ordain remedy against the practice that was grown in use, to stop and damp informations upon penal laws, by procuring informations by collusion to be put in by the confederates of the delinquents, to be faintly prosecuted, and let fall at pleasure; and pleading them in bar of the informations, which were prosecuted with effect.

He made also laws for the correction of the mint, and counterfeiting of foreign coin current. And that no payment in gold should be made to any merchant-stranger, the better to keep treasure within the realm, for that gold was the metal that lay in the least room.

He made also statutes for the maintenance of drapery, and the keeping of wools within the realm; and not only so, but for stinting and limiting the prices of cloth, one for the finer, and another for the

coarser sort. Which I note, both because it was a rare thing to set prices by statute, especially upon our home commodities; and because of the wise model of this act, not prescribing prices, but stinting them not to exceed a rate; that the clothier might drape accordingly as he might afford.

Divers other good statutes were made that parliament, but these were the principal. And here I do desire those into whose hands this work shall fall, that they do take in good part my long insisting upon the laws that were made in this king's reign. Whereof I have these reasons; both because it was the pre-eminent virtue and merit of this king to whose memory I do honour; and because it hath some correspondence to my person; but chiefly because, in my judgment, it is some defect even in the best writers of history, that they do not often enough summarily deliver and set down the most memorable laws that passed in the times whereof they writ, being indeed the principal acts of peace. For though they may be had in original books of law themselves; yet that informeth not the judgment of kings and counsellors, and persons of estate, so well as to see them described, and entered in the table and portrait of the times.

II

At this time the king began again to be haunted with spirits, by the magic and curious arts of the lady Margaret; who raised up the ghost of Richard duke of York, second son to king Edward the Fourth, to walk and vex the king. This was a finer counterfeit stone than Lambert Simnel; better done, and worn upon greater hands; being graced after with the wearing of a king of France, and a king of Scotland, not of a duchess of Burgundy only. And for Simnel, there was not much in him, more than that he was a handsome boy, and did not shame his robes. But this youth, of whom we are now to speak, was such a mercurial, as the like hath seldom been known; and could make his own part, if at any time he chanced to be out. Wherefore this being one of the strangest examples of a personation that ever was in elder or later times; it deserveth to be discovered, and related at the full. Although the king's manner of showing things by pieces, and by dark lights, hath so muffled it, that it hath left it almost as a mystery to this day.

The lady Margaret, whom the king's friends called Juno, because she was to him as Juno was to Aeneas, stirring both heaven and hell to do him mischief, for a foundation of her particular practices against

him, did continually, by all means possible, nourish, maintain, and divulge the flying opinion, that Richard duke of York, second son to Edward the Fourth, was not murdered in the Tower, as was given out, but saved alive. For that those who were employed in that barbarous fact, having destroyed the elder brother, were stricken with remorse and compassion towards the younger, and set him privily at liberty to seek his fortune. This lure she cast abroad, thinking that this fame and belief together with the fresh example of Lambert Simnel, would draw at one time or other some birds to strike upon it. She used likewise a farther diligence, not committing all to chance; for she had some secret espials, like to the Turk's commissioners for children of tribute, to look abroad for handsome and graceful youths, to make Plantagenets, and dukes of York. At the last she did light on one, in whom all things met, as one would wish, to serve her turn for a counterfeit of Richard duke of York.

This was Perkin Warbeck, whose adventures we shall now describe. For first, the years agreed well. Secondly, he was a youth of fine favour and shape. But more than that, he had such a crafty and bewitching fashion, both to move pity, and to induce belief, as was like a kind of fascination and enchantment to those that saw him or heard him. Thirdly, he had been from his childhood such a wanderer, or, as the king called him, such a landloper, as it was extreme hard to hunt out his nest and parents. Neither again could any man, by company or conversing with him, be able to say or detect well what he was, he did so flit from place to place. Lastly, there was a circumstance, which is mentioned by one that wrote in the same time, that is very likely to have made somewhat to the matter: which is, that king Edward the Fourth was his godfather. Which as it is somewhat suspicious for a wanton prince to become gossip in so mean a house, and might make a man think, that he might indeed have in him some base blood of the house of York; so at the least, though that were not, it might give the occasion to the boy, in being called king Edward's godson, or perhaps in sport king Edward's son, to entertain such thoughts into his head. For tutor he had none, for ought that appears, as Lambert Simnel had, until he came unto the lady Margaret who instructed him.

Thus therefore it came to pass: There was a townsman of Tournay, that had borne office in that town, whose name was John Osbeck, a convert jew, married to Catherine de Faro, whose business drew him to live for a time with his wife at London in king Edward the

Fourth's days. During which time he had a son by her, and being known in court, the king, either out of the religious nobleness, because he was a convert, or upon some private acquaintance, did him the honour to be godfather to his child, and named him Peter. But afterwards, proving a dainty and effeminate youth, he was commonly called by the diminutive of his name, Peterkin or Perkin. For as for the name of Warbeck, it was given him when they did but guess at it, before examinations had been taken. But yet he had been so much talked on by that name, as it stuck by him after his true name of Osbeck was known. While he was a young child, his parents returned with him to Tournay. Then was he placed in a house of a kinsman of his, called John Stenbeck, at Antwerp, and so roved up and down between Antwerp and Tournay, and other towns of Flanders, for a good time; living much in English company, and having the English tongue perfect. In which time, being grown a comely youth, he was brought by some of the espials of the lady Margaret into her presence. Who viewing him well, and seeing that he had a face and personage that would bear a noble fortune; and finding him otherwise of a fine spirit and winning behaviour; thought she had now found a curious piece of marble to carve out an image of the duke of York. She kept him by her a great while, but with extreme secrecy. The while she instructed him by many cabinet conferences. First, in princely behaviour and gesture; teaching him how he should keep state, and yet with a modest sense of his misfortunes. Then she informed him of all the circumstances and particulars that concerned the person of Richard duke of York, which he was to act; describing unto him the personages, lineaments, and features of the king and queen his pretended parents; and of his brother, and sisters, and divers others, that were nearest him in his childhood; together with all passages, some secret, some common, that were fit for a child's memory, until the death of king Edward. Then she added the particulars of the time from the king's death, until he and his brother were committed to the Tower, as well during the time he was abroad, as while he was in sanctuary. As for the times while he was in the Tower, and the manner of his brother's death, and his own escape; she knew they were things that a very few could control. And therefore she taught him only to tell a smooth and likely tale of those matters; warning him not to vary from it. It was agreed likewise between them, what account he should give of his peregrination abroad, intermixing many things which were true, and such as they knew others could testify,

for the credit of the rest; but still making them to hang together with the part he was to play. She taught him likewise how to avoid sundry captious and tempting questions, which were like to be asked of him. But in this she found him of himself so nimble and shifting, as she trusted much to his own wit and readiness; and therefore laboured the less in it. Lastly, she raised his thoughts with some present rewards, and farther promises; setting before him chiefly the glory and fortune of a crown if things went well, and a sure refuge to her court, if the worst should fall. After such time as she thought he was perfect in his lesson, she began to cast herself from what coast this blazing star should first appear, and at what time it must be upon the horizon of Ireland; for there had the like meteor strong influence before. The time of the apparition to be, when the king should be engaged into war with France. But well she knew, that whatsoever should come from her, would be suspected. And therefore, if he should go out of Flanders immediately into Ireland, she might be thought to have some hand in it. And besides, the time was not yet ripe; for that the two kings were then upon terms of peace. Therefore she wheeled about; and to put all suspicion afar off; and loth to keep him any longer by her, for that she knew secrets are not long-lived, she sent him unknown into Portugal with the lady Brampton, an English lady, that embarked for Portugal at that time; with some *privado* of her own, to have an eye upon him; and there he was to remain, and to expect her farther directions. In the mean time she omitted not to prepare things for his better welcome and accepting, not only in the kingdom of Ireland, but in the court of France. He continued in Portugal about a year; and by that time the king of England called his parliament, as hath been said, and declared open war against France. Now did the sign reign, and the constellation was come, under which Perkin should appear. And therefore he was straight sent unto by the duchess to go for Ireland, according to the first designment. In Ireland he did arrive at the town of Cork. When he was thither come, his own tale was, when he made his confession afterwards, that the Irishmen, finding him in some good clothes, came flocking about him, and bare him down that he was the Duke of Clarence that had been there before. And after that he was Richard the Third's base son. And lastly, that he was Richard duke of York, second son of Edward the Fourth. But that he, for his part, renounced all these things, and offered to swear upon the holy evangelists, that he was no such man; till at last they forced it upon him, and bad him fear nothing, and

so forth. But the truth is, that immediately upon his coming into Ireland, he took upon him the said person of the duke of York, and drew unto him complices and partakers by all the means he could devise. Insomuch as he wrote his letters unto the earls of Desmond and Kildare, to come in to his aid, and be of his party; the originals of which letters are yet extant.

Somewhat before this time, the duchess had also gained unto her a near servant of king Henry's own, one Stephen Frion, his secretary for the French tongue; an active man, but turbulent and discontented. This Frion had fled over to Charles, the French king, and put himself into his service, at such time as he began to be in open enmity with the king. Now king Charles, when he understood of the person and attempts of Perkin, ready of himself to embrace all advantages against the king of England, instigated by Frion, and formerly prepared by the lady Margaret, forthwith dispatched one Lucas and this Frion, in the nature of ambassadors to Perkin, to advertise him of the king's good inclination to him, and that he was resolved to aid him to recover his right against king Henry, an usurper of England and an enemy of France; and wished him to come over unto him at Paris. Perkin thought himself in heaven now that he was invited by so great a king in so honourable a manner. And imparting unto his friends in Ireland for their encouragement, how fortune called him, and what great hopes he had, sailed presently into France. When he was come to the court of France, the king received him with great honour; saluted, and styled him by the name of the duke of York; lodged him, and accommodated him in great state. And the better to give him the representation and the countenance of a prince, assigned him a guard for his person, whereof the lord Congresall was captain. The courtiers likewise, though it be ill mocking with the French, applied themselves to their king's bent, seeing there was reason of state for it. At the same time there repaired unto Perkin divers Englishmen of quality; Sir George Neville, Sir John Taylor, and about one hundred more; and amongst the rest, this Stephen Frion, of whom we spake, who followed his fortune both then and for a long time after, and was indeed his principal counsellor and instrument in all his proceedings. But all this on the French king's part was but a trick, the better to bow king Henry to peace. And therefore upon the first grain of incense, that was sacrificed upon the altar of peace at Boloign, Perkin was smoked away. Yet would not the French king deliver him up to king Henry, as he was aboured to do, for his

honour's sake, but warned him away and dismissed him. And Perkin on his part was as ready to be gone, doubting he might be caught up under-hand. He therefore took his way into Flanders, unto the duchess of Burgundy; pretending that having been variously tossed by fortune, he directed his course thither as to a safe harbour: no ways taking knowledge that he had ever been there before, but as if that had been his first address. The duchess, on the other part, made it as new and strange, to see him; pretending, at the first, that she was taught and made wise by the example of Lambert Simnel, how she did admit of any counterfeit stuff; though even in that, she said, she was not fully satisfied. She pretended at the first, and that was ever in the presence of others, to pose him and sift him, thereby to try whether he were indeed the very duke of York or no. But seeming to receive full satisfaction by his answers, she then feigned herself to be transported with a kind of astonishment, mixt of joy and wonder, at his miraculous deliverance; receiving him as if he were risen from death to life: and inferring, that God, who had in such wonderful manner preserved him from death, did likewise reserve him for some great and prosperous fortune. As for his dismission out of France, they interpreted it, not as if he were detected or neglected for a counterfeit deceiver; but contrariwise, that it did show manifestly unto the world, that he was some great matter; for that it was his abandoning that, in effect, made the peace; being no more but the sacrificing of a poor distressed prince unto the utility and ambition of two mighty monarchs. Neither was Perkin, for his part, wanting to himself, either in gracious or princely behaviour, or in ready and apposite answers, or in contenting and caressing those that did apply themselves unto him, or in pretty scorn and disdain to those that seemed to doubt of him; but in all things did notably acquit himself; insomuch as it was generally believed, as well amongst great persons, as amongst the vulgar, that he was indeed duke Richard. Nay, himself, with long and continued counterfeiting, and with oft telling a lie, was turned by habit almost into the thing he seemed to be; and from a liar to a believer. The duchess therefore, as in a case out of doubt, did him all princely honour, calling him always by the name of her nephew, and giving him the delicate title of the white rose of England: and appointed him a guard of thirty persons, halberdiers, clad in a party-coloured livery of murrey and blue, to attend his person. Her court likewise, and generally the Dutch and strangers, in their usage towards him, expressed no less respect.

The news hereof came blazing and thundering over into England, that the duke of York was sure alive. As for the name of Perkin Warbeck, it was not at that time come to light, but all the news ran upon the duke of York; that he had been entertained in Ireland, bought and sold in France, and was now plainly avowed, and in great honour in Flanders. These fames took hold of divers; in some upon discontent; in some upon ambition; in some upon levity and desire of change; and in some few upon conscience and belief; but in most upon simplicity; and in divers out of dependence upon some of the better sort, who did in secret favour and nourish these bruits. And it was not long ere these rumours of novelty had begotten others of scandal and murmur against the king and his government, taxing him for a great taxer of his people, and discountenancer of his nobility. The loss of Britain, and the peace with France, were not forgotten. But chiefly they fell upon the wrong that he did his queen, in that he did not reign in her right. Wherefore they said that God had now brought to light a masculine branch of the house of York, that would not be at his courtesy, howsoever he did depress his poor lady. And yet, as it fareth in the things which are current with the multitude, and which they affect, these fames grew so general, as the authors were lost in the generality of speakers. They being like running weeds that have no certain root; or like footings up and down, impossible to be traced; but after a while these ill humours drew to a head, and settled secretly in some eminent persons; which were, Sir William Stanley, lord chamberlain of the king's household, the lord Fitzwalter, Sir Simon Mountfort, and Sir Thomas Thwaites. These entered into a secret conspiracy to favour duke Richard's title.

* * *

Upon Allhallows-day even, being now the tenth year of the king's reign, the king's second son Henry was created duke of York; and as well the duke, as divers others, noblemen, knights-bachelors, and gentlemen of quality, were made knights of the Bath, according to the ceremony. Upon the morrow after twelfth-day, the king removed from Westminster, where he had kept his Christmas, to the Tower of London. This he did as soon as he had advertisement that Sir Robert Clifford, in whose bosom or budget most of Perkin's secrets were laid up, was come into England. And the place of the Tower was chosen to that end, that if Clifford should accuse any of the great ones, they might, without suspicion, or noise, or sending abroad of warrants, be

presently attached; the court and prison being within the cincture of one wall. After a day or two, the king drew unto him a selected council, and admitted Clifford to his presence; who first fell down at his feet, and in all humble manner craved the king's pardon; which the king then granted, though he were indeed secretly assured of his life before. Then commanded to tell his knowledge, he did amongst many others, of himself, not interrogated, impeach Sir William Stanley, the lord chamberlain of the king's household.

The king seemed to be much amazed at the naming of this lord, as if he had heard the news of some strange and fearful prodigy. To hear a man that had done him service of so high a nature, as to save his life, and set the crown upon his head; a man that enjoyed, by his favour and advancement, so great a fortune both in honour and riches; a man, that was tied unto him in so near a band of alliance, his brother having married the king's mother; and lastly, a man to whom he had committed the trust of his person, in making him his chamberlain: that this man, no ways disgraced, no ways discontent, no ways put in fear, should be false unto him. Clifford was required to say over again and again, the particulars of his accusation; being warned, that in a matter so unlikely, and that concerned so great a servant of the king's, he should not in any wise go too far. But the king finding that he did sadly and constantly, without hesitation or varying, and with those civil protestations that were fit, stand to that that he had said, offering to justify it upon his soul and life, he caused him to be removed. And after he had not a little bemoaned himself unto his council there present, gave order that Sir William Stanley should be restrained in his own chamber where he lay before in the square tower: and the next day he was examined by the lords. Upon his examination he denied little of that wherewith he was charged, nor endeavoured much to excuse or extenuate his fault: so that, not very wisely, thinking to make his offence less by confession, he made it enough for condemnation. It was conceived, that he trusted much to his former merits, and the interest that his brother had in the king. But those helps were overweighed by divers things that made against him, and were predominant in the king's nature and mind. First, an over-merit; for convenient merit, unto which reward may easily reach, doth best with kings. Next, the sense of his power; for the king thought, that he that could set him up, was the more dangerous to pull him down. Thirdly, the glimmering of a confiscation; for he was the richest subject for value in the kingdom: there being found in his castle of Holt forty

thousand marks in ready money and plate, besides jewels, household-stuff, stocks upon his grounds, and other personal estate, exceeding great. And for his revenue in land and fee, it was three thousand pounds a year of old rent, a great matter in those times. Lastly, the nature of the time; for if the king had been out of fear of his own estate, it was not unlike he would have spared his life. But the cloud of so great a rebellion hanging over his head, made him work sure. Wherefore after some six weeks' distance of time, which the king did honourably interpose, both to give space to his brother's intercession, and to show to the world that he had a conflict with himself what he should do: he was arraigned of high treason, and condemned, and presently after beheaded.

END

THE EARL OF CLARENDON

1609–1674

The first passage is from book four of The History of the Rebellion and Civil Wars in England, *which was published, posthumously, in 1702–04. It deals with the attempt of the opposition, headed by Pym, to push through and publish, as propaganda for the country at large, the Grand Remonstrance, in which the whole of the King's misdoings were listed. The debate was complicated by the fact that the opposition to the court was not itself united. The portrait of Charles I is taken from book eleven. I have used the text established by W. D. Macray, and published in six volumes, in 1888.*

The text and composition of the History *are fully discussed by C. Firth in three articles in the* English Historical Review, *1904. G. Huehns has edited a useful volume of selections in the Oxford World's Classics series (1955). Among the studies of Clarendon as a writer, the most illuminating is an article by L. C. Knights, "Reflections on Clarendon's* History of the Rebellion" *in* Scrutiny, *1948.*

Clarendon's account of the Remonstrance debate may be compared with J. H. Hexter's, in his The Reign of King Pym *(1941).*

I

ABOUT the time the news came of the King's being to begin his journey from Scotland upon a day appointed, and that he had settled all things in that kingdom to the general satisfaction, the committee for preparing the Remonstrance offered their report to the House, which caused the draught they offered to be read. It contained a very bitter

representation of the illegal things which had been done from the first hour of the King's coming to the crown to that minute, with all those sharp reflections which could be made upon the King himself, the Queen, and Council; and published all the unreasonable jealousies of the present government, of the introducing Popery, and all other particulars which might disturb the minds of the people, which were enough discomposed.

The House seemed generally to dislike it; many saying, 'that it was very unnecessary and unseasonable: unnecessary, all those grievances being already fully redressed, and the liberty and property of the subject being as well secured for the future as can possibly be done: and then, that it was very unseasonable, after the King had gratified them with granting every thing which they had desired of him, and after so long absence in the settling the disorders in another kingdom, which he had happily composed, to be now welcomed home with such a volume of reproaches for what others had done amiss and which he himself had reformed.' Notwithstanding all which, all the other party appeared passionately concerned that it might not be rejected, and enlarged themselves with as high expressions against the government as at first; with many insinuations 'that we were in danger of being deprived of all the good Acts which we had gained if great care and vigilance was not used to disappoint some counsels which were still entertained;' making doubtful glances and reflections upon the rebellion in Ireland, (with which they perceived many good men were easily amused), and in the end prevailed 'that a day should be appointed when the House should be resolved into a grand committee, and the Remonstrance to be then retaken into consideration:' and in the mean time they employed all their credit and interest with particular men, to persuade them that the passing that Remonstrance was most necessary for the preservation and maintenance of all those good laws which they had already made; giving several reasons to several persons, according to their natures and inclinations; assuring many that they intended it only for the mortification of the Court, and manifestation that the malignant party which appeared to be growing up in the House could not prevail, and then, that it should remain still in the clerk's hands and never be published.

And by these and the like arts they promised themselves that they should easily carry it: so that the day it was to be resumed, they entertained the House all the morning with other debates, and towards noon called for the Remonstrance; and it being urged by some that it was

too late to enter upon it with much difficulty they consented that it should be entered upon the next morning at nine of the clock, and every clause should be debated, the Speaker in the chair; for they would not have the House resolved into a Committee, which they believed would spend too much time. Oliver Cromwell (who at that time was little taken notice of) asked the lord Falkland, 'Why he would have it put off, for that day would quickly have determined it?' He answered, 'There would not have been time enough, for sure it would take some debate.' The other replied, 'A very sorry one:' they supposing, by the computation they had made, that very few would oppose it.

But he quickly found he was mistaken: for, the next morning, the debate being entered upon about nine of the clock in the morning, it continued all that day; and candles being called for when it grew dark, (neither side being very desirous to adjourn it till the next day; though it was evident very many withdrew themselves out of pure faintness, and disability to attend the conclusion,) the debate continued till after it was twelve of the clock, with much passion; and the House being then divided upon the passing or not passing it, it was carried for the affirmative by nine voices and no more: and as soon as it was declared, Mr. Hambden moved 'that there might be an order entered for the present printing it;' which produced a sharper debate than the former. It appeared then, that they did not intend to send it up to the House of Peers for their concurrence, but that it was upon the matter an appeal to the people, and to infuse jealousies into their minds. It had never been the custom to publish any debates or determinations of the House which [were] not regularly first transmitted to the House of Peers, not was it thought, in truth, that the House had authority to give warrant for the printing of any thing; all which was offered by Mr. Hyde with some warmth, as soon as the motion was made for the printing it; and he said 'he did believe the printing it in that manner was not lawful, and he feared it would produce mischievous effects; and therefore desired the leave of the House that, if the question should be put and carried in the affirmative, he might have liberty to enter his protestation.' Which he no sooner said than Geffry Palmer (a man of great reputation, and much esteemed in the House) stood up and made the same motion for himself, that he might likewise protest, when immediately together many afterwards, without distinction and in some disorder, cried out, 'They did protest:' so that there was after scarce any quiet and regular debate. But the House by

degrees being quieted, they all consented, about two of the clock in the morning, to adjourn till two of the clock the next afternoon. And as they went out of the House the lord Falkland asked Oliver Cromwell, 'Whether there had been a debate?' to which he answered, 'that he would take his word another time,' and whispered him in his ear, with some asseveration, 'that if the Remonstrance had been rejected he would have sold all he had the next morning, and never have seen England more; and he knew there were many other honest men of the same resolution.' So near was the poor kingdom at that time to its deliverance!

And, however they got this victory, they did not in a long time recover the spirits they lost, and the agony they had sustained, whilst it was in suspense; and they discerned well enough that the House had not at that time half its members, though they had provided that not a man of their party was absent, and that they had even then carried it by the hour of the night, which drove away a greater number of old and infirm opposers than would have made those of the negative superior in number; so that they had little hope in a fuller House to prevail in any of their unjust designs, except they found some other expedient, by hopes or fears, to work upon the affections of the several members.

In order to which, they spent most part of the next day in their private consultations how to chastise some of those who had most offended them the day before, and resolved, in the first place, not to suffer that precedent to be introduced into the House, 'that men should protest against the sense of the House:' which it is true had not been used in the House of Commons. And this subject was the more grateful to them because they should hereby take revenge upon Mr. Hyde, whom they perfectly hated above any man, and to whose activity they imputed the trouble they had sustained the day before; and he was the first who made the protestation, that is, asked leave to do it, which produced the other subsequent clamour, that was indeed in some disorder. But here they differed amongst themselves; all the leading violent men, who bore the greatest sway, were most glad of the occasion, as it gave them opportunity to be rid of Mr. Hyde, which they passionately desired: but sir John Hotham, Cholmely, and Stapleton, who never severed, and had a numerous train which attended their motions, remembered the service Mr. Hyde had done against the court of York, (the overthrowing whereof was their peculiar glory,) and would not consent that they should question him, but were ready to concur with

them in the prosecution of any other of the protesters, whereof there was number enough. This made so great difference amongst them that for the present they agreed no further than that they would that afternoon only provide that the next morning they would fall upon the matter; and so they might consult together at night what person they would sacrifice.

And so, about three of the clock, when the House met, Mr. Pimm lamented the disorder of the night before, which, he said, might probably have engaged the House in blood, and proceeded principally by the offering a protestation, which had never before been offered in that House, and was a transgression that ought to be severely examined, that mischief hereafter might not result from that precedent: and therefore proposed that the House would the next morning enter upon that examination, and in the meantime men might recollect themselves, and they who used to take notes might peruse their memorials, that the persons who were the chief causers of the disorder might be named, and defend themselves as best they could. And with this resolution the House rose; the vexation of the night before being very visible in the looks and countenance of many. And that night's deliberation, nor all the artifice or importunity that could be used, could not remove the obstinate Northern men from their resolution: and they declared positively that if they prosecuted Mr. Hyde, they and all their friends would engage in his defence: but the others would not incur the danger or inconvenience of such a schism; and so they unanimously agreed upon a third person whom they would accuse.

The next morning they first enlarged upon the offence itself; of 'the mischief it had liked to have produced, and of the mischief it would unavoidably produce if the custom or liberty of it was ever introduced; that it was the first time it had ever been offered in that House; and that care ought to be taken that it should be the last, by the severe judgment of the House upon those persons who had begun the presumption.'

Mr. Hyde, who had then known nothing of the private consultation, and had many reasons to believe himself to be designed, stood up (notwithstanding some signs made to him at a distance by his Northern friends, which he understood not) and said 'it concerned him to justify what he had done, being the first man who mentioned the protestation:' upon which there was a general noise and clamour 'to withdraw,' and as great 'to speak': upon which he proceeded, and said 'he was not old enough to know the ancient customs of that House; but that he well

knew it was a very ancient custom in the House of Peers, and leave was never denied to any man who asked that he might protest, and enter his dissent, against any judgment of the House to which he would not be understood to have given his consent: that he did not understand any reason why a commoner should not have the same liberty, if he desired not to be involved in any vote which he thought might possibly be inconvenient to him. That he had not offered his protestation against the Remonstrance, though he had opposed [it] all he could, because it remained still within those walls; that he had only desired leave to protest against the printing it, which he thought was not in many respects lawful for them to do, and might prove very pernicious to the public peace.'

They were very much offended with all he said and his confidence in speaking; and Mr. Strowde could not contain himself from saying, 'that that gentleman had confessed that he had first proposed the protestation,' and therefore desired he might withdraw, which many others likewise called for: till Sir John Hotham appeared with some warmth against it; and young Hotham, his son, accused Geffry Palmer of giving the cause of disorder, by saying '*I do protest*,' without asking the leave of the House, and encouraging men to cry out every man, '*I do protest*' whereupon they all fell into that noise and confusion; and so, without much more discourse, Mr. Palmer was called upon 'to explain'. Which as he was about to do, Mr. Hyde (who loved him much, and had rather have suffered himself than that he should) spake to the orders of the House, and said that 'it was against the orders and practice of the House that any man should be called upon to explain for any thing he said in the House two days before, when it could not be presumed that his own memory could recollect all the words he had used, or that any body else could charge him with them;' and appealed to the House whether there was any precedent of the like. And there is no doubt there never had been; and it was very irregular. But they were too positively resolved not to be diverted; and, after two hours' debate, Mr. Palmer himself desiring that, to save the House further trouble, he might answer, and withdraw, which he did, and when it drew towards night, after many hours' debate it was ordered that he should be committed to the Tower; the angry men pressing with all their power that he might be expelled the House, having borne him a long grudge for the civility he shewed in the prosecution of the earl of Strafford, that is, that he had not used the same reproachful language which the others had done: but they

were at last glad to compound for his bare commitment to the Tower, from whence he was within few days enlarged, and returned again to the House. And in the close of that day and the rising of the House, without much opposition, they obtained an order for the printing their Remonstrance. . . .

I know not how those men have already answered it to their own consciences, or how they will answer it to Him who can discern their consciences, who, having assumed their country's trust, and, it may be, with great earnestness laboured to procure that trust, by their supine laziness, negligence and absence were the first inlets to these inundations, and so contributed to those licenses which have overwhelmed us. For by this means, a handful of men, much inferior in the beginning in number and interest, came to give laws to the major part; and, to shew that three diligent persons are a greater number in arithmetic, as well as a more significant number in logic, than ten unconcerned, they, by plurality of voices, in the end converted or reduced the whole body to their opinions. It is true, men of activity and faction, in any design, have many advantages that a composed and settled council, though industrious enough, usually have not, and some that gallant men cannot give themselves leave to entertain; for, besides their through considering and forming their counsels before they begin to execute, they contract a habit of ill nature and uningenuity, necessary to their affairs and the temper of those upon whom they are to work, that liberal-minded men would not persuade themselves to entertain, even for the prevention of all the mischief the others intend. And whoever observed the ill arts these men used, to prevail upon the people in general; their absurd, ridiculous lying, to win the affections and corrupt the understandings of the weak, and the bold scandals to confirm the wilful; the boundless promises they presented to the ambitious, and their gross, abject flatteries and applications to the vulgar-spirited; would hardly give himself leave to use those weapons for the preservation of the three kingdoms.

The King besides had at that time a greater disadvantage (besides the concurrence of ill and extraordinary accidents) than himself or any of his progenitors had ever had before; having no servant of the House of Commons of interest, ability and reputation, and of faithfulness and affection to his service. . . . So whilst these men and their consorts with the greatest deliberation consulted and disposed themselves to compass confusion, they who, out of the most abstracted sense of

loyalty to the King and duty to their country, severed from any relations to the King, or hopes from the Court, preserved their own innocence, and endeavoured to uphold the good old frame of government, received neither countenance or conduct from those who were naturally to have taken care of that province. And sure the raging and fanatic distempers of the House of Commons (to which all other distempers are to be imputed) must most properly be attributed to the want of good ministers of the Crown in that assembly, who, being unawed by any guilt of their own, could have watched other men's, and informed, encouraged, and governed those who stood well inclined to the public peace.

To which purpose, if that stratagem (though none of the best) of winning men by places had been practised as soon as the resolution was taken at York to call a Parliament, (in which it was apparent dangerous attempts would be made, and that the Court could not be able to resist those attempts,) and if Mr. Pimm, Mr. Hambden, and Mr. Hollis, had been then preferred with Mr. St. John, before they were desperately embarked in their desperate designs, and had innocence enough about them to trust the King and be trusted by him, having yet contracted no personal animosities against him, it is very possible that they might either have been made instruments to have done good service, or at least been restrained from endeavouring to subvert the royal building, for supporting whereof they were placed as principal pillars.

But the rule the King gave himself, (very reasonable at another time,) that they should first do service and compass this or that thing for him before they should receive favour, was then very unseasonable: since, besides that they could not in truth do him that service without the qualification, it could not be expected they would desert that side by the power of which they were sure to make themselves considerable without an unquestionable mark of interest in the other, by which they were to keep up their power and reputation. And so, whilst the King expected they should manifest their inclinations to his service by their temper and moderation in those proceedings that most offended him, and they endeavoured by doing all the hurt they could to make evident the power they had to do him good, he grew so far disobliged and provoked that he could not in honour gratify them, and they so obnoxious and guilty that they could not think themselves secure in his favour: and thence, according to the policy and method

of injustice, combined to oppress that power they had injured, and to raise a security for themselves by disenabling the King to question their transgressions.

II

The several unheard of insolences which this excellent prince was forced to submit to at the other times he was brought before that odious judicatory, his majestic behaviour under so much insolence, and resolute insisting upon his own dignity, and defending it by manifest authorities in the law as well as by the clearest deductions from reason, the pronouncing that horrible sentence upon the most innocent person in the world, the execution of that sentence by the most execrable murder that ever was committed since that of our blessed Saviour, and the circumstances thereof; the application and interposition that was used by some noble persons to prevent that woeful murder, and the hypocrisy with which that interposition was deluded; the saint-like behaviour of that blessed martyr, and his Christian courage and patience at his death; are all particulars so well known, and have been so much enlarged upon in a treatise peculiarly applied to that purpose, that the farther mentioning it in this place would but afflict and grieve the reader, and make the relation itself odious; and therefore no more shall be said here of that lamentable tragedy, so much to the dishonour of the nation and the religion professed by it.

But it will not be unnecessary to add the short character of his person, that posterity may know the inestimable loss which the nation then underwent, in being deprived of a prince whose example would have had a greater influence upon the manners and piety of the nation than the most strict laws can have. To speak first of his private qualifications as a man, before the mention of his princely and royal virtues; he was, if ever any, the most worthy of the title of an honest man; so great a lover of justice, that no temptation could dispose him to a wrongful action, except it were so disguised to him that he believed it to be just. He had a tenderness and compassion of nature, which restrained him from ever doing a hard-hearted thing; and therefore he was so apt to grant pardon to malefactors, that his judges represented to him the damage and insecurity to the public that flowed from such his indulgence; and then he restrained himself from pardoning either murders or highway robberies, and quickly discerned the fruits of his severity by a wonderful reformation of those enormities. He was very punctual and regular in his devotions; so that he was never

known to enter upon his recreations or sports, though never so early in the morning, before he had been at public prayers; so that on hunting-days his chaplains were bound to a very early attendance. And he was likewise very strict in observing the hours of his private cabinet devotions; and was so severe an exactor of gravity and reverence in all mention of religion, that he could never endure any light or profane word in religion, with what sharpness of wit soever it was covered: and though he was well pleased and delighted with reading verses made upon any occasion, no man durst bring before him any thing that was profane or unclean; that kind of wit had never any countenance then. He was so great an example of conjugal affection, that they who did not imitate him in that particular did not brag of their liberty: and he did not only permit but direct his bishops to prosecute those scandalous vices in the ecclesiastical courts, against persons of eminence and near relation to his service.

His kingly virtues had some mixture and allay that hindered them from shining in full lustre, and from producing those fruits they should have been attended with. He was not in his nature bountiful, though he gave very much: which appeared more after the duke of Buckingham's death, after which those showers fell very rarely; and he paused too long in giving, which made those to whom he gave less sensible of the benefit. He kept state to the full, which made his Court very orderly; no man presuming to be seen in a place where he had no pretence to be. He saw and observed men long before he received any about his person, and did not love strangers, nor very confident men. He was a patient hearer of causes, which he frequently accustomed himself to at the Council board; and judged very well, and was dextrous in the mediating part: so that he often put an end to causes by persuasion, which the stubbornness of men's humours made dilatory in courts of justice.

He was very fearless in his person, but not enterprising; and had an excellent understanding, but was not confident enough of it; which made him oftentimes change his own opinion for a worse, and follow the advice of a man that did not judge so well as himself. And this made him more irresolute than the conjuncture of his affairs would admit. If he had been of a rougher and more imperious nature, he would have found more respect and duty; and his not applying some severe cures to approaching evils proceeded from the lenity of his nature and the tenderness of his conscience, which in all cases of blood made him choose the softer way, and not hearken to severe counsels,

how reasonably soever urged. This only restrained him from pursuing his advantage in the first Scots' expedition, when, humanly speaking, he might have reduced that nation to the most slavish obedience that could have been wished. But no man can say he had then many who advised him to it, but the contrary, by a wonderful indisposition all his Council had to fighting or any other fatigue. He was always an immoderate lover of the Scottish nation, having not only been born there, but educated by that people, and besieged by them always, having few English about him until he was king; and the major number of his servants being still of those, who he thought could never fail him; and then no man had such an ascendant over him, by the lowest and humblest insinuations, as duke Hambleton had.

As he excelled in all other virtues, so in temperance he was so strict, that he abhorred all deboshry to that degree, that, at a great festival solemnity, where he once was, when very many of the nobility of the English and Scots were entertained, being told by one who withdrew from thence, what vast draughts of wine they drank, and that there was one earl who had drank most of the rest down and was not himself moved or altered, the King said that he deserved to be hanged; and that earl coming shortly into the room where his majesty was, in some gaiety, to show how unhurt he was from that battle, the King sent one to bid him withdraw from his majesty's presence; nor did he in some days after appear before the King.

There were so many miraculous circumstances contributed to his ruin, that men might well think that heaven and earth conspired it, and that the stars designed it. Though he was, from the first declension of his power, so much betrayed by his own servants, that there were very few who remained faithful to him, yet that treachery proceeded not from any treasonable purpose to do him any harm, but from particular and personal animosities against other men. And afterwards, the terror all men were under of the Parliament, and the guilt they were conscious of themselves, made them watch all opportunities to make themselves gracious to those who could do them good; and so they became spies upon their master, and from one piece of knavery were hardened and confirmed to undertake another, till at last they had no hope of preservation but by the destruction of their master. And after all this, when a man might reasonably believe that less than a universal defection of three nations could not have reduced a great King to so ugly a fate, it is most certain that in that very hour when he was thus wickedly murdered in the sight of the sun, he had as great

a share in the hearts and affections of his subjects in general, was as much beloved, esteemed, and longed for by the people in general of the three nations, as any of his predecessors had ever been. To conclude: he was the worthiest gentleman, the best master, the best friend, the best husband, the best father, and the best Christian, that the age in which he lived had produced. And if he was not the best King, if he was without some parts and qualities which have made some kings great and happy, no other prince was ever unhappy who was possessed of half his virtues and endowments, and so much without any kind of vice.

DAVID HUME

1711–1776

The first two passages, which contain much that is central to Hume's analysis of the constitutional and party issues that led up to the civil war, were originally part of the text, but when Hume revised the History of England *he put them as notes in the back, "in order to avoid, as much as possible, the style of dissertation in the body of his history." The success of these pioneer passages of analysis, and of the third section, taken from the beginning of chapter 56, can be appreciated by comparing them with the recent account of early Stuart England and the composition of parties given in C. V. Wedgwood's* The King's Peace *(1955). The fourth section is from chapter 59, and the last from the conclusion to chapter 62, on the Commonwealth. "At this era" is the moment of the restoration of Charles II in 1660. The last line is a neat reminder of how much "the Whig interpretation of history" owes to this Tory history.*

On Hume as a historian, see G. H. Sabine, "Hume's contribution to historical method," in Philosophical Review, *1906, E. C. Mossner, "An Apology for David Hume, Historian," in* Publications of the Modern Language Association of America, *1941 and H. R. Trevor-Roper in* David Hume: a Symposium, *ed. D. F. Pears (1963). Mossner has also written the best biography,* Life of Hume *(1954). Macaulay's savage estimate is in the* Edinburgh Review, *vol. 94.*

I

So low, at that time, ran the inclination towards liberty, that Elizabeth, the last of that arbitrary line, herself no less arbitrary, was yet

the most renowned and most popular of all the sovereigns that had filled the throne of England. It was natural for James to take the government as he found it, and to pursue her measures, which he heard so much applauded; nor did his penetration extend so far as to discover, that neither his circumstances nor his character could support so extensive an authority. His narrow revenues and little frugality began now to render him dependent on his people, even in the ordinary course of administration; their increasing knowledge discovered to them that advantage which they had obtained; and made them sensible of the inestimable value of civil liberty. And as he possessed too little dignity to command respect, and too much good-nature to impress fear, a new spirit discovered itself every day in the parliament; and a party watchful of a free constitution was regularly formed in the house of commons.

But notwithstanding these advantages acquired to liberty, so extensive was royal authority, and so firmly established in all its parts, that it is probable the patriots of that age would have despaired of ever resisting it, had they not been stimulated by religious motives, which inspire a courage unsurmountable by any human obstacle.

The same alliance which has ever prevailed between kingly power and ecclesiastical authority, was now fully established in England; and while the prince assisted the clergy in suppressing schismatics and innovators, the clergy, in return, inculcated the doctrine of an unreserved submission and obedience to the civil magistrate. The genius of the church of England, so kindly to monarchy, forwarded the confederacy; its submission to episcopal jurisdiction; its attachment to ceremonies, to order, and to a decent pomp and splendor of worship; and, in a word, its affinity to the tame superstition of the catholics, rather than to the wild fanaticism of the puritans.

On the other hand, opposition to the church, and the persecutions under which they laboured, were sufficient to throw the puritans into the country party and to beget political principles little favourable to the high pretensions of the sovereign. The spirit too of enthusiasm; bold, daring and uncontrolled, strongly disposed their minds to adopt republican tenets; and inclined them to arrogate, in their actions and conduct, the same liberty which they assumed in their rapturous flights and ecstasies. Ever since the first origin of that sect, through the whole reign of Elizabeth as well as of James, *puritanical* principles had been understood in a double sense, and expressed the opinions favourable both to political and to ecclesiastical liberty. And as the court, in order

to discredit all parliamentary opposition, affixed the denomination of puritans to its antagonists; the religious puritans willingly adopted this idea, which was so advantageous to them, and which confounded their cause with that of the patriots or country party. Thus were the civil and ecclesiastical factions regularly formed; and the humour of the nation during that age running strongly towards fanatical extravagancies, the spirit of civil liberty gradually revived from its lethargy, and by means of its religious associate, from which it reaped more advantage than honour, it secretly enlarged its dominion over the greater part of the kingdom.

II

In the ancient constitution, before the beginning of the seventeenth century, the meetings of parliament were precarious, and were not frequent. The sessions were short, and the members had no leisure, either to get aquainted with each other, or with public business. The ignorance of the age made men more submissive to that authority which governed them. And above all, the large demesnes of the crown, with the small expence of government during that period, rendered the prince almost independent, and taught the parliament to preserve great submission and duty towards him.

In our present constitution, many accidents which have rendered governments everywhere, as well as in Great Britain, much more burthensome than formerly, have thrown into the hands of the crown the disposal of a large revenue, and have enabled the king, by the private interest and ambition of the members, to restrain the public interest and ambition of the body. While the opposition (for we must still have an opposition, open or disguised) endeavours to draw every branch of administration under the cognizance of parliament, the courtiers reserve a part to the disposal of the crown; and the royal prerogative, though deprived of its ancient powers, still maintains a due weight in the balance of the constitution.

It was the fate of the house of Stuart to govern England at a period, when the former source of authority was already much diminished, and before the latter began to flow in any tolerable abundance. Without a regular and fixed foundation, the throne perpetually tottered; and the prince sat upon it anxiously and precariously. Every expedient used by James and Charles in order to support their dignity, we have seen attended with sensible inconveniences. The majesty of the crown, derived from ancient powers and prerogatives, procured respect, and

checked the approaches of insolent intruders: but it begat in the king so high an idea of his own rank and station, as made him incapable of stooping to popular courses, or submitting in any degree to the control of parliament. The alliance with the hierarchy strengthened law by the sanction of religion: but it enraged the puritanical party, and exposed the prince to the attacks of enemies, numerous, violent, and implacable. The memory too of these two kings, from like causes, has been attended, in some degree, with the same infelicity, which pursued them during the whole course of their lives. Though it must be confessed, that their skill in government was not proportioned to the extreme delicacy of their situation; a sufficient indulgence has not been given them, and all the blame, by several historians, has been unjustly thrown on *their* side. Their violations of law, particularly those of Charles, are in some few instances, transgressions of a plain limit, which was marked out to royal authority. But the encroachments of the commons, though in the beginning less positive and determinate, are no less discernible by good judges, and were equally capable of destroying the just balance of the constitution. While they exercised the powers transmitted to them, in a manner more independent, and less compliant, than had ever before been practised; the kings were, perhaps imprudently, but, as they imagined, from necessity, tempted to assume powers which had scarcely ever been exercised, or had been exercised in a different manner by the crown. And from the shock of these opposite pretensions, together with religious controversy, arose all the factions, convulsions, and disorders, which attended that period.

III

When two names, so sacred in the English constitution as those of KING and PARLIAMENT, were placed in opposition; no wonder the people were divided in their choice, and were agitated with the most violent animosities and factions.

The nobility, and more considerable gentry, dreading a total confusion of rank from the fury of the populace, inlisted themselves in defence of the monarch, from whom they received, and to whom they communicated, their lustre. Animated with the spirit of loyalty, derived from their ancestors, they adhered to the ancient principles of the constitution, and valued themselves on exerting the maxims, as well as inheriting the possessions, of the old English families. And while they passed their time mostly at their country-seats, they were surprised to hear of opinions prevailing, with which they had ever been

unacquainted, and which implied not a limitation, but an abolition almost total, of monarchical authority.

The city of London, on the other hand, and most of the great corporations, took part with the parliament, and adopted with zeal those democratical principles on which the pretentions of that assembly were founded. The government of cities which even under absolute monarchies is commonly republican, inclined them to this party: the small hereditary influence, which can be retained over the industrious inhabitants of towns; the natural independence of citizens; and the force of popular currents over those more numerous associations of mankind; all these causes gave, there, authority to the new principles propagated throughout the nation. Many families too, which had lately been enriched by commerce, saw with indignation, that, notwithstanding their opulence, they could not raise themselves to a level with the ancient gentry: they therefore adhered to a power, by whose success they hoped to acquire rank and consideration. And the new splendour and glory of the Dutch commonwealth, where liberty so happily supported industry, made the commercial part of the nation desire to see a like form of government established in England.

The genius of the two religions, so closely at this time interwoven with politics, corresponded exactly to these divisions. The presbyterian religion was new, republican, and suited to the genius of the populace: the other had an air of greater show and ornament, was established on ancient authority, and bore an affinity to the kingly and aristocratical parts of the constitution. The devotees of presbytery became of course zealous partisans of the parliament: the friends of the episcopal church valued themselves on defending the rights of monarchy.

Some men also there were of liberal education, who, being either careless or ignorant of those disputes bandied about by the clergy on both sides, aspired to nothing but an easy enjoyment of life, amidst the jovial entertainment and social intercourse of their companions. All these flocked to the king's standard, where they breathed a freer air, and were exempted from that rigid preciseness and melancholy austerity, which reigned among the parliamentary party.

Never was a quarrel more unequal than seemed at first that between the contending parties: almost every advantage lay against the royal cause. The king's revenue had been seized, from the beginning, by the parliament, who issued out to him, from time to time, small sums for his present subsistence; and as soon as he withdrew to York, they totally stopped all payments. London and all the seaports, except New-

castle, being in their hands, the customs yielded them a certain and considerable supply of money; and all contributions, loans, and impositions, were more easily raised from the cities which possessed the ready money, and where men lived under their inspection, than they could be levied by the king in those open countries, which after some time declared for him.

The seamen naturally followed the disposition of the seaports to which they belonged: and the earl of Northumberland, lord admiral, having embraced the party of the parliament, had appointed, at their desire, the earl of Warwick to be his lieutenant, who at once established his authority in the fleet, and kept the entire dominion of the sea in the hands of that assembly.

All the magazines of arms and ammunition were from the first seized by the parliament; and their fleet intercepted the greater part of those which were sent by the queen from Holland. The king was obliged, in order to arm his followers, to borrow the weapons of the train-bands, under promise of restoring them as soon as peace should be settled in the kingdom.

The veneration for parliaments was at this time extreme throughout the nation. The custom of reviling those assemblies for corruption, as it had no pretence, so was it unknown, during all former ages. Few or no instances of their encroaching ambition or selfish claims had hitherto been observed. Men considered the house of commons in no other light than as the representatives of the nation, whose interest was the same with that of the public, who were the eternal guardians of law and liberty, and whom no motive, but the necessary defence of the people, could ever engage in an opposition to the crown. The torrent, therefore, of general affection ran to the parliament. What is the great advantage of popularity, the privilege of affixing epithets, fell of course to that party. The king's adherents were the *Wicked* and the *Malignant*: Their adversaries were the *Godly* and *Well-affected*. And as the force of the cities was more united than that of the country, and at once gave shelter and protection to the parliamentary party, who could easily suppress the royalists in their neighbourhood, almost the whole kingdom, at the commencement of the war, seemed to be in the hands of the parliament.

What alone gave the king some compensation for all the advantages possessed by his adversaries, was the nature and qualities of his adherents. More bravery and activity were hoped for, from the generous spirit of the nobles and gentry, than from the base disposition of the

multitude. And as the men of estates, at their own expence, levied and armed their tenants, besides an attachment to their masters, greater force and courage were to be expected in these rustic troops, than in the vicious and enervated populace of cities.

The neighbouring states of Europe, being engaged in violent wars, little interested themselves in these civil commotions; and this island enjoyed the singular advantage (for such it surely was) of fighting out its own quarrels without the interposition of foreigners.

IV

The tragical death of Charles begat a question, whether the people, in any case, were entitled to judge and to punish their sovereign; and most men, regarding chiefly the atrocious usurpation of the pretended judges, and the merit of the virtuous prince who suffered, were inclined to condemn the republican principle as highly seditious and extravagant: but there still were a few who, abstracting from the particular circumstances of this case, were able to consider the question in general, and were inclined to moderate, not contradict, the prevailing sentiment. Such might have been their reasoning. If ever, on any occasion, it were laudable to conceal truth from the populace, it must be confessed, that the doctrine of resistance affords such an example; and that all speculative reasoners ought to observe, with regard to this principle, the same cautious silence, which the laws in every species of government have ever prescribed to themselves. Government is instituted in order to restrain the fury and injustice of the people; and being always founded on opinion, not on force, it is dangerous to weaken, by these speculations, the reverence which the multitude owe to authority, and to instruct them beforehand, that the case can ever happen, when they may be freed from their duty of allegiance. Or should it be found impossible to restrain the license of human disquisitions, it must be acknowledged, that the doctrine of obedience ought alone to be *inculcated*, and that the exceptions, which are rare, ought seldom or never to be mentioned in popular reasonings and discourses. Nor is there any danger, that mankind, by this prudent reserve, should universally degenerate into a state of abject servitude. When the exception really occurs, even though it be not previously expected and descanted on, it must, from its very nature, be so obvious and undisputed, as to remove all doubt, and over-power the restraint, however great, imposed by teaching the general doctrine of obedience. But between resisting a prince and dethroning him there is a wide interval;

and the abuses of power, which can warrant the latter violence, are greater and more enormous than those which will justify the former. History, however, supplies us with examples even of this kind; and the reality of the supposition, though, for the future, it ought ever to be little looked for, must, by all candid inquirers, be acknowledged in the past. But between dethroning a prince and punishing him, there is another very wide interval; and it were not strange, if even men of the most enlarged thought should question, whether human nature could ever in any monarch reach that height of depravity, as to warrant, in revolted subjects, this last act of extraordinary jurisdiction. That illusion, if it be an illusion, which teaches us to pay a sacred regard to the persons of princes, is so salutary, that to dissipate it by the formal trial and punishment of a sovereign, will have more pernicious effects upon the people, than the example of justice can be supposed to have a beneficial influence upon princes, by checking their career of tyranny. It is dangerous also by these examples, to reduce princes to despair, or bring matters to such extremities against persons endowed with great power, as to leave them no resource, but in the most violent and most sanguinary counsels. This general position being established, it must however be observed, that no reader, almost of any party or principle, was ever shocked, when he read, in ancient history, that the Roman senate voted Nero, their absolute sovereign, to be a public enemy, and, even without trial, condemned him to the severest and most ignominious punishment; a punishment from which the meanest Roman citizen was, by the laws, exempted. The crimes of that bloody tyrant are so enormous that they break through all rules; and extort a confession, that such a dethroned prince is no longer superior to his people, and can no longer plead, in his own defence, laws, which were established for conducting the ordinary course of administration. But when we pass from the case of Nero to that of Charles, the great disproportion, or rather total contrariety, of character immediately strikes us; and we stand astonished, that, among a civilized people, so much virtue could ever meet with so fatal a catastrophe. History, the great mistress of wisdom, furnishes examples of all kinds; and every prudential, as well as moral precept, may be authorised by those events, which her enlarged mirror is able to present to us. From the memorable revolutions which passed in England during this period, we may naturally deduce the same useful lesson, which Charles himself, in his later years, inferred; that it is dangerous for princes, even from the appearance of necessity, to assume more authority than the laws have allowed

them. But it must be confessed, that these events furnish us with another instruction, no less natural, and no less useful, concerning the madness of the people, the furies of fanaticism, and the danger of mercenary armies.

V

At this era, it may be proper to stop a moment and take a general survey of the age, so far as regards manners, finances, arms, commerce, arts and sciences. The chief use of history is, that it affords materials for disquisitions of this nature; and it seems the duty of an historian to point out the proper inferences and conclusions . . .

The commerce and industry of England increased extremely during the peaceable period of Charles's reign: The trade to the East-Indies and to Guinea became considerable. The English possessed almost the sole trade with Spain. Twenty thousand cloths were annually sent to Turkey. Commerce met with interruption, no doubt from the civil wars and convulsions which afterwards prevailed; though it soon recovered after the establishment of the commonwealth. The war with the Dutch, by distressing the commerce of so formidable a rival, served to encourage trade in England: The Spanish war was to an equal degree pernicious. All the effects of the English merchants, to an immense value, were confiscated in Spain. The prevalence of democratical principles engaged the country gentlemen to bind their sons apprentices to merchants; and commerce has ever since been more honourable in England than in any other European kingdom. The exclusive companies, which formerly confined trade, were never expressly abolished by any ordinance of parliament during the commonwealth; but as men payed no regard to the prerogative whence the charters of these companies were derived, the monopoly was gradually invaded, and commerce increased by the increase of liberty. Interest in 1650 was reduced to six per cent.

The customs in England, before the civil wars, are said to have amounted to 500,000 pounds a year: A sum ten times greater than during the best period in queen Elizabeth's reign: But there is probably some exaggeration in this matter.

The post-house in 1653 was farmed at 10,000 pounds a-year, which was deemed a considerable sum for the three kingdoms. Letters paid only about half their present postage.

From 1619 to 1638, there had been coined 6,900,042 pounds. From 1638 to 1657, the coinage amounted to 7,733,521 pounds. Dr. Daven-

ant has told us from the registers of the mint, that between 1558 and 1659, there had been coined 19,832,476 pounds in gold and silver.

The first mention of tea, coffee, and chocolate, is about 1660. Asparagus, artichoaks, cauliflower, and a variety of sallads, were about the same time introduced into England.

The colony of New England increased by means of the puritans, who fled thither in order to free themselves from the constraint which Laud and the church party had imposed upon them; and, before the commencement of the civil wars, it is supposed to have contained 25,000 souls. For a like reason, the catholics, afterwards, who found themselves exposed to many hardships, and dreaded still worse treatment, went over to America in great numbers, and settled the colony of Maryland.

Before the civil wars, learning and the fine arts were favoured at court, and a good taste began to prevail in the nation. The king loved pictures, sometimes handled the pencil himself, and was a good judge of art. The pieces of foreign masters were bought up at a vast price; and the value of pictures doubled in Europe by the emulation between Charles and Philip IV of Spain, who were touched with the same elegant passion. Vandyke was caressed and enriched at court. Inigo Jones was master of the king's buildings; though afterwards persecuted by the parliament, on account of the part which he had in rebuilding St. Paul's, and for obeying some orders of the council, by which he was directed to pull down houses, in order to make room for that edifice. Laws, who had not been surpassed by any musician before him, was much beloved by the king, who called him the father of music. Charles was a good judge of writing, and was thought by some more anxious with regard to purity of style than became a monarch. Notwithstanding his narrow revenue, and his freedom from all vanity, he lived in such magnificence, that he possessed four and twenty palaces, all of them elegantly and completely furnished; insomuch that, when he removed from one to another, he was not obliged to transport any thing along with him.

Cromwell, though himself a barbarian, was not insensible to literary merit. Usher, notwithstanding his being a bishop, received a pension from him. Marvel and Milton were in his service. Waller, who was his relation, was caressed by him. That poet always said, that the protector himself was not so wholly illiterate as was commonly imagined. He gave a hundred pounds a-year to the divinity professor at Oxford; and an historian mentions this bounty as an instance of his love of literature.

He intended to have erected a college at Durham for the benefit of the northern counties.

Civil wars, especially when founded on principles of liberty, are not commonly unfavourable to the arts of eloquence and composition; or rather, by presenting nobler and more interesting objects, they amply compensate that tranquillity of which they bereave the muses. The speeches of the parliamentary orators during this period are of a strain much superior to what any former age had produced in England; and the force and compass of our tongue were then first put to trial. It must, however, be confessed, that the wretched fanaticism which so much infected the parliamentary party, was no less destructive of taste and science, than of all law and order. Gaiety and wit were proscribed: human learning despised: freedom of inquiry detested: cant and hyprocrisy alone encouraged. It was an article positively insisted on in the preliminaries to the treaty of Uxbridge, that all playhouses should for ever be abolished. Sir John Davenant, says Whitlocke, speaking of the year 1658, published an opera, notwithstanding the nicety of the times. All the king's furniture was put to sale: His pictures, disposed of at very low prices, enriched all the collections in Europe: the cartoons, when complete, were only appraised at 300 pounds, though the whole collection of the king's curiosities was sold at above 50,000. Even the royal palaces were pulled in pieces and the materials of them sold. The very library and medals at St. James's were intended by the generals to be brought to auction, in order to pay the arrears of some regiments of cavalry quartered near London: but Selden, apprehensive of the loss, engaged his friend Whitlocke, then lord-keeper for the commonwealth, to apply for the office of librarian. This expedient saved that valuable collection.

It is, however, remarkable, that the greatest genius by far that shone out in England during this period, was deeply engaged with these fanatics, and even prostituted his pen in theological controversy, in factious disputes, and in justifying the most violent measures of the party. This was John Milton, whose poems are admirable, though liable to some objections; his prose writings disagreeable though not altogether defective in genius. Nor all his poems equal: his *Paradise Lost,* his *Comus,* and a few others, shine out amidst some flat and insipid compositions: even in the *Paradise Lost*, his capital performance, there are very long passages, amounting to near a third of the work, almost wholly destitute of harmony and elegance, nay, of all vigour of

imagination. This natural inequality in Milton's genius was much increased by the inequalities in his subject; of which some parts are of themselves the most lofty that can enter into human conception; others would have required the most laboured elegance of composition to support them. It is certain that this author, when in a happy mood, and employed on a noble subject, is the most wonderfully sublime of any poet in any language; Homer and Lucretius and Tasso not excepted. More concise than Homer, more simple than Tasso, more nervous than Lucretius; had he lived in a later age, and learned to polish some rudeness in his verses; had he enjoyed better fortune, and possessed leisure to watch the returns of genius in himself, he had attained the pinnacle of perfection, and borne away the palm of epic poetry.

It is well known, that Milton never enjoyed in his lifetime the reputation which he deserved. His *Paradise Lost* was long neglected: prejudices against an apologist for the regicides, and against a work not wholy purged from the cant of former times, kept the ignorant world from perceiving the prodigious merit of that performance. Lord Somers, by encouraging a good edition of it, about twenty years after the author's death, first brought it into request; and Tonson, in his dedication of a smaller edition, speaks of it as a work just beginning to be known. Even during the prevalence of Milton's party, he seems never to have been much regarded; and Whitlocke talks of one Milton, as he calls him, a blind man, who was employed in translating a treaty with Sweden into Latin. These forms of expression are amusing to posterity, who consider how obscure Whitlocke himself, though lord-keeper and ambassador, and indeed a man of great abilities and merit, has become in comparison of Milton.

It is not strange that Milton received no encouragement after the restoration: It is more to be admired that he escaped with his life. Many of the cavaliers blamed extremely that lenity towards him, which was so honourable in the king, and so advantageous to posterity. It is said, that he had saved Davenant's life during the protectorship; and Davenant in return afforded him like protection after the restoration; being sensible, that men of letters ought always to regard their sympathy of taste as a more powerful band of union, than any difference of party or opinion as a source of animosity. It was during a state of poverty, blindness, disgrace, danger, and old age, that Milton composed his wonderful poem, which not only surpassed all the performances of his contemporaries, but all the compositions which had flowed

from his pen during the vigour of his age and the height of his prosperity. This circumstance is not the least remarkable of all those which attend that great genius. He died in 1674, aged 66 . . .

No English author in that age was more celebrated both abroad and at home, than Hobbes: in our time, he is much neglected: a lively instance, how precarious all reputations founded on reasoning and philosophy! A pleasant comedy, which paints the manners of the age, and exposes a faithful picture of nature, is a durable work, and is transmitted to the latest posterity. But a system, whether physical or metaphysical, commonly owes its success to its novelty; and is no sooner canvassed with impartiality than its weakness is discovered. Hobbes's politics are fitted only to promote tyranny, and his ethics to encourage licentiousness. Though an enemy to religion, he partakes nothing of the spirit of scepticism; but is as positive and dogmatical as if human reason, and his reason in particular, could attain a thorough conviction in these subjects. Clearness and propriety of style are the chief excellencies of Hobbes's writings. In his own person he is represented to have been a man of virtue; a character no-wise surprising, notwithstanding his libertine system of ethics. Timidity is the principal fault with which he is reproached: he lived to an extreme old age, yet could never reconcile himself to the thoughts of death. The boldness of his opinions and sentiments forms a remarkable contrast to this part of his character. He died in 1679, aged 91.

Harrington's *Oceana* was well adapted to that age, when the plans of imaginary republics were the daily subjects of debate and conversation; and even in our time, it is justly admired as a work of genius and invention. The idea, however, of a perfect and immortal commonwealth will always be found as chimerical as that of a perfect and immortal man. The style of this author wants ease and fluency; but the good matter, which his work contains, makes compensation. He died in 1677, aged 66.

Harvey is entitled to the glory of having made, by reasoning alone, without any mixture of accident, a capital discovery in one of the most important branches of science. He had also the happiness of establishing at once his theory on the most solid and convincing proofs; and posterity has added little to the arguments suggested by his industry and ingenuity. His treatise of the circulation of the blood is farther embellished by that warmth and spirit which so naturally accompany the genius of invention. This great man was much favored by Charles I, who gave him the liberty of using all the deer in the royal forests for

perfecting his discoveries on the generation of animals. It was remarked, that no physician in Europe, who had reached forty years of age, ever, to the end of his life, adopted Harvey's doctrine of the circulation of the blood, and that his practice in London diminished extremely, from the reproach drawn upon him by that great and signal discovery. So slow is the progress of truth in very science, even when not opposed by factious or superstitious prejudices! He died in 1657, aged 79.

This age affords great materials for history; but did not produce any accomplished historian. Clarendon, however, will always be esteemed an entertaining writer, even independent of our curiosity to know the facts which he relates. His style is prolix and redundant, and suffocates us by the length of its periods: but it discovers imagination and sentiment, and pleases us at the same time that we disapprove of it. He is more partial in appearance than in reality: for he seems perpetually anxious to apologise for the king; but his apologies are often well grounded. He is less partial in his relation of facts, than in his account of characters: he was too honest a man to falsify the former; his affections were easily capable, unknown to himself, of disguising the latter. An air of probity and goodness runs through the whole work; as these qualities did in reality embellish the whole life of the author. He died in 1674, aged 66.

These are the chief performances which engage the attention of posterity.

WILLIAM ROBERTSON

1721–1793

As these two passages from The History of America *are chosen to show Robertson's skill as a narrator and an analyst, it may be worth showing how, in the Preface, he justifies the lengthy bibliography with which the work commences. Here the* érudit, *the professional exponent of an expanding subject, defends himself from the Enlightenment emphasis on learning lightly borne.*

> *The historian who records the events of his own time, is credited in proportion to the opinion which the public entertains with respect to his means of information and his veracity. He who delineates the transactions of a remote period, has no title to claim assent, unless he produces evidence in proof of his assertions. Without this, he may write an amusing tale, but cannot be said to have composed an authentic history. In those sentiments I have been confirmed by the opinion of an Author [Gibbon] whom his industry, erudition, and discernment, have deservedly placed in a high rank among the most eminent historians of the age. Emboldened by a hint from him, I have published a catalogue of the Spanish books which I have consulted. This practice was frequent in the last century [not Bacon nor Raleigh; Camden in his* Britannia, *not in the* Annals*], and was considered as an evidence of laudable industry in an author; in the present, it may, perhaps, be deemed the effect of ostentation; but . . . to any person who may choose to follow me in this path of inquiry, the catalogue must be very useful.*

The first passage is from book 2, and may be compared with the account of Columbus's first voyage given in Samuel Eliot Morrison's

Admiral of the Ocean Sea, *1946. The second is from book 8, where Robertson analyzed the effect of the Spanish settlements "upon the countries of which they took possession, the maxims which they adopted in forming their new colonies, the interior structure and policy of these, together with the influence of their progressive improvement upon the parent state, and upon the commercial intercourse of nations." Robertson's explanation of why Spain did not derive more advantage from her New World wealth can be compared with the brief survey given in R. Trevor Davies,* The Golden Century of Spain, 1501–1621 *(rev. ed. 1954).*

Little attention has been paid recently to Robertson, but see R. A. Humphrey's lecture Robertson and His History of America *(1954) and the chapter on Robertson in J. B. Black,* The Art of History *(1926).*

I

NEXT MORNING, being Friday the third day of August, in the year one thousand four hundred and ninety-two, Columbus set sail, a little before sun-rise, in presence of a vast crowd of spectators, who sent up their supplications to Heaven for the prosperous issue of the voyage, which they wished, rather than expected. Columbus steered directly for the Canary Islands, and arrived there without any occurrence that would have deserved notice on any other occasion. But, in a voyage of such expectation and importance, every circumstance was the object of attention. The rudder of the Pinta broke loose, the day after she left the harbour, and that accident alarmed the crew, no less superstitious than unskilful, as a certain omen of the unfortunate destiny of the expedition. Even in the short run to the Canaries, the ships were found to be so crazy and ill appointed, as to be very improper for a navigation which was expected to be both long and dangerous. Columbus refitted them, however, to the best of his power, and having supplied himself with fresh provisions he took his departure from Gomera, one of the most westerly of the Canary Islands, on the sixth day of September.

Here the voyage of discovery may properly be said to begin; for Columbus holding his course due west, left immediately the usual track of navigation, and stretched into unfrequented and unknown seas. The first day, as it was very calm, he made but little way; but on the second, he lost sight of the Canaries; and many of the sailors, dejected already and dismayed, when they contemplated the boldness of the undertak-

ing, began to beat their breasts, and to shed tears, as if they were never more to behold land. Columbus comforted them with assurances of success, and the prospect of vast wealth, in those opulent regions whither he was conducting them. This early discovery of the spirit of his followers taught Columbus, that he must prepare to struggle, not only with the unavoidable difficulties which might be expected from the nature of the undertaking, but with such as were likely to arise from the ignorance and timidity of the people under his command; and he perceived that the art of governing the minds of men would be no less requisite for accomplishing the discoveries which he had in view, than naval skill and undaunted courage. Happily for himself, and for the country by which he was employed, he joined to the ardent temper and inventive genius of a projector, virtues of another species, which are rarely united with them. He possessed a thorough knowledge of mankind, an insinuating address, a patient perseverance in executing any plan, the perfect government of his own passions, and the talent of acquiring an ascendant over those of other men. All these qualities, which formed him for command, were accompanied with that superior knowledge of his profession, which begets confidence in times of difficulty and danger. To unskilful Spanish sailors, accustomed only to coasting voyages in the Mediterranean, the maritime science of Columbus, the fruit of thirty years experience, improved by an acquaintance with all the inventions of the Portuguese, appeared immense. As soon as they put to sea, he regulated every thing by his sole authority; he superintended the execution of every order; and allowing himself only a few hours for sleep, he was at all other times upon deck. As his course lay through seas which had not formerly been visited, the sounding-line, or instruments for observation, were continually in his hands. After the example of the Portuguese discoverers, he attended to the motion of tides and currents, watched the flight of birds, the appearance of fishes, of sea-weeds, and of every thing that floated on the waves, and entered every occurrence, with a minute exactness, in the journal which he kept. As the length of the voyage could not fail of alarming sailors habituated only to short excursions, Columbus endeavoured to conceal from them the real progress which they made. With this view, though they run eighteen leagues on the second day after they left Gomera, he gave out that they had advanced only fifteen, and he uniformly employed the same artifice of reckoning short during the whole voyage. By the fourteenth of September, the fleet was above two hundred leagues to the west of the Canary Isles, at a

greater distance from land than any Spaniard had been before that time. There they were struck with an appearance no less astonishing than new. They observed that the magnetic needle, in their compasses, did not point exactly to the polar star, but varied towards the west; and as they proceeded, this variation increased. This appearance, which is now familiar, though it still remains one of the mysteries of nature, into the cause of which the sagacity of man hath not been able to penetrate, filled the companions of Columbus with terror. They were now in a boundless unknown ocean, far from the usual course of navigation; nature itself seemed to be altered, and the only guide which they had left was about to fail them. Columbus, with no less quickness than ingenuity, invented a reason for this appearance, which, though it did not satisfy himself, seemed so plausible to them, that it dispelled their fears, or silenced their murmurs.

He still continued to steer due west, nearly in the same latitude with the Canary Islands. In this course he came within the sphere of the trade wind, which blows invariably from east to west, between the tropics and a few degrees beyond them. He advanced before this steady gale with such uniform rapidity, that it was seldom necessary to shift a sail. When about four hundred leagues to the west of the Canaries, he found the sea so covered with weeds, that it resembled a meadow of vast extent; and in some places they were so thick, as to retard the motion of the vessels. This strange appearance occasioned new alarm and disquiet. The sailors imagined that they were now arrived at the utmost boundary of the navigable ocean; that these floating weeds would obstruct their farther progress, and concealed dangerous rocks, or some large tract of land, which had sunk, they knew not how, in that place. Columbus endeavoured to persuade them, that what had alarmed, ought rather to have encouraged them, and was to be considered as a sign of approaching land. At the same time, a brisk gale arose, and carried them forward. Several birds were seen hovering about the ship, and directed their flight towards the west. The desponding crew resumed some degree of spirit, and began to entertain fresh hopes.

Upon the first of October they were, according to the admiral's reckoning, seven hundred and seventy leagues to the west of the Canaries; but lest his men should be intimidated by the prodigious length of the navigation, he gave out that they had proceeded only five hundred and eighty-four leagues; and, fortunately for Columbus, neither his own pilot, nor those of the other ships, had skill sufficient to correct this error, and discover the deceit. They had now been above

three weeks at sea; they had proceeded far beyond what former navigators had attempted or deemed possible; all their prognostics of discovery, drawn from the flight of birds and other circumstances, had proved fallacious; the appearances of land, with which their own credulity or the artifice of their commander had from time to time flattered and amused them, had been altogether illusive, and their prospect of success seemed now to be as distant as ever. These reflections occurred often to men, who had no other object or occupation, than to reason and discourse concerning the intention and circumstances of their expedition. They made impression, at first, upon the ignorant and timid, and extending, by degrees, to such as were better informed or more resolute, the contagion spread at length from ship to ship. From secret whispers or murmurings, they proceeded to open cabals and public complaints. They taxed their sovereign with inconsiderate credulity, in paying such regard to the vain promises and rash conjectures of an indigent foreigner, as to hazard the lives of so many of her own subjects, in prosecuting a chimerical scheme. They affirmed that they had fully performed their duty, by venturing so far in an unknown and hopeless course, and could incur no blame, for refusing to follow, any longer, a desperate adventurer to certain destruction. They contended, that it was necessary to think of returning to Spain, while their crazy vessels were still in a condition to keep the sea, but expressed their fears that the attempt would prove vain, as the wind, which had hitherto been so favourable to their course, must render it impossible to sail in the opposite direction. All agreed that Columbus should be compelled by force to adopt a measure on which their common safety depended. Some of the more audacious proposed, as the most expeditious and certain method for getting rid at once of his remonstrances, to throw him into the sea, being persuaded that, upon their return to Spain, the death of an unsuccessful projector would excite little concern, and be inquired into with no curiosity.

Columbus was fully sensible of his perilous situation. He had observed, with great uneasiness, the fatal operation of ignorance and of fear in producing disaffection among his crew, and saw that it was now ready to burst out into open mutiny. He retained, however, perfect presence of mind. He affected to seem ignorant of their machinations. Notwithstanding the agitation and solicitude of his own mind, he appeared with a cheerful countenance, like a man satisfied with the progress which he had made, and confident of success. Sometimes

he employed all the arts of insinuation to soothe his men. Sometimes he endeavoured to work upon their ambition or avarice, by magnificent descriptions of the fame and wealth which they were about to acquire. On other occasions, he assumed a tone of authority, and threatened them with vengeance from their sovereign, if, by their dastardly behaviour they should defeat this noble effort to promote the glory of God, and to exalt the Spanish name above that of every other nation. Even with seditious sailors, the words of a man whom they had been accustomed to reverence, were weighty and persuasive, and not only restrained them from those violent excesses, which they meditated, but prevailed with them to accompany their admiral for some time longer.

As they proceeded, the indications of approaching land seemed to be more certain and excited hope in proportion. The birds began to appear in flocks, making towards the southwest. Columbus, in imitation of the Portuguese navigators, who had been guided, in several of their discoveries, by the motion of the birds, altered his course from due west towards that quarter whither they pointed their flight. But, after holding on for several days in this new direction, without any better success than formerly, having seen no object, during thirty days, but the sea and the sky, the hopes of his companions subsided faster than they had risen; their fears revived with additional force; impatience, rage, and despair, appeared in every countenance. All sense of subordination was lost: the officers, who had hitherto concurred with Columbus in opinion, and supported his authority, now took part with the private men; they assembled tumultuously on the deck, expostulated with their commander, mingled threats with their expostulations, and required him instantly to tack about and to return to Europe. Columbus perceived that it would be of no avail to have recourse to any of his former arts, which having been tried so often, had lost their effect; and that it was impossible to rekindle any zeal for the success of the expedition among men, in whose breasts fear had extinguished every generous sentiment. He saw that it was no less vain to think of employing either gentle or severe measures, to quell a mutiny so general and so violent. It was necessary, on all these accounts, to soothe passions which he could no longer command, and to give way to a torrent to be checked. He promised solemnly to his men that he would comply with their request, provided they would accompany him, and obey his commands for three days longer, and if, during that time, land were not discovered, he would then abandon the enterprise, and direct his course towards Spain.

Enraged as the sailors were, and impatient to turn their faces again towards their native country, this proposition did not appear to them unreasonable. Nor did Columbus hazard much in confining himself to a term so short. The presages of discovering land were now so numerous and promising, that he deemed them infallible. For some days the sounding-line reached the bottom, and the soil which it brought up indicated land to be at no great distance. The flocks of birds increased, and were composed not only of sea fowl, but of such land birds as could not be supposed to fly far from the shore. The crew of the Pinta observed a cane floating, which seemed to have been newly cut, and likewise a piece of timber artificially carved. The sailors aboard the Nigna took up the branch of a tree with red berries, perfectly fresh. The clouds around the setting sun assumed a new appearance; the air was more mild and warm, and, during the night, the wind became unequal and variable. From all these symptoms, Columbus was so confident of being near land, that on the evening of the eleventh of October, after public prayers for success, he ordered the sails to be furled, and the ships to lie to, keeping strict watch, lest they should be driven ashore in the night. During this interval of suspence and expectation, no man shut his eyes, all kept upon deck, gazing intently towards that quarter where they expected to discover the land, which had been so long the object of their wishes.

About two hours before midnight, Columbus standing on the forecastle, observed a light at a distance, and privately pointed it out to Pedro Guttierez, a page of the queen's wardrobe. Guttierez perceived it, and calling to Salcedo, comptroller of the fleet, all three saw it in motion, as if it were carried from place to place. A little after midnight, the joyful sound of *land, land* was heard from the Pinta, which kept always ahead of the other ships. But, having been so often deceived by fallacious appearances, every man was now become slow of belief, and waited, in all the anguish of uncertainty and impatience, for the return of day. As soon as morning dawned, all doubts and fears were dispelled. From every ship an island was seen about two leagues to the north, whose flat and verdant fields, well stored with wood, and watered with many rivulets, presented the aspect of a delightful country. The crew of the Pinta instantly began the Te Deum, as a hymn of thanksgiving to God, and were joined by those of the other ships, with tears of joy and transports of congratulation. This office of gratitude to Heaven was followed by an act of justice to their commander. They threw themselves at the feet of Columbus, with feelings of self-

condemnation mingled with reverence. They implored him to pardon their ignorance, incredulity, and insolence, which had created him so much unnecessary disquiet, and had so often obstructed the prosecution of his well-concerted plan; and passing, in the warmth of their admiration, from one extreme to another, they now pronounced the man, whom they had so lately reviled and threatened, to be a person inspired by Heaven with sagacity and fortitude more than human, in order to accomplish a design, so far beyond the ideas and conception of all former ages.

II

When the importation into Spain of those various articles from her colonies, first became active and considerable, her interior industry and manufactures were in a state so prosperous, that with the product of these she was able both to purchase the commodities of the New World, and to answer its growing demands. Under the reigns of Ferdinand and Isabella, and Charles V, Spain was one of the most industrious countries in Europe. Her manufactures in wool, and flax, and silk, were so extensive, as not only to furnish what was sufficient for her own consumption, but to afford a surplus for exportation. When a market for them, formerly unknown, and to which she alone had access, opened in America, she had recourse to her domestic store, and found there an abundant supply. This new employment must naturally have added vivacity to the spirit of industry. Nourished and invigorated by it, the manufactures, the population, and the wealth of Spain might have gone on increasing in the same proportion with the growth of her colonies. Nor was the state of the Spanish marine at this period less flourishing than that of its manufactures. In the beginning of the sixteenth century, Spain is said to have possessed above a thousand merchant ships, a number probably far superior to that of any nation in Europe in that age. By the aid which foreign trade and domestic industry give reciprocally to each other in their progress, the augmentation of both must have been rapid and extensive, and Spain might have received the same accession of opulence and vigour from her acquisitions in the New World, that other powers have derived from their colonies there.

But various causes prevented this. The same thing happens to nations as to individuals. Wealth, which flows in gradually, and with moderate increase, feeds and nourishes that activity which is friendly to commerce, and calls it forth into vigourous and well-conducted

exertions; but when opulence pours in suddenly, and with too full a stream, it overturns all sober plans of industry, and brings along with it a taste for what is wild and extravagant, and daring in business or in action. Such was the great and sudden augmentation of power and revenue, that the possession of America brought into Spain, and some symptoms of its pernicious influence upon the political operations of that monarchy soon began to appear. For a considerable time, however, the supply of treasure from the New World was scanty and precarious, and the genius of Charles V conducted public measures with such prudence, that the effects of this influence were little perceived. But when Philip II ascended the Spanish throne, with talents far inferior to those of his father, and remittances from the colonies became a regular and considerable branch of revenue, the fatal operation of this rapid change in the state of the kingdom, both on the monarch and his people, was at once conspicuous. Philip, possessing that spirit of unceasing assiduity, which often characterises the ambition of men of moderate talents, entertained such an high opinion of his own resources, that he thought nothing too arduous for him to undertake. Shut up himself in the solitude of the Escurial, he troubled and annoyed all the nations around him. He waged open war with the Dutch and English; he encouraged and aided a rebellious faction in France; he conquered Portugal, and maintained armies and garrisons in Italy, Africa, and both the Indies. By such a multiplicity of great and complicated operations, pursued with ardour during the course of a long reign, Spain was drained both of men and money. Under the weak administration of his successor, Philip III, the vigour of the nation continued to decrease, and sunk into the lowest decline, when the inconsiderate bigotry of that monarch expelled at once a near million of his most industrious subjects, at the very time when the exhausted state of the kingdom required some extraordinary exertion of political wisdom to augment its numbers, and to revive its strength. Early in the seventeenth century, Spain felt such a diminution in the number of her people, that from inability to recruit her armies, she was obliged to contract her operations. Her flourishing manufactures were fallen into decay. Her fleets, which had been the terror of all Europe, were ruined. Her extensive foreign commerce was lost. The trade between different parts of her own dominions was interrupted, and the ships which attempted to carry it on, were taken and plundered by the enemies whom she once despised. Even agriculture, the primary object of industry in every prosperous state, was neglected, and one of the

most fertile countries in Europe hardly raised what was sufficient for the support of its own inhabitants.

In proportion as the population and manufactures of the parent state declined, the demands of her colonies continued to increase. The Spaniards, like their monarchs, intoxicated with the wealth which poured in annually upon them, deserted the paths of industry, to which they had been accustomed, and repaired with eagerness to those regions from which this opulence issued. By this rage of emigration, another drain was opened, and the strength of the colonies augmented by exhausting that of the mother-country. All those emigrants, as well as the adventurers who had at first settled in America, depended absolutely upon Spain for almost every article of necessary consumption. Engaged in more alluring and lucrative pursuits, or prevented by restraints which government imposed, they could not turn their own attention towards establishing the manufactures requisite for comfortable subsistence. They received (as I have observed in another place) their clothing, their furniture, whatever ministers to the ease or luxury of life, and even their instruments of labour, from Europe. Spain, thinned of people, and decreasing in industry, was unable to supply their growing demands. She had recourse to her neighbours. The manufactures of the Low Countries, of England, of France, and of Italy, which her wants called into existence, or animated with new vivacity, furnished in abundance whatever she required. In vain did the fundamental law, concerning the exclusion of foreigners from trade with America, oppose this innovation. Necessity, more powerful than any statute, defeated its operations, and constrained the Spaniards themselves to concur in eluding it. The English, the French, and Dutch, relying on the fidelity and honour of Spanish merchants, who lend their names to cover the deceit, send out their manufactures to America, and receive the exorbitant price for which they are sold there, either in specie, or in the rich commodities of the New World. Neither the dread of danger, nor the allurement of profit, ever induced a Spanish factor to betray or defraud the person who confided in him; and that probity, which is the pride and distinction of the nation, contributes to its ruin. In a short time, not above a twentieth part of the commodities exported to America was of Spanish growth or fabric. All the rest was the property of foreign merchants, though entered in the name of Spaniards. The treasure of the New World may be said henceforward not to have belonged to Spain. Before it reached Europe, it was anticipated as the price of goods pur-

chased from foreigners. That wealth which, by an internal circulation, would have spread through each vein of industry, and have conveyed life and movement to every branch of manufacture, flowed out of the kingdom with such a rapid course, as neither enriched nor animated it. On the other hand, the artizans of rival nations, encouraged by this quick sale of their commodities, improved so much in skill and industry, as to be able to afford them at a rate so low, that the manufactures of Spain, which could not vie with theirs, either in quality or cheapness of work, were still farther depressed. This destructive commerce drained off the riches of the nation faster and more completely, than even the extravagant schemes of ambition carried on by its monarchs. Spain was so much astonished and distressed, at beholding her American treasures vanish almost as soon as they were imported, that Philip III, unable to supply what was requisite in circulation, issued an edict, by which he endeavoured to raise copper money to a value in currency nearly equal to that of silver; and the lord of the Peruvian and Mexican mines was reduced to a wretched expedient, which is the last resource of petty impoverished states.

Thus the possessions of Spain in America have not proved a source of population and of wealth to her, in the same manner as those of other nations. In the countries of Europe, where the spirit of industry subsists in full vigour, every person settled in such colonies as are similar in their situation to those of Spain is supposed to give employment to three or four at home in supplying his wants. But wherever the mother-country cannot afford this supply, every emigrant may be considered as a citizen lost to the community, and strangers must reap all the benefit of answering his demands.

EDWARD GIBBON

1737–1794

Of these four passages, the first two are from the beginning, and the second two from the end of chapter 50, on Mahomet. I have included only a selection of the footnotes to these passages. Text and notes are chosen to give a representative glimpse of the range and quality of Gibbon's mind in a setting perhaps less familiar than Rome or the Danube.

Of a copious literature, most useful are: A. Momigliano, "Gibbon's Contribution to Historical Method," in Contributo alla storia degli Studi Classici *(Rome, 1955) and Christopher Dawson, "Edward Gibbon," in* Dynamics of World History *(1957). The most perceptive (and best written) biography is by G. M. Young,* Gibbon *(1948). It is also the shortest.*

I

AFTER PURSUING, above six hundred years, the fleeting Caesars of Constantinople and Germany, I now descend, in the reign of Heraclius, on the eastern borders of the Greek monarchy. While the state was exhausted by the Persian war, and the church was distracted by the Nestorian and Monophysite sects, Mahomet, with the sword in one hand and the Koran in the other, erected his throne on the ruins of Christianity and of Rome. The genius of the Arabian prophet, the manners of his nation, and the spirit of his religion involve the causes of the decline and fall of the Eastern empire; and our eyes are curiously intent on one of the most memorable revolutions which have

impressed a new and lasting character on the nations of the globe.(1)

In the vacant space between Persia, Syria, Egypt, and Æthiopia, the Arabian peninsula(2) may be conceived as a triangle of spacious but irregular dimensions. From the northern point of Beles on the Euphrates, a line of fifteen hundred miles is terminated by the straights of Babelmandeb and the land of frankincense. About half this length may be allowed for the middle breadth from east to west, from Bassora to Suez, from the Persian Gulf to the Red Sea. The sides of the triangle are gradually enlarged, and the southern basis presents a front of a thousand miles to the Indian ocean. The entire surface of the peninsula exceeds in a fourfold proportion that of Germany or France; but the far greater part has been justly stigmatized with the epithets of the *stony* and the *sandy*. Even the wilds of Tartary are decked by the hand of nature with lofty trees and luxuriant herbage; and the lonesome traveller derives a sort of comfort and society from the presence of vegetable life. But in the dreary waste of Arabia, a boundless level of sand is intersected by sharp and naked mountains, and the face of the desert, without shade or shelter, is scorched by the direct and intense rays of a tropical sun. Instead of refreshing breezes, the winds, particularly from the south-west, diffuse a noxious and even deadly vapour; the hillocks of sand which they alternately raise and scatter are compared to the billows of the ocean; and whole caravans, whole armies, have been lost and buried in the whirlwind. The common benefits of water are an object of desire and contest; and such is the scarcity of wood that some art is requisite to preserve and propagate the element of fire. Arabia is destitute of navigable rivers, which fertilize the soil and convey its produce to the adjacent regions; the torrents that fall from the hills are imbibed by the thirsty earth; the rare and hardy plants, the tamarind or the acacia, that strike their roots into the clefts of the rocks, are nourished by the dews of the night; a scanty supply of rain is collected in cisterns and aqueducts; the wells and springs are the secret treasure of the desert; and the pilgrim of Mecca, after many a dry and sultry march, is disgusted by the taste of the waters, which have rolled over a bed of sulphur or salt. Such is the general and genuine picture of the climate of Arabia. The experience of evil enhances the value of any local or partial enjoyments. A shady grove, a green pasture, a stream of fresh water, are sufficient to attract a colony of sedentary Arabs to the fortunate spots which can afford food and refreshment to themselves and their cattle, and which encourage their industry in the

cultivation of the palm-tree and the vine. The high lands that border on the Indian ocean are distinguished by their superior plenty of wood and water; the air is more temperate, the fruits are more delicious, the animals and the human race more numerous; the fertility of the soil invites and rewards the toil of the husbandman; and the peculiar gifts of frankincense and coffee have attracted, in different ages, the merchants of the world. If it be compared with the rest of the peninsula, this sequestered region may truly deserve the appellation of the *happy;* and the splendid colouring of fancy and fiction has been suggested by contrast and countenanced by distance. It was for this earthly paradise that nature had reserved her choicest favours and her most curious workmanship; the incompatible blessings of luxury and innocence were ascribed to the natives; the soil was impregnated with gold and gems, and both the land and sea were taught to exhale the odours of aromatic sweets. This division of the *sandy,* the *stony,* and the *happy,* so familiar to the Greeks and Latins, is unknown to the Arabians themselves; and it is singular enough that a country, whose language and inhabitants had ever been the same, should scarcely retain a vestige of its ancient geography. The maritime districts of *Bahrein* and *Oman* are opposite to the realm of Persia. The kingdom of *Yemen* displays the limits, or at least the situation, of Arabia Felix; the name of *Neged* is extended over the inland space; and the birth of Mahomet has illustrated the province of *Hejaz* along the coast of the Red Sea.

The measure of population is regulated by the means of subsistence; and the inhabitants of this vast peninsula might be out-numbered by the subjects of a fertile and industrious province. Along the shores of the Persian gulf, of the ocean, and even of the Red Sea, the *Icthyophagi,* or fish-eaters, continued to wander in quest of their precarious food. In this primitive and abject state, which ill deserves the name of society, the human brute, without arts or laws, almost without sense or language, is poorly distinguished from the rest of the animal creation. Generations and ages might roll away in silent oblivion, and the helpless savage was restrained from multiplying his race by the wants and pursuits which confined his existence to the narrow margin of the sea-coast. But in an early period of antiquity the great body of the Arabs had emerged from this scene of misery; and, as the naked wilderness could not maintain a people of hunters, they rose at once to the more secure and plentiful condition of the pastoral life. The same life is uniformly pursued by the roving tribes

of the desert, and in the portrait of the modern *Bedoweens* we may trace the features of their ancestors, who, in the age of Moses or Mahomet, dwelt under similar tents, and conducted their horses and camels and sheep to the same springs and the same pastures. Our toil is lessened, and our wealth is encreased, by our dominion over the useful animals; and the Arabian shepherd had acquired the absolute possession of a faithful friend and a laborious slave. Arabia, in the opinion of the naturalist, is the genuine and original country of the *horse;* the climate most propitious, not indeed to the size, but to the spirit and swiftness, of that generous animal. The merit of the Barb, the Spanish, and the English breed is derived from a mixture of Arabian blood; the Bedoweens preserve, with superstitious care, the honours and the memory of the purest race; the males are sold at a high price, but the females are seldom alienated; and the birth of a noble foal was esteemed, among the tribes, as a subject of joy and mutual congratulation. These horses are educated in the tents, among the children of the Arabs, with a tender familiarity, which trains them in the habits of gentleness and attachment. They are accustomed only to walk and to gallop; the sensations are not blunted by the incessant abuse of the spur and the whip; their powers are reserved for the moments of flight and pursuit; but no sooner do they feel the touch of the hand or the stirrup than they dart away with the swiftness of the wind; and if their friend be dismounted in the rapid career, they instantly stop till he has recovered his seat. In the sands of Africa and Arabia the *camel* is a sacred and precious gift. That strong and patient beast of burthen can perform, without eating or drinking, a journey of several days; and a reservoir of fresh water is preserved in a large bag, a fifth stomach of the animal, whose body is imprinted with the marks of servitude. The larger breed is capable of transporting a weight of a thousand pounds; and the dromedary, of a lighter and more active frame, outstrips the fleetest courser in the race. Alive or dead, almost every part of the camel is serviceable to man; her milk is plentiful and nutritious; the young and tender flesh has the taste of veal; a valuable salt is extracted from the urine; the dung supplies the deficiency of fuel; and the long hair, which falls each year and is renewed, is coarsely manufactured into the garments, the furniture, and the tents, of the Bedoweens. In the rainy seasons they consume the rare and insufficient herbage of the desert; during the heats of summer and the scarcity of winter, they remove their en-

campments to the sea-coast, the hills of Yemen, or the neighbourhood of the Euphrates, and have often extorted the dangerous licence of visiting the banks of the Nile and the villages of Syria and Palestine. The life of a wandering Arab is a life of danger and distress; and though sometimes, by rapine or exchange, he may appropriate the fruits of industry, a private citizen in Europe is in the possession of more solid and pleasing luxury than the proudest emir who marches in the field at the head of ten thousand horse.

II

The religion of the Arabs, as well as of the Indians, consisted in the worship of the sun, the moon, and the fixed stars; a primitive and specious mode of superstition. The bright luminaries of the sky display the visible image of a Deity: their number and distance convey to a philosophic, or even a vulgar, eye the idea of boundless space: the character of eternity is marked on these solid globes, that seem incapable of corruption or decay: the regularity of their motions may be ascribed to a principle of reason or instinct; and their real or imaginary influence encourages the vain belief that the earth and its inhabitants are the object of their peculiar care. The science of astronomy was cultivated at Babylon; but the school of the Arabs was a clear firmament and a naked plain. In their nocturnal marches, they steered by the guidance of the stars; their names, and order, and daily station were familiar to the curiosity and devotion of the Bedoween; and he was taught by experience to divide in twenty-eight parts the zodiac of the moon, and to bless the constellations who refreshed with salutary rains the thirst of the desert. The reign of the heavenly orbs could not be extended beyond the visible sphere; and some metaphysical powers were necessary to sustain the transmigration of souls and the resurrection of bodies; a camel was left to perish on the grave, that he might serve his master in another life; and the invocation of departed spirits implies that they were still endowed with consciousness and power. I am ignorant, and I am careless, of the blind mythology of the barbarians; of the local deities, of the stars, the air, and the earth, of their sex or titles, their attributes or subordination. Each tribe, each family, each independent warrior, created and changed the rites and the object of his fantastic worship; but the nation, in every age, has bowed to the religion, as well as to the language, of Mecca.

III

At the conclusion of the life of Mahomet, it may perhaps be expected that I should balance his faults and virtues, that I should decide whether the title of enthusiast or impostor more properly belongs to that extraordinary man. Had I been intimately conversant with the son of Abdallah, the talk would still be difficult, and the success uncertain: at the distance of twelve centuries, I darkly contemplate his shade through a cloud of religious incense; and, could I truly delineate the portrait of an hour, the fleeting resemblance would not equally apply to the solitary of mount Hera, to the preacher of Mecca, and to the conqueror of Arabia. The author of a mighty revolution appears to have been endowed with a pious and contemplative disposition: so soon as marriage had raised him above the pressure of want, he avoided the paths of ambition and avarice; and till the age of forty, he lived with innocence, and would have died without a name. The unity of God is an idea most congenial to nature and reason; and a slight conversation with the Jews and Christians would teach him to despise and detest the idolatry of Mecca. It was the duty of a man and a citizen to impart the doctrine of salvation, to rescue his country from the dominion of sin and error. The energy of a mind incessantly bent on the same object would convert a general obligation into a particular call; the warm suggestings of the understanding or the fancy would be felt as the inspirations of heaven; the labour of thought would expire in rapture and vision; and the inward sensation, the invisible monitor, would be described with the form and attributes of an angel of God.(3) From enthusiasm to imposture the step is perilous and slippery; the dæmon of Socrates affords a memorable instance, how a wise man may deceive himself, how a good man may deceive others, how the conscience may slumber in a mixed and middle state between self-illusion and voluntary fraud. Charity may believe that the original motives of Mahomet were those of pure and genuine benevolence; but a human missionary is incapable of cherishing the obstinate unbelievers who reject his claims, despise his arguments, and persecute his life; he might forgive his personal adversaries, he may lawfully hate the enemies of God; the stern passions of pride and revenge were kindled in the bosom of Mahomet, and he sighed, like the prophet of Nineveh, for the destruction of the rebels whom he had condemned. The injustice of Mecca and the choice of Medina transformed the citizen into a prince,

the humble preacher into the leader of armies; but his sword was consecrated by the example of the saints; and the same God who afflicts a sinful world with pestilence and earthquakes might inspire for their conversion or chastisement the valour of his servants. In the exercise of political government, he was compelled to abate of the stern rigour of fanaticism, to comply in some measure with the prejudices and passions of his followers, and to employ even the vices of mankind as the instruments of their salvation. The use of fraud and perfidy, of cruelty and injustice, were often subservient to the propagation of the faith; and Mahomet commanded or approved the assassination of the Jews and idolaters who had escaped from the field of battle. By the repetition of such acts, the character of Mahomet must have been gradually stained; and the influence of such pernicious habits would be poorly compensated by the practice of the personal and social virtues which are necessary to maintain the reputation of a prophet among his sectaries and friends. Of his last years, ambition was the ruling passion; and a politician will suspect that he secretly smiled (the victorious impostor!) at the enthusiasm of his youth and the credulity of his proselytes. A philosopher will observe that *their* credulity and *his* success would tend more strongly to fortify the assurance of his divine mission, that his interest and religion were inseparably connected, and that his conscience would be soothed by the persuasion that he alone was absolved by the Deity from the obligation of positive and moral laws. If he retained any vestige of his native innocence, the sins of Mahomet may be allowed as an evidence of his sincerity. In the support of truth, the arts of fraud and fiction may be deemed less criminal; and he would have started at the foulness of the means, had he not been satisfied of the importance and justice of the end. Even in a conqueror or a priest, I can surprise a word or action of unaffected humanity; and the decree of Mahomet that, in the sale of captives, the mothers should never be separated from their children may suspend or moderate the censure of the historian.

The good sense of Mahomet despised the pomp of royalty; the apostle of God submitted to the menial offices of the family; he kindled the fire, swept the floor, milked the ewes, and mended with his own hands his shoes and his woollen garment. Disdaining the penance anu merit of an hermit, he observed, without effort or vanity, the abstemious diet of an Arab and a soldier. On solemn occasions he feasted his companions with rustic and hospitable plenty; but in

his domestic life many weeks would elapse without a fire being kindled on the hearth of the prophet. The interdiction of wine was confirmed by his example; his hunger was appeased with a sparing allowance of barley bread; he delighted in the taste of milk and honey; but his ordinary food consisted of dates and water. Perfumes and women were the two sensual enjoyments which his nature required and his religion did not forbid; and Mahomet affirmed that the fervour of his devotion was increased by these innocent pleasures. The heat of the climate inflames the blood of the Arabs; and their libidinous complexion has been noticed by the writers of antiquity. Their incontinence was regulated by the civil and religious laws of the Koran; their incestuous alliances were blamed; the boundless license of polygamy was reduced to four legitimate wives or concubines; their rights both of bed and of dowry were equitably determined; the freedom of divorce was discouraged, adultery was condemned as a capital offence, and fornication, in either sex, was punished with an hundred stripes. Such were the calm and rational precepts of the legislator; but in his private conduct Mahomet indulged the appetites of a man and abused the claims of a prophet. A special revelation dispensed him from the laws which he had imposed on his nation; the female sex, without reserve, was abandoned to his desires; and this singular prerogative excited the envy, rather than the scandal, the veneration, rather than the envy, of the devout Musulmans. If we remember the seven hundred wives and three hundred concubines of the wise Solomon, we shall applaud the modesty of the Arabian, who espoused no more than seventeen or fifteen wives; eleven are enumerated who occupied at Medina their separate apartments round the house of the apostle, and enjoyed in their turns the favour of his conjugal society. What is singular enough, they were all widows, excepting only Ayesha, the daughter of Abubeker. *She* was doubtless a virgin, since Mahomet consummated his nuptials (such is the premature ripeness of the climate) when she was only nine years of age. The youth, the beauty, the spirit of Ayesha gave her a superior ascendant; she was beloved and trusted by the prophet; and after his death, the daughter of Abubeker was long revered as the mother of the faithful. Her behaviour had been ambiguous and indiscreet; in a nocturnal march, she was accidentally left behind; and in the morning Ayesha returned to the camp with a man. The temper of Mahomet was inclined to jealousy; but a divine revelation assured him of her innocence: he chastised her accusers, and published a law of domestic peace that no

woman should be condemned unless four male witnesses had seen her in the act of adultery. In his adventures with Zeineb, the wife of Zeid, and with Mary, an Egyptian captive, the amorous prophet forgot the interest of his reputation. At the house of Zeid, his freedman and adopted son, he beheld, in a loose undress, the beauty of Zeineb, and burst forth into an ejaculation of devotion and desire. The servile or grateful freedman understood the hint, and yielded, without hesitation to the love of his benefactor. But as the filial relation had excited some doubt and scandal, the angel Gabriel descended from heaven to ratify the deed, to annul the adoption, and gently to reprove the apostle for distrusting the indulgence of his God. One of his wives, Hafsa, the daughter of Omar, surprised him on her own bed in the embraces of his Egyptian captive: she promised secrecy and forgiveness; he swore that he would renounce the possession of Mary. Both parties forgot their engagements; and Gabriel again descended with a chapter of the Koran, to absolve him from his oath, and to exhort him freely to enjoy his captives and concubines without listening to the clamours of his wives. In a solitary retreat of thirty days, he laboured, alone with Mary, to fulfil the commands of the angel. When his love and revenge were satiated, he summoned to his presence his eleven wives, reproached their disobedience and indiscretion, and threatened them with a sentence of divorce both in this world and in the next: a dreadful sentence, since those who had ascended the bed of the prophet were for ever excluded from the hope of a second marriage. Perhaps the incontinence of Mahomet may be palliated by the tradition of his natural or preternatural gifts: (4) he united the manly virtue of thirty of the children of Adam; and the apostle might rival the thirteenth labour of the Grecian Hercules. A more serious and decent excuse may be drawn from his fidelity to Cadijah. During the twenty-four years of their marriage, her youthful husband abstained from the right of polygamy, and the pride or tenderness of the venerable matron was never insulted by the society of a rival. After her death, he placed her in the rank of the four perfect women, with the sister of Moses, the mother of Jesus, and Fatima, the best beloved of his daughters. "Was she not old?" said Ayesha, with the insolence of a blooming beauty; "has not God given you a better in her place?" "No, by God," said Mahomet, with an effusion of honest gratitude, "there never can be a better! She believed in me, when men despised me; she relieved my wants, when I was poor and persecuted by the world."

IV

The talents of Mahomet are entitled to our applause, but his success has perhaps too strongly attracted our admiration. Are we surprised that a multitude of proselytes should embrace the doctrine and the passions of an eloquent fanatic? In the heresies of the church, the same seduction has been tried and repeated from the time of the apostles to that of the reformers. Does it seem incredible that a private citizen should grasp the sword and the sceptre, subdue his native country, and erect a monarchy by his victorious arms? In the moving picture of the dynasties of the East, an hundred fortunate usurpers have arisen from a baser origin, surmounted more formidable obstacles, and filled a larger scope of empire and conquest. Mahomet was alike instructed to preach and to fight, and the union of these opposite qualities, while it enhanced his merit, contributed to his success: the operation of force and persuasion, of enthusiasm and fear, continually acted on each other, till every barrier yielded to their irresistible power. His voice invited the Arabs to freedom and victory, to arms and rapine, to the indulgence of their darling passions in this world and the other; the restraints which he imposed were requisite to establish the credit of the prophet and to exercise the obedience of the people; and the only objection to his success was his rational creed of the unity and perfections of God. It is not the propagation but the permanency of his religion that deserves our wonder: the same pure and perfect impression which he engraved at Mecca and Medina is preserved, after the revolutions of twelve centuries, by the Indian, the African, and the Turkish proselytes of the Koran. If the Christian apostles, St. Peter or St. Paul, could return to the Vatican, they might possibly inquire the name of the Deity who is worshipped with such mysterious rites in that magnificent temple: at Oxford or Geneva, they would experience less surprise; but it might still be incumbent on them to peruse the catechism of the church, and to study the orthodox commentators on their own writings and the words of their Master. But the Turkish dome of St. Sophia, with an increase of splendour and size, represents the humble tabernacle erected at Medina by the hands of Mahomet. The Mahometans have uniformly withstood the temptation of reducing the object of their faith and devotion to a level with the senses and imagination of man. "I believe in one God, and Mahomet the apostle of God," is the sim-

ple and invariable profession of Islam. The intellectual image of the Deity has never been degraded by any visible idol; the honours of the prophet have never transgressed the measure of human virtue; and his living precepts have restrained the gratitude of his disciples within the bounds of reason and religion. The votaries of Ali have indeed consecrated the memory of their hero, his wife, and his children; and some of the Persian doctors pretend that the divine essence was incarnate in the person of the Imams; but their superstition is universally condemned by the Sonnites; and their impiety has afforded a seasonable warning against the worship of saints and martyrs. The metaphysical questions on the attributes of God and the liberty of man have been agitated in the schools of the Mahometans as well as in those of the Christians; but among the former they have never engaged the passions of the people or disturbed the tranquillity of the state. The cause of this important difference may be found in the separation or union of the regal and sacerdotal characters. It was the interest of the caliphs, the successors of the prophet and commanders of the faithful, to repress and discourage all religious innovations: the order, the discipline, the temporal and spiritual ambition of the clergy are unknown to the Moslems; and the sages of the law are the guides of their conscience and the oracles of their faith. From the Atlantic to the Ganges, the Koran is acknowledged as the fundamental code, not only of theology but of civil and criminal jurisprudence; and the laws which regulate the actions and the property of mankind are guarded by the infallible and immutable sanction of the will of God. This religious servitude is attended with some practical disadvantage; the illiterate legislator had been often misled by his own prejudices and those of his country; and the institutions of the Arabian desert may be ill adapted to the wealth and numbers of Ispahan and Constantinople. On these occasions, the Cadhi respectfully places on his head the holy volume, and substitutes a dexterous interpretation, more apposite to the principles of equity and the manners and policy of the times.

His beneficial or pernicious influence on the public happiness is the last consideration in the character of Mahomet. The most bitter or most bigotted of his Christian or Jewish foes will surely allow that he assumed a false commission to inculcate a salutary doctrine, less perfect only than their own. He piously supposed, as the basis of his religion, the truth and sanctity of *their* prior revelations, the virtues

and miracles of their founders. The idols of Arabia were broken before the throne of God; the blood of human victims was expiated by prayer and fasting and alms, the laudable or innocent arts of devotion; and his rewards and punishments of a future life were painted by the images most congenial to an ignorant and carnal generation. Mahomet was perhaps incapable of dictating a moral and political system for the use of his countrymen; but he breathed among the faithful a spirit of charity and friendship, recommended the practice of the social virtues, and checked, by his laws and precepts, the thirst of revenge and the oppression of widows and orphans. The hostile tribes were united in faith and obedience, and the valour which had been idly spent in domestic quarrels was vigorously directed against a foreign enemy. Had the impulse been less powerful, Arabia, free at home and formidable abroad, might have flourished under a succession of her native monarchs. Her sovereignty was lost by the extent and rapidity of conquest. The colonies of the nation were scattered over the East and West, and their blood was mingled with the blood of their converts and captives. After the reign of three caliphs the throne was transported from Medina to the valley of Damascus and the banks of the Tigris; the holy cities were violated by impious war; Arabia was ruled by the rod of a subject, perhaps of a stranger; and the Bedoweens of the desert, awakening from their dream of dominion, resumed their old and solitary independence.(5)

NOTES

(1) As in this and the following chapter I shall display much Arabic learning, I must profess my total ignorance of the Oriental tongues, and my gratitude to the learned interpreters, who have transfused their science into the Latin, French, and English languages. Their collections, versions, and histories, I shall occasionally notice.

(2) The geographers of Arabia may be divided into three classes: 1. The *Greeks* and *Latins,* whose progressive knowledge may be traced in Agatharcides (de Mari Rubro, in Hudson, Geograph. Minor. tom. i), Diodorus Siculus (tom. i. l. ii. p. 159–167, l. iii. p. 211–216, edit. Wesseling), Strabo (l. xvi. p. 1112–1114, from Eratosthenes; p. 1122–1132, from Artemidorus), Pliny (Hist. Natur. v. 12, vi. 32.), and Ptolemy (Descript. et Tabulæ Urbium, in Hudson, tom. iii.). 2. The *Arabic writers,* who have treated the subject with the zeal of patriotism

or devotion: the extracts of Pocock (Specimen Hist. Arabum, p. 125–128), from the Geography of the Sherif al Edrissi, render us still more dissatisfied with the version or abridgment (p. 24–27. 44–56. 108, &c. 119, &c.) which the Maronites have published under the absurd title of Geographia Nubiensis (Paris, 1619); but the Latin and French translators, Greaves (in Hudson, tom. iii.) and Galland (Voyage de la Palestine par La Roque, p. 265–346), have opened to us the Arabia of Abulfeda, the most copious and correct account of the peninsula, which may be enriched, however from the Bibliothèque Orientale of d'Herbelot, p. 120. et alibi passim. 3. The *European travellers;* among whom Shaw (p. 438–455) and Niebuhr (Description, 1773, Voyages, tom. i. 1776) deserve an honourable distinction: Busching (Géographie par Berenger, tom. viii. p. 416–510) has compiled with judgment; and d'Anville's Maps (Orbis Veteribus Notus, and 1re Partie de l'Asie) should lie before the reader, with his Géographie Ancienne, tom. ii. p. 208–231.

(3) The Christians, rashly enough, have assigned to Mahomet a tame pigeon, that seemed to descend from heaven and whisper in his ear. As this pretended miracle is urged by Grotius (de Veritate Religionis Christianæ), his Arabic translator, the learned Pocock, enquired of him the names of his authors; and Grotius confessed that it is unknown to the Mahometans themselves. Lest it should provoke their indignation and laughter, the pious *lie* is suppressed in the Arabic version; but it has maintained an edifying place in the numerous editions of the Latin text (Pocock, Specimen Hist. Arabum, p. 186, 187. Reland, de Religion. Moham. l. ii. c. 39. p. 259–262).

(4) Sibi robur ad generationem, quantum triginta viri habent, inesse jactaret: ita ut unica hora posset undecim foeminis *satisfacere*, ut ex Arabum libris refert Stus. Petrus Paschasius, c. 2. (Maracci, Prodromus Alcoran, p. iv, p. 55. See likewise, Observations de Belon, l. iii. c. 10. fol. 179. recto). Al Jannabi (Gagnier, tom. iii. p. 487) records his own testimony that he surpassed all men in conjugal vigour; and Abulfeda mentions the exclamation of Ali, who washed his body after his death, "O propheta, certe penis tuus cælum versus erectus est" (in Vit. Mohammed. p. 140).

(5) The writers of the Modern Universal History (vol. i. and ii.) have compiled, in 850 folio pages, the life of Mahomet and the annals of the caliphs. They enjoyed the advantage of reading, and sometimes

correcting, the Arabic text; yet, notwithstanding their high-sounding boasts, I cannot find, after the conclusion of my work, that they have afforded me much (if any) additional information. The dull mass is not quickened by a spark of philosophy or taste: and the compilers indulge the criticism of acrimonious bigotry against Boulainvilliers, Sale, Gagnier, and all who have treated Mahomet with favour, or even justice.

SIR WALTER SCOTT

1771–1832

These passages are from chapters 5 and 6 of The Heart of Midlothian *(1818) and chapter 5 of* The Fortunes of Nigel *(1822). The description of the Porteous riot in 1736 was influenced by accounts of French revolutionary mobs and surely influenced Carlyle's description of the storming of the Bastille. Captain Porteous and his City Guard had opened fire on the crowd during the hanging of a man who had won general sympathy because of Porteous's harsh behavior to him before he mounted the scaffold. Porteous was judged responsible for the deaths that resulted, and was sentenced to be hanged. When Butler, a local schoolmaster, came up to Edinburgh, word had been spread that a reprieve had arrived for Porteous, and a mob gathered to exact justice for itself.*

Scott's biographer Lockhart said that "Scott amused some leisure hours with writing a series of 'Private Letters' supposed to have been discovered in the repositories of a Noble English Family, and giving a picture of manners in town and country during the early part of the reign of James I." This was the origin of Nigel, *the vivid local color of which was assisted by Scott's editorial labors on early seventeenth-century pamphlets. The passage given here is from chapter 5. The goldsmith, Heriot, has come to show the monarch a piece of plate.*

Scott's views on history and the writing of historical fiction can best be seen in the epistle prefaced to Ivanhoe, *which was dedicated to a character destined to as great a fame as any of his fictional creations, the Rev. Doctor Dryasdust, F.A.S.*

I

WHILE this was going on, Butler could not, even if he had been willing, avoid making remarks on the individuals who seemed to lead this singular mob. The torchlight, while it fell on their forms, and left him in the shade, gave him an opportunity to do so without their observing him. Several of those who appeared most active were dressed in sailors' jackets, trousers, and sea-caps; others in large loose-bodied greatcoats, and slouched hats, and there were several who, judging from their dress, should have been called women, whose rough deep voices, uncommon size, and masculine deportment and mode of walking, forbade them being so interpreted. They moved as if by some well-concerted plan of arrangement. They had signals by which they knew, and nicknames by which they distinguished each other. Butler remarked, that the name of Wildfire was used among them, to which one stout Amazon seemed to reply.

The rioters left a small party to observe the West Port, and directed the Waiters, as they valued their lives, to remain within their lodge, and make no attempt for that night to repossess themselves of the gate. They then moved with rapidity along the low street called the Cowgate, the mob of the city everywhere rising at the sound of their drum, and joining them. When the multitude arrived at the Cowgate Port, they secured it with as little opposition as the former, made it fast, and left a small party to observe it. It was afterwards remarked, as a striking instance of prudence and precaution, singularly combined with audacity, that the parties left to guard those gates did not remain stationary on their posts, but flitted to and fro, keeping so near the gates as to see that no efforts were made to open them, yet not remaining so long as to have their persons closely observed. The mob, at first only about one hundred strong, now amounted to thousands, and were increasing every moment. They divided themselves so as to ascend with more speed the various narrow lanes which lead up from the Cowgate to the High Street; and still beating to arms as they went, and calling on all true Scotsmen to join them, they now filled the principal street of the city.

The Netherbow Port might be called the Temple Bar of Edinburgh, as intersecting the High Street at its termination, it divided Edinburgh, properly so called, from the suburb named the Canongate, as Temple Bar separates London from Westminster. It was of the utmost im-

portance to the rioters to possess themselves of this pass, because there was quartered in the Canongate at that time a regiment of infantry, commanded by Colonel Moyle, which might have occupied the city by advancing through this gate, and would possess the power of totally defeating their purpose. The leaders therefore hastened to the Netherbow Port, which they secured in the same manner, and with as little trouble, as the other gates, leaving a party to watch it, strong in proportion to the importance of the post.

The next object of these hardy insurgents was at once to disarm the City Guard, and to procure arms for themselves; for scarce any weapons but staves and bludgeons had been seen among them. The Guard-house was a long, low, ugly building (removed in 1787), which to a fanciful imagination might have suggested the idea of a long black snail crawling up the middle of the High Street, and deforming its beautiful esplanade. This formidable insurrection had been so unexpected, that there were no more than the ordinary sergeant's guard of the city corps upon duty; even these were without any supply of powder and ball; and sensible enough what had raised the storm, and which way it was rolling, could hardly be supposed very desirous to expose themselves by a valiant defence to the animosity of so numerous and desperate a mob, to whom they were on the present occasion much more than usually obnoxious.

There was a sentinel upon guard, who (that one town guard soldier might do his duty on that eventful evening) presented his piece, and desired the foremost of the rioters to stand off. The young Amazon, whom Butler had observed particularly active, sprung upon the soldier, seized his musket, and after a struggle succeeded in wrenching it from him, and throwing him down on the causeway. One or two soldiers, who endeavoured to turn out to the support of their sentinel, were in the same manner seized and disarmed, and the mob without difficulty possessed themselves of the Guard-house, disarming and turning out of doors the rest of the men on duty. It was remarked, that, notwithstanding the city soldiers had been the instruments of the slaughter which this riot was designed to revenge, no ill-usage or even insult was offered to them. It seemed as if the vengeance of the people disdained to stoop at any head meaner than that which they considered as the source and origin of their injuries.

On possessing themselves of the guard, the first act of the multitude was to destroy the drums, by which they supposed an alarm might be conveyed to the garrison in the castle; for the same reason they

now silenced their own, which was beaten by a young fellow, son to the drummer of Portsburgh, whom they had forced upon that service. Their next business was to distribute among the boldest of the rioters the guns, bayonets, partisans, halberds, and battle or Lochaber axes. Until this period the principal rioters had preserved silence on the ultimate object of their rising, as being that which all knew, but none expressed. Now, however, having accomplished all the preliminary parts of their design, they raised a tremendous shout of "Porteous! Porteous! To the Tolbooth! To the Tolbooth!"

They proceeded with the same prudence when the object seemed to be nearly in their grasp, as they had done hitherto when the success was more dubious. A strong party of the rioters, drawn up in front of the Luckenbooths, and facing down the street, prevented all access from the eastward, and the west end of the defile formed by the Luckenbooths was secured in the same manner; so that the Tolbooth was completely surrounded, and those who undertook the task of breaking it open effectually secured against the risk of interruption.

The magistrates, in the meanwhile, had taken the alarm, and assembled in a tavern, with the purpose of raising some strength to subdue the rioters. The deacons, or presidents of the trades, were applied to, but declared there was little chance of their authority being respected by the craftsmen, where it was the object to save a man so obnoxious. Mr. Lindsay, member of Parliament for the city., volunteered the perilous task of carrying a verbal message from the Lord Provost to Colonel Moyle, the commander of the regiment lying in the Canongate, requesting him to force the Netherbow Port, and enter the city to put down the tumult. But Mr. Lindsay declined to charge himself with any written order, which, if found on his person by an enraged mob, might have cost him his life; and the issue of the application was, that Colonel Moyle, having no written requisition from the civil authorities, and having the fate of Porteous before his eyes as an example of the severe construction put by a jury on the proceedings of military men acting on their own responsibility, declined to encounter the risk to which the Provost's verbal communication invited him.

More than one messenger was despatched by different ways to the Castle, to require the commanding officer to march down his troops, to fire a few cannon-shot, or even to throw a shell among the mob, for the purpose of clearing the streets. But so strict and watchful were the various patrols whom the rioters had established in different parts

of the street, that none of the emissaries of the magistrates could reach the gate of the Castle. They were, however, turned back without either injury or insult, and with nothing more of menace than was necessary to deter them from again attempting to accomplish their errand.

The same vigilance was used to prevent everybody of the higher, and those which, in this case, might be deemed the more suspicious orders of society, from appearing in the street, and observing the movements, or distinguishing the persons, of the rioters. Every person in the garb of a gentleman was stopped by small parties of two or three of the mob, who partly exhorted, partly required of them, that they should return to the place from whence they came. Many a quadrille table was spoiled that memorable evening; for the sedan-chairs of ladies, even of the highest rank, were interrupted in their passage from one point to another, in despite of the laced footmen and blazing flambeaux. This was uniformly done with a deference and attention to the feelings of the terrified females, which could hardly have been expected from the vedettes of a mob so desperate. Those who stopped the chair usually made the excuse, that there was much disturbance on the streets, and that it was absolutely necessary for the lady's safety that the chair should turn back. They offered themselves to escort the vehicles which they had thus interrupted in their progress, from the apprehension, probably, that some of those who had casually united themselves to the riot might disgrace their systematic and determined plan of vengeance, by those acts of general insult and license which are common on similar occasions.

Persons are yet living who remember to have heard from the mouths of ladies thus interrupted on their journey in the manner we have described, that they were escorted to their lodgings by the young men who stopped them, and even handed out of their chairs, with a polite attention far beyond what was consistent with their dress which was apparently that of journeymen mechanics.(1) It seemed as if the conspirators, like those who assassinated the Cardinal Beatoun in former days, had entertained the opinion, that the work about which they went was a judgment of Heaven, which, though unsanctioned by the usual authorities, ought to be proceeded in with order and gravity.

While their outposts continued thus vigilant, and suffered themselves neither from fear nor curiosity to neglect that part of the duty assigned to them, and while the main guards to the east and west secured them against interruption, a select body of the rioters thundered at

the door of the jail, and demanded instant admission. No one answered, for the outer keeper had prudently made his escape with the keys at the commencement of the riot, and was nowhere to be found. The door was instantly assailed with sledge-hammers, iron crows, and the coulters of ploughs, ready provided for the purpose, with which they prized, heaved, and battered for some time with little effect; for, being of double oak planks, clenched, both end-long and athwart, with broad-headed nails, the door was so secured as to yield to no means of forcing, without the expenditure of much time. The rioters, however, appeared determined to gain admittance. Gang after gang relieved each other at the exercise, for, of course, only a few could work at a time; but gang after gang retired, exhausted with their violent exertions, without making much progress in forcing the prison door. Butler had been led up near to this the principal scene of action; so near, indeed that he was almost deafened by the unceasing clang of the heavy forehammers against the iron-bound portals of the prison. He began to entertain hopes, as the task seemed protracted, that the populace might give it over in despair, or that some rescue might arrive to disperse them. There was a moment at which the latter seemed probable.

The magistrates having assembled their officers, and some of the citizens who were willing to hazard themselves for the public tranquillity, now sallied forth from the tavern where they held their sitting, and approached the point of danger. Their officers went before them with links and torches, with a herald to read the Riot Act, if necessary. They easily drove before them the outposts and vedettes of the rioters; but when they approached the line of guard which the mob, or rather, we should say, the conspirators, had drawn across the street in the front of the Luckenbooths, they were received with an unintermitted volley of stones, and, on their nearer approach, the pikes, bayonets, and Lochaber axes, of which the populace had possessed themselves, were presented against them. One of their ordinary officers, a strong resolute fellow, went forward, seized a rioter, and took from him a musket; but, being unsupported, he was instantly thrown on his back in the street, and disarmed in his turn. The officer was too happy to be permitted to rise and run away without receiving any farther injury; which afforded another remarkable instance of the mode in which these men had united a sort of moderation towards all others, with the most inflexible inveteracy against the object of their resentment. The magistrates, after vain attempts to make themselves heard and obeyed,

possessing no means of enforcing their authority, were constrained to abandon the field to the rioters, and retreat in all speed from the showers of missiles that whistled around their ears.

The passive resistance of the Tolbooth-gate promised to do more to baffle the purpose of the mob than the active interference of the magistrates. The heavy sledge-hammers continued to din against it without intermission, and with a noise which, echoed from the lofty buildings around the spot, seemed enough to have alarmed the garrison in the Castle. It was circulated among the rioters, that the troops would march down to disperse them, unless they could execute their purpose without loss of time; or that, even without quitting the fortress, the garrison might obtain the same end by throwing a bomb or two upon the street.

Urged by such motives for apprehension, they eagerly relieved each other at the labour of assailing the Tolbooth door; yet such was its strength, that it still defied their efforts. At length, a voice was heard to pronounce the words, "Try it with fire". The rioters with a unanimous shout, called for combustibles, and as all their wishes seemed to be instantly supplied, they were soon in possession of two or three empty tar-barrels. A huge red glaring bonfire speedily arose close to the door of the prison, sending up a tall column of smoke and flame against its antique turrets and strongly-grated windows, and illuminating the ferocious and wild gestures of the rioters who surrounded the place, as well as the pale and anxious groups of those, who from windows in the vicinage, watched the progress of this alarming scene. The mob fed the fire with whatever they could find fit for the purpose. The flames roared and crackled among the heaps of nourishment piled on the fire, and a terrible shout soon announced that the door had kindled, and was in the act of being destroyed. The fire was suffered to decay, but, long ere it was quite extinguished, the most forward of the rioters rushed, in their impatience, one after another, over its yet smouldering remains. Thick showers of sparkles rose high in the air, as man after man bounded over the glowing embers, and disturbed them in their passage. It was now obvious to Butler, and all others who were present, that the rioters would be instantly in possession of their victim, and have it in their power to work their pleasure upon him, whatever that might be.

The unhappy object of this remarkable disturbance had been that day delivered from the apprehension of a public execution, and his joy was the greater, as he had some reason to question whether govern-

ment would have run the risk of unpopularity by interfering in his favour, after he had been legally convicted by the verdict of a jury, of a crime so very obnoxious. Relieved from this doubtful state of mind, his heart was merry within him, and he thought, in the emphatic words of Scripture on a similar occasion, that surely the bitterness of death was past. Some of his friends, however, who had watched the manner and behaviour of the crowd when they were made acquainted with the reprieve, were of a different opinion. They augured from the unusual sternness and silence with which they bore their disappointment, that the populace nourished some scheme of sudden and desperate vengeance; and they advised Porteous to lose no time in petitioning the proper authorities, that he might be conveyed to the Castle under a sufficient guard, to remain there in security until his ultimate fate should be determined. Habituated, however by his office, to overawe the rabble of the city, Porteous could not suspect them of an attempt so audacious as to storm a strong and defensible prison; and, despising the advice by which he might have been saved, he spent the afternoon of the eventful day in giving an entertainment to some friends who visited him in jail, several of whom, by the indulgence of the Captain of the Tolbooth, with whom he had an old intimacy, arising from their official connection, were even permitted to remain to supper with him, though contrary to the rules of the jail.

It was, therefore, in the hour of unalloyed mirth, when this unfortunate wretch was "full of bread," hot with wine, and high in mistimed and ill-grounded confidence, and, alas! with all his sins full blown, when the first distant shouts of the rioters mingled with the song of merriement and intemperance. The hurried call of the jailer to the guests, requiring them instantly to depart, and his yet more hasty intimation that a dreadful and determined mob had possessed themselves of the city gates and guard-house, were the first explanation of these fearful clamours.

Porteous might, however, have eluded the fury from which the force of authority could not protect him, had he thought of slipping on some disguise, and leaving the prison along with his guests. It is probable that the jailer might have connived at his escape, or even that, in the flurry of this alarming contingency, he might not have observed it. But Porteous and his friends alike wanted presence of mind to suggest or execute such a plan of escape. The former hastily fled from a place where their own safety seemed compromised, and the latter, in a state resembling stupefaction, awaited in his apart-

ment the termination of the enterprise of the rioters. The cessation of the clang of instruments with which they had at first attempted to force the door, gave him momentary relief. The flattering hopes, that the military had marched into the city, either from the Castle or from the suburbs, and that the rioters were intimidated and dispersing, were soon destroyed by the broad and glaring light of the flames, which, illuminating through the grated window every corner of his apartment, plainly showed that the mob, determined on their fatal purpose, had adopted a means of forcing entrance equally desperate and certain.

The sudden glare of light suggested to the stupefied and astonished object of popular hatred, the possibility of concealment or escape. To rush to the chimney, to ascend it at the risk of suffocation, were the only means which seem to have occurred to him; but his progress was speedily stopped by one of those iron gratings, which are, for the sake of security, usually placed across the vents of buildings designed for imprisonment. The bars, however, which impeded his farther progress, served to support him in the situation which he had gained, and he seized them with the tenacious grasp of one who esteemed himself clinging to his last hope of existence. The lurid light, which had filled the apartment, lowered and died away; the sound of shouts was heard within the walls, and on the narrow and winding stair, which, cased within one of the turrets, gave access to the upper apartments of the prison. The huzza of the rioters was answered by a shout wild and desperate as their own, the cry, namely, of the imprisoned felons, who, expecting to be liberated in the general confusion, welcomed the mob as their deliverers. By some of these the apartment of Porteous was pointed out by his enemies. The obstacle of the lock and bolts was soon overcome, and from his hiding-place the unfortunate man heard his enemies search every corner of the apartment, with oaths and maledictions, which would but shock the reader if we recorded them, but which served to prove, could it have admitted of doubt, the settled purpose of soul with which they sought his destruction.

A place of concealment so obvious to suspicion and scrutiny as that which Porteous had chosen, could not long screen him from detection. He was dragged from his lurking-place, with a violence which seemed to argue an intention to put him to death on the spot. More than one weapon was directed towards him, when one of the rioters, the same whose female disguise had been particularly noticed by Butler, inter-

fered in an authoritative tone. "Are ye mad?" he said, "or would ye execute an act of justice as if it were a crime and a cruelty? This sacrifice will lose half its savour if we do not offer it at the very horns of the altar. We will have him die where a murderer should die, on the common gibbet—We will have him die where he spilled the blood of so many innocents!"

A loud shout of applause followed the proposal, and the cry, "To the gallows with the murderer!—To the Grassmarket with him!" echoed on all hands.

"Let no man hurt him," continued the speaker; "let him make his peace with God, if he can; we will not kill both his soul and body."

"What time did he give better folk for preparing their account?" answered several voices. "Let us mete to him with the same measure he measured to them."

But the opinion of the spokeman better suited the temper of those he addressed, a temper rather stubborn than impetuous, sedate though ferocious, and desirous of colouring their cruel and revengeful action with a show of justice and moderation.

That tumult was now transferred from the inside to the outside of the Tolbooth. The mob had brought their destined victim forth, and were about to conduct him to the common place of execution, which they had fixed as the scene of his death. The leader, whom they distinguished by the name of Madge Wildfire, had been summoned to assist at the procession by the impatient shouts of his confederates.

"I will ensure you five hundred pounds," said the unhappy man, grasping Wildfire's hand,—"five hundred pounds for to save my life."

The other answered in the same undertone, and returning his grasp with one equally convulsive, "Five hundredweight of coined gold should not save you. —Remember Wilson!"

A deep pause of a minute ensued, when Wildfire added, in a more composed tone, "Make your peace with Heaven. —Where is the clergyman?"

Butler, who, in great terror and anxiety, had been detained within a few yards of the Tolbooth door, to wait the event of the search after Porteous, was now brought forward, and commanded to walk by the prisoner's side, and to prepare him for immediate death. His answer was a supplication that the rioters would consider what they did. "You are neither judges nor jury," said he. "You cannot have, by the laws of

God or man, power to take away the life of a human creature, however deserving he may be of death. If it is murder even in a lawful magistrate to execute an offender otherwise than in the place, time, and manner, which the judges' sentence prescribes, what must it be in you, who have no warrant for interference but your own wills? In the name of Him who is all mercy, show mercy to this unhappy man, and do not dip your hands in his blood, nor rush into the very crime which you are desirous of avenging!"

"Cut your sermon short—you are not in your pulpit," answered one of the rioters.

"If we hear more of your clavers," said another, "we are like to hang you up beside him."

"Peace, hush!" said Wildfire. "Do the good man no harm—he discharges his conscience, and I like him the better."

He then addressed Butler. "Now, sir, we have patiently heard you, and we just wish you to understand, in the way of answer, that you may as well argue to the ashler work and iron stanchels of the Tolbooth as think to change our purpose—Blood must have blood. We have sworn to each other by the deepest oaths ever were pledged, that Porteous shall die the death he deserves so richly; therefore, speak no more to us, but prepare him for death as well as the briefness of his change will permit."

They had suffered the unfortunate Porteous to put on his night-gown and slippers, as he had thrown off his coat and shoes, in order to facilitate his attempted escape up the chimney. In this garb he was now mounted on the hands of two of the rioters, clasped together, so as to form what is called in Scotland, "The King's Cushion." Butler was placed close to his side, and repeatedly urged to perform a duty always the most painful which can be imposed on a clergyman deserving of the name, and now rendered more so by the peculiar and horrid circumstances of the criminal's case. Porteous at first uttered some supplications for mercy, but when he found that there was no chance that these would be attended to, his military education, and the natural stubbornness of his disposition, combined to support his spirits.

"Are you prepared for this dreadful end?" said Butler, in a faltering voice. "O turn to Him, in whose eyes time and space have no existence, and to whom a few minutes are as a lifetime, and a lifetime as a minute."

"I believe I know what you would say," answered Porteous sullenly. "I was bred a soldier; if they will murder me without time, let my sins as well as my blood lie at their door."

"Who was it," said the stern voice of Wildfire, "that said to Wilson at this very spot, when he could not pray, owing to the galling agony of his fetters, that his pains would soon be over?—I say to you to take your own tale home; and if you cannot profit by the good man's lessons, blame not them that are still more merciful to you than you were to others."

The procession now moved forward with a slow and determined pace. It was enlightened by many blazing links and torches; for the actors of this work were so far from affecting any secrecy on the occasion, that they seemed even to court observation. Their principal leaders kept close to the person of the prisoner, whose pallid yet stubborn features were seen distinctly by the torchlight, as his person was raised considerably above the concourse which thronged around him. Those who bore swords, muskets, and battleaxes, marched on each side, as if forming a regular guard to the procession. The windows, as they went along were filled with the inhabitants, whose slumbers had been broken by this unusual disturbance. Some of the spectators muttered accents of encouragement; but in general they were so much appalled by a sight so strange and audacious, that they looked on with a sort of stupefied astonishment. No one offered, by act or word, the slightest interruption.

The rioters, on their part, continued to act with the same air of deliberate confidence and security which had marked all their proceedings. When the object of their resentment dropped one of his slippers, they stopped, sought for it, and replaced it upon his foot with great deliberation.(2) As they descended the Bow towards the fatal spot where they designed to complete their purpose, it was suggested that there should be a rope kept in readiness. For this purpose the booth of a man who dealt in cordage was forced open, a coil of rope fit for their purpose was selected to serve as a halter, and the dealer next morning found that a guinea had been left on his counter in exchange; so anxious were the perpetrators of this daring action to show that they meditated not the slightest wrong or infraction of law, excepting so far as Porteous was himself concerned.

Leading, or carrying along with them, in this determined and regular manner, the object of their vengeance, they at length reached the place of common execution, the scene of his crime, and destined spot

of his sufferings. Several of the rioters (if they should not rather be described as conspirators) endeavoured to remove the stone which filled up the socket in which the end of the fatal tree was sunk when it was erected for its fatal purpose; others sought for the means of constructing a temporary gibbet, the place in which the gallows itself was deposited being reported too secure to be forced, without much loss of time. Butler endeavoured to avail himself of the delay afforded by these circumstances, to turn the people from their desperate design. "For God's sake," he exclaimed, "remember it is the image of your Creator which you are about to deface in the person of this unfortunate man! Wretched as he is, and wicked as he may be, he has a share in every promise of Scripture, and you cannot destroy him in impenitence without blotting his name from the Book of Life—Do not destroy soul and body; give time for preparation."

"What time had they," returned a stern voice, "whom he murdered on this very spot?—The laws both of God and man call for his death."

"But what, my friends," insisted Butler, with a generous disregard to his own safety—"what hath constituted you his judges?"

"We are not his judges," replied the same person; "he has been already judged and condemned by lawful authority. We are those whom Heaven, and our righteous anger, have stirred up to execute judgment, when a corrupt government would have protected a murderer."

"I am none," said the unfortunate Porteous; "that which you charge upon me fell out in self-defence, in the lawful exercise of my duty."

"Away with him—away with him!" was the general cry. "Why do you trifle away time in making a gallows?—that dyester's pole is good enough for the homicide."

The unhappy man was forced to his fate with remorseless rapidity. Butler, separated from him by the press, escaped the last horrors of his struggles. Unnoticed by those who had hitherto detained him as a prisoner, he fled from the fatal spot, without much caring in what direction his course lay. A loud shout proclaimed the stern delight with which the agents of this deed regarded its completion. Butler, then, at the opening into the low street called the Cowgate, cast back a terrified glance, and, by the red and dusky light of the torches, he could discern a figure wavering and struggling as it hung suspended above the heads of the multitude, and could even observe men striking at it with their Lochaber axes and partisans. The sight was of a nature to double his horror, and to add wings to his flight.

II

No word was spoken on either side, but one of the ushers looked first to Heriot, and then to a little door half-covered by the tapestry, which seemed to say, as plain as a look could, "Lies your business that way?" The citizen nodded; and the court-attendant, moving on tiptoe, and with as much caution as if the floor had been paved with eggs, advanced to the door, opened it gently, and spoke a few words in a low tone. The broad Scottish accent of King James was heard in reply, "Admit him instanter, Maxwell. Have you hairboured sae lang at the Court, and not learned that gold and silver are ever welcome?"

The usher signed to Heriot to advance, and the honest citizen was presently introduced into the cabinet of the Sovereign.

The scene of confusion amid which he found the King seated was no bad picture of the state and quality of James's own mind. There was much that was rich and costly in cabinet pictures and valuable ornaments; but they were arranged in a slovenly manner, covered with dust, and lost half their value, or at least their effect, from the manner in which they were presented to the eye. The table was loaded with huge folios, amongst which lay light books of jest and ribaldry; and, amongst notes of unmercifully long orations and essays on king-craft were mingled miserable roundels and ballads by the Royal 'Prentice, as he styled himself, in the art of poetry, and schemes for the general pacification of Europe with a list of the names of the King's hounds and remedies against canine madness.

The King's dress was of green velvet, quilted so full as to be dagger-proof, which gave him the appearance of clumsy and ungainly protuberance; while its being buttoned awry communicated to his figure an air of distortion. Over his green doublet he wore a sad-coloured night-gown, out of the pocket of which peeped his hunting-horn. His high-crowned grey hat lay on the floor, covered with dust, but encircled by a carcanet of large balas rubies; and he wore a blue velvet nightcap, in the front of which was placed the plume of a heron, which had been struck down by a favourite hawk in some critical moment of the flight, in remembrance of which the King wore this highly-honoured feather.

But such inconsistencies in dress and appointments were mere outward types of those which existed in the royal character—rendering it a subject of doubt amongst his contemporaries, and bequeathing it as a problem to future historians. He was deeply learned, without possessing useful knowledge; sagacious in many individual cases, without

having real wisdom, fond of his power, and desirous to maintain and augment it, yet willing to resign the direction of that, and of himself, to the most unworthy favourites; a big and bold assertor of his rights in words, yet one who tamely saw them trampled on in deeds; a lover of negotiations, in which he was always outwitted; and one who feared war, where conquest might have been easy. He was fond of his dignity, while he was perpetually degrading it by undue familiarity; capable of much public labour, yet often neglecting it for the meanest amusement; a wit, though a pedant; and a scholar, though fond of the conversation of the ignorant and uneducated. Even his timidity of temper was not uniform, and there were moments of his life, and those critical, in which he showed the spirit of his ancestors. He was laborious in trifles, and a trifler where serious labour was required; devout in his sentiments, and yet too often profane in his language; just and beneficent by nature, he yet gave way to the iniquities and oppression of others. He was penurious respecting money which he had to give from his own hand, yet inconsiderately and unboundedly profuse of that which he did not see. In a word, those good qualities which displayed themselves in particular cases and occasions, were not of a nature sufficiently firm and comprehensive to regulate his general conduct; and, showing themselves as they occasionally did, only entitled James to the character bestowed on him by Sully—that he was the wisest fool in Christendom.

That the fortunes of this monarch might be as little a piece as his character, he, certainly the least able of the Stewarts, succeeded peaceably to that kingdom, against the power of which his predecessors had, with so much difficulty, defended his native throne; and lastly, although his reign appeared calculated to ensure to Great Britain that lasting tranquillity and internal peace which so much suited the King's disposition, yet during that very reign were sown those seeds of dissension which, like the teeth of the fabulous dragon, had their harvest in a bloody and universal civil war.

NOTES

(1) A near relation of the author's used to tell of having been stopped by the rioters, and escorted home in the manner described. On reaching her own home, one of the attendants, in appearance a baxter, i.e., a baker's lad, handed her out of her chair, and took leave with a bow, which, in the lady's opinion, argued breeding that could hardly be learned beside the oven.

(2) This little incident, characteristic of the extreme composure of the extraordinary mob, was witnessed by a lady, who disturbed, like others, from her slumbers, had gone to the window. It was told to the author by the lady's daughter.

HENRY HALLAM

1777–1859

The first passage is from the beginning of the concluding chapter of the View of the State of Europe during the Middle Ages, *"On the state of society." It is a good example of his Enlightenment attitude to medieval history. The second passage is from part 2 of the same chapter. The third passage is from chapter 9 of the* Constitutional History *and discusses the nature of the rival parties on the eve of the civil war; it may be compared with Hume's analysis beginning on page 142. I include one characteristic footnote.*

Not much has been written on Hallam. The useful article in the Dictionary of National Biography *is by Leslie Stephen; and see the article on Hallam by C. C. Weston in* Essays in Honour of R. L. Schuyler, *edited by Herman Ausubel (1951).*

I

IT HAS BEEN the object of every preceding chapter of this work, either to trace the civil revolutions of states during the period of the Middle Ages, or to investigate, with rather more minute attention, their political institutions. There remains a large tract to be explored, if we would complete the circle of historical information, and give to our knowledge that copiousness and clear perception, which arise from comprehending a subject under numerous relations. The philosophy of history embraces far more than the wars and treaties, the factions and cabals of common political narration; it extends to whatever illustrates the character of the human species in a particular period, to their

reasonings and sentiments, their arts and industry. Nor is this comprehensive survey merely interesting to the speculative philosopher; without it, the statesman would form very erroneous estimates of events, and find himself constantly misled in any analogical application of them to present circumstances. Nor is it an uncommon source of error to neglect the general signs of the times, and to deduce a prognostic from some partial coincidence with past events, where a more enlarged comparison of all the facts that ought to enter into the combination would destroy the whole parallel. The philosophical student, however, will not follow the antiquary into his minute details; and though it is hard to say what may not supply matter for a reflecting mind, there is always some danger of losing sight of grand objects in historical disquisition, by too laborious a research into trifles. I may possibly be thought to furnish, in some instances, an example of the error I condemn. But in the choice and disposition of topics to which the present chapter relates, some have been omitted on account of their comparative insignificance, and others on account of their want of connexion with the leading subject. Even of those treated I can only undertake to give a transient view; and must bespeak the reader's candour to remember, that passages which, separately taken, may often appear superficial, are but parts of the context of a single chapter, as the chapter itself is of an entire work.

The Middle Ages, according to the division I have adopted, comprize about one thousand years, from the invasion of France by Clovis to that of Naples by Charles VIII. This period, considered as to the state of society, has been esteemed dark through ignorance, and barbarous through poverty and want of refinement. And although this character is much less applicable to the two last centuries of the period, than to those which preceded its commencement, yet we cannot expect to feel in respect of ages at best imperfectly civilized and slowly progressive, that interest which attends a more perfect development of human capacities, and more brilliant advances in improvement. The first moiety indeed of these ten ages is almost absolutely barren, and presents little but a catalogue of evils. The subversion of the Roman empire, and devastation of its provinces by barbarous nations, either immediately preceded, or were coincident with the commencement of the middle period. We begin in darkness and calamity; and though the shadows grow fainter as we advance, yet we are to break off our pursuit as the morning breathes upon us, and the twilight reddens into the lustre of day.

II

I should leave this slight survey of œconomical history still more imperfect, were I to make no observation on the relative values of money. Without something like precision in our notions upon this subject, every statistical inquiry becomes a source of confusion and error. But considerable difficulties attend the discussion. These arise principally from two causes; the inaccuracy or partial representations of historical writers, on whom we are accustomed too implicitly to rely, and the change of manners, which renders a certain command over articles of purchase less adequate to our wants than it was in former ages . . .

It is by no means required that I should here offer a table of values, which, as to every country except England, I have no means of constructing, and which, even as to England, would be subject to many difficulties. But a reader, unaccustomed to these investigations, ought to have some assistance in comparing the prices of ancient times with those of his own. I will therefore, without attempting to ascend very high, for we have really no sufficient data as to the period immediately subsequent to the conquest, much less that which preceded, endeavour at a sort of approximation for the thirteenth and fifteenth centuries. In the reigns of Henry III and Edward I previously to the first debasement of the coin by the latter in 1301, the ordinary price of a quarter of wheat appears to have been about four shillings, and that of barley and oats in proportion. A sheep was rather sold high at a shilling, and an ox might be reckoned at ten or twelve. The value of cattle is of course dependent upon their breed and condition; and we have unluckily no early account of butcher's meat; but we can hardly take a less multiple than about thirty for animal food, and eighteen or twenty for corn, in order to bring the prices of the thirteenth century to a level with those of the present day. Combining the two, and setting the comparative dearness of cloth against the cheapness of fuel and many other articles, we may perhaps consider any given sum under Henry III and Edward I as equivalent in general command over commodities to about twenty-four or twenty-five times their nominal value at present. Under Henry VI, the coin had lost one-third of its weight in silver, which caused a proportional increase of money prices; but, so far as I can perceive, there had been no diminution in the value of that metal. We have not much information as to the fertility of the mines which supplied Europe during the Middle Ages; but it is probable

that the drain of silver towards the East, joined to the ostentatious splendour of courts, might fully absorb the usual produce. By the statutes of 15 H.VI.c.2. the price up to which wheat might be exported is fixed at 6s.8d., a point no doubt above the average; and the private documents of that period, which are sufficiently numerous, lead to a similar result. Sixteen will be a proper multiple, when we would bring the general value of money in this reign to our present standard.

But after ascertaining the proportional values of money at different periods by a comparison of the prices in several of the chief articles of expenditure, which is the only fair process, we shall sometimes be surprised at incidental facts of this class which seem irreducible to any rule. These difficulties arise not so much from the relative scarcity of particular commodities, which it is for the most part easy to explain, as from the change in manners and in the usual mode of living. We have reached in this age so high a pitch of luxury, that we can hardly believe or comprehend the frugality of ancient times; and have in general formed mistaken notions as to the habits of expenditure which then prevailed. Accustomed to judge of feudal and chivalrous ages by works of fiction, or by historians who embellish their writings with accounts of occasional festivals and tournaments, and sometimes inattentive enough to transfer the manners of the seventeenth to the fourteenth century, we are not at all aware of the usual simplicity with which the gentry lived under Edward I or even Henry VI. They drank little wine; they had no foreign luxuries; they rarely or never kept male servants, except for husbandry; their horses, as we may guess by the price, were indifferent; they seldom travelled beyond their county. And even their hospitality must have been greatly limited, if the value of manors were really no greater than we find it in many surveys. Twenty-four seems a sufficient multiple when we would raise a sum mentioned by a writer under Edward I to the same real value expressed in our present money, but an income of £10 or £20 was reckoned a competent estate for a gentleman; at least the lord of a single manor would seldom have enjoyed more. A knight who possessed £150 per annum passed for extremely rich. Yet this was not equal in command over commodities to £4000 at present. But this income was comparatively free from taxation, and its expenditure lightened by the services of his villeins. Such a person however must have been among the most opulent of country-gentlemen. Sir John Fortescue speaks of five pounds a year as 'a fair living for a yeoman',

a class of whom he is not at all inclined to diminish the importance. So, when Sir William Drury, one of the richest men in Suffolk, bequeaths in 1493 fifty marks to each of his daughters, we must not imagine that this was of greater value than four or five hundred pounds at this day, but remark the family pride, and want of ready money, which induced country gentlemen to leave their younger children in poverty. Or, if we read that the expense of a scholar at the university in 1514 was but five pounds annually, we should err in supposing that he had the liberal accommodation which the present age deems indispensable, but consider how much could be afforded for about sixty pounds, which will be not far from the proportion. And what would a modern lawyer say to the following entry in the churchwarden's accounts of St. Margaret, Westminster, for 1476: 'Also paid to Roger Fylpott, learned in the law, for his counsel giving, 3s.8d., *with fourpence for his dinner*.' Though fifteen times the fee might not seem altogether inadequate at present, five shillings would hardly furnish the table of a barrister, even if the fastidiousness of our manners would admit of his accepting such a dole. But this fastidiousness, which considers certain kinds of remuneration degrading to a man of liberal condition, did not prevail in those simple ages. It would seem rather strange that a young lady should learn needlework and good-breeding in a family of superior rank, paying for her board; yet such was the laudable custom of the fifteenth and even sixteenth centuries, as we perceive by the Paston Letters, and even later authorities.

There is one very unpleasing remark which every one who attends to the subject of prices will be induced to make, that the labouring classes, especially those engaged in agriculture, were better provided with the means of subsistence in the reign of Edward III or of Henry VI than they are at present. In the fourteenth century, Sir John Cullum observes, a harvest man had four-pence a day, which enabled him in a week to buy a comb of wheat; but to buy a comb of wheat, a man must now (1784) work ten or twelve days. So, under Henry VI, if meat was at a farthing and a half the pound, which I suppose was about the truth, a labourer earning three-pence a day, or eighteen pence in the week, could buy a bushel of wheat, at six shillings the quarter, and twenty-four pounds of meat for his family. A labourer at present, earning twelve shillings a week, can only buy half a bushel of wheat, at eighty shillings the quarter, and twelve pounds of meat at seven-pence. Several acts of parliament regulate the wages that

might be paid to labourers of different kinds. Thus the statute of labourers in 1350, fixed the wages of reapers during harvest at threepence a day without diet, equal to five shillings at present; that of 23 H.VI.c.12 in 1444, fixed the reapers' wages at five-pence, and those of common workmen in building at 3½d. equal to 6s.8d. and 4s.8d.; that of 11 H.VII.c.22 in 1496, leaves the wages of labourers in harvest as before, but rather increases those of ordinary workmen. The yearly wages of a chief hind or shepherd by the act of 1444 were £1.4s. equivalent to about £20, those of a common servant in husbandry, 18s.4d. with meat and drink; they were somewhat augmented by the statute of 1496. Yet, although these wages are regulated, as a maximum, by acts of parliament, which may naturally be supposed to have had a view rather towards diminishing than enhancing the current rate, I am not fully convinced that they were not rather beyond it; private accounts at least do not always correspond with these statutable prices. And it is necessary to remember, that the uncertainty of employment, natural to so imperfect a state of husbandry, must have diminished the labourer's means of subsistence. Extreme dearth, not more owing to adverse seasons than to improvident consumption, was frequently endured. But after every allowance of this kind, I should find it difficult to resist the conclusion, that however the labourer has derived benefit from the cheapness of manufactured commodities, and from many inventions of common utility, he is much inferior in ability to support a family to his ancestors three or four centuries ago. I know not why some have supposed that meat was a luxury seldom obtained by the labourer. Doubtless he could not have procured as much as he pleased. But, from the greater cheapness of cattle, as compared with corn, it seems to follow, that a more considerable portion of this ordinary diet consisted of animal food than at present. It was remarked by Sir John Fortescue, that the English lived far more upon an animal diet than their rivals the French; and it was natural to ascribe their superior strength and courage to this cause. I should feel much satisfaction in being convinced that no deterioration in the state of the labouring classes has really taken place; yet it cannot, I think, appear extraordinary to those who reflect, that the whole population of England, in the year 1377, did not much exceed 2,300,000 souls, about one-fifth of the results upon the last enumeration, an increase with which that of the fruits of the earth cannot be supposed to have kept an even pace.

III

In weighing the merits of this great contest, in judging whether a thoroughly upright and enlightened man would rather have listed under the royal or parliamentary standard, there are two political postulates, the concession of which we may require: one, that civil war is such a calamity as nothing but the most indispensable necessity can authorise any party to bring on; the other, that the mixed government of England by king, lords, and commons, was to be maintained in preference to any other form of polity. The first of these can hardly be disputed; and though the denial of the second would certainly involve no absurdity, yet it may justly be assumed where both parties avowed their adherence to it as a common principle. Such as prefer a despotic or a republican form of government will generally, without much further enquiry, have made their election between Charles the First and the parliament. We do not argue from the creed of the English constitution to those who have abandoned its communion.

There was so much in the conduct and circumstances of both parties in the year 1642, to excite disapprobation and distrust, that a wise and good man could hardly unite cordially with either of them. On the one hand, he would entertain little doubt of the king's desire to overthrow by force or stratagem whatever had been effected in parliament, and to establish a plenary despotism; his arbitrary temper, his known principles of government, the natural sense of wounded pride and honour, the instigations of a haughty woman, the solicitations of favourites, the promises of ambitious men, were all at work to render his new position as a constitutional sovereign, even if unaccompanied by fresh indignities and encroachments, too grievous and mortifying to be endured. He had already tampered in a conspiracy to over-awe, if not to disperse, the parliament; he had probably obtained large promises, though very little to be trusted, from several of the presbyterian leaders in Scotland during his residence there in the summer of 1641; he had attempted to recover his ascendancy by a sudden blow in the affair of the five members; he had sent the queen out of England, furnished with the crown-jewels, for no other probable end than to raise men and procure arms in foreign countries; he was now about to take the field with an army, composed in part of young gentlemen disdainful of a puritan faction that censured their licence, and of those soldiers of fortune, reckless of public principle, and averse to civil

control, whom the war in Germany had trained, and partly of the catholics, a wealthy and active body devoted to the crown, from which alone they had experienced justice or humanity, and from whose favour and gratitude they now expected the most splendid returns. Upon neither of these parties could a lover of his country and her liberties look without alarm; and though he might derive more hope from those better spirits, who had withstood the prerogative in its exorbitance, as they now sustained it in its decline, yet it could not be easy to foretell that they would preserve sufficient influence to keep steady the balance of power, in the contingency of any decisive success of the royal arms.

But, on the other hand, the house of commons presented still less favourable prospects. We should not indeed judge over severely some acts of a virtuous indignation in the first moments of victory, or those heats of debate, without some excesses of which a popular assembly is in danger of falling into the opposite extreme of phlegmatic security. But, after every allowance has been made, he must bring very heated passions to the records of those times, who does not perceive in the conduct of that body a series of glaring violations, not only of positive and constitutional, but of those higher principles which are paramount to all immediate policy. Witness the ordinance for disarming recusants passed by both houses in August 1641, and that in November, authorising the earl of Leicester to raise men for the defence of Ireland without warrant under the great seal; both manifest encroachments on the executive power; and the enormous extension of privilege, under which every person accused on the slightest testimony of disparaging their proceedings, or even of introducing new-fangled ceremonies in the church, a matter wholly out of their cognizance, was dragged before them as a delinquent, and lodged in their prison. Witness the outrageous attempts to intimidate the minority of their own body in the commitment of Mr. Palmer, and afterwards of sir Ralph Hopton, to the Tower, for such language used in debate as would not have excited any observation in ordinary times:—their continual encroachments on the rights and privileges of the lords, as in their intimation that, if bills thought by them necessary for the public good should fall in the upper house, they must join with the minority of the lords in representing the same to the king; or in the impeachment of the duke of Richmond for words, and those of the most trifling nature, spoken in the upper house;—their despotic violation of the rights of the people, in imprisoning those who presented or prepared respectful

petitions in behalf of the established constitution, while they encouraged those of a tumultuous multitude at their bar in favour of innovation; (1)—their usurpation at once of the judicial and legislative powers in all that related to the church, particularly by their committee for scandalous ministers, under which denomination, adding reproach to injury, they subjected all who did not reach the standard of puritan perfection to contumely and vexation, and ultimately to expulsion from their lawful property. Witness the impeachment of the twelve bishops for treason, on account of their protestation against all that should be done in the house of lords during their compelled absence through fear of the populace; a protest not perhaps entirely well expressed, but abundantly justifiable in its argument by the plainest principles of law. These great abuses of power, becoming daily more frequent, as they became less excusable, would make a sober man hesitate to support them in a civil war, wherein their success must not only consummate the destruction of the crown, the church, and the peerage, but expose all who had dissented from their proceedings, as it ultimately happened, to an oppression less severe perhaps, but far more sweeping, than that which had rendered the star-chamber odious.

But it may reasonably also be doubted whether, in staking their own cause on the perilous contingencies of war, the house of commons did not expose the liberties for which they professedly were contending, to a far greater risk than they could have incurred even from peace with an insidious court. For let any one ask himself what would have been the condition of the parliament, if by the extension of that panic which in fact seized upon several regiments, or by any of those countless accidents which determine the fate of battles, the king had wholly defeated their army at Edgehill? Is it not probable, nay, in such supposition, almost demonstrable, that in those first days of the civil war, before the parliament had time to discover the extent of its own resources, he would have found no obstacle to his triumphal entry into London? And, in such circumstances, amidst the defection of the timid and lukewarm, the consternation of the brawling multitude, and the exultation of his victorious troops, would the triennial act itself, or those other statutes which he had very reluctantly conceded, have stood secure? Or, if we believe that the constitutional supporters of his throne, the Hertfords, the Falklands, the Southamptons, the Spencers, would still have had sufficient influence to shield from violent hands that palladium which they had assisted to place in the building, can there be a stronger argument against the necessity of taking up

arms for the defence of liberties, which, even in the contingency of defeat, could not have been subverted?

There were many indeed at that time, as there have been ever since, who, admitting all the calamities incident to civil war, of which this country reaped the bitter fruits for twenty years, denied entirely that the parliament went beyond the necessary precautions for self-defence, and laid the whole guilt of the aggression at the king's door. He had given, it was said, so many proofs of a determination to have recourse to arms, he had displayed so insidious an hostility to the privileges of parliament, that, if he should be quietly allowed to choose and train soldiers, under the name of a militia, through hired servants of his own nomination, the people might find themselves either robbed of their liberties by surprise, or compelled to struggle for them in very unfavourable circumstances. The commons, with more loyal respect perhaps than policy, had opposed no obstacle to his deliberate journey towards the north, which they could have easily prevented, though well aware that he had no other aim but to collect an army; was it more than ordinary prudence to secure the fortified town of Hull with its magazine of arms from his grasp, and to muster the militia in each county under the command of lieutenants in whom they could confide, and to whom, from their rank and personal character, he could frame no just objection?

These considerations are doubtless not without weight, and should restrain such as may not think them sufficient from too strongly censuring those, who, deeming that either civil liberty or the ancient constitution must be sacrificed, persisted in depriving Charles the First of every power, which, though pertaining to a king of England, he could not be trusted to exercise. We are, in truth, after a lapse of ages, often able to form a better judgment of the course that ought to have been pursued in political emergencies than those who stood nearest to the scene. Not only have we our knowledge of the event to guide and correct our imaginary determinations; but we are free from those fallacious rumours, those pretended secrets, those imperfect and illusive views, those personal prepossessions, which in every age warp the political conduct of the most well-meaning. The characters of individuals, so frequently misrepresented by flattery or party rage, stand out to us revealed by the tenor of their entire lives, or by the comparison of historical anecdotes, and that more authentic information which is reserved for posterity. Looking as it were from an eminence, we can take a more comprehensive range, and class better

the objects before us in their due proportions and in their bearings on one another. It is not easy for us even now to decide, keeping in view the maintenance of the entire constitution, from which party in the civil war greater mischief was to be apprehended; but the election was, I am persuaded, still more difficult to be made by contemporaries. No one, at least, who has given any time to the study of that history, will deny that among those who fought in opposite battalions at Edge-hill and Newbury, or voted in the opposite parliaments of Westminster and Oxford, there were many who thought much alike on general theories of prerogative and privilege, divided only perhaps by some casual prejudice, which had led these to look with greater distrust on courtly insidiousnes, and those with greater indignation at popular violence. We cannot believe that Falkland and Colepepper differed greatly in their constitutional principles from Whitelock and Pierpoint, or that Hertford and Southampton were less friends to a limited monarchy than Essex and Northumberland.

There is, however, another argument sometimes alledged of late, in justification of the continued attacks on the king's authority; which is the most specious, as it seems to appeal to what are now denominated the Whig principles of the constitution. It has been said that, sensible of the maladministration the nation had endured for so many years (which, if the king himself were to be deemed by constitutional fiction ignorant of it, must at least be imputed to evil advisers), the house of commons sought only that security which, as long as a sound spirit continues to actuate its members, it must ever require—the appointment of ministers in whose fidelity to the public liberties it could better confide; that by carrying frankly into effect those counsels which he had unwisely abandoned upon the earl of Bedford's death, and bestowing the responsible offices of the state on men approved for patriotism, he would both have disarmed the jealousy of his subjects and ensured his own prerogative, which no ministers are prone to impair.

Those who are struck by these considerations may not, perhaps, have sufficiently reflected on the changes which the king had actually made in his administration since the beginning of the parliament. Besides those already mentioned, Essex, Holland, Say, and St. John, he had, in the autumn of 1641, conferred the post of secretary of state on lord Falkland, and that of master of the rolls on sir John Colepepper; both very prominent in the redress of grievances and punishment of delinquent ministers during the first part of the session, and whose attach-

ment to the cause of constitutional liberty there was no sort of reason to distrust. They were indeed in some points of a different way of thinking from Pym and Hampden, and had doubtless been chosen by the king on that account. But it seems rather beyond the legitimate bounds of parliamentary opposition to involve the kingdom in civil war, simply because the choice of the crown has not fallen on its leaders. The real misfortune was, that Charles did not rest in the advice of his own responsible ministers, against none of whom the house of commons had any just cause of exception. The theory of our constitution in this respect was very ill-established; and, had it been more so, there are perhaps few sovereigns, especially in circumstances of so much novelty, who would altogether conform to it. But no appointment that he could have made from the patriotic bands of parliament would have furnished a security against the intrigues of his bed-chamber or the influence of the queen.

The real problem that we have to resolve, as to the political justice of the civil war, is not the character, the past actions, or even the existing designs, of Charles; not even whether he had justly forfeited his crown as his son was deemed to have done for less violence and less insincerity; not even, I will add, whether the liberties of his subjects could have been absolutely secure under his government; but whether the risk attending his continuance upon the throne with the limited prerogatives of an English sovereign were great enough to counterbalance the miseries of protracted civil war, the perils of defeat, and the no less perils, as experience showed, of victory. Those who adopt the words spoken by one of our greatest orators, and quoted by another, "There was ambition, there was sedition, there was violence; but no man shall persuade me that it was not the cause of liberty on one side, and of tyranny on the other," have for themselves decided this question. But, as I know (and the history of eighteen years is my witness) how little there was on one side of such liberty as a wise man would hold dear, so I am not yet convinced that the great body of the royalists, the peers and gentry of England, were combating for the sake of tyranny. I cannot believe them to have so soon forgotten their almost unanimous discontent at the king's arbitrary government in 1640, or their general concurrence in the first salutary measures of the parliament. I cannot think that the temperate and constitutional language of the royal declarations and answers to the house of commons in 1642, known to have proceeded from the pen of Hyde, and as superior to those on the opposite side in argument as

they were in eloquence, was intended for the willing slaves of tyranny. I cannot discover in the extreme reluctance of the royalists to take up arms, and their constant eagerness for an accommodation, (I speak not of mere soldiers, but of the greater and more important portion of that party), that zeal for the king's re-establishment in all his abused prerogatives which some connect with the very names of a royalist or a cavalier.

It is well observed by Burnet, in answer to the vulgar notion that Charles I was undone by his concessions, that, but for his concessions, he would have had no party at all. This is, in fact, the secret of what seems to astonish the parliamentary historian, May, of the powerful force that the king was enabled to raise, and the protracted resistance he opposed. He had succeeded, according to the judgment of many real friends of the constitution, in putting the house of commons in the wrong. Law, justice, moderation, once ranged against him, had gone over to his banner. His arms might reasonably be called defensive, if he had no other means of preserving himself from the condition, far worse than captivity, of a sovereign compelled to a sort of suicide upon his own honour and authority. For, however it may be alleged that a king is bound in conscience to sacrifice his power to the public will, yet it could hardly be inexcusable not to have practised this disinterested morality; especially while the voice of his people was by no means unequivocal, and while the major part of one house of parliament adhered openly to his cause.

It is indeed a question perfectly distinguishable from that of the abstract justice of the king's cause, whether he did not too readily abandon his post as a constitutional head of the parliament; whether, with the greater part of the peers, and a very considerable minority in the commons, resisting in their places at Westminster all violent encroachments on his rights, he ought not rather to have sometimes persisted in a temperate though firm assertion of them, sometimes had recourse to compromise and gracious concession, instead of calling away so many of his adherents to join his arms as left neither numbers nor credit with those who remained. There is a remarkable passage in lord Clarendon's life, not to quote Whitelock and other writers less favourable to Charles, where he intimates his own opinion that the king would have had a fair hope of withstanding the more violent faction, if, after the queen's embarkation for Holland in February 1642, he had returned to Whitehall; admitting, at the same time, the hazards and inconveniences to which this course was liable. That he

resolved on trying the fortune of arms, his noble historian insinuates to have been the effect of the queen's influence, with whom, before her departure, he had concerted his future proceedings. Yet, notwithstanding the deference owing to contemporary opinions, I cannot but suspect that Clarendon has, in this instance as in some other passages, attached too great an importance to particular individuals, measuring them rather by their rank in the state, than by that capacity and energy of mind, which, in the levelling hour of revolution, are the only real pledges of political influence. He thought it of the utmost consequence to the king that he should gain over the earls of Essex and Northumberland, both, or at least the former, wavering between the two parties, though voting entirely with the commons. Certainly the king's situation required every aid, and his repulsive hardness towards all who had ever given him offence displayed an obstinate unconciliating character, which deprived him of some support he might have received. But the subsequent history of these two celebrated earls, and indeed of all the moderate adherents to the parliament, will hardly lead us to believe that they could have afforded the king any protection. Let us suppose that he had returned to Whitehall, instead of proceeding towards the north. It is evident that he must either have passed the bill for the militia, or seen the ordinances of both houses carried into effect without his consent. He must have consented to the abolition of episcopacy, or at least have come into some compromise which would have left the bishops hardly a shadow of their jurisdiction and pre-eminence. He must have driven from his person those whom he best loved and trusted. He would have found it impossible to see again the queen, without awakening distrust and bringing insult on them both. The royalist minority of parliament, however considereable in numbers, was lukewarm and faint-hearted. That they should have gained strength so as to keep a permanent superiority over their adversaries, led as they were by statesmen so bold and profound as Hampden, Pym, St. John, Cromwell, and Vane, is what, from the experience of the last twelve months, it was unreasonable to anticipate. But, even if the commons had been more favourably inclined, it would not have been in their power to calm the mighty waters that had been moved from their depths. They had permitted the populace to mingle in their discussions, testifying pleasure at its paltry applause, and encouraging its tumultuous aggressions on the minority of the legislature. What else could they expect than that, so soon as they ceased to satisfy the city apprentices, or the trained bands raised under

their militia bill, they must submit to that physical strength which is the ultimate arbiter of political contentions?

Thus, with evil auspices, with much peril of despotism on the one hand, with more of anarchy on the other, amidst the apprehensions and sorrows of good men, the civil war commenced in the summer of 1642. I might now perhaps pass over the period that intervened, until the restoration of Charles II, as not strictly belonging to a work which undertakes to relate the progress of the English constitution. But this would have left a sort of chasm that might disappoint the reader; and as I have already not wholly excluded our more general political history, without a knowledge of which the laws and government of any people must be unintelligible, it will probably not be deemed an unnecessary digression, if I devote one chapter to the most interesting and remarkable portion of British history.

NOTE

(1) Clarendon, 322. Among other petitions presented at this time, the noble author inserts one from the porters of London. Mr. Brodie asserts of this, that "it is nowhere to be found or alluded to, so far as I recollect, except in Clarendon's History; and I have no hesitation in pronouncing it a forgery by that author, to disgrace the petitions which so galled him and his party. The journals of the commons give an account of every petition; and I have gone over them *with the utmost care*, in order to ascertain whether such a petition ever was presented, and yet cannot discover a trace of it." (iii. 306) This writer is much too precipitate and passionate. No sensible man will believe Clarendon to have committed so foolish and useless a forgery; and as to Mr. B.'s diligent perusal of the journals, this petition is fully noticed, though not inserted at length, on the 3d of February.

THOMAS CARLYLE

1795–1881

This description of the storming of the Bastille is from chapters 6 and 7 of The French Revolution, *part 1, book 5. The few factual errors in Carlyle's account are pointed out in the footnotes to C. R. L. Fletcher's edition (1902). It is interesting to read George Rudé's* The Crowd in the French Revolution *(1959) in connection with this passage.*

The most useful discussions of Carlyle as a historian are: L. M. Young, Thomas Carlyle and the Art of History *(1939); H. Ben-Israel, "Carlyle and the French Revolution," in* The Historical Journal, *1958; E. Neff,* The Poetry of History *(1947).*

ALL MORNING, since nine, there has been a cry every where: To the Bastille! Repeated 'deputations of citizens' have been here, passionate for arms; whom De Launay has got dismissed by soft speeches through portholes. Towards noon, Elector Thuriot de la Rosière gains admittance; finds De Launay indisposed for surrender; nay disposed for blowing up the place rather. Thuriot mounts with him to the battlements: heaps of paving-stones, old iron and missiles lie piled; cannon all duly levelled; in every embrasure a cannon,—only drawn back a little! But outwards, behold, O Thuriot, how the multitude flows on, welling through every street: tocsin furiously pealing, all drums beating the *générale:* the Suburb Saint-Antoine rolling hitherward wholly, as one man! Such vision (spectral yet real) thou, O Thuriot, as from thy Mount of Vision, beholdest in this moment: prophetic of what

other Phantasmagories, and loud-gibbering Spectral Realities, which thou yet beholdest not, but shalt! "*Que voulez-vous?*" said De Launay, turning pale at the sight, with an air of reproach, almost of menace. "Monsieur," said Thuriot, rising into the moral-sublime, "what mean *you?* Consider if I could not precipitate *both* of us from this height,"—say only a hundred feet, exclusive of the walled ditch! Whereupon De Launay fell silent. Thuriot shows himself from some pinnacle, to comfort the multitude becoming suspicious, fremescent: then descends; departs with protest; with warning addressed also to the Invalides,—on whom, however, it produces but a mixed indistinct impression. The old heads are none of the clearest; besides, it is said, De Launay has been profuse of beverages *(prodigua des buissons).* They think, they will not fire,—if not fired on, if they can help it; but must, on the whole, be ruled considerably by circumstances.

Wo to thee, De Launay, in such an hour, if thou canst not, taking some one firm decision, *rule* circumstances! Soft speeches will not serve; hard grapeshot is questionable; but hovering between the two is *un*questionable. Ever wilder swells the tide of men; their infinite hum waxing ever louder, into imprecations, perhaps into crackle of stray musketry,—which latter, on walls nine feet thick, cannot do execution. The Outer Drawbridge has been lowered for Thuriot; new *deputation of citizens* (it is the third, and noisiest of all) penetrates that way into the Outer Court: soft speeches producing no clearance of these, De Launay gives fire; pulls up his Drawbridge. A slight sputter;—which has *kindled* the too combustible chaos; made it a roaring fire-chaos! Bursts forth Insurrection, at sight of its own blood (for there were deaths by that sputter of fire), into endless rolling explosion of musketry, distraction, execration;—and over head, from the Fortress, let one great gun, with its grapeshot, go booming, to show what we *could* do. The Bastille is besieged!

On, then, all Frenchmen, that have hearts in your bodies! Roar with all your throats, of cartilage and metal, ye Sons of Liberty; stir spasmodically whatsoever of utmost faculty is in you, soul, body, or spirit; for it is the hour! Smite, thou Louis Tournay, cartwright of the Marais, old-soldier of the Regiment Dauphiné; smite at that Outer Drawbridge chain, though the fiery hail whistles round thee! Never, over nave or felloe, did thy axe strike such a stroke. Down with it, man; down with it to Orcus: let the whole accursed Edifice sink thither, and Tyranny be swallowed up forever! Mounted, some say, on the roof of the guardroom, some 'on bayonets stuck into joints of

the wall,' Louis Tournay smites, brave Aubin Bonnemère (also an old soldier) seconding him: the chain yields, breaks; the huge Drawbridge slams down, thundering (*avec fracas*). Glorious: and yet, alas, it is still but the outworks. The Eight grim Towers, with their Invalide musketry, their paving-stones and cannon-mouths, still soar aloft intact;—Ditch yawning impassable, stone-faced; the inner Drawbridge with its *back* towards us: the Bastille is still to take!

To describe this Siege of the Bastille (thought to be one of the most important in History) perhaps transcends the talent of mortals. Could one but, after infinite reading, get to understand so much as the plan of the building! But there is open Esplanade, at the end of the Rue Saint-Antoine; there are such Forecourts, *Cour Avancé, Cour de l'Orme,* arched Gateway (where Louis Tournay now fights); then new drawbridges, dormant bridges, rampart-bastions, and the grim Eight Towers: a labyrinthic Mass, high-frowning there, of all ages from twenty years to four hundred and twenty;—beleaguered, in this its last hour, as we said, by mere Chaos come again! Ordnance of all calibres; throats of all capacities; men of all plans, every man his own engineer: seldom since the war of Pygmies and Cranes was there seen so anomalous a thing. Half-pay Élie is home for a suit of regimentals; no one would heed him in coloured clothes: half-pay Hulin is haranguing Gardes Françaises in the Place de Grève. Frantic Patriots pick up the grapeshots; bear them, still hot (or seemingly so), to the Hôtel-de-Ville:—Paris, you perceive, is to be burnt! Flesselles is 'pale to the very lips,' for the roar of the multitude grows deep. Paris wholly has got to the acme of its frenzy; whirled, all ways, by panic madness. At every street-barricade, there whirls simmering a minor whirlpool,—strengthening the barricade, since God knows what is coming; and all minor whirlpools play distractedly into that grand Fire-Mahlstrom which is lashing round the Bastille.

And so it lashes and it roars. Cholat the wine-merchant has become an impromptu cannoneer. See Georget, of the Marine Service, fresh from Brest, ply the King of Siam's cannon. Singular (if we were not used to the like): Georget lay, last night, taking his ease at his inn; the King of Siam's cannon also lay, knowing nothing of *him,* for a hundred years. Yet now, at the right instant, they have got together, and discourse eloquent music. For, hearing what was toward, Georget sprang from the Brest Diligence, and ran. Gardes Françaises also will be here, with real artillery: were not the walls so thick!—Upwards from the Esplanade, horizontally from all neighbouring roofs and

windows, flashes one irregular deluge of musketry, without effect. The Invalides lie flat, firing comparatively at their ease from behind stone; hardly through portholes, show the tip of a nose. We fall, shot; and make no impression!

Let conflagration rage; of whatsoever is combustible! Guardrooms are burnt, Invalides mess-rooms. A distracted 'Peruke-maker with two fiery torches' is for burning 'the saltpetres of the Arsenal;'—had not a woman run screaming; had not a Patriot, with some tincture of Natural Philosophy, instantly struck the wind out of him (butt of musket on pit of stomach), over-turned barrels, and stayed the devouring element. A young beautiful lady, seized escaping in these Outer Courts, and thought falsely to be De Launay's daughter, shall be burnt in De Launay's sight; she lies swooned on a paillasse: but again a Patriot, it is brave Aubin Bonnemère the old soldier, dashes in, and rescues her. Straw is burnt; three cartloads of it, hauled thither, go up in white smoke: almost to the choking of Patriotism itself; so that Élie had, with singed brows, to drag back one cart; and Réole the 'gigantic haberdasher' another. Smoke as of Tophet; confusion as of Babel; noise as of the Crack of Doom!

Blood flows; the aliment of new madness. The wounded are carried into houses of the Rue Cerisaie; the dying leave their last mandate not to yield till the accursed Stronghold fall. And yet, alas, how fall? The walls are so thick! Deputations, three in number, arrive from the Hôtel-de-Ville; Abbé Fauchet (who was of one) can say with what almost superhuman courage of benevolence. These wave their Town-flag in the arched Gateway; and stand, rolling their drum; but to no purpose. In such Crack of Doom, De Launay cannot hear them, dare not believe them: they return, with justified rage, the whew of lead still singing in their ears. What to do? The Firemen are here, squirting with their fire-pumps on the Invalides cannon, to wet the touch-holes; they unfortunately cannot squirt so high; but produce only clouds of spray. Individuals of classical knowledge propose *catapults*. Santerre, the sonorous Brewer of the Suburb Saint-Antoine, advises rather that the place be fired, by a 'mixture of phosphorus and oil-of-turpentine spouted up through forcing pumps:' O Spinola-Santerre, hast thou the mixture *ready?* Every man his own engineer! And still the fire-deluge abates not: even women are firing, and Turks; at least one woman (with her sweetheart), and one Turk. Gardes Françaises have come: real cannon, real cannoneers. Usher Maillard is busy; half-pay Élie, half-pay Hulin rage in the midst of thousands.

How the great Bastille Clock ticks (inaudible) in its Inner Court there, at its ease, hour after hour; as if nothing special, for it or the world, were passing! It tolled One when the firing began; and is now pointing towards Five, and still the firing slakes not.—Far down, in their vaults, the seven Prisoners hear muffled din as of earthquakes; their Turnkeys answer vaguely.

Wo to thee, De Launay, with thy poor hundred Invalides! Broglie is distant, and his ears heavy: Besenval hears, but can send no help. One poor troop of Hussars has crept, reconnoitering cautiously along the Quais, as far as the Pont Neuf. "We are come to join you," said the Captain; for the crowd seems shoreless. A large-headed dwarfish individual, of smoke-bleared aspect, shambles forward, opening his blue lips, for there is sense in him; and croaks: "Alight then, and give up your arms!" The Hussar-Captain is too happy to be escorted to the Barriers, and dismissed on parole. Who the squat individual was? Men answer, It is M. Marat, author of the excellent pacific *Avis au Peuple!* Great truly, O thou remarkable Dogleech, is this thy day of emergence and new-birth: and yet this same day come four years—! —But let the curtains of the Future hang.

What shall De Launay do? One thing only De Launay could have done: what he said he would do. Fancy him sitting, from the first, with lighted taper, within arm's length of the Powder-Magazine; motionless, like old Roman Senator, or Bronze Lampholder; coldly apprising Thuriot, and all men, by a slight motion of his eye, what his resolution was:—Harmless he sat there, while unharmed; but the King's Fortress, meanwhile, could, might, would, or should, in nowise be surrendered, save to the King's Messenger: one old man's life is worthless, so it be lost with honour; but think, ye brawling *canaille,* how will it be when a whole Bastille springs skyward!—In such statuesque, taper-holding attitude, one fancies De Launay might have left Thuriot, the red Clerks of the Basoche, Curé of Saint-Stephen and all the tag-rag-and-bobtail of the world, to work their will.

And yet, withal, he could not do it. Hast thou considered how each man's heart is so tremulously responsive to the hearts of all men; has thou noted how omnipotent is the very sound of many men? How their shriek of indignation palsies the strong soul; their howl of contumely withers with the unfelt pangs? The Ritter Gluck confessed that the ground-tone of the noblest passage, in one of his noblest Operas, was the voice of the Populace he had heard at Vienna, crying to their

Kaiser: Bread! Bread! Great is the combined voice of men; the utterance of their *instincts,* which are truer than their *thoughts:* it is the greatest man encounters, among the sounds and shadows which make up this World of Time. He who can resist that, has his footing somewhere *beyond* Time. De Launay could not do it. Distracted, he hovers between two; hopes in the middle of despair; surrenders not his Fortress; declares that he will blow it up, seizes torches to blow it up, and does not blow it. Unhappy old De Launay, it is the death-agony of thy Bastille and thee! Jail, Jailoring and Jailor, all three, such as they may have been, must finish.

For four hours now has the World-Bedlam roared; call it the World-Chimaera, blowing fire! The poor Invalides have sunk under their battlements, or rise only with reversed muskets: they have made a white flag of napkins; go beating the *chamade,* or seeming to beat, for one can hear nothing. The very Swiss at the Portcullis look weary of firing; disheartened in the fire-deluge: a porthole at the drawbridge is opened, as by one that would speak. See Huissier Maillard, the shifty man! On his plank, swinging over the abyss of that stone Ditch; plank resting on parapet, balanced by weight of Patriots,—he hovers perilous: such a Dove towards such an Ark! Deftly, thou shifty Usher: one man already fell; and lies smashed, far down there, against the masonry! Usher Maillard falls not: deftly, unerring he walks, with outspread palm. The Swiss holds a paper through his porthole; the shifty Usher snatches it, and returns. Terms of surrender: Pardon, immunity to all! Are they accepted?—"*Foi d'officier,* On the word of an officer," answers half-pay Hulin,—or half-pay Élie, for men do not agree on it, "they are!" Sinks the drawbridge,—Usher Maillard bolting it when down; rushes-in the living deluge: the Bastille is fallen! *Victoire! La Bastille est prise!*

Why dwell on what follows? Hulin's *foi d'officier* should have been kept, but could not. The Swiss stand drawn up, disguised in white canvass smocks; the Invalides without disguise; their arms all piled against the wall. The first rush of victors, in ecstasy that the death-peril is passed, 'leaps joyfully on their necks;' but new victors rush, and ever new, also in ecstasy not wholly of joy. As we said, it was a living deluge, plunging headlong: had not the Gardes Françaises, in their cool military way, 'wheeled round with arms levelled,' it would have plunged suicidally, by the hundred or the thousand, into the Bastille-ditch.

And so it goes plunging through court and corridor; billowing un-

controllable, firing from windows—on itself; in hot frenzy of triumph, of grief and vengeance for its slain. The poor Invalides will fare ill; one Swiss, running off in his white smock, is driven back, with a death-thrust. Let all Prisoners be marched to the Townhall, to be judged!—Alas, already one poor Invalide has his right hand slashed off him; his maimed body dragged to the Place de Grève, and hanged there. The same right hand, it is said, turned back De Launay from the Powder-Magazine, and saved Paris.

De Launay, 'discovered in grey frock with poppy-coloured riband,' is for killing himself with the sword of his cane. He shall to the Hôtel-de-Ville; Hulin, Maillard and others escorting him; Élie marching foremost 'with the capitulation paper on his sword's point.' Through roarings and cursings; through hustlings, clutchings, and at last through strokes! Your escort is hustled aside, felled down; Hulin sinks exhausted on a heap of stones. Miserable De Launay! He shall never enter the Hôtel-de-Ville: only his 'bloody hair-queue, held up in a bloody hand;' that shall enter, for a sign. The bleeding trunk lies on the steps there; the head is off through the streets; ghastly, aloft on a pike.

Rigorous De Launay has died; crying out, "O friends, kill me fast!" Merciful De Losme must die; though Gratitude embraces him, in this fearful hour, and will die for him; it avails not Brothers, your wrath is cruel! Your Place de Grève is become a Throat of the Tiger; full of mere fierce bellowings, and thirst of blood. One other officer is massacred; one other Invalide is hanged on the Lamp-iron; with difficulty, with generous perseverance, the Gardes Françaises will save the rest. Provost Flesselles, stricken long since with the paleness of death, must descend from his seat, 'to be judged at the Palais Royal:'—alas, to be shot dead, by an unknown hand, at the turning of the first street!—

O evening sun of July, how, at this hour, thy beams fall slant on reapers amid peaceful woody fields; on old women spinning in cottages; on ships far out in the silent main; on Balls at the Orangerie of Versailles, where high-rouged Dames of the Palace are even now dancing with double-jacketed Hussar Officers,—and also on this roaring Hell-porch of a Hôtel-de-Ville! Babel Tower, with the confusion of tongues, were not Bedlam added with the conflagration of thoughts, was no type of it. One forest of distracted steel bristles, endless, in front of an Electoral Committee; points itself, in horrid radii, against

this and the other accused breast. It was the Titans warring with Olympus; and they, scarcely crediting it, have *conquered:* prodigy of prodigies; delirious,—as it could not but be. Denunciation, vengeance; blaze of triumph on a dark ground of terror; all outward, all inward things fallen into one general wreck of madness!

Electoral Committee? Had it a thousand throats of brass, it would not suffice. Abbé Lefèvre, in the Vaults down below, is black as Vulcan, distributing that 'five thousand-weight of Powder;' with what perils, these eight-and-forty hours! Last night, a Patriot, in liquor, insisted on sitting to smoke on the edge of one of the Powder-barrels: there smoked he, independent of the world,—till the Abbé 'purchased his pipe for three francs,' and pitched it far.

Élie, in the grand Hall, Electoral Committee looking on, sits 'with drawn sword bent in three places;' with battered helm, for he was of the Queen's Regiment, Cavalry: with torn regimentals, face singed and soiled; comparable, some think, to 'an antique warrior;'—judging the people; forming a list of Bastille Heroes. O Friends, stain not with blood the greenest laurels ever gained in this world: such is the burden of Élie's song: could it but be listened to. Courage, Élie! Courage, ye Municipal Electors! A declining sun; the need of victuals, and of telling news, will bring assuagement, dispersion: all earthly things must end.

Along the streets of Paris circulate Seven Bastille Prisoners, borne shoulder-high; seven Heads on pikes; the Keys of the Bastille; and much else. See also the Gardes Françaises, in their stedfast military way, marching home to their barracks, with the Invalides and Swiss kindly enclosed in hollow square. It is one year and two months since these same men stood unparticipating, with Brennus d'Agoust at the Palais de Justice, when Fate overtook D'Eprémémil; and now they have participated; and will participate. Not Gardes Françaises henceforth, but *Centre Grenadiers of the National Guard:* men of iron discipline and humour—not without a kind of thought in them!

Likewise ashlar stones of the Bastille continue thundering through the dusk; its paper archives shall fly white. Old secrets come to view; and long-buried Despair finds voice. Read this portion of an old Letter: 'If for my consolation Monseigneur would grant me, for the sake of God and the Most Blessed Trinity, that I could have news of my dear wife; were it only her name on a card, to show that she is alive! It were the greatest consolation I could receive; and I should forever

bless the greatness of Monseigneur.' Poor Prisoner, who namest thyself Quéret-Démery, and hast no other history,—she is *dead,* that dear wife of thine, and thou art dead! 'Tis fifty years since thy breaking heart put this question; to be heard now first, and long heard, in the hearts of men.

But so does the July twilight thicken; so must Paris, as sick children, and all distracted creatures do, brawl itself finally into a kind of sleep. Municipal Electors, astonished to find their heads still uppermost, are home: only Moreau de Saint-Méry of tropical birth and heart, of coolest judgment; he, with two others, shall sit permanent at the Town-hall. Paris sleeps; gleams upward the illuminated City: patrols go clashing, without common watchword; there go rumours; alarms of war, to the extent of 'fifteen thousand men marching through the Suburb Saint-Antoine,'—who never got it marched through. Of the day's distraction judge by this of the night: Moreau de Saint-Méry, 'before rising from his seat, gave upwards of three thousand orders.' What a head; comparable to Friar Bacon's Brass Head! Within it lies all Paris. Prompt must the answer be, right or wrong; in Paris is no other Authority extant. Seriously, a most cool clear head;—for which also thou, O brave Saint-Méry, in many capacities, from august Senator to Merchant's-Clerk, Book-dealer, Vice-King; in many places, from Virginia to Sardinia, shalt, ever as a brave man, find employment.

Besenval has decamped, under cloud of dusk, 'amid a great affluence of people,' who did not harm him; he marches, with faint-growing tread, down the left bank of the Seine, all night,—towards infinite space. Re-summoned shall Besenval himself be; for trial, for difficult acquittal. His King's-troops, his Royal-Allemand, are gone hence forever.

The Versailles Ball and lemonade is done; the Orangerie is silent except for nightbirds. Over in the Salle des Menus, Vice-president Lafayette, with unsnuffed lights, 'with some Hundred or so of Members, stretched on tables round him,' sits erect; out-watching the Bear. This day, a second solemn Deputation went to his Majesty; a second and then a third: with no effect. What will the end of these things be?

In the Court, all is mystery, not without whisperings of terror; though ye dream of lemonade and epaulettes, ye foolish women! His Majesty, kept in happy ignorance, perhaps dreams of double-barrels

and the Woods of Meudon. Late at night, the Duke de Liancourt, having official right of entrance, gains access to the Royal Apartments; unfolds, with earnest clearness, in his constitutional way, the Job's-news. *"Mais,"* said poor Louis, *"c'est une révolte,* Why, that is a revolt!"—"Sire," answered Laincourt, "it is not a revolt,—it is a revolution."

THOMAS BABINGTON MACAULAY

1800–1859

With Macaulay's third chapter (1848), from which this passage is taken, social history came of age, and the beginnings made by Hume, Robertson, and Hallam were suddenly developed to something not very different from the sort of panoramic survey of a nation's life with which we are familiar from G. M. Trevelyan's England in the Age of Queen Anne *(1930), and Miss C. V. Wedgewood's* The King's Peace *(1955). Macaulay devoted especial pains to the collection of material for this last chapter and to its arrangement. There are similar descriptions of Ireland in chapter 12, and of Scotland in chapter 13.*

An essential work is Sir Charles Firth's A Commentary on Macaulay's History of England *(1938), and the magnificent* Life of Macaulay *by his nephew, G. O. Trevelyan (1876). See also: W. C. Abbott,* Adventures in Reputation *(1935); R. L. Schuyler, "Macaulay and His History: One Hundred Years After," in* Political Science Quarterly, *1948; Andrew Browning, "Lord Macaulay," in* The Historical Journal, *1959.*

THE POSITION of London, relatively to the other towns of the empire, was, in the time of Charles the Second, far higher than at present. For at present the population of London is little more than six times the population of Manchester or of Liverpool. In the days of Charles the Second the population of London was more than seventeen times the population of Bristol or of Norwich. It may be doubted whether

any other instance can be mentioned of a great kingdom in which the first city was more than seventeen times as large as the second. There is reason to believe that, in 1685, London had been, during about half a century, the most populous capital in Europe. The inhabitants, who are now at least nineteen hundred thousand, were then probably little more than half a million.(1) London had in the world only one commercial rival, now long ago outstripped, the mighty and opulent Amsterdam. English writers boasted of the forest of masts and yard-arms which covered the river from the Bridge to the Tower, and of the stupendous sums which were collected at the Custom House in Thames Street. There is, indeed, no doubt that the trade of the metropolis then bore a far greater proportion than at present to the whole trade of the country; yet to our generation the honest vaunting of our ancestors must appear almost ludicrous. The shipping which they thought incredibly great appears not to have exceeded seventy thousand tons. This was, indeed, then more than a third of the whole tonnage of the kingdom, but is now less than a fourth of the tonnage of Newcastle, and is nearly equalled by the tonnage of the steam vessels of the Thames. The customs of London amounted, in 1685, to about three hundred and thirty thousand pounds a year. In our time the net duty paid annually, at the same place, exceeds ten millions.(2)

Whoever examines the maps of London which were published towards the close of the reign of Charles the Second will see that only the nucleus of the present capital then existed. The town did not, as now, fade by imperceptible degrees into the country. No long avenues of villas, embowered in lilacs and laburnums, extended from the great centre of wealth and civilisation almost to the boundaries of Middlesex and far into the heart of Kent and Surrey. In the east, no part of the immense line of warehouses and artificial lakes which now stretches from the Tower to Blackwall had even been projected. On the west, scarcely one of those stately piles of building which are inhabited by the noble and wealthy was in existence; and Chelsea, which is now peopled by more than forty thousand human beings, was a quiet country village with about a thousand inhabitants.(3) On the north, cattle fed, and sportsmen wandered with dogs and guns, over the site of the borough of Marylebone, and over far the greater part of the space now covered by the boroughs of Finsbury and the Tower Hamlets. Islington was almost a solitude; and poets loved to contrast its silence and repose with the din and turmoil of the monster London.(4)

On the south the capital is now connected with its suburb by several bridges, not inferior in magnificence and solidity to the noblest works of the Caesars. In 1685, a single line of irregular arches, overhung by piles of mean and crazy houses, and garnished, after a fashion worthy of the naked barbarians of Dahomy, with scores of mouldering heads, impeded the navigation of the river.

Of the metropolis, the City, properly so called, was the most important division. At the time of the Restoration it had been built, for the most part, of wood and plaster; the few bricks that were used were ill baked; the booths where goods were exposed to sale projected far into the streets, and were overhung by the upper stories. A few specimens of this architecture may still be seen in those districts which were not reached by the great fire. That fire had, in a few days, covered a space of little less than a square mile with the ruins of eighty-nine churches and of thirteen thousand houses. But the City had risen again with a celerity which had excited the admiration of neighbouring countries. Unfortunately the old lines of the streets had been to a great extent preserved; and those lines, originally traced in an age when even princesses performed their journeys on horseback, were often too narrow to allow wheeled carriages to pass each other with ease, and were therefore ill adapted for the residence of wealthy persons in an age when a coach and six was a fashionable luxury. The style of building was, however, far superior to that of the City which had perished. The ordinary material was brick, of much better quality than had formerly been used. On the sites of the ancient parish churches had arisen a multitude of new domes, towers, and spires which bore the mark of the fertile genius of Wren. In every place save one the traces of the great devastation had been completely effaced. But the crowds of workmen, the scaffolds, and the masses of hewn stone were still to be seen where the noblest of Protestant temples was slowly rising on the ruins of the old Cathedral of Saint Paul.(5)

The whole character of the City has, since that time, undergone a complete change. At present the bankers, the merchants, and the chief shopkeepers repair thither on six mornings of every week for the transaction of business: but they reside in other quarters of the metropolis, or at suburban country seats surrounded by shrubberies and flower gardens. This revolution in private habits has produced a political revolution of no small importance. The City is no longer regarded by the wealthiest traders with that attachment which every man naturally feels for his home. It is no longer associated in their minds with

domestic affections and endearments. The fireside, the nursery, the social table, the quiet bed are not there. Lombard Street and Threadneedle Street are merely places where men toil and accumulate. They go elsewhere to enjoy and to expend. On a Sunday, or in an evening after the hours of business, some courts and alleys, which a few hours before had been alive with hurrying feet and anxious faces, are as silent as the glades of a forest. The chiefs of the mercantile interest are no longer citizens. They avoid, they almost contemn, municipal honours and duties. Those honours and duties are abandoned to men who, though useful and highly respectable, seldom belong to the princely commercial houses of which the names are renowned throughout the world.

In the seventeenth century the City was the merchant's residence. Those mansions of the great old burghers which still exist have been turned into counting houses and warehouses: but it is evident that they were originally not inferior in magnificence to the dwellings which were then inhabited by the nobility. They sometimes stand in retired and gloomy courts, and are accessible only by inconvenient passages: but their dimensions are ample, and their aspect stately. The entrances are decorated with richly carved pillars and canopies. The staircases and landing places are not wanting in grandeur. The floors are sometimes of wood, tessellated after the fashion of France. The palace of Sir Robert Clayton, in the Old Jewry, contained a superb banqueting room wainscoted with cedar, and adorned with battles of gods and giants in fresco.(6) Sir Dudley North expended four thousand pounds, a sum which would then have been important to a Duke, on the rich furniture of his reception rooms in Basinghall Street.(7) In such abodes, under the last Stuarts, the heads of the great firms lived splendidly and hospitably. To their dwelling place they were bound by the strongest ties of interest and affection. There they had passed their youth, had made their friendships, had courted their wives, had seen their children grow up, had laid the remains of their parents in the earth, and expected that their own remains would be laid. That intense patriotism which is peculiar to the members of societies congregated within a narrow space was, in such circumstances, strongly developed. London was, to the Londoner, what Athens was to the Athenian of the age of Pericles, what Florence was to the Florentine of the fifteenth century. The citizen was proud of the grandeur of his city, punctilious about her claims to respect, ambitious of her offices, and zealous for her franchises.

At the close of the reign of Charles the Second the pride of the Londoners was smarting from a cruel mortification. The old charter had been taken away; and the magistracy had been remodelled. All the civic functionaries were Tories: and the Whigs, though in numbers and in wealth superior to their opponents, found themselves excluded from every local dignity. Nevertheless, the external splendour of the municipal government was not diminished, nay, was rather increased by this change. For, under the administration of some Puritans who had lately borne rule, the ancient fame of the City for good cheer had declined: but under the new magistrates, who belonged to a more festive party, and at whose boards guests of rank and fashion from beyond Temple Bar were often seen, the Guildhall and the halls of the great companies were enlivened by many sumptuous banquets. During these repasts, odes, composed by the poet laureate of the corporation, in praise of the King, the Duke, and the Mayor, were sung to music. The drinking was deep, the shouting loud. An observant Tory, who had often shared in these revels, has remarked that the practice of huzzaing after drinking healths dates from this joyous period.(8)

The magnificence displayed by the first civic magistrate was almost regal. The gilded coach, indeed, which is now annually admired by the crowd, was not yet a part of his state. On great occasions he appeared on horseback, attended by a long cavalcade inferior in magnificence only to that which, before a coronation, escorted the sovereign from the Tower to Westminster. The Lord Mayor was never seen in public without his rich robe, his hood of black velvet, his gold chain, his jewel, and a great attendance of harbingers and guards.(9) Nor did the world find anything ludicrous in the pomp which constantly surrounded him. For it was not more than became the place which, as wielding the strength and representing the dignity of the City of London, he was entitled to occupy in the state. That City, being then not only without equal in the country, but without second, had, during five and forty years, exercised almost as great an influence on the politics of England as Paris has, in our own time, exercised on the politics of France. In intelligence London was greatly in advance of every other part of the kingdom. A government, supported and trusted by London, could in a day obtain such pecuniary means as it would have taken months to collect from the rest of the island. Nor were the military resources of the capitol to be despised. The power which the Lord Lieutenants exercised in other parts of the kingdom was in London entrusted to a Commission of eminent citizens. Under the

orders of this Commission were twelve regiments of foot and two regiments of horse. An army of drapers' apprentices and journeymen tailors, with common councilmen for captains and aldermen for colonels, might not indeed have been able to stand its ground against regular troops; but there were then very few regular troops in the kingdom. A town, therefore, which could send forth, at an hour's notice, thousands of men, abounding in natural courage, provided with tolerable weapons, and not altogether untinctured with martial discipline, could not but be a valuable ally and a formidable enemy. It was not forgotten that Hampden and Pym had been protected from lawless tyranny by the London trainbands; that, in the great crisis of the civil war, the London trainbands had marched to raise the siege of Gloucester; or that, in the movement against the military tyrants which followed the downfall of Richard Cromwell, the London trainbands had borne a signal part. In truth, it is no exaggeration to say that, but for the hostility of the City, Charles the First would never have been vanquished, and that, without the help of the City, Charles the Second could scarcely have been restored.

These considerations may serve to explain why, in spite of that attraction which had, during a long course of years, gradually drawn the aristocracy westward, a few men of high rank had continued, till a very recent period, to dwell in the vicinity of the Exchange and of the Guildhall. Shaftsbury and Buckingham, while engaged in bitter and unscrupulous opposition to the government, had thought that they could nowhere carry on their intrigues so conveniently or so securely as under the protection of the City magistrates and the City militia. Shaftsbury had therefore lived in Aldersgate Street, at a house which may still be easily known by pilasters and wreaths, the graceful work of Inigo. Buckingham had ordered his mansion near Charing Cross, once the abode of the Archbishops of York, to be pulled down; and, while streets and alleys which are still named after him were raising on that site, chose to reside in Dowgate.(10)

These, however, were rare exceptions. Almost all the noble families of England had long migrated beyond the walls. The district where most of their town houses stood lies between the City and the regions which are now considered as fashionable. A few great men still retained their hereditary hotels in the Strand. The stately dwellings on the south and west of Lincoln's Inn Fields, the Piazza of Covent Garden, Southampton Square, which is now called Bloomsbury Square, and King's Square, in Soho Fields, which is now called Soho Square, were among the favourite spots. Foreign princes were carried to see

Bloomsbury Square, as one of the wonders of England.(11) Soho Square, which had just been built, was to our ancestors a subject of pride with which their posterity will hardly sympathise. Monmouth Square had been the name while the fortunes of the Duke of Monmouth flourished; and on the southern side towered his mansion. The front, though ungraceful, was lofty and richly adorned. The walls of the principal apartments were finely sculptured with fruit, foliage, and armorial bearings, and were hung with embroidered satin.(12) Every trace of this magnificence has long disappeared; and no aristocratical mansion is to be found in that once aristocratical quarter. A little way north from Holborn, and on the verge of the pastures and cornfields, rose two celebrated palaces, each with an ample garden. One of them, then called Southampton House, and subsequently Bedford House, was removed about fifty years ago to make room for a new city, which now covers, with its squares, streets, and churches, a vast area, renowned in the seventeenth century for peaches and snipes. The other, Montague House, celebrated for its frescoes and furniture, was, a few months after the death of Charles the Second, burned to the ground, and was speedily succeeded by a more magnificent Montague House, which, having been long the repository of such various and precious treasures of art, science, and learning as were scarcely ever before assembled under a single roof, has now given place to an edifice more magnificent still.(13)

Nearer to the Court, on a space called Saint James's Fields, had just been built Saint James's Square and Jermyn Street. Saint James's Church had recently been opened for the accommodation of the inhabitants of this new quarter.(14) Golden Square, which was in the next generation inhabited by lords and ministers of state, had not yet been begun. Indeed the only dwellings to be seen on the north of Piccadilly were three or four isolated and almost rural mansions, of which the most celebrated was the costly pile erected by Clarendon, and nick-named Dunkirk House. It had been purchased after its founder's downfall by the Duke of Albermarle. The Clarendon Hotel and Albemarle Street still preserve the memory of the site.

He who then rambled to what is now the gayest and most crowded part of Regent Street found himself in a solitude, and was sometimes so fortunate as to have shot at a woodcock.(15) On the north the Oxford road ran between hedges. Three or four hundred yards to the south were the garden walls of a few great houses which were considered as quite out of town. On the west was a meadow renowned

for a spring from which, long afterwards, Conduit Street was named. On the east was a field not to be passed without a shudder by any Londoner of that age. There, as in a place far from the haunts of men, had been dug twenty years before, when the great plague was raging, a pit into which the dead carts had nightly shot corpses by scores. It was popularly believed that the earth was deeply tained with infection, and could not be disturbed without imminent risk to human life. No foundations were laid there till two generations had passed without any return of the pestilence, and till the ghastly spot had long been surrounded by buildings.(16)

We should greatly err if we were to suppose that any of the streets and squares then bore the same aspect as at present. The great majority of houses, indeed, have, since that time, been wholly, or in great part, rebuilt. If the most fashionable parts of the capital could be placed before us, such as they then were, we should be disgusted by their squalid appearance, and poisoned by their noisome atmosphere.

In Covent Garden a filthy and noisy market was held close to the dwellings of the great. Fruit women screamed, carters fought, cabbage stalks and rotten apples accumulated in heaps at the thresholds of the Countess of Berkshire and of the Bishop of Durham.(17)

The centre of Lincoln's Inn Fields was an open space where the rabble congregated every evening, within a few yards of Cardigan House and Winchester House, to hear mountebanks harangue, to see bears dance, and to set dogs at oxen. Rubbish was shot in every part of the area. Horses were exercised there. The beggars were as noisy and importunate as in the worst governed cities of the Continent. A Lincoln's Inn mumper was a proverb. The whole fraternity knew the arms and liveries of every charitably disposed grandee in the neighbourhood, and, as soon as his lordship's coach and six appeared, came hopping and crawling in crowds to persecute him. These disorders lasted, in spite of many accidents, and of some legal proceedings, till, in the reign of George the Second, Sir Joseph Jekyll, Master of the Rolls, was knocked down and nearly killed in the middle of the square. Then at length palisades were set up, and a pleasant garden laid out.(18)

Saint James's Square was a receptacle for all the offal and cinders, for all dead cats and dead dogs of Westminster. At one time a cudgel player kept the ring there. At another time an impudent squatter settled himself there, and built a shed for rubbish under the windows of the gilded saloons in which the first magnates of the realm, Norfolk,

Ormond, Kent, and Pembroke, gave banquets and balls. It was not till these nuisances had lasted through a whole generation, and till much had been written about them, that the inhabitants applied to Parliament for permission to put up rails, and to plant trees.(19)

When such was the state of the region inhabited by the most luxurious portion of society, we may easily believe that the great body of the population suffered what would now be considered as insupportable grievances. The pavement was detestable: all foreigners cried shame upon it. The drainage was so bad that in rainy weather the gutters soon became torrents. Several facetious poets have commemorated the fury with which these black rivulets roared down Snow Hill and Ludgate Hill, bearing to Fleet Ditch a vast tribute of animal and vegetable filth from the stalls of butchers and greengrocers. This flood was profusely thrown to right and left by coaches and carts. To keep as far from the carriage road as possible was therefore the wish of every pedestrian. The mild and timid gave the wall. The bold and athletic took it. If two roisterers met, they cocked their hats in each other's faces, and pushed each other about till the weaker was shoved towards the kennel. If he was a mere bully he sneaked off, muttering that he should find a time. If he was pugnacious, the encounter probably ended in a duel behind Montague House.(20)

The houses were not numbered. There would indeed have been little advantage in numbering them; for of the coachmen, chairmen, porters, and errand boys of London, a very small proportion could read. It was necessary to use marks which the most ignorant could understand. The shops were therefore distinguished by painted or sculptured signs, which gave a gay and grotesque aspect to the streets. The walk from Charing Cross to Whitechapel lay through an endless succession of Saracens' Heads, Royal Oaks, Blue Bears, and Golden Lambs, which disappeared when they were no longer required for the direction of the common people.

When the evening closed in, the difficulty and danger of walking about London became serious indeed. The garret windows were opened, and pails were emptied, with little regard to those who were passing below. Falls, bruises, and broken bones were of constant occurrence. For, till the last year of the reign of Charles the Second, most of the streets were left in profound darkness. Thieves and robbers plied their trade with impunity: yet they were hardly so terrible to peaceable citizens as another class of ruffians. It was a favourite amusement of dissolute young gentlemen to swagger by night about

the town, breaking windows, upsetting sedans, beating quiet men, and offering rude caresses to pretty women. Several dynasties of these tyrants had, since the Restoration, domineered over the streets. The Muns and Tityre Tus had given place to the Hectors, and the Hectors had been recently succeeded by the Scourers. At a later period arose the Nicker, the Hawcubite, and the yet more dreaded name of Mohawk.(21) The machinery for keeping the peace was utterly contemptible. There was an Act of Common Council which provided that more than a thousand watchmen should be constantly on the alert in the city, from sunset to sunrise, and that every inhabitant should take his turn of duty. But this Act was negligently executed. Few of those who were summoned left their homes; and those few generally found it more agreeable to tipple in alehouses than to pace the streets.(22)

It ought to be noticed that, in the last year of the reign of Charles the Second, began a great change in the police of London, a change which has perhaps added as much to the happiness of the body of the people as revolutions of much greater fame. An ingenious projector, named Edward Heming, obtained letters patent conveying to him, for a term of years, the exclusive right of lighting up London. He undertook, for a moderate consideration, to place a light before every tenth door, on moonless nights, from Michaelmas, to Lady Day, and from six to twelve of the clock. Those who now see the capital all the year round, from dusk to dawn, blazing with a splendour beside which the illuminations for La Hogue and Blenheim would have looked pale, may perhaps smile to think of Heming's lanterns, which glimmered feebly before one house in ten during a small part of one night in three. But such was not the feeling of his contemporaries. His scheme was enthusiastically applauded, and furiously attacked. The friends of improvement extolled him as the greatest of all the benefactors of his city. What, they asked, were the boasted inventions of Archimedes, when compared with the achievement of the man who had turned the nocturnal shades into noon day? In spite of these eloquent eulogies the cause of darkness was not left undefended. There were fools in that age who opposed the introduction of what was called the new light as strenuously as fools in our age have opposed the introduction of vaccination and railroads, as strenuously as the fools of an age anterior to the dawn of history doubtless opposed the introduction of the plough and of alphabetical writing. Many years after the date of Heming's patent there were extensive districts in which no lamp was seen.(23)

We may easily imagine what, in such times, must have been the state of the quarters of London which were peopled by the outcasts of society. Among those quarters one had attained a scandalous preeminence. On the confines of the City and the Temple had been founded, in the thirteenth century, a House of Carmelite Friars, distinguished by their white hoods. The precinct of this house had, before the Reformation, been a sanctuary for criminals, and still retained the privilege of protecting debtors from arrest. Insolvents consequently were to be found in every dwelling, from cellar to garret. Of these a large proportion were knaves and libertines, and were followed to their asylum by women more abandoned than themselves. The civil power was unable to keep order in a district swarming with such inhabitants; and thus Whitefriars became the favourite resort of all who wished to be emancipated from the restraints of the law. Though the immunities legally belonging to the place extended only to cases of debt, cheats, false witnesses, forgers, and highwaymen found refuge there. For amidst a rabble so desperate no peace officer's life was in safety. At the cry of "Rescue", bullies with swords and cudgels, and termagant hags with spits and broomsticks, poured forth by hundreds; and the intruder was fortunate if he escaped back into Fleet Street, hustled, stripped, and pumped upon. Even the warrant of the Chief Justice of England could not be executed without the help of a company of musketeers. Such relics of the barbarism of the darkest ages were to be found within a short walk of the chambers where Somers was studying history and law, of the chapel where Tillotson was preaching, of the coffee house where Dryden was passing judgment on poems and plays, and of the hall where the Royal Society was examining the astronomical system of Isaac Newton. (24)

Each of the two cities which made up the capital of England had its own centre of attraction. In the metropolis of commerce the point of convergence was the Exchange; in the metropolis of fashion the Palace. But the Palace did not retain its influence so long as the Exchange. The Revolution completely altered the relations between the Court and the higher classes of society. It was by degrees discovered that the King, in his individual capacity, had very little to give; that coronets and garters, bishoprics and embassies, lordships of the Treasury and tellerships of the Exchequer, nay, even charges in the royal stud and bedchamber, were really bestowed, not by him, but by his advisers. Every ambitious and covetous man perceived that he would consult his own interest far better by acquiring the dominion of a

Cornish borough, and by rendering good service to the ministry during a critical session, than by becoming the companion, or even the minion of his prince. It was therefore in the antechambers, not of George the First and of George the Second, but of Walpole and of Pelham, that the daily crowd of courtiers was to be found. It is also to be remarked that the same Revolution, which made it impossible that our Kings should use the patronage of the state merely for the purpose of gratifying their personal predilections, gave us several Kings unfitted by their education and habits to be gracious and affable hosts. They had been born and bred on the Continent. They never felt themselves at home in our island. If they spoke our language, they spoke it inelegantly and with effort. Our national character they never fully understood. Our national manners they hardly attempted to acquire. The most important part of their duty they performed better than any ruler who had preceded them: for they governed strictly according to law: but they could not be the first gentlemen of the realm, the heads of polite society. If ever they unbent, it was in a very small circle where hardly an English face was to be seen; and they were never so happy as when they could escape for a summer to their native land. They had indeed their days of reception for our nobility and gentry; but the reception was mere matter of form, and became at last as solemn a ceremony as a funeral.

Not such was the court of Charles the Second. Whitehall, when he dwelt there, was the focus of political intrigue and of fashionable gaiety. Half the jobbing and half the flirting of the metropolis went on under his roof. Whoever could make himself agreeable to the prince, or could secure the good offices of the mistress, might hope to rise in the world without rendering any service to the government, without being even known by sight to any minister of state. This courtier got a frigate, and that a company; a third, the pardon of a rich offender; a fourth, a lease of crown land on easy terms. If the King notified his pleasure that a briefless lawyer should be made a judge, or that a libertine baronet should be made a peer, the gravest counsellors, after a little murmuring, submitted.(25) Interest, therefore, drew a constant press of suitors to the gates of the palace; and those gates always stood wide. The King kept open house every day, and all day long, for the good society of London, the extreme Whigs only excepted. Hardly any gentleman had any difficulty in making his way to the royal presence. The levee was exactly what the word imports. Some men of quality came every morning to stand round their

master, to chat with him while his wig was combed and cravat tied, and to accompany him in his early walk through the Park. All persons who had been properly introduced might, without any special invitation, go to see him dine, sup, dance, and play at hazard, and might have the pleasure of hearing him tell stories, which indeed he told remarkably well, about his flight from Worcester, and about the misery which he had endured when he was a state prisoner in the hands of the canting meddling preachers of Scotland. Bystanders whom His Majesty recognised often came in for a courteous word. This proved a far more successful kingcraft than any that his father or grandfather had practised. It was not easy for the most austere republican of the school of Marvel to resist the fascination of so much goodhumour and affability: and many a veteran Cavalier, in whose heart the remembrance of unrequited sacrifices and services had been festering during twenty years, was compensated in one moment for wounds and sequestrations by his sovereign's kind nod, and "God bless you, my old friend!"

Whitehall naturally became the chief staple of news. Whenever there was a rumour that anything important had happened or was about to happen, people hastened thither to obtain intelligence from the fountain head. The galleries presented the appearance of a modern club room at an anxious time. They were full of people enquiring whether the Dutch mail was in, what tidings the express from France had brought, whether John Sobiesky had beaten the Turks, whether the Doge of Genoa was really at Paris. These were matters about which it was safe to talk aloud. But there were subjects concerning which information was asked and given in whispers. Had Halifax got the better of Rochester? Was there to be a Parliament? Was the Duke of York really going to Scotland? Had Monmouth really been summoned from the Hague? Men tried to read the countenance of every minister as he went through the throng to and from the royal closet. All sorts of auguries were drawn from the tone in which His Majesty spoke to the Lord President, or from the laugh with which His Majesty honoured a jest of the Lord Privy Seal; and in a few hours the hopes and fears inspired by such slight indications had spread to all the coffee houses from Saint James's to the Tower.(26)

The coffee house must not be dismissed with a cursory mention. It might indeed at that time have been not improperly called a most important political institution. No Parliament had sat for years. The municipal council of the City had ceased to speak the sense of the

citizens. Public meetings, harangues, resolutions, and the rest of the modern machinery of agitation had not yet come into fashion. Nothing resembling the modern newspaper existed. In such circumstances the coffee houses were the chief organs through which the public opinion of the metropolis vented itself.

The first of these establishments had been set up, in the time of the Commonwealth, by a Turkey merchant, who had acquired among the Mahometans a taste for their favourite beverage. The convenience of being able to make appointments in any part of the town, and of being able to pass evenings socially at a very small charge, was so great that the fashion spread fast. Every man of the upper or middle class went daily to his coffee house to learn the news and to discuss it. Every coffee house had one or more orators to whose eloquence the crowd listened with admiration, and who soon became, what the journalists of our time have been called, a fourth Estate of the realm. The Court had long seen with uneasiness the growth of this new power in the state. An attempt had been made, during Danby's administration, to close the coffee houses. But men of all parties missed their usual places of resort so much that there was an universal outcry. The government did not venture, in opposition to a feeling so strong and general, to enforce a regulation of which the legality might well be questioned. Since that time ten years had elapsed, and during those years the number and influence of the coffee houses had been constantly increasing. Foreigners remarked that the coffee house was that which especially distinguished London from all other cities; that the coffee house was the Londoner's home, and that those who wished to find a gentleman commonly asked, not whether he lived in Fleet Street or Chancery Lane, but whether he frequented the Grecian or the Rainbow. Nobody was excluded from these places who laid down his penny at the bar. Yet every rank and profession, and every shade of religious and political opinion, had its own headquarters. There were houses near Saint James's Park where fops congregated, their heads and shoulders covered with black or flaxen wigs, not less ample than those which are now worn by the Chancellor and by the Speaker of the House of Commons. The wig came from Paris; and so did the rest of the fine gentleman's ornaments, his embroidered coat, his fringed gloves, and the tassel which upheld his pantaloons. The conversation was in that dialect which, long after it had ceased to be spoken in fashionable circles, continued in the mouth of Lord Foppington, to excite the mirth of theatres.(27) The atmosphere was like that of a perfumer's

shop. Tobacco in any other form than that of richly scented snuff was held in abomination. If any clown, ignorant of the usages of the house, called for a pipe, the sneers of the whole assembly and the short answers of the waiters soon convinced him that he had better go somewhere else. Nor, indeed, would he have had far to go. For, in general, the coffee rooms reeked with tobacco like a guardroom; and strangers sometimes expressed their surprise that so many people should leave their own firesides to sit in the midst of eternal fog and stench. Nowhere was the smoking more constant than at Will's. That celebrated house, situated between Covent Garden and Bow Street, was sacred to polite letters. There the talk was about poetical justice and the unities of place and time. There was a faction for Perrault and the moderns, a faction for Boileau and the ancients. One group debated whether Paradise Lost ought not to have been in rhyme. To another an envious poetaster demonstrated that Venice Preserved ought to have been hooted from the stage. Under no roof was a greater variety of figures to be seen. There were Earls in stars and garters, clergymen in cassocks and bands, pert Templars, sheepish lads from the Universities, translators and indexmakers in ragged coats of frieze. The great press was to get near the chair where John Dryden sate. In winter that chair was always in the warmest nook by the fire; in summer it stood in the balcony. To bow to the Laureate, and to hear his opinion of Racine's last tragedy or of Bossu's treatise on epic poetry, was thought a privilege. A pinch from his snuff box was an honour sufficient to turn the head of a young enthusiast. There were coffee houses where the first medical men might be consulted. Doctor John Radcliffe, who, in the year 1685, rose to the largest practice in London, came daily, at the hour when the Exchange was full, from his house in Bow Street, then a fashionable part of the capital, to Garraway's and was to be found, surrounded by surgeons and apothecaries, at a particular table. There were Puritan coffee houses where no oath was heard, and where lankhaired men discussed election and reprobation through their noses; Jew coffee houses where darkeyed money changers from Venice and from Amsterdam greeted each other; and Popish coffee houses where, as good Protestants believed, Jesuits planned, over their cups, another great fire, and cast silver bullets to shoot the King.(28)

These gregarious habits had no small share in forming the character of the Londoner of that age. He was, indeed, a different being from the rustic Englishman. There was not then the intercourse which now

exists between the two classes. Only very great men were in the habit of dividing the year between town and country. Few esquires came to the capital thrice in their lives. Nor was it yet the practice of all citizens in easy circumstances to breathe the fresh air of the fields and woods during some weeks of every summer. A cockney, in a rural village, was stared at as much as if he had intruded into a Kraal of Hottentots. On the other hand, when the lord of a Lincolnshire or Shropshire manor appeared in Fleet Street, he was as easily distinguished from the resident population as a Turk or a Lascar. His dress, his gait, his accent, the manner in which he gazed at the shops, stumbled into the gutters, ran against the porters, and stood under the waterspouts, marked him out as an excellent subject for the operations of swindlers and banterers. Bullies jostled him into the kennel. Hackney coachmen splashed him from head to foot. Thieves explored with perfect security the huge pockets of his horseman's coat, while he stood entranced by the splendour of the Lord Mayor's show. Moneydroppers, sore from the cart's tail, introduced themselves to him, and appeared to him the most honest friendly gentlemen that he had ever seen. Painted women, the refuse of Lewkner Lane and Whetstone Park, passed themselves on him for countesses and maids of honour. If he asked his way to Saint James's, his informants sent him to Mile End. If he went into a shop, he was instantly discerned to be a fit purchaser of everything that nobody else would buy, of secondhand embroidery, copper rings, and watches that would not go. If he rambled into any fashionable coffee house, he became a mark for the insolent derision of fops and the grave waggery of Templars. Enraged and mortified, he soon returned to his mansion, and there, in the homage of his tenants and the conversation of his boon companions, found consolation for the vexations and humiliations which he had undergone. There he was once more a great man, and saw nothing above himself except when at the assizes he took his seat on the bench near the Judge, or when at the muster of the militia he saluted the Lord Lieutenant.

NOTES

(1) According to King 530,000.(1848.) In 1851 the population of London exceeded 2,300,000.(1857.)

(2) Macpherson's History of Commerce; Chalmers's Estimate; Chamberlayne's State of England, 1684. The tonnage of the steamers belonging to the port of London was, at the end of 1847, about 60,000

tons. The customs of the port, from 1842 to 1845, very nearly averaged 11,000,000*l*.(1848.) In 1854 the tonnage of the steamers of the port of London amounted to 138,000 tons, without reckoning vessels of less than fifty tons.(1857.)

(3) Lyson's Environs of London. The baptisms at Chelsea, between 1680 and 1690, were only 42 a year.

(4) Cowley, Discourse of Solitude.

(5) The fullest and most trustworthy information about the state of the buildings of London at this time is to be derived from the maps and drawings in the British Museum and in the Pepysian Library. The badness of the bricks in the old buildings of London is particularly mentioned in the Travels of the Grand Duke Cosmo. There is an account of the works at Saint Paul's in Ward's London Spy. I am almost ashamed to quote such nauseous balderdash; but I have been forced to descend even lower, if possible in search of materials.

(6) Evelyn's Diary, Sept. 20, 1672.

(7) Roger North's Life of Sir Dudley North.

(8) North's Examen. This amusing writer has preserved a specimen of the sublime raptures in which the Pindar of the City indulged:—

"The worshipful Sir John Moor!
After age that name adore!"

(9) Chamberlayne's State of England, 1684; Angliae Metropolis, 1690; Seymour's London, 1734.

(10) North's Examen, 116; Wood, Ath. Ox. Shaftsbury; The Duke of B.'s Litany.

(11) Travels of the Grand Duke Cosmo.

(12) Chamberlayne's State of England, 1684; Pennant's London; Smith's Life of Nollekens.

(13) Evelyn's Diary, Oct. 10, 1683; Jan. 19, 1685/6.

(14) Stat. 1 Jac.II. c.22; Evelyn's Diary, Dec. 7, 1684.

(15) Old General Oglethorpe, who died in 1785, used to boast that he had shot birds here in Anne's reign. See Pennant's London, and the Gentleman's Magazine for July 1785.

(16) The pest field will be seen in maps of London as late as the end of George the First's reign.

(17) See a very curious plan of Covent Garden made about 1690, and

engraved for Smith's History of Westminster. See also Hogarth's Morning, painted while some of the houses in the Piazza were still occupied by people of fashion.

(18) London Spy; Tom Brown's Comical View of London and Westminster; Turner's Propositions for the employing of the Poor, 1678; Daily Courant and Daily Journal of June 7, 1733; Case of Michael v Allestree, in 1676, 2 Levinz, p. 172. Michael had been run over by two horses which Allestree was breaking in Lincoln's Inn Fields. The declaration set forth that the defendant "porta deux chivals ungovernable en un coach, et improvide, inacute, et absque debita consideratione ineptitudinis loci la eux drive pur eux faire tractable et apt pur un coach, quels chivals, pur ceo que, per leur ferocite, ne poient estre rule, curre sur le plaintiff et le noie."

(19) Stat. 12 Geo.I. c.25; Commons' Journals, Feb. 25. March 2. 1725/6; London Gardener, 1712; Evening Post, March 23, 1731. I have not been able to find this number of the Evening Post; I therefore quote it on the faith of Mr. Malcolm, who mentions it in his History of London.

(20) Lettres sur les Anglois, written early in the reign of William the Third; Swift's City Shower; Gay's Trivia. Johnson used to relate a curious conversation which he had with his mother about giving and taking the wall.

(21) Oldham's Imitation of the 3d Satire of Juvenal, 1682; Shadwell's Scourers, 1690. Many other authorities will readily occur to all who are acquainted with the popular literature of that and the succeeding generation. It may be suspected that some of the Tityre Tus, like good Cavaliers, broke Milton's windows shortly after the Restoration. I am confident that he was thinking of those pests of London when he dictated the noble lines:—

> "And in luxurious cities, when the noise
> Of riot ascends above their loftiest towers,
> And injury and outrage, and when night
> Darkens the streets, then wander forth the sons
> Of Belial, flown with insolence and wine."

(22) Seymour's London.

(23) Angliae Metropolis, 1690, Sect. 17. entitled, "Of the new lights"; Seymour's London.

(24) Stowe's Survey of London; Shadwell's Squire of Alsatia; Ward's London Spy; Stat. 8 & 9 Gul.III. cap.27.

(25) See Sir Roger North's account of the way in which Wright was made a judge, and Clarendon's account of the way in which Sir George Savile was made a peer.

(26) The sources from which I have drawn my information about the state of the Court are too numerous to recapitulate. Among them are the Despatches of Barillon, Van Citters, Ronquillo, and Adda, the Travels of the Grand Duke Cosmo, the works of Roger North, the Diaries of Pepys, Evelyn, and Teonge, and the Memoirs of Grammont and Reresby.

(27) The chief peculiarity of this dialect was that, in a large class of words, the O was pronounced like A. Thus Lord was pronounced Lard. See Vanbrugh's Relapse. Lord Sunderland was a great master of this court tune, as Roger North calls it; and Titus Oates affected it in the hope of passing for a fine gentleman. Examen, 77.254.

(28) Lettres sur les Anglois; Tom Brown's Tour; Ward's London Spy; The Character of a Coffee House, 1673; Rules and Orders of the Coffee House, 1674; Coffee Houses vindicated, 1675; A Satyr against Coffee; North's Examen, 138; Life of Guildford, 152; Life of Sir Dudley North, 149; Life of Dr. Radcliffe, published by Curll in 1715. The liveliest description of Will's is in the City and Country Mouse. There is a remarkable passage about the influence of the coffee house orators in Halstead's Succinct Genealogies, printed in 1685.

HENRY THOMAS BUCKLE

1821–1862

Buckle believed that three factors had reduced man's taste for war: gunpowder, free trade, and steam. He was wrong, but the investigation demonstrates the sort of large conjecture he thought historians ought to make and, were this information wide enough, might make with increasing accuracy. He knew the foundations for scientific history were weak, but he could not help demonstrating how it ought to be written. The free trade argument, which I omit, is based on the assumption that a bullionist theory necessitates international rivalry while the theories of Adam Smith, who "has, by the publication of one single work, contributed more towards the happiness of man, than has been effected by the united abilities of all the statesmen and legislators of whom history has preserved an authentic record," have helped men to see that peaceful relations between states aid the prosperity of all. I have added all the footnotes to the first section, dealing with gunpowder. Footnotes may have elevated Buckle, at times, no higher than a soapbox lifts an orator in Hyde Park, but it is important to realize on how wide a reading his text is based. He warned the reader, after this discussion, that it "is merely an approach towards demonstration: and the complete demonstration must be reserved for the future volumes of this work." He brought out a second volume in 1861, but died next year with this demonstration, and so many others, incomplete.

Contemporary discussion can be followed in J. M. Robertson, Buckle and His Critics *(1895). In* A Victorian Eminence *(1958), Giles St. Aubyn provides a sympathetic account of Buckle's life and work.*

THUS STRIKING is the contrast between the military genius of ancient times, and the military genius of modern Europe. The causes of this decay are clearly traceable to the circumstance that, owing to the immense increase of intellectual employments, few men of ability will now enter a profession into which, in antiquity, men of ability eagerly crowded, as supplying the best means of exercising those faculties which, in more civilized countries, are turned to a better account. This, indeed, is a very important change; and thus to transfer the most powerful intellects from the arts of war to the arts of peace, has been the slow work of many centuries, the gradual, but constant, encroachments of advancing knowledge. To write the history of those encroachments would be to write the history of the human intellect—a task impossible for any single man adequately to perform. But the subject is one of such interest, and has been so little studied, that though I have already carried this analysis farther than I had intended, I cannot refrain from noticing what appear to me to be the three leading ways in which the warlike spirit of the ancient world has been weakened by the progress of European knowledge.

The first of these arose out of the invention of Gunpowder; which, though a warlike contrivance, has in its results been eminently serviceable to the interests of peace.(1) This important invention is said to have been made in the thirteenth century;(2) but was not in common use until the fourteenth, or even the beginning of the fifteenth, century. Scarcely had it come into operation, when it worked a great change in the whole scheme and practice of war. Before this time, it was considered the duty of nearly every citizen to be prepared to enter the military service, for the purpose either of defending his own country, or of attacking others.(3) Standing armies were entirely unknown; and in their place there existed a rude and barbarous militia, always ready for battle and always unwilling to engage in those peaceful pursuits which were then universally despised. Nearly every man being a soldier, the military profession, as such, had no separate existence; or, to speak more properly, the whole of Europe composed one great army, in which all other professions were merged. To this the only exception was the ecclesiastical profession; but even that was affected by the general tendency, and it was not at all uncommon to see large bodies of troops led to the field by bishops and abbots, to most of whom the arts of war were in those days perfectly familiar.(4) At all events, between these two professions men were necessarily divided:

the only avocations were war and theology; and if you refused to enter the church, you were bound to serve in the army. As a natural consequence, everything of real importance was altogether neglected. There were, indeed, many priests and many warriors, many sermons and many battles.(5) But, on the other hand, there was neither trade, nor commerce, nor manufactures; there was no science, no literature: the useful arts were entirely unknown; and even the highest ranks of society were unacquainted, not only with the most ordinary comforts, but with the commonest decencies of civilized life.

But so soon as gunpowder came into use, there was laid the foundation of a great change. According to the old system, a man had only to possess, what he generally inherited from his father, either a sword or a bow, and he was ready equipped for the field.(6) According to the new system, new means were required, and the equipment became more costly and more difficult. First, there was the supply of gunpowder;(7) then there was the possession of muskets, which were expensive weapons, and considered difficult to manage.(8) Then, too, there were other contrivances to which gunpowder naturally gave rise, such as pistols, bombs, mortars, shells, mines, and the like.(9) All these things, by increasing the complication of the military art, increased the necessity of discipline and practice; while, at the same time, the change that was being effected in the ordinary weapons deprived the great majority of men of the possibility of procuring them. To suit these altered circumstances, a new system was organized: and it was found advisable to train up bodies of men for the sole purpose of war, and to separate them as much as possible from those other employments in which formerly all soldiers were occasionally engaged. Thus it was that there arose standing armies; the first of which were formed in the middle of the fifteenth century,(10) almost immediately after gunpowder was generally known. Thus, too, there arose the custom of employing mercenary troops; of which we find a few earlier instances, though the practice was not fully established until the latter part of the fourteenth century.(11)

The importance of this movement was soon seen, by the change it effected in the classification of European society. The regular troops being, from their discipline, more serviceable against the enemy, and also more immediately under the control of the government, it naturally followed that, as their merits became understood, the old militia should fall, first into disrepute, then be neglected, and then sensibly diminish. At the same time, this diminution in the number of un-

disciplined soldiers deprived the country of a part of its warlike resources, and therefore made it necessary to pay more attention to the disciplined ones, and to confine them more exclusively to their military duties. Thus it was that a division was first broadly established between the soldier and the civilian; and there arose a separate military profession,(12) which, consisting of a comparatively small number of the total amount of citizens, left the remainder to settle in some other pursuit.(13) In this way immense bodies of men were gradually weaned from their old warlike habits; and being, as it were, forced into civil life, their energies became available for the general purposes of society, and for the cultivation of those arts of peace which had formerly been neglected. The result was, that the European mind, instead of being, as heretofore, solely occupied either with war or with theology, now struck out into a middle path, and created those great branches of knowledge to which modern civilization owes its origin. In each successive generation this tendency towards a separate organization was more marked; the utility of a division of labour became clearly recognised; and by this means knowledge itself advanced, the authority of this middle or intellectual class correspondingly increased. Each addition to its power lessened the weight of the other two classes, and checked those superstitious feelings and that love of war, on which, in an early state of society, all enthusiasm is concentrated. The evidence of the growth and diffusion of this intellectual principle is so full and decisive, that it would be possible, by combining all the branches of knowledge, to trace nearly the whole of its consecutive steps. At present, it is enough to say, that, taking a general view, this third, or intellectual, class, first displayed an independent, though still a vague, activity in the fourteenth and fifteenth centuries; that in the sixteenth century, this activity, assuming a distinct form, showed itself in religious outbreaks; that in the seventeenth century, its energy, becoming more practical, was turned against the abuses of government, and caused a series of rebellions, from which hardly any part of Europe escaped; and finally, that in the eighteenth and nineteenth centuries, it has extended its aim to every department of public and private life, diffusing education, teaching legislators, controlling kings, and, above all, settling on a sure foundation that supremacy of Public Opinion, to which not only constitutional princes, but even the most despotic sovereigns, are now rendered strictly amenable.

These, indeed, are vast questions; and, without some knowledge of them, no one can understand the present condition of European so-

ciety, or form the least idea of its future prospects. It is, however, sufficient that the reader can now perceive the way in which so slight a matter as the invention of gunpowder diminished the warlike spirit, by diminishing the number of persons to whom the practice of war was habitual. There were, no doubt, other and collateral circumstances which tended in the same direction; but the use of gunpowder was the most effectual, because, by increasing the difficulty and expense of war, it made a separate military profession indispensable; and thus, curtailing the action of the military spirit, left an overplus, an unemployed energy, which soon found its way to the pursuits of peace, infused into them a new life, and began to control that lust of conquest, which, though natural to a barbarous people, is the great enemy of knowledge, and is the most fatal of those diseased appetites by which even civilized countries are too often afflicted.

The second intellectual movement, by which the love of war has been lessened, is much more recent, and has not yet produced the whole of its natural effects. I allude to the discoveries made by Political Economy: a branch of knowledge with which even the wisest of the ancients had not the least acquaintance, but which possesses an importance it would be difficult to exaggerate, and is, moreover, remarkable, as being the only subject immediately connected with the art of government that has yet been raised to a science.

* * *

The third great cause by which the love of war has been weakened, is the way in which discoveries respecting the application of Steam to the purposes of travelling have facilitated the intercourse between different countries, and thus aided in destroying that ignorant contempt which one nation is too apt to feel for another. Thus, for instance, the miserable and impudent falsehoods which a large class of English writers formerly directed against the morals and private character of the French, and, to their shame be it said, even against the chastity of French women, tended not a little to embitter the angry feelings then existing between the two first countries of Europe; irritating the English against the French vices, irritating the French against the English calumnies. In the same way, there was a time when every honest Englishman firmly believed that he could beat ten Frenchmen; a class of beings whom he held in sovereign contempt, as a lean and stunted race, who drank claret instead of brandy, who lived entirely off frogs; miserable infidels, who heard mass every Sunday, who bowed

down before idols, and who even worshipped the Pope. On the other hand, the French were taught to despise us, as rude unlettered barbarians, without either taste or humanity; surly, ill-conditioned men, living in an unhappy climate, where a perpetual fog, only varied by rain, prevented the sun from ever being seen; suffering from so deep and inveterate a melancholy, that physicians had called it the English spleen; and under the influence of this cruel malady constantly committing suicide, particularly in November, when we were well known to hang and shoot ourselves by thousands.

Whoever has looked much into the older literature of France and England, knows that these were the opinions which the two first nations of Europe, in the ignorance and simplicity of their hearts, held respecting each other. But the progress of improvement, by bringing the two countries into close and intimate contact, has dissipated these foolish prejudices, and taught each people to admire, and, what is still more important, to respect each other. And the greater the contact, the greater the respect. For, whatever theologians may choose to assert, it is certain that mankind at large has far more virtue than vice, and that in every country good actions are more frequent than bad ones. Indeed, if this were otherwise, the preponderance of evil would long since have destroyed the human race, and not even have left a single man to lament the degeneracy of his species. An additional proof of this is the fact, that the more nations associate with each other, and the more they see and know of their fellow-creatures, the more quickly do ancient enmities disappear. This is because an enlarged experience proves that mankind is not so radically bad as we from our infancy are taught to believe. But if vices were really more frequent than virtues, the result would be, that the increasing amalgamation of society would increase our bad opinion of others; because, though we may love our own vices, we do not generally love the vices of our neighbours. So far, however, is this from being the actual consequence, that it has always been found that those whose extensive knowledge makes them best acquainted with the general course of human actions, are precisely those who take the most favourable view of them. The greatest observer and the most profound thinker is invariably the most lenient judge. It is the solitary misanthrope, brooding over his fancied wrongs, who is most prone to depreciate the good qualities of our nature, and exaggerate its bad ones. Or else it is some foolish and ignorant monk, who, dreaming away his existence in an idle solitude, flatters his own vanity by denouncing the vices of others; and thus

declaiming against the enjoyments of life, revenges himself on that society from which by his own superstition he is excluded. These are the sort of men who insist most strongly on the corruption of our nature, and on the degeneracy into which we have fallen. The enormous evil which such opinions have brought about, is well understood by those who have studied the history of countries in which they are, and have been, most prevalent. Hence it is that, among the innumerable benefits derived from advancing knowledge, there are few more important than those improved facilities of communication, which, by increasing the frequency with which nations and individuals are brought into contact, have, to an extraordinary extent, corrected their prejudices, raised the opinion which each forms of the other, diminished their mutual hostility, and thus diffusing a more favourable view of our common nature, have stimulated us to develop those boundless resources of the human understanding, the very existence of which it was once considered almost a heresy to assert.

This is precisely what has occurred in modern Europe. The French and English people have, by the mere force of increased contact, learned to think more favourably of each other, and to discard that foolish contempt in which both nations formerly indulged. In this, as in all cases, the better one civilized country is acquainted with another, the more it will find to respect and to imitate. For of all the causes of national hatred, ignorance is the most powerful. When you increase the contact, you remove the ignorance, and thus you diminish the hatred. This is the true bond of charity; and it is worth all the lessons which moralists and divines are able to teach. They have pursued their vocation for centuries, without producing the least effect in lessening the frequency of war. But it may be said without the slightest exaggeration, that every new railroad which is laid down, and every fresh steamer which crosses the Channel, are additional guarantees for the preservation of that long and unbroken peace which, during forty years, has knit together the fortunes and the interests of the two most civilized nations of the earth. . . .

Such are the three great modes or channels by which the progress of knowledge has weakened the old warlike spirit; and the way in which they have effected this has, I trust, been clearly pointed out. The facts and arguments which I have brought forward, have, I can conscientiously say, been subjected to careful and repeated scrutiny; and I am quite unable to see on what possible ground their accuracy is to be impugned. That they will be disagreeable to certain classes,

I am well aware; but the unpleasantness of a statement is hardly to be considered a proof of its falsehood. The sources from which the evidence has been derived are fully indicated; and the arguments, I hope, fairly stated. And from them there results a most important conclusion. From them we are bound to infer, that the two oldest, greatest, most inveterate, and most widely-spread evils which have ever been known, are constantly, though, on the whole, slowly, diminishing; and that their diminution has been effected, not at all by moral feelings, nor by moral teachings, but solely by the activity of the human intellect, and by the inventions and discoveries which, in a long course of successive ages, man has been able to make.

NOTES

(1) The consequences of the invention of gunpowder are considered very superficially by Frederick Schlegel (*Lectures on the History of Literature*, vol. ii. pp. 37, 38) and by Dugald Stewart (*Philosophy of the Mind*, vol. i. p. 262). They are examined with much greater ability, though by no means exhaustively, in *Smith's Wealth of Nations*, Book v. chap. i. pp. 292, 296, 297; *Herder's Ideen zur Geschichte der Menschheit*, vol. iv. p. 301; *Hallam's Middle Ages*, vol. ii. p. 470.

(2) From the following authorities, it appears impossible to trace it further back than the thirteenth century; and it is doubtful whether the Arabs were, as is commonly supposed, the inventors: *Humboldt's Cosmos*, vol. ii. p. 590; *Koch, Tableaux des Révolutions*, vol. i. p. 242; *Beckmann's History of Inventions*, 1846, vol. ii. p. 505; *Histoire Lit. de la France*, vol. i. p. 236; *Thompson's History of Chemistry*, vol. i. p. 36; *Hallam's Middle Ages*, vol. i. p. 341. The statements in *Erman's Siberia*, vol. i. pp. 370, 371, are more positive than the evidence we are possessed of will justify; but there can be no doubt that a sort of gunpowder was at an early period used in China, and in other parts of Asia.

(3) *Vattel, le Droit des Gens,* vol. ii. p. 129; *Lingard's History of England*, vol. ii. pp. 356, 357. Among the Anglo Saxons, 'all free men and proprietors of land, except the ministers of religion, were trained to the use of arms, and always held ready to take the field at a moment's warning.' *Eccleston's English Antiquities*, p. 62. 'There was no distinction between the soldier and the citizen.' *Palgrave's Anglo-Saxon Commonwealth*, vol. i. p. 200.

(4) On these warlike ecclesiastics, compare *Grose's Military Antiq.*, vol. i. pp. 67–8; *Lingard's Hist. of England*, vol. ii. pp. 26, 183, vol. iii. p. 14; *Turner's Hist. of England*, vol. iv. p. 458, vol. v. pp. 92, 402, 406; *Mosheim's Eccl. History*, vol. i. pp. 173, 193, 241; *Crichton's Scandinavia*, Edinb. 1838, vol. i. p. 220. Such opponents were the more formidable, because in those happy days it was sacrilege for a layman to lay hands on a bishop. In 1095 his Holiness the Pope caused a council to declare, 'Quod qui apprehenderit episcopum omnino exlex fiat.' *Matthaei Paris Historia Major*, p. 18. As the context contains no limitation of this, it would follow that a man became spiritually outlawed if he, even in self-defence, took a bishop a prisoner.

(5) As Sharon Turner observes of England under the Anglo-Saxon government, 'war and religion were the absorbing subjects of this period.' *Turner's History of England*, vol. iii. p. 263. And a recent scientific historian says of Europe generally: 'alle Künste und Kenntnisse, die sich nicht auf das edle Kriegs-, Rauf-und Raubhandwerk bezogen, waren überflüssig und schädlich. Nur etwas Theologie war vonnöthen, um die Erde mit dem Himmel zu verbinden'. *Winckler, Geschichte der Botanik*, 1854, p. 56.

(6) In 1181, Henry II of England ordered that every man should have either a sword or bow; which he was not to sell, but leave to his heir: 'caeteri autem omnes haberent wanbasiam, capellum ferreum, lanceam et gladium, vel arcum et sagittas: et prohibuit ne aliquis arma sua venderet vel invadiaret; sed cum moreretur, daret illa propinquiori haeredi suo.' *Rog. de Hov. Annal, in Scriptores post Bedam*, p. 348 rev. In the reign of Edward I., it was ordered that every man possessing land to the value of forty shillings should keep 'a sword, bow and arrows, and a dagger. . . . Those who were to keep bows and arrows might have them out of the forest.' *Grose's Military Antiquities*, vol. ii. pp. 301, 302. Compare *Geijer's History of the Swedes*, part i. p. 94. Even late in the fifteenth century, there were at the Universities of Oxford and Cambridge, 'in each from four to five thousand scholars, all grown up, carrying swords and bows, and in great part gentry.' *Sir William Hamilton on the History of Universities*, in *Hamilton's Philosoph. Discussions*, p. 414. One of the latest attempts made to revive archery was a warrant issued by Elizabeth in 1596, and printed by Mr. Collier in the *Egerton Papers*, pp. 217–220, edit. Camden Soc. 1840. In the south-west of England, bows and arrows did not finally

disappear from the muster-rolls till 1599; and in the meantime the musket gained ground. See *Yonge's Diary*, edit. Camden Soc. 1848, p. xvii.

(7) It is stated by many writers that no gunpowder was manufactured in England until the reign of Elizabeth. *Camden's Elizabeth*, in *Kennett's History,* vol. ii. p. 388, London, 1719; *Strickland's Queens of England*, vol. vi. p. 223, Lond. 1843; *Grose's Military Antiquities*, vol. i. p. 378. But Sharon Turner (*History of England,* vol. vi. pp. 490, 491, Lond. 1839) has shown, from an order of Richard III in the Harleian manuscripts, that it was made in England in 1483; and Mr. Eccleston (*English Antiquities*, p. 182, Lond. 1847) states, that the English both made and exported it as early as 1411: compare p. 202. At all events, it long remained a costly article; and even in the reign of Charles I, I find a complaint of its dearness, 'whereby the train-bands are much discouraged in their exercising.' *Parliament Hist*., vol. ii. p. 655. In 1686, it appears from the *Clarendon Correspondence*, vol. i. p. 413, that the wholesale price ranged from about £2.10s. to £3. per barrel. On the expense of making it in the present century, see *Liebig and Kopp's Reports on Chemistry*, vol. iii. p. 325, Lond. 1852.

(8) The muskets were such miserable machines, that, in the middle of the fifteenth century, it took a quarter of an hour to charge and fire one. *Hallam's Middle Ages*, vol. i. p. 342. Grose (*Military Antiquities*, vol. i. p. 146, vol. ii. pp. 292, 337) says, that the first mention of muskets in England is in 1471; and that rests for them did not become obsolete until the reign of Charles I. In the recent edition of *Beckmann's History of Inventions*, Lond. 1846, vol. ii. p. 535, it is strangely supposed that muskets were 'first used at the battle of Pavia.' Compare *Daniel, Histoire de la Milice*, vol. i. p. 464, with *Smythe's Military Discourses*, in *Ellis's Original Letters*, p. 53, edit. Camden Society.

(9) Pistols are said to have been invented early in the sixteenth century. *Grose's Military Antiq*., vol. i. pp. 102, 146. Gunpowder was first employed in mining towns in 1487. *Prescott's Hist. of Ferdinand and Isabella,* vol. ii. p. 32; *Koch, Tableaux des Révolutions,* vol. i. p. 243; *Daniel, Histoire de la Milice Française*, vol. i. p. 574. Daniel (*Milice Française*, vol. i. pp. 580, 581) says that bombs were not invented till 1588; the same thing is asserted in *Biographie Universelle*, vol. xv. p. 248: but, according to Grose (*Military Antiq.,* vol. i. p. 387), they are mentioned by Valturinus in 1472. On the general condition of the French artillery in the sixteenth century, see *Relations des Ambassa-*

deurs Venitiens, vol. i. pp. 94, 476, 478, Paris, 1838, 4to: a curious and valuable publication. There is some doubt as to the exact period in which cannons were first known; but they were certainly used in war before the middle of the fourteenth century. See *Bohlen, das alte Indien*, vol. ii. p. 63; *Daniel, Histoire de la Milice*, vol. i. pp. 441, 442.

(10) *Blackstone's Commentaries*, vol. i. p. 413; *Daniel, Hist. de la Milice*, vol. i. p. 210, vol. ii. pp. 491, 493; *Oeuvres de Turgot*, vol. viii. p. 228.

(11) The leading facts respecting the employment of mercenary troops are indicated with great judgment by Mr. Hallam, in his *Middle Ages*, vol. i. p. 328–337.

(12) Grose (*Military Antiquities*, vol. i. pp. 310, 311) says, that until the sixteenth century, English soldiers had no professional dress, but 'were distinguished by badges of their leader's arms, similar to those now worn by watermen.' It was also early in the sixteenth century that there first arose a separate military literature. *Daniel, Hist. de la Milice*, vol. i. p. 380: 'Les auteurs, qui ont écrit en détail sur la discipline militaire: or ce n'est guères que sous François I, et sous l'Empereur Charles V, que les Italiens, les François, les Espagnols et les Allemans ont commencé à écrire sur ce sujet.'

(13) The change from the time when every layman was a soldier, is very remarkable. Adam Smith (*Wealth of Nations*, book v. chap. i. p. 291) says, 'Among the civilized nations of modern Europe, it is commonly computed, that not more than the one-hundredth part of the inhabitants of any country can be employed as soldiers, without ruin to the country which pays the expense of their service.' The same proportion is given in *Sadler's Law of Population*, vol. i. p. 292; and in *Grandeur et Décadence des Romains*, chap. iii—*Oeuvres de Montesquieu*—p. 130: also in *Sharpe's History of Egypt*, vol. i. p. 105; and in *Alison's History of Europe*, vol. xii. p. 318.

JAMES ANTHONY FROUDE

1818–1894

The execution of Mary, Queen of Scots, is one of the set pieces of English literature, not merely of English history, and it is an indication of the unique effectiveness of Froude's style that it fits with complete naturalness into his narrative as a whole, and this in a volume which follows (and frequently paraphrases) the sources particularly closely. Froude can be said to have invented the modern narrative style and remains a model of how to work from a basis of dense documentation, and use much direct quotation, without sacrificing ease and a direct, personal tone. This passage comes from chapter 71 in the last volume of his History of England, *first published in 1870.*

Froude's lectures "The Science of History" and "Scientific method as applied to history" are printed in Short Studies on Great Subjects, *volumes 1 and 2 (various editions). I do not know of any adequate work on Froude's historical method since F. Harrison's "The Historical Method of Froude," in* The Nineteenth Century, *vol. 44, 1898.*

MEANWHILE as the weeks had passed on, Mary Stuart's confidence had returned. She had nerved herself for the worst and had dared it. Believre had written, entreating her to make her peace with the Queen before it was too late; her fate was still in her own hands. But she feared that she might be betrayed. A confession would disqualify her for the martyr's attitude which, if she was to die, she meant to assume; and though she interpreted a sound of hammers in the hall into the

erection of a scaffold, she had remained defiant. Day had followed day, and she had heard no more. She understood Elizabeth as well as Elizabeth understood her. Her almoner had been permitted to resume his duties, and the unwelcome offer of an English minister had not been again obtruded upon her. She had written Elizabeth one of her most pathetic letters, protesting and swearing her innocence, attributing the accusations against her to a conspiracy of the Puritans, hinting in her old way that she had secrets of the gravest moment to impart to her if she could but communicate with her in private, and addressing her in a tone in which affection and tender reproach were melted into resignation.

No answer had been sent, but she had counted justly on the effect it would produce. 'There has been a letter,' said Leicester, 'which hath wrought tears.'

The blow when it came at last therefore came suddenly. Beale rode hard—for unless, which is unlikely, he trusted the letter to Kent to a second hand he called at Wrest on his way down—and he arrived at Fotheringay on Sunday evening. The purpose of his coming was not made known in the castle. Early on Monday he went in search of Lord Shrewsbury, while a message was despatched to the Sheriff of Northamptonshire to be in attendance on Wednesday morning. On Monday evening the Earl of Kent came. Shrewsbury appeared on Tuesday before noon, and when the early castle dinner was over, they sent a servant to the Queen of Scots with a request to be admitted to her presence.

Shrewsbury had not seen her since she had passed from under his charge. He had not been on the Commission which tried her; illness had prevented him from attending the last Parliament, and he had taken no public part in the prosecution; and although he had signified privately as his personal opinion that her death was necessary, it could not have been without emotion that he was once more brought into a brief relation with her in so terrible a form. Kent was an austere Puritan, to whom she was merely a wicked woman overtaken at last by the punishment which she had too long deserved and escaped.

Briefly, solemnly, and sternly they delivered their awful message. They informed her that they had received a commission under the great seal to see her executed, and she was told that she must prepare to suffer on the following morning.

She was dreadfully agitated. For a moment she refused to believe them. Then, as the truth forced itself upon her, tossing her head in

disdain and struggling to control herself, she called her physician and began to speak to him of money that was owed to her in France. At last it seems that she broke down altogether, and they left her with a fear either that she would destroy herself in the night, or that she would refuse to come to the scaffold, and that it might be necessary to drag her there by violence.

The end had come. She had long professed to expect it, but the clearest expectation is not certainty. The scene for which she had affected to prepare she was to encounter in its dread reality, and all her busy schemes, her dreams of vengeance, her visions of a revolution, with herself ascending out of the convulsion and seating herself on her rival's throne—all were gone. She had played deep, and the dice had gone against her.

Yet in death, if she encountered it bravely, victory was still possible. Could she but sustain to the last the character of a calumniated suppliant accepting heroically for God's sake and her creed's the concluding stroke of a long series of wrongs, she might stir a tempest of indignation which, if it could not save herself, might at least overwhelm her enemy. Persisting, as she persisted to the last, in denying all knowledge of Babington, it would be affectation to credit her with a genuine feeling of religion; but the imperfection of her motive exalts the greatness of her fortitude. To an impassioned believer death is comparatively easy.

Her chaplain was lodged in a separate part of the castle. The Commissioners, who were as anxious that her execution should wear its real character as she was herself determined to convert it into a martyrdom, refused, perhaps unwisely, to allow him access to her, and offered her again the assistance of an Anglican Dean. They gave her an advantage over them which she did not fail to use. She would not let the Dean come near her. She sent a note to the chaplain telling him that she had meant to receive the sacrament, but as it might not be she must content herself with a general confession. She bade him watch through the night and pray for her. In the morning when she was brought out she might perhaps see him, and receive his blessing on her knees. She supped cheerfully, giving her last meal with her attendants a character of sacred parting; afterwards she drew aside her apothecary M. Gorion, and asked him if she might depend upon his fidelity. When he satisfied her that she might trust him, she said she had a letter and two diamonds which she wished to send to Mendoza. He undertook to melt some drug and conceal them in it where they would never be looked for, and

promised to deliver them faithfully. One of the jewels was for Mendoza himself; the other and the largest was for Philip. It was to be a sign that she was dying for the truth, and was meant also to bespeak his care for her friends and servants. Every one of them so far as she was able, without forgetting a name, she commended to his liberality. Arundel, Paget, Morgan, the Archbishop of Glasgow, Westmoreland, Throgmorton, the Bishop of Ross, her two secretaries, the ladies who had shared the trials of her imprisonment, she remembered them all, and specified the sums which she desired Philip to bestow on them. And as Mary Stuart then and throughout her life never lacked gratitude to those who had been true to her, so then as always she remembered her enemies. There was no cant about her, no unreal talk of forgiveness of injuries. She bade Gorion tell Philip it was her last prayer that he should persevere, notwithstanding her death, in the invasion of England. It was God's quarrel, she said, and worthy of his greatness; and as soon as he had conquered it, she desired him not to forget how she had been treated by Cecil, and Leicester, and Walsingham; by Lord Huntingdon, who had ill-used her fifteen years before at Tutbury; by Sir Amyas Paulet, and Secretary Wade.

Her last night was a busy one. As she said herself, there was much to be done and the time was short. A few lines to the King of France were dated two hours after midnight. They were to insist for the last time that she was innocent of the conspiracy, that she was dying for religion, and for having asserted her right to the crown; and to beg that out of the sum which he owed her, her servants' wages might be paid, and masses provided for her soul. After this she slept for three or four hours, and then rose and with the most elaborate care prepared to encounter the end.

At eight in the morning the Provost-marshal knocked at the outer door which communicated with her suite of apartments. It was locked and no one answered, and he went back in some trepidation lest the fears might prove true which had been entertained the preceding evening. On his returning with the sheriff however a few minutes later, the door was open, and they were confronted with the tall majestic figure of Mary Stuart standing before them in splendour. The plain grey dress had been exchanged for a robe of black satin; her jacket was of black satin also, looped and slashed and trimmed with velvet. Her false hair was arranged studiously with a coif, and over her head and falling down over her back was a white veil of delicate lawn. A crucifix of gold hung from her neck. In her hand she held a crucifix of ivory,

and a number of jewelled paternosters was attached to her girdle. Led by two of Paulet's gentlemen, the Sheriff walking before her, she passed to the chamber of presence in which she had been tried, where Shrewsbury, Kent, Paulet, Drury, and others were waiting to receive her. Andrew Melville, Sir Robert's brother, who had been master of her household, was kneeling in tears. 'Melville,' she said, 'you should rather rejoice than weep that the end of my troubles is come. Tell my friends I die a true Catholic. Commend me to my son. Tell him I have done nothing to prejudice his kingdom of Scotland, and so, good Melville, farewell.' She kissed him, and turning asked for her chaplain du Preau. He was not present. There had been a fear of some religious melodrama which it was thought well to avoid. Her ladies, who had attempted to follow her, had been kept back also. She could not afford to leave the account of her death to be reported by enemies and Puritans, and she required assistance for the scene which she meditated. Missing them she asked for the reason of their absence, and said she wished them to see her die. Kent said he feared they might scream or faint, or attempt perhaps to dip their handkerchiefs in her blood. She undertook that they should be quiet and obedient. 'The Queen,' she said, 'would never deny her so slight a request;' and when Kent still hesitated, she added with tears, 'You know I am cousin to your Queen, of the blood of Henry the Seventh, a married Queen of France, and anointed Queen of Scotland.'

It was impossible to refuse. She was allowed to take six of her own people with her, and select them herself. She chose her physician Burgoyne, Andrew Melville, the apothecary Gorion, and her surgeon, with two ladies, Elizabeth Kennedy and and Curle's young wife Barbara Mowbray, whose child she had baptized.

'Allons donc,' she then said—'Let us go,' and passing out attended by the Earls, and leaning on the arm of an officer of the guard, she descended the great staircase to the hall. The news had spread far through the country. Thousands of people were collected outside the walls. About three hundred knights and gentlemen of the county had been admitted to witness the execution. The tables and forms had been removed, and a great wood fire was blazing in the chimney. At the upper end of the hall, above the fire-place, but near it, stood the scaffold, twelve feet square and two feet and a half high. It was covered with black cloth; a low rail ran round it covered with black cloth also, and the Sheriff's guard of halberdiers were ranged on the floor below on the four sides to keep off the crowd. On the scaffold was

the block, black like the rest; a square black cushion was placed behind it, and behind the cushion a black chair; on the right were two other chairs for the Earls. The axe leant against the rail, and two masked figures stood like mutes on either side at the back. The Queen of Scots as she swept in seemed as if coming to take a part in some solemn pageant. Not a muscle of her face could be seen to quiver; she ascended the scaffold with absolute composure, looked round her smiling, and sat down. Shrewsbury and Kent followed and took their places, the Sheriff stood at her left hand, and Beale then mounted a platform and read the warrant aloud.

In all the assembly Mary Stuart appeared the person least interested in the words which were consigning her to death.

'Madam,' said Lord Shrewsbury to her, when the reading was ended, 'you hear what we are commanded to do.'

'You will do your duty,' she answered, and rose as if to kneel and pray.

The Dean of Peterborough, Dr. Fletcher, approached the rail. 'Madam,' he began, with a low obeisance, 'the Queen's most excellent Majesty;' 'Madam, the Queen's most excellent Majesty'—thrice he commenced his sentence, wanting words to pursue it. When he repeated the words a fourth time, she cut him short.

'Mr. Dean,' she said, 'I am a Catholic, and must die a Catholic. It is useless to attempt to move me, and your prayers will avail me but little.'

'Change your opinion, Madam,' he cried, his tongue being loosed at last; 'repent of your sins, settle your faith in Christ, by him to be saved.'

'Trouble not yourself further, Mr. Dean,' she answered; 'I am settled in my own faith, for which I mean to shed my blood.'

'I am sorry, Madam,' said Shrewsbury, 'to see you so addicted to Popery.'

'That image of Christ you hold there,' said Kent, 'will not profit you if he be not engraved in your heart.'

She did not reply, and turning her back on Fletcher knelt for her own devotions.

He had been evidently instructed to impair the Catholic complexion of the scene, and the Queen of Scots was determined that he should not succeed. When she knelt he commenced an extempore prayer in which the assembly joined. As his voice sounded out in the hall she raised her own, reciting with powerful deep-chested tones the penitential Psalms in Latin, introducing English sentences at intervals, that

the audience might know what she was saying, and praying with especial distinctness for her holy father the Pope.

From time to time, with conspicuous vehemence, she struck the crucifix against her bosom, and then, as the Dean gave up the struggle, leaving her Latin, she prayed in English wholly, still clear and loud. She prayed for the Church which she had been ready to betray, for her son, whom she had disinherited, for the Queen whom she had endeavoured to murder. She prayed God to avert his wrath from England, that England which she had sent a last message to Philip to beseech him to invade. She forgave her enemies, whom she had invited Philip not to forget, and then, praying to the saints to intercede for her with Christ, and kissing the crucifix and crossing her own breast, 'Even as thy arms, oh Jesus,' she cried, 'were spread upon the cross, so receive me into thy mercy and forgive my sins.'

With these words she rose; the black mutes stepped forward, and in the usual form begged her forgiveness.

'I forgive you,' she said, 'for now I hope you shall end all my troubles.' They offered their help in arranging her dress. 'Truly, my Lords,' she said with a smile to the Earls, 'I never had such grooms waiting on me before.' Her ladies were allowed to come up upon the scaffold to assist her; for the work to be done was considerable, and had been prepared with no common thought.

She laid her crucifix on her chair. The chief executioner took it as a perquisite, but was ordered instantly to lay it down. The lawn veil was lifted carefully off, not to disturb the hair, and was hung upon the rail. The black robe was next removed. Below it was a petticoat of crimson velvet. The black jacket followed, and under the jacket was a body of crimson satin. One of her ladies handed her a pair of crimson sleeves, with which she hastily covered her arms; and thus she stood on the black scaffold with the black figures all around her, blood-red from head to foot.

Her reasons for adopting so extraordinary a costume must be left to conjecture. It is only certain that it must have been carefully studied, and that the pictorial effect must have been appalling.

The women, whose firmness had hitherto borne the trial, began now to give way, spasmodic sobs bursting from them which they could not check. 'Nc criez vous,' she said, 'j'ay promis pour vous.' Struggling bravely, they crossed their breasts again and again, she crossing them in turn and bidding them pray for her. Then she knelt on the cushion. Barbara Mowbray bound her eyes with a handkerchief.

'Adieu,' she said, smiling for the last time and waving her hand to them. 'Adieu, au revoir.' They stepped back from off the scaffold and left her alone. On her knees she repeated the Psalm, In te, Domine, confido, 'In Thee, O Lord, have I put my trust.' Her shoulders being exposed, two scars became visible, one on either side, and the Earls being now a little behind her, Kent pointed to them with his white wand and looked enquiringly at his companion. Shrewsbury whispered that they were the remains of two abscesses from which she had suffered while living with him at Sheffield.

When the psalm was finished she felt for the block, and laying down her head muttered: 'In manus, Domine tuas, commendo animam meam.' The hard wood seemed to hurt her, for she placed her hands under her neck. The executioners gently removed them, lest they should deaden the blow, and then one of them holding her slightly, the other raised the axe and struck. The scene had been too trying even for the practised headsman of the Tower. His arm wandered. The blow fell on the knot of the handkerchief, and scarcely broke the skin. She neither spoke nor moved. He struck again, this time effectively. The head hung by a shred of skin, which he divided without withdrawing the axe; and at once a metamorphosis was witnessed, strange as was ever wrought by wand of fabled enchanter. The coif fell off and the false plaits. The laboured illusion vanished. The lady who had knelt before the block was in the maturity of grace and loveliness. The executioner, when he raised the head, as usual, to show it to the crowd, exposed the withered features of a grizzled, wrinkled old woman.

'So perish all enemies of the Queen,' said the Dean of Peterborough. A loud Amen rose over the hall. 'Such end,' said the Earl of Kent, rising and standing over the body, 'to the Queen's and the Gospel's enemies.'

Orders had been given that everything which she had worn should be immediately destroyed, that no relics should be carried off to work imaginary miracles. Sentinels stood at the doors who allowed no one to pass out without permission; and after the first pause, the Earls still keeping their places, the body was stripped. It then appeared that a favourite lapdog had followed its mistress unperceived, and was concealed under her clothes; when discovered it gave a short cry, and seated itself between the head and the neck, from which the blood was still flowing. It was carried away and carefully washed, and then beads, Paternoster, handkerchief—each particle of dress which the blood had touched, with the cloth on the block and on the scaffold,

was burnt in the hall fire in the presence of the crowd. The scaffold itself was next removed; a brief account of the execution was drawn up, with which Henry Talbot, Lord Shrewsbury's son, was sent to London, and then every one was dismissed. Silence settled down on Fotheringay, and the last scene of the life of Mary Stuart, in which tragedy and melodrama were so strangely intermingled, was over.

A spectator, who was one of her warmest admirers, describes her bearing as infinitely transcending the power of the most accomplished actor to represent. The association of the stage was perhaps unconsciously suggested by what was in fact, notwithstanding the tremendous reality with which it closed, the most brilliant acting throughout. The plain grey dress would have sufficed, had she cared only to go through with simplicity the part which was assigned her. She intended to produce a dramatic sensation, and she succeeded. The self-possession was faultless, the courage splendid. Never did any human creature meet death more bravely; yet, in the midst of the admiration and pity which cannot be refused her, it is not to be forgotten that she was leaving the world with a lie upon her lips. She was a bad woman, disguised in the livery of a martyr, and, if in any sense at all she was suffering for her religion, it was because she had shown herself capable of those detestable crimes which in the sixteenth century appeared to be the proper fruits of it.

To assume and to carry through the character of a victim of religious intolerance, to exhibit herself as an example of saintliness, suffering for devotion to the truth, would be to win the victory over Elizabeth, even in defeat and death to fasten upon her the reputation of a persecutor, which she had most endeavoured to avoid, to stamp her name with infamy, and possibly drag her down to destruction.

Nor can it be said that she failed. She could not indeed stay the progress of the Reformation, make England a province of Spain, or arrest the dissolution of an exploded creed; but she became a fitting tutelary saint for the sentimental Romanism of the modern world. She has had her revenge, if not on Elizabeth living, yet on her memory in the annals of her country, and English history will continue, probably to the end of time, to represent the treatment of Mary Stuart, which, if it erred at all, erred from the beginning on the side of leniency and weakness, as the one indelible stain on the reputation of the great Queen.

'Who now doubts,' writes an eloquent modern writer, 'that it would have been wiser in Elizabeth to spare her life?' Rather, the political

wisdom of a critical and difficult act has never in the world's history been more signally justified. It cut away the only interest on which the Scotch and English Catholics could possibly have combined. It determined Philip upon the undisguised pursuit of the English throne, and it enlisted against him and his projects the passionate patriotism of the English nobility, who refused to be tempted, even by their creed, to betray the independence of their country. At once and for ever it destroyed the hope that the Spanish Armada would find a party to welcome it. The entire Catholic organization, as directed against England, was smitten with paralysis; and the Queen found herself, when the invader arrived at last, supported by the loyal enthusiasm of an undivided nation.

WILLIAM STUBBS

1825–1901

This character of Henry II is taken from the beginning of the preface to volume two of Stubbs's edition of The Chronicle of "Benedict of Peterborough" *in the Rolls series (1867). In the same year he gave his inaugural lecture at Oxford in which he described himself as "a worker at history." The preface brilliantly gives the lie to any Dryasdust implications in this phrase.*

The best of Stubbs's prefaces are brought together in Historical Introductions to the Rolls Series, *edited by A. Hassall (1902). On Stubbs as a historian see Helen Cam, "Stubbs Seventy Years later," in* Cambridge Historical Journal, *1948; J. G. Edwards,* William Stubbs, *Historical Association pamphlet (1952).*

IT IS ALMOST a matter of necessity for the student of history to work out for himself some definite idea of the characters of the great men of the period he is employed upon. History cannot be well read as a chess problem, and the man who tries to read it so is not worthy to read it at all. Its scenes cannot be realised, its lessons cannot be learned, if the actors are looked on merely as puppets. A living interest must invest those who played a part in making the world what it is: those whose very existence has left indelible traces on its history must have had characteristics worthy of the most careful investigation.

Such a judgment as may be formed in the nineteenth century, of a king of the twelfth may well seem unsatisfactory. With the utmost

pains it is hard to persuade ourselves that a true view is obtained, or is even obtainable. We know too little of his personal actions to be able in many cases to distinguish between them and those of his advisers; or to say whether he was a man of weak will or of strong; whether his good deeds proceeded from fear or from virtue, or from the love of praise; whether his bad ones were the workings of hasty impulse, or the breaking out of concealed habit, or the result of a long struggle between good motives and evil passions.

Neither can we accept the delineations of contemporary writers without carefully testing them at every step. They are almost always superficial, but if that were the only fault we might be content to accept them as the verdict of ordinary judges, and it is always satisfactory to know what a man's contemporaries thought of him, even if they were neither close observers nor judicious critics. But their descriptions are seldom to be trusted even in this respect, for they betray almost universally a bias for or against the hero. The one in a thousand who is so far removed from personal feeling as to wish to take a philosophical or consistent view, is probably too far removed from acquaintance to be able to distinguish the truth from falsehood. The contemporary historian cannot view the career of his leading character as a whole; he sees it too closely, or else he sees it through a distorting medium. Hence the unsearchableness of the king's heart is so often given by mediaeval writers as the reason for measures the bent of which they do not see, and as to which, for the want of acquaintance with other acts of the same kind, they cannot generalise.

The heart of kings is unsearchable; but on the other hand their freedom of action is, or rather was in the middle ages, uncontrolled by external restraints. In them, as in no other men, can the outward conduct be safely assumed to be the unrestrained expression of the inward character. It is from observing the general current of the life, from the examination of the recorded acts of it, that the only reasonable view of the character can be obtained. Standing too far off in time and mode of thought to be in much danger of imputing modern principles and motives, we can generalise somewhat as to the inward life of a man if we know what his outward life was; and then we can compare our conclusion with the judgment of contemporaries, and see whether such men as they were would be likely to think as they have done of such a man as we have described to ourselves.

If we know enough of the facts of a man's life we can draw such a picture. Character that is not shown in act is not strong enough to

be worthy of the name. The man whose character is worthy study must be one whose acts bear the marks of character. In the view of a long life, some generalisations can almost always be drawn, from the repetition of acts, from the uniformity or uncertainty of policy. A king who lets his advisers act for him in one case will show the like weakness in others; will act in different ways under different personal influences. But one who all his life chooses his counsellors on one principle, and follows with them a uniform line of policy, chooses them because he approves their policy, or rather because they will carry out his own. And that policy, if such be traceable, is the expression of the strongest principles of his own character; it may be confused or perplexed by his minor traits, but it cannot be suppressed by them, and if it exists it will be seen in operation.

A careful reading of the history of the three centuries of Angevin kings might almost tempt one to think that the legend of their diabolical origin and hereditary curse was not a mere fairy tale, but the mythical expression of some political foresight or of a strong historical instinct. But, in truth, no such theory is needed; the vices of kings, like those of other men, carry with them their present punishment; whilst with them, even more signally than with other men, the accumulation of subsequent misery is distinctly conspicuous, and is seen to fall with a weight more overwhelming the longer their strength or their position has kept it poised.

It was not that their wickedness was of a monstrous kind; such wickedness indeed was not a prominent feature in the character of the mediaeval devil; nor was it mere capricious cruelty or wanton mischief. Neither were their misfortunes of the appalling sort wrought out by the Furies of Attic tragedy. Of such misery there were not wanting instances, but not enough to give more than an occasional luridness to the picture. Nor was it, as in the case of the Stewarts, that the momentum of inherited misfortune and misery had become a conscious influence under which no knightly or kingly qualities could maintain hope, and a meaner nature sought a refuge in recklessness. All the Plantagenet kings were high-hearted men, rather rebellious against circumstances than subservient to them. But the long pageant shows us uniformly, under so great a variety of individual character, such signs of great gifts and opportunities thrown away, such unscrupulousness in action, such uncontrolled passion, such vast energy and strength wasted on unworthy aims, such constant failure and final disappointment, in spite of constant successes and brilliant

achievements, as remind us of the conduct and luck of those unhappy spirits who, throughout the middle ages, were continually spending superhuman strength in building in a night inaccessible bridges and uninhabitable castles, or purchasing with untold treasures souls that might have been had for nothing, and invariably cheated of their reward.

Only two in the whole list strike us as free from the hereditary sins: Edward I and Henry VI, the noblest and the unhappiest of the race; and of these the former owes his real greatness in history, not to the success of his personal ambition, but to the brilliant qualities brought out by the exigencies of his affairs; whilst on the latter, both as a man and as a king, fell the heaviest crash of accumulated misery. None of the others seem to have had a wish to carry out the true grand conception of kingship. And thus it is with the extinction of the male line of Plantagenet that the social happiness of the English people begins. Even Henry VII, though, perhaps, as selfish a man as any of his predecessors, and certainly less cared for or beloved, seems to open an era during which the vices of the monarchs have been less disastrous to their subjects than before, and the prosperity of the state has increased in no proportion to the ability of the kings.

And yet no two of these princes were alike in the constituent proportions of their temperament. The leading feature of one was falsehood, of another cruelty, of another licentiousness, of another unscrupulous ambition: one was the slave of women, another of unworthy favourites; one a raiser of taxes, another a shedder of the blood of his people. Yet there was not one thoroughly contemptible person in the list. Many had redeeming qualities, some had great ones; all had a certain lion-like nobility, some had a portion of the real elements of greatness. Some were wise; all were brave; some were pure in life, some gentle as well as strong; but is it too hard to say that all were thoroughly selfish, all were in the main unfortunate?

In the character of Henry II are found all the characteristics of this race. Not the greatest, nor the wisest, nor the worst, nor the most unfortunate, he still unites all these in their greatest relative proportions. Not so impetuous as Richard, or Edward III, or Henry V; not so wise as Edward I; not so luxurious as John or Edward IV; not so false as Henry III, nor so greedy as Henry IV, nor so cruel as the princes of the house of York; he was still eminently wise and brave, eminently cruel, lascivious, greedy, and false, and eminently unfor-

tunate also, if the ruin of all the selfish aims of his sagacious plans, the disappointment of his affections, and the sense of having lost his soul for nothing, can be called misfortune.

It would be a great mistake to view the personal and political character of Henry as one of unmingled vice. It was a strange compound of inconsistent qualities rather than a balance of opposing ones, yet the inconsistencies were so compounded as to make him restless rather than purposeless, and the opposing qualities were balanced sufficiently to suffer him to carry out a consistent policy. His fortunes, therefore, bear the impress of the man. He was a brave and consummate warrior, yet he never carried on war on a large scale, or hesitated to accept the first overtures of peace. He was impetuous and unscrupulous, yet he never tempted fortune. He was violent in hatred, yet moderate in revenge; a lover of good men, a corrupter of innocent women; at once religious and profane, lawless and scrupulous of right; a maker of good laws, and a seller of justice; the most patient and provoking of husbands; the most indulgent and exacting of fathers; playing with the children, whose ingratitude was breaking his heart, the great game of statecraft as if they had been pawns. He was tyrannical in mood without being a tyrant either in principle or in the exigencies of policy. In power and character, by position and alliances, the arbiter of Western Europe in both war and peace, he never waged a great war or enjoyed a sound peace; he never until his last year made an unsatisfactory peace or fought an unsuccessful battle. The most able and successful politician of his time, and thoroughly unscrupulous about using his power for his own ends, he yet died in a position less personally important than any that he had occupied during the thirty-five years of his reign, and, on the whole, less powerful than he began. Yet if we could distinguish between the man and the king, between personal selfishness and official or political statesmanship, between the ruin of his personal aims and the real success of his administrative conceptions, we might conclude by saying that altogether he was great and wise and successful.

In so mixed a character it would be strange if partial judges could not find much to praise and much to blame. In the eyes of a friend the abilities of Henry excuse his vices, and the veriest experiments of political sagacity wear the aspect of inventions of profound philanthropic devotion. To the enemy the same measures are the transparent disguise of a crafty and greedy spirit anxious only for selfish aggrandisement. The constitutional historian cannot help looking with

reverence on one under whose hand the foundations of liberty and national independence were so clearly marked and so deeply laid that in the course of one generation the fabric was safe for ever from tyrants or conquerors. The partisan of ecclesiastical immunities or monastic discipline can see in him only the apostate and the persecutor. The pure moralist inclines to scrutinise personal vices and to give too little credit to political merit. It is by such that the character of Henry has for the most part been written. Whilst we accept the particulars in which they agree, we may, without pretending to be free from prejudice, attempt to draw from our own survey of his acts a more probable theory of the man and of his work on the age and nation.

Interpreted by the history of his acts, the main purpose of Henry's life is clear. That was the consolidation of the kingly power in his own hands. Putting aside the disproportioned estimate of his ambition formed by contemporary writers, and encouraged perhaps by some careless or ostentatious words of his own, we see in that purpose no very towering idea of conquest, or shortsighted appetite for tyranny. If ambition were ever really his ruling passion, it was one which he concealed so well that its definite object cannot be guessed, which at an early period of his reign he must have dismissed as impracticable, and which never led him to forego by precipitate ardour one of the advantages that might be secured by delay and moderation. He may have had such an aim, he may have thought of the empire, or that the deliverance of Spain or Palestine was reserved for his arms; but that he really did so we have not the most shadowy evidence. We know that he was a powerful, unscrupulous man, a man of vast energy and industry, of great determination, the last man in the world to be charged with infirmity of purpose; but we also know that he knew mankind and had read history, and we see that as the actual results of his plans were of no immoderate dimensions, so also the details of his designs were carried out with a care and minuteness only credible on the supposition that they were ends in themselves. We need not suppose gratuitously that he intended to base on the foundation of consolidated power a fabric of conquest that would demand half a dozen lives to complete.

Such a theory as I have stated at once gives him a fitting aim for a moderate sensible ambition, and explains the relation between the influences of passion and policy by which he was actually swayed. His moral character, his self-will and self-indulgence, his licentious

habits, his paroxysms of rage, his covetousness, faithlessness, and cruelty, did not come into any violent collision with his political schemes, or if they threatened to do so were kept (except perhaps in the single exception of the forest laws) in abeyance until the pressing necessity of policy was satisfied. That they were so restrained proves that this leading purpose is not to be regarded as imaginary. That they did sway him on almost every recorded occasion of his life in which they did not clash with his purpose is so certain as to prevent us from listening for a moment to any theory which would represent him as a beneficent, unselfish ruler. His ambition may not have been the one which his moral character and circumstances might lead us to expect; but to say this is merely to repeat that that character was rather a compound of inconsistent qualities than a balance of opposing forces.

Take for example his relations with France, the conquest of which is the only conceivable and was the most feasible object of the ambition with which he may be credited. In such a purpose his passions and his unscrupulous policy would have run in the utmost harmony—pride, passion, revenge, the lust of dominion, the love of power. He hated Lewis the Seventh, he had every right to hate him, both as injurer and as injured. He was more or less at variance with him as long as he lived; he knew him to be weak and contemptible, and yet to be the source of all his own deepest unhappiness. At many periods of his reign Lewis and France lay at his mercy. The net of alliances was spread all around him. Italy, Spain, Flanders, were in close alliance with Henry. From 1168 to 1180 the position of Henry the Lion in Germany was such as must have prevented Lewis from looking for any help from the house of Hohenstaufen, even if he and the emperor had not been the champions of rival popes. If the King of England and ruler of half of France abstained from taking what a man of vulgar ambition would have taken, what Edward III and Henry V nearly succeeded in taking, we are not indeed to ignore other possible reasons for his forbearance, but the most probable reason is that he did not want it.

Such possible reasons may be suggested, but for the most part they are much too weak to stand before a resolute passionate ambition, and the certainty that they must have occurred to so clear-headed a man as Henry tells that the ambition they served to restrain could not have been of such a nature, if it existed at all; but it is needless to speculate upon them. Unscrupulous as men were, the idea of

unrighteous conquest from a Christian prince did not enter into the ordinary morality of the age. They fought for the settlement of quarrels, or for the decision of doubtful claims, or for rivalry, or for the love of war, but not for illegal conquest. In Henry's own wars this fact is clear, he never waged a war but on the ground of a legal claim. Further than this, his own feudal superstition, if it is not worthy of a higher name, with regard to the person of Lewis, was so strong as to exercise a visible restraint on his actual hatred. His political common sense might well have told him that the force which was enough to crush Lewis was not strong enough to hold France. The difficulties he experienced in ruling the dominions which he already possessed, and the variety of nationalities already crowded under one sceptre, were considerations that could not have escaped him, and they were just the considerations which, powerless before the lust of dominion, would commend themselves most forcibly to his characteristic caution.

The real object of Henry's external ambition was the consolidation of his dominions. To effect this but a moderate extension was necessary. These dominions on the continent were a long territory of varying breadth, the cohesion of which was of course weakest at its narrowest part. The reduction of Brittany from the condition of nominal to that of real dependence, and the extinction of any formidable power in Angoumois, La Marche, Saintonge, and Limousin, were necessary for the maintenance of the desired unity of estates. Second in importance was the enforcement of feudal claims over Toulouse and Auvergne, which might be more useful as independent allies than as unwilling vassals. The recovery of the Vexin and the establishment of Eleanor's rights over Berry gave a strength to the frontier and an apparent compactness to the mass; but these, like Brittany, Henry chose to secure by marriages rather than by arms; and in the same way the only considerable acquisition which he contemplated was attempted in the abortive proposal for the marriage of John with the heiress of Savoy and Maurienne.

In the pursuit of his object Henry went to work very much in the way in which a rich man in the eighteenth century created an estate and founded a family. He was anxious to increase the mass of his inheritance and his local influence by advantageous marriages and judicious purchases. He was scarcely less anxious to extinguish copyholds and buy up small interloping freeholders. In the choice of his acquisitions, that stood first in his consideration which could be brought within a ring fence. If Henry II occasionally had recourse

to chicanery and oppression, he has not wanted followers on both a large and a small scale whom his moderation even in these points might put to shame.

The character of his insular acquisitions was determined on a similar principle. Wales, Ireland, and Scotland were all desirable conquests, but no great cost should be spent on them. If internal divisions could be turned to profit, or if the scheme of aggression could be made available for the diversion of uneasy spirits from home, Henry was ready to take advantage of the circumstances, but would not waste much treasure or many men. In each of these cases he had a legal claim; to Ireland by the gift of Pope Adrian IV; to Scotland and Wales by his inheritance of the ancient supremacy of the Anglo-Saxon kings, and the simple application of feudal principles to that inheritance. The case with regard to Ireland was even stronger, if we consider him as succeeding to the like ancient claim to supremacy, and as at once the nominee of the sovereign of all islands and the invited arbiter of domestic quarrels. Yet, according to Robert de Monte, the original design upon Ireland was formed for the purpose of finding a kingdom for William Longespee of Anjou, and the final conquest was carried out in order to provide a suitable settlement for John. William the Lion and David of North Wales were reconciled by a royal or quasi-royal marriage. Galloway was not attacked until a like bond had proved too slight or too frail to hold it.

Henry's division of his dominions among his sons was a measure which, as his own age did not understand it, later ones may be excused for mistaking; but the object of it was, as may be inferred from his own recorded words, to strengthen and equalise the pressure of the ruling hand in different provinces of various laws and nationalities. The sons were to be the substitutes, not the successors of their father; the eldest as the accepted or elected sharer of the royal name, as feudal superior to his brothers, and first in the royal councils, stood in the same relation to his father as the king of the Romans to the emperor; he might rule with a full delegated power, or perhaps with inchoate independence, but the father's hand was to guide the helm of state. Unhappily the young brood of the eagle of the broken covenant were the worst possible instruments for the working of a large and complex policy; the last creatures in the world to be made useful in carrying on a form of government which the experience of all ages has tried and found wanting.

Yet how grand a scheme of western confederation might be deduced

from the consideration of the position of Henry's children, how great a dream of conquest may after all have been broken by the machinations of Lewis and Eleanor! What might not a crusade have effected headed by Henry II, with his valiant sons, the first warriors of the age, with his sons-in-law Henry the Lion, William of Sicily, and Alfonso of Castile; with Philip of France, the brother-in-law of his sons, Frederick Barbarossa, his distant kinsman and close ally, the princes of Champagne and Flanders, his cousins? In it the grand majestic chivalry of the emperor, the wealth of Sicily, the hardy valour and practical skill of Spain, the hereditary crusading ardour of the land of Godfrey of Bouillon and Stephen of Blois, the statesmanlike vigour and simple piety of the great Saxon hero, under the guidance of the craft and sagacity, the mingled impetuosity and caution of Henry II, might have presented Europe to Asia in a guise which she has never yet assumed. Yet all the splendour of the family confederation, all the close-woven widespread web that fortune and sagacity had joined to weave, end in the cruel desertion, the baffled rage, the futile curses of the chained leopard in the last scene at Chinon. The lawful sons, the offspring, the victims, and the avengers of a heartless policy, the loveless children of a loveless mother, have left the last duties of an affection they did not feel to the hands of a bastard, the child of an early, obscure, misplaced, degrading, but not a mercenary love.

The same idea of consolidating the kingly power is apparent in the legal and social measures of Henry II. His position was in these respects, indeed, more fortunate than in his foreign relations. He had not here to originate a policy which was to unite heterogeneous provinces, but inherited the experience of a century, the able ministers of his grandfather, and the plans which had been initiated in the reigns of William the Conqueror and William Rufus. But it certainly is not in the power of an ordinary administrator to adapt and develop the ideas of others, and embody them in a policy of his own. What credit Henry loses for originality he more than recovers when we consider the energy, skill, and industry with which he pursued his main object.

The bent of his internal policy may be described as the substitution of the king's government for the state of things which had prevailed more or less ever since the Conquest, which was partly coeval with the existence of the Norman race, partly owing to the incrustation of feudal institutions; against which the Conqueror had had to struggle, which William Rufus had to repress by the strong hand, which Henry

I by dint of time and skill had but in a degree weakened, and which had regained in the anarchy of Stephen's reign all the power that it had lost under his predecessor.

The idea of a kingly government administered by the king's servants, in which the action of the feudal nobility where it existed was simply ministerial, and was not, so far as the executive was concerned, even necessary to the maintenance of the plan, was the true remedy for the evils of anarchy inherent in the Norman state. Such a system could not be devised by a weak or ambitious head, or worked by feeble or indolent hands. Nor could it be brought to maturity or to easy action in one man's lifetime. The elements of discord were not extinguished in Henry's reign; they broke out whenever any other trouble distracted the king's energy or divided his power. Still he was in the main successful, and left to his successors the germ of a uniform administration of justice and system of revenue. His ministers, who at the beginning of his reign were little more than officers of his household, at the end of it were the administrators of the country. The position of England in the affairs of Europe was, from this time, owing, not to the foreign possessions of the sovereign, but to the compactness of her organisation, and the facility with which the national strength and resources could be handled.

It does not matter much whether we consider the several measures of Henry's administrative reforms as parts of a matured definite scheme, or as the expedients and experiments of an adroit manager. The more carefully we study the remaining monuments of the earlier reigns, or the character of Henry's ministers, the more we may be convinced that his genius was rather adaptive and digestive than originative. When on the other hand we examine the actual results of his reforms as exemplified in the succeeding reigns, the more certainly we see the difference between the earlier fragmentary attempts at legislation and the definite system which Henry left behind him; but on any view the industry, energy, and readiness of his working were qualities of the man himself.

It is obvious that Henry's great design as well as the subordinate parts of it may, taken apart from the general tenour of his character, be read in two ways, or rather that two opposing views of his character may be drawn from the bare consideration of his objects and measures. It may seem that he wished to create a tyranny, to overthrow every vestige of independence among the clergy and nobles, and to provide himself from the proceeds of taxation with means of carrying out

personal selfish designs. He might be a man who could endure no opposition, and to whom it was enough to make a thing intolerable that it should be originated by any other than himself. Such a reading would explain much of his avarice, cruelty, and greediness in acquiring territory.

Or it might be argued that as so many of his schemes did actually result in the amelioration of the condition of his subjects, as his judicial reforms were the basis on which the next generation was enabled to raise the earlier stages of civil liberty; and as his ecclesiastical measures have in nearly every particular been sanctioned and adopted by the practice of later ages, he is therefore entitled to the praise of a well-intentioned, benevolent ruler, as well as to the credit of a far-sighted statesman.

Both of these views have been advocated, the first by some of his contemporaries, and those who in later times have approached the history from their point of prejudice; the latter by those who, both anciently and recently, have been inclined to look with too professional an eye on the character of his reforms. I have stated already that I think neither of them tenable; and as it is at present Henry's personal character that is before me, I will give the reasons.

As to the first theory, which, in the mouths of his contemporaries, seems so condemnatory, it must be said that gratuitous baseness was no part of Henry's character, if we may judge by his actions. He was thoroughly unscrupulous and unprincipled, but he was not a tyrant; he was not wantonly cruel or oppressive. His crimes against public law and order, such as they were, were not purposeless, nor is it in any way necessary to suppose that he had that intolerance of all opposition which pursues tyranny for its own sake. He had definite aims, and followed them unrelentingly; whatever could be made to minister to their furtherance was forced to its use. As his passions gave way to his policy, so the minor measures of his policy were sometimes compelled to give way to the occasional exigencies of his great design. But where there was no definite object he was not a tyrant.

The theory that he was a benevolent governor or a far-sighted statesman is not supported, either by the apparent purpose of his reforms, or by their actual result. It requires no particular benevolence to teach a king that his subjects are more contented when justice is fairly administered than when violence reigns unrepressed; and that where they are contented they are more likely to be industrious, and more able

to pay taxes; that where they have more at stake they are more ready to make sacrifices to purchase security; but this is no lesson of far-sighted statesmanship, for it is the simplest principle of the art of government. If there were any sign of benevolence, any glimpse of the love of his people apparent in his actions, he ought by all means to have the credit of it; if there were any such general tone in his private life it might be allowed to give the key of interpretation of his public life, and a harmony to his whole character. But his life was violent and lawless; his personal design, wherever it clashed with his established measures, set them at once aside.

Again, such parts of his system as have been approved by the voice of late posterity, such as, especially, the restrictions on papal power and on ecclesiastical immunities, are capable of very simple discussion. There is no need to enter into a question of the personal merit of S. Thomas of Canterbury, or of the exact point for which he held out, and for which, in fact, he perished. We may respect the stout-heartedness of the prelate without approving his cause, or we may approve his cause without shutting our eyes to the violent and worldly spirit in which he conducted it; but when we find that in this cause all the piety and wisdom of three centuries saw the championship of Divine truth and justice against secular usurpation, we are not surely wrong in supposing that the Constitutions of Clarendon were dated three centuries too soon. Was Henry really three centuries before his age? If the answer is affirmative, we deny his character as a statesman, and reduce him to a theorist. In truth, it was as ancient customs that he wished to restore them, not to force them as innovations. His mistake was not that he anticipated the age of the Reformation, but that he neglected to consider that such was the rapid progress of papal assumption, and its acceptance, both in England and on the continent, since the age of Hildebrand, that his 'ancestral rights' were really left high and dry behind the advancing flood which he vainly thought to stem. The policy to which feudal antiquity had been forced to yield was really powerless against the increasing tide of ecclesiastical authority. The point which eluded the sagacity of Henry was identical with that which the Conqueror himself had overlooked when he established ecclesiastical courts to take cognisance of the secular offences of the clergy. Both saw the impossibility of reconciling royal supremacy with the claims of feudal antiquity; but in ecclesiastical matters William yielded to, or perhaps helped on, the first trickling of the stream which Henry had to withstand in its full force. It was

as necessary to William to strengthen as it was to Henry to weaken the power of the clergy. Henry should not have expected to find in Becket one who would at once fill the seat and reverse the measures of Lanfranc.

In his secular and ecclesiastical reforms alike, he had an object to gain which demanded unusual measures; and he, without scruple and without remorse, tried to enforce them by all means, fair and foul. If he was not a mere tyrant, he was a man who was never deterred by any considerations but those of expediency from trying to win his game.

It seems, then, that there is a third and a truer reading of this eventful life, one which makes no demand on our credulity like the second, and which requires no harsh construction of simple actions like the first. Henry wished to create, at home and abroad, a strong government. In this itself there was nothing deserving the name of tyrannical; at the worst it was less of a tyranny than that which had been in use in the three Norman reigns, and had been exercised on both sides in the contests of that of Stephen. As governments were in those days, any might be accounted good which was conducted on the principle of law, not on caprice. The notions of constitutional sovereignty and liberty were still locked up in the libraries, or in embryo in the brains of the clergy.

Such a theory makes Henry neither an angel nor a devil. He was a man of strong nature; strong will, strong affections, and strong passions. His ambition was not a wanton one. He began his reign without any temptation to be oppressive; but from the beginning we can read his purpose of being master in his own house. The humbling of the barons was no hard task; the initiation of law and order was an easy consequence; but the attempt to apply the principles of law and order to the clergy, in a way that was not sanctioned by the public opinion of his day, and which made his ablest counsellor his most inveterate foe, brought up an opposition which called into play all the violence of his nature. It was not that his character changed, but that circumstances brought out what was in him in a stronger light. After Becket's death, the circumstances became even stronger still, and brought out in a still stronger light the same characteristics.

By that most disastrous event all the elements of opposition were restored to life. Lewis had now a cause which to his weak and wicked conscience, justified all the meanness and falsehood that he could use against his rival. The clergy dared not side with the king in such a quarrel. The barons took immediate advantage of the general dis-

affection. The king's sons lighted the flames of war. Not, I think, that there is any evidence to show that the death of S. Thomas was actually or nominally the pretext for revolt; but it was a breaking up of the restraints which had so far been effectual; and all who had grievances were ready and able to take advantage of the shock.

Under the circumstances, Henry did not show himself a hero, but he behaved as a moderate and politic conqueror. It was not revenge, but the restoration of the strength of his government that he desired. He did not break off his plans of reform: year after year saw some wise change introduced into the legal or military administration; and practically he managed the church without any glaring scandal. He ruled for himself, not for his people; but he did not rule cruelly or despotically. His character contained much that was tyrannical, but his policy was not such as to curse him with the name of tyrant.

Is Henry, then, to have no credit for his sagacious measures? Yes; the credit due to a man who, having come to his crown with a power limited by circumstances rather than by law, and having overcome those circumstances, has chosen to sacrifice somewhat of the licence of despotism for the safety of order; has chosen to place his power on the basis of public security and common justice. Such merit was his, although, doubtless, the love of power was stronger in him than the love of order. His wisdom was not less wisdom because it was the wisdom of a selfish man.

In the elaborate descriptions of Henry II which are given by Peter of Blois, Giraldus Cambrensis, and Ralph Niger, we cannot doubt that we have the accurate delineation of the man as he appeared through the different mediums of liking and dislike. The main lines of the portraits are the same, though they are seen as it were through variously-coloured glass. They are well-marked and defined, as we might expect in the most superficial view of such a man. But although well-marked and strongly defined, they do not combine, even under the hand of a professed panegyrist, into the outlines of a hero.

We see a hard-headed, industrious, cautious, subtle, restless man; fixed in purpose, versatile in expedients; wonderfully rapid in execution; great in organising, without being himself methodical; one who will always try to bind others, whilst leaving himself free; who never prefers good faith to policy or appearances to realities; who trusts rather to time and circumstances than to the goodwill of others; by inclination parsimonious and retiring, but on occasion lavish and

magnificent; liberal in almsgiving, splendid in building, but not giving alms without an ulterior object, nor spending money on buildings, except where he can get his money's worth. As with treasure, so with men, he was neither extravagant nor sparing; rather economical than humane; pitiful after the slaughter of battle, but not chary of human life where it could be spent with effect.

He had the one weakness of great minds, without which no man ever reached greatness: never to be satisfied without doing or taking part himself in everything that was to be done; and he had not what may be called the strength of little minds, inability to see good in what he did not himself devise.

He was eloquent, affable, polite, jocose; so persuasive in address that few could resist the charm of his manner. He had the royal prerogative of never forgetting names and faces; he loved to encourage the retiring and to repel the presuming. He was a most excellent and bountiful master. He was very faithful, both in friendships and enmities, where they did not interfere with his policy.

He was not without elegant tastes; he loved the reading of history, delighted in the conversation of acute and learned men like his uncles the kings of Jerusalem, and his sons-in-law William of Sicily and Henry of Saxony. He had a wonderful memory, well stored with the lessons of past times, and with the experiences of constant journeys, on which he was careful to see everything that was to be seen.

He had little regard for more than the merest forms of religion; like Napoleon Bonaparte, he heard mass daily, but without paying decent attention to the ceremony. During the most solemn part of the service he was whispering to his courtiers, or scribbling, or looking at pictures. His vows to God he seems to have thought might be evaded as easily as his covenants with men; his undertaking to go on crusade was commuted for money payments, and his promised religious foundations were carried out at the expense of others. His regard to personal morality was of much the same value and extent. He was at no period of his life a faithful husband; and when he had finally quarrelled with Eleanor he sank into sad depths of licentiousness.

He was an able, plausible, astute, cautious, unprincipled man of business. His temper was violent, and he was probably subject to the outrageous paroxysms of passion which are attributed to his Norman ancestors, and which, if they have not been exaggerated by the his-

torians, must have been fearful proofs of a profane and cruel disposition, on which discipline had imposed no restraints.

His personal appearance did not approach the heroic. He was slightly above the middle height, square and substantial, with a decided tendency to corpulence. His head was round, and well proportioned; his hair approaching to red, sprinkled in his later years with white, but always kept very short as a precaution against baldness. His face is described by one authority as fiery, by another as lion-like. His eyes were grey, and full of expression, but rather prominent, and occasionally bloodshot. His nose was well formed, and denoted no more pride or fastidiousness than was becoming to a king.

He had a short bull neck, a broad square chest, the arms of a boxer, and the legs of a horseman (the author does not say whether of a groom or a cavalier). His feet were highly arched, but his hands were clumsy and coarse.

He paid very little attention to dress, and never wore gloves but when he went hawking. He took a great deal of exercise, being both restless by habit and anxious to keep down his tendency to fat. He was a great hunter and hawker; he never sat except at meals or on horseback. He transacted all business standing, greatly to the detriment of his legs. He was very moderate in both meat and drink, cared very little for appearances, loved order in others without observing it himself; he was a good and kind master, who chose his servants well, but neither trusted them too much, nor ever forgave their neglect of his interests.

The picture is not a pleasant one; in spite of his refined taste and his polite address he must have looked generally like a rough, passionate, uneasy man. But his frame, though not elegant, was very serviceable, qualified him for great exertion, and was proof against privation or fatigue. He was an adroit and formidable man at arms, but there was little at first sight to denote either the courteous knight or the skilful general, or the self-possessed intriguer, or the ingenious organiser, or the versatile administrator, or the profound politician.

But if the character of Henry contained none of the elements of real greatness, if the leading principle of it was one which is actually incompatible with the highest degree of excellence in a ruler, the position of the nation he governed was such, and the influence exercised upon it by his character and the events of his reign was so salutary, as to make him one of the most conspicuous actors in the drama of English history. He was a link in the chain of great men by whom,

through good and evil, the English nation was drawn on to constitutional government. He was the man the time required. It was a critical time, and his actions and policy determined the crisis in a favourable way. He stands with Alfred, Canute, William the Conqueror, and Edward I, one of the conscious creators of English greatness.

SAMUEL GARDINER

1829–1902

Gardiner intended his history to run from 1603 to 1660, but after sixteen volumes (from 1869 to 1901) illness prevented him from going further than 1656. This description of the battle of Marston Moor is taken from chapter 18 of volume one, published in 1886, of the series entitled History of the Great Civil War, 1642–1649, *and I quote it to show that Gardiner's caution and personal reserve did not prevent him from writing descriptive pieces that are worthy to put beside Macaulay's celebrated battle scenes. He was diffident on this point, and in the preface to this volume emphasized that "I cannot describe battles which I have not seen as if I had; yet, if to describe a battle as if he saw it is no part of the historian's task, he need not therefore turn aside from the duty of describing it with truthfulness, as far as his materials allow him to do so, and I have therefore thought it right to visit the fields on which all the important struggles of the war took place. I am only afraid that I have often given my narrative the appearance of greater accuracy than is attainable, and I must therefore ask my readers to supply a chorus of doubt, and to keep in mind that they read, not an account of that which certainly happened, but of that which appears to me to have happened after such inquiry as I have been able to make." Gardiner's bicycle trips enabled him to draw the first battle diagrams which take an accurate account of topography. The map of Marston Moor is omitted here, as are the footnotes. Gardiner's account of the battle may be compared with that of A. Woolrych, in* Battles of the English Civil War *(1961).*

On Gardiner, see C. H. Firth, Quarterly Review, *April 1902 and R. G. Usher,* Critical Studies of the Historical Method of Gardiner *(1912).*

THE CONTROVERSY as to the possibility of making peace with Charles which had long been smouldering in Parliament had thus been transferred to the camp. All subsequent experience, indeed, went to show that Vane and Cromwell were in the right in coming to the conclusion that it was impossible to expect any reasonable security for the maintenance of Puritanism if Charles were re-established on the throne. Yet the very horror with which men of ordinary capacity, like Manchester and the elder Fairfax, regarded any meddling with the occupancy of the throne might have served as a warning against the enormous difficulties in the way of those who should attempt permanently to settle the government on a revolutionary basis. The England of that day could neither be governed by Charles I nor without a king, and the dread which was entertained of any attempt to dispense with Charles was in reality the expression of a widely felt belief that security for property and life would disappear with the overthrow of the throne. Vane and Cromwell were right in their judgment of Charles, but Manchester and Fairfax had a firmer hold on the possibilities of that future which would arise as soon as Charles was in his coffin.

For the present, however, the business of the Generals was to take York; not to settle how England was to be governed. On the 13th Newcastle offered to treat for the surrender of the city. His demand for permission to march out with bag and baggage, and for security that the clergy should be allowed to carry on 'the altar service' in the cathedral, having been promptly rejected, the besiegers were further encouraged by the capture of messengers sent out to inform Rupert that York could only hold out for six days longer.

It was the object of the Parliamentary commanders to enter York, if possible, before the six days elapsed. For some time a mine had been in progress which was expected to effect a practicable breach. Its explosion had been entrusted to Crawford, the Scottish Major-General of Manchester's army, who, three months before, had come into collision with Cromwell. Anxious in his vanity to secure the credit of the capture of the city, Crawford fired the mine on the 17th without

giving notice either to Leven or Fairfax. Manchester's troops, having been warned, gallantly rushed at the breach, but they were promptly overpowered and driven out, in consequence of the enforced failure of the other two commanders to second them by assaults on the sides of the fortifications opposite to their respective quarters.

A delay of some days was thus secured by the garrison. Rupert might surely be expected to hasten to its succour; and if he had needed a spur, he would have found it in a letter written to him by his uncle before that march from Bewdley to Oxford which led to the fight at Cropredy Bridge. "Now," wrote Charles, "I must give you the true state of my affairs, which, if their condition be such as enforces me to give you more peremptory commands than I would willingly do, you must not take it ill. If York be lost I shall esteem my crown little less, unless supported by your sudden march to me, and a miraculous conquest in the South, before the effects of the Northern power can be found here; but if York be relieved, and you beat the rebels' armies of both kingdoms which were before it, then, but otherways not, I may possibly make a shift upon the defensive to spin out time until you come to assist me; wherefore I command and conjure you, by the duty and affection which I know you bear me, that, all new enterprises laid aside, you immediately march according to your first intention, with all your force, to the relief of York; but if that be either lost or have freed themselves from the besiegers, or that for want of powder you cannot undertake that work, that you immediately march with your whole strength directly to Worcester, to assist me and my army, without which, or your having relieved York by beating the Scots, all the successes you can afterwards have most infallibly will be useless to me."

Whatever may have been the precise meaning of these painfully involved sentences, there could be no doubt what interpretation would be put upon them by Rupert. "Before God," said Culpepper to Charles when he heard that the letter had been sent, "you are undone, for upon this peremptory order he will fight whatever comes on't."

Since the failure of the mine the besiegers of York had been looking anxiously for Rupert's coming. The six days which Newcastle declared to be the utmost duration of his resistance passed away, and there were no signs of surrender. At last the three Generals learnt that Rupert had completed his preparations and was actually on the [illegible]ve. On the 28th tidings arrived that he had crossed the range of [illegible]ich divides Yorkshire from Lancashire. On the 30th it was

known that he had reached Knaresborough, and was therefore about twelve miles from York. The Generals had already summoned Denbigh and Meldrum to their aid, but neither Denbigh nor Meldrum would be at Wakefield before July 3, and unless reinforcements arrived it would be ruinous to be caught between Rupert's army and Newcastle's garrison, as Meldrum had been caught in March at Newark, and as Waller in the preceding summer had been caught at Devizes. On the morning of July 1, therefore, the whole besieging force marched off towards Marston Moor, on the road to Knaresborough, hoping to bar the way to York. Its leaders had learnt the lesson that it was useless to besiege a fortified town with an enemy unbeaten in the field.

The tactics of the Parliamentary Generals were simple—too simple to baulk Rupert of his design. Sweeping round to the left by Boroughbridge, and crossing the Swale at Thornton Bridge, he wheeled sharply to the right, and, driving off a guard placed by Manchester over the bridge of boats which had been thrown over the Ouse at the commencement of the siege, crossed that river into a place of safety. Halting for the night outside York, on its northern side, he sent orders to Newcastle to come out and meet him on the following morning.

While Newcastle was pondering over this message the Parliamentary Generals were holding serious debate on Marston Moor. York was lost, and the turn of the Eastern Association would come next. To defend those trusty counties the army fell back on the morning of the 2nd in the direction of Tadcaster and Cawood. The infantry had almost reached Tadcaster when a message arrived from Fairfax, who, with David Leslie and Cromwell, was still guarding with horse the long ridge which slopes down to Marston Moor, to tell them that Rupert's cavalry was gathering in front of them, and that a conflict was imminent. If Rupert meant to fight and not to manoeuvre, there was no reason why he should not be gratified. The Parliamentary infantry was hurried back, and by two in the afternoon had established itself amidst the rye which waved on the summit of the ridge. Some attempt was made by a party of Royalists, probably under Lord Byron, to win ground on the extreme left of the Parliamentary ground at Tockwith, but the attempt was repulsed and the assailants driven back upon the moor.

The Royalists, on their part, had been slow to gather to the field. Rupert was burning for the fight, but Newcastle, always unadventurous, and vexed at Rupert's appointment to be his superior officer, was by no means so ardent. His men, too, had broken into mutiny,

crying aloud for pay. When the two Generals met Rupert was already on the march. "My Lord," said the Prince, as soon as the first compliments had been exchanged, "I hope we shall have a glorious day." Newcastle replied that it would be better not to fight at all. The enemies' commanders were on bad terms with one another, and their army would break up before long. Reinforcements under Clavering were already on their way from the North. It may be that Newcastle was wounded by Rupert's abrupt manner, but there was nothing in the military antecedents of the courtly Marquis to lead Rupert to treat him with respect. He had frittered away great opportunities before, and he seemed bent on frittering them away again. The fiery young Prince cut him short by announcing that he had a letter from the King 'with a positive and absolute command to fight the enemy.' Before this announcement Newcastle withdrew all objections. "Happen what will," he said to his friends, who told him it was unworthy of him to be commanded by Rupert, "I will not shun to fight, for I have no other ambition but to live and die a loyal subject to his Majesty."

No doubt the King's letter was not so plain of interpretation as Rupert asserted, but it does not follow that Rupert was obviously in the wrong in calling for a battle. He had never yet met the horsemen whom he had not scattered, and, as the events of that evening were to prove, if he had personally been as successful on Marston Moor as he had been on every field stricken since the war began, the victory would have been won along the whole line, and there can be no serious doubt that that victory would have given to Charles once more an undisputed throne. As for Newcastle's projected war of manoeuvre, it was at least as likely to turn against him as in his favour.

All through the summer afternoon, with rain-showers falling heavily at times, the two armies faced one another; the Parliamentary soldiers on the summit or slope of the long hill outnumbering their opponents, and being distinguished by white handkerchiefs or white pieces of paper in their caps. Baillie, who was, under Leven, at the head of the Scottish infantry, held the centre of the line. On his right were the Fairfaxes, Sir Thomas commanding, under his father, his own horse on the extreme right, a reserve of Scottish cavalry being posted behind his own regiments, whilst there was also a reserve of Scottish infantry behind those led by Lord Fairfax in person. On the left was Manchester's army of the Eastern Association, the infantry being commanded by Crawford, and the cavalry, supported by some Scottish

dragoons and by three regiments of Scottish horse under David Leslie, being led by Cromwell.

The Royalist centre was under the command of Eythin, the professional soldier who had come to England from the German wars as General King, and who had long been the military adviser of Newcastle. On the left, opposite the Fairfaxes, was a strong body of horse, under Goring, whilst Rupert himself took up his post on the right. With a soldier's instinct Rupert had singled out Cromwell as the one soldier worthy of his steel. "Is Cromwell there?" he is reported to have asked of a prisoner. "And will they fight?" continued Rupert as soon as he was informed of his presence. "If they will, they shall have fighting enough." Rupert bade the prisoner return to his own people to bear this message. "If it please God," was Cromwell's answer when he heard it, "so shall he."

It was weary waiting amidst the rye, but Leven did not judge it prudent to attack. A long ditch ran along the edge where the moor skirted the hill, and that ditch was occupied by Rupert's musketeers. About four in the afternoon Eythin brought up some 3,000 of Newcastle's foot. The cautious veteran was struck with surprise at the rashness of the Prince. The Royalist line was drawn up close to the enemy, with only the long ditch between, which neither side had as yet ventured to cross, but which was unlikely to prove an insuperable obstacle to a dashing commander. Rupert, heedless of the fault which he had committed, gaily asked Eythin how he liked the marshalling of his army, pointing to a paper on which he had sketched the position of the troops. "By God, sir," answered Eythin, "it is very fine in the paper, but there is no such thing in the field!" Rupert, so far as can be gathered from the fragmentary information which has reached us, contemplated an attack upon the enemy as soon as Eythin arrived. The old soldier would not hear of beginning a battle so late in the day, and found fault with Rupert for placing his men so near the enemy. "They may be drawn," said Rupert, with unwonted meekness, "to a further distance." "No, sir," replied Eythin, "it is too late." Risky as his position was, Rupert did not seem to understand his danger. "We will charge them," he said to Newcastle, "to-morrow morning!" It was now between six and seven, and Rupert, calling for provisions, dismounted and began to eat his supper. A large number of his followers did the like. Newcastle strolled towards his coach to solace himself with a pipe. Before he had time to take a whiff the battle had begun.

It may well be that the Parliamentarians on the hill marked these signs of unpreparedness. In an instant horse and foot dashed forward, the horsemen of the Eastern Association leading the way over the ditch. Rupert had neither the advantage of being the first to charge nor the advantage of a defensible position. In a moment he had recovered his vigour so far as recovery was possible and flew at Cromwell's horse. His first regiment was beaten and driven back, but the charge was well supported. Cromwell was slightly wounded in the neck, and for an instant his whole force recoiled. The reserves under David Leslie hastened up and loosened Rupert's hold. Cromwell and Leslie forced their way steadily onwards, pushing Rupert's hitherto unconquered cavalry before them, and at last scattering them 'like a little dust.'

In the centre the Parliamentarians were hardly less successful. In front of Crawford, who, as Major-General, commanded Manchester's foot, the ditch had been filled up, and the Royalists opposed to him had drawn aside towards their own left to avoid the unsheltered position. There was therefore a gap between the right of their foot and the left of Rupert's horse. Into this gap Crawford dashed, and then, wheeling sharply round, threw himself on the flank of the Royalist infantry. Its hold upon the ditch was loosened, and Baillie, with his Scots, poured over it to attack them in front. Yet, pushed back as the main Royalist battle was, it did not break into flight as Rupert had fled before Cromwell, and under a dark pall of smoke, made luminous where the guns flashed and roared, the wild work of slaughter bestrewed the moor with the dying and the dead.

Whilst the Scottish foot were struggling thus manfully, a great disaster had happened on the Parliamentary right, where the Yorkshire men were fighting under the two Fairfaxes. On that side the moor was covered with furze, and the enemy was only to be reached by way of a narrow lane, which ran at right angles with the positions of the two armies. The passage was the more difficult as a ditch ran on one side of the lane and a hedge on the other, and both hedge and ditch were already lined by the musketeers of the Royalist army. In that part of the field, too, fought Newcastle's Whitecoats, the chosen regiment which had been raised on the edge of the Northern moors, and which had clothed itself in a uniform of undyed cloth, vowing to dye it red in the blood of the enemy.

Whilst Lord Fairfax was struggling with difficulty through the lane, his son, picking his way as well as he could farther to the right amongst

the furze, charged Goring's horse. Sir Thomas, indeed, with his immediate followers, broke through, but the main body of his cavalry was utterly routed. Dashing back upon the Yorkshire infantry on their flank, the frightened horsemen trod them down or scattered them irretrievably. One Scottish regiment of horse under Lord Eglinton alone maintained its steadiness, whilst the Scottish foot, placed in reserve behind Lord Fairfax, shared in the general ruin. The hillside and the roads which led to Tadcaster were choked by the flying rout. The sabres of Goring's horse had full work among the fugitives, till the victors wheeled round to betake themselves, not to the attack of the enemies' regiments which remained unbroken, but to the tempting plunder of the baggage. As the runaways swept past Tadcaster in panting confusion exultant Royalists sped on the news of victory, and bells rang and bonfires blazed at Oxford and wherever Charles's name was held in honour.

On the field it seemed as if the news so prematurely believed would be justified by the event. Not all of Goring's cavalry had followed him in the charge and in the pursuit, and enough remained behind, under Sir Charles Lucas, to join their comrades on foot in pressing hard upon the Scottish infantry in the centre. Taken in front and flank, the hardy Scots were exposed to a trial the most severe which on that day befell any part of the Parliamentary army. Twice they repelled attack, but each time their ranks were thinned. Whole regiments broke and fled. Old Leven toiled in vain to restore order. "Although," he cried out to the fugitives, "you run from your enemies, yet leave not your General." It was all to no purpose, and at last the veteran, believing that all was lost, set spurs to his horse, galloping for dear life's sake to Wetherby, and through Wetherby, as some reports averred, even to Leeds. Yet though Leven fled, his subordinate, Baillie, kept the field. Under him fought the regiment of Lord Lindsay, and that which bore the name of Lord Maitland, but which was under the command of Lieutenant-Colonel Pitscottie, whilst a third in reserve under Lumsdaine moved up in support and maintained the unequal fight. A third attack was repulsed, and some ground was even gained. Yet so desperate a struggle could not last much longer. Unless help came the three heroic regiments which maintained the honour of the Scottish name would be swept away.

The needed help was already at hand. The younger Fairfax, staggering from the effect of a wound on his face, had flung away the white handkerchief, which would expose him to death or capture from the

stragglers in the rear of the Royalist army, and groped his way behind the fight to the spot where Cromwell was already halting his victorious horsemen, and peering through the smoke to discern, if possible, how the battle was going elsewhere. As at Gainsborough, Cromwell had kept his men well in hand; and Crawford, too, had preserved unbroken the ranks of the infantry of the Eastern Association. Learning the tale of misfortune from the lips of Fairfax, he took his measures promptly. Sending a party to follow up Rupert's flying squadrons, and leaving David Leslie to deal with the Whitecoats, whilst Crawford supported Baillie, he betook himself to the lane's end through which Fairfax had emerged. Fronting southwards, as Goring's horse had fronted at the beginning of the battle, he caught the disordered Royalist cavalry on their way back from pursuit and plunder. The disadvantage of the ground, the narrow way through the lane, the furze bushes on either side, told heavily against the confused mass of horsemen, and Goring's Cavaliers were redased [reduced?] back into hopeless ruin by the serried ranks of the Puritan troopers.

In the centre David Leslie had flown at the Whitecoats. That faithful band retreated into an enclosure, resolved, like the King's Red Regiment at Edgehill, to die where they stood. They had their wish. Scarcely one of their number left the field alive. On the other side Baillie and Crawford advanced steadily against the remainder of the Royalist infantry, and when Cromwell and David Leslie, having accomplished each his own immediate task, came up to aid, all resistance was at an end.

The Parliamentary victory was complete. Four thousand Royalists had been slain. Colours enough, as a contemporary publication expressed it, 'to make surplices for all the cathedrals in England, were they white,' had fallen into the hands of the victors. What was more to the purpose, the great force to which they had been opposed had ceased to exist as an army. The mutual jealousies of the Royalist commanders were inflamed too highly to bear the strain of defeat. Rupert threw the blame on the sluggishness of Newcastle, and Newcastle threw the blame on the rashness of Rupert. The courtly Marquis, who was more at home in a riding-school than on a field of battle, had yet borne himself bravely in the fight. When the fight was over he thought more of himself than of his master's cause. Abandoning all hope, like a fair-weather warrior as he was, on the day after the battle he rode off to Scarborough, to ship himself for a secure retreat on the Continent. With him were Eythin and a crowd of dissatisfied officers, who

thought it no shame to desert their King. "I will not endure the laughter of the Court," was the only explanation of his misconduct which Newcastle chose to give.

Rupert was made of sterner stuff. Collecting about 6,000 horse who still remained together, he rode out of the gates of York, not to fly, but to retrieve, if it were yet possible, the great disaster. With no relieving army in the field York was plainly untenable, and on July 16 the garrison left in it, under Sir Thomas Glenham, surrendered to the conquerors of Marston Moor. A few isolated fortresses would still have to be besieged and captured, but the defeat of Rupert virtually placed the whole of the North at the mercy of the Parliamentary Generals.

JOHN RICHARD GREEN

1837–1883

This account of the West Saxon move from Hampshire toward London comes from chapter 3 of The Making of England *(1881). The map and footnotes are omitted, but I have made the trifling alterations to the text which Green would have incorporated in a second edition had he lived. They are made in the margins of his own copy in the Library of Jesus College, Oxford. Green's account may be compared with that of Sir Frank Stenton,* Anglo-Saxon England, *Oxford History of England Series (2nd edition, 1947).*

Green's letters were edited by Leslie Stephen in 1901, and this is the best source for his life. And see R. L. Schuyler, "John Richard Green and His Short History," *in* Political Science Quarterly, *1949.*

WHAT BROKE this inaction, whether the Britons had grown weaker, or whether fresh reinforcements had strengthened their opponents, we do not know. We hear only that Cynric, whom Cerdic's death left King of the West-Saxons, again took up the work of invasion in 552 by a fresh advance on the west. Winchester was the meeting-point of five Roman Roads; and of these one struck directly westward, along the northern skirts of the woodlands that filled the space between the lower Itchen and the mid-valley of the Avon, to the fortress of Old Sarum. Celt and Roman alike had seen the military value of the height from which the eye sweeps nowadays over the grassy meadows of the Avon to the arrowy spire of Salisbury; and admirable as the

position was in itself, it had been strengthened at a vast cost of labour. The camp on the summit of the knoll was girt in by a trench hewn so deeply in the chalk that from the inner side of it the white face of the rampart rose a hundred feet high, while strong outworks protected the approaches to the fortress from the west and from the east. Arms must have been useless against such a stronghold as this; and, though the Britons were 'put to flight' before its investment, the reduction of Sorbiodunum was probably due rather to famine or want of water than to the sword.

But its fall brought with the easy winning of the district which it guarded, as well as the downs on whose edge stood the strange monument, then as now an object of wonder, to which the conquerors as they marched beside its mystic circle gave the name of the Hanging Stones, Stonehenge. The Gewissas passed over the Stratford, or paved ford by which the road they had followed from Winchester passed the river, to the westernmost reaches of the Gwent, the district we now know as Salisbury Plain. To the south of them as they marched, behind the lower Avon and its little affluent of the Nadder, a broken and woodland country whose memory lingers in Cranbourne Chase screened the later Dorsetshire from their arms; but in their front the open downs offered no line of defence, and the Gewissas could push along the road from Old Sarum unhindered till they reached the steep slope down which the upland fell into the valley of the Frome. How roughly their march was checked at this point by the dense forests which filled the Frome valley we see from the fact that these woodlands remained in British hands for more than a hundred years; and the significant name of 'Mere' preserves for us the memory of the border-bound which the Gewissas were forced to draw along the western steeps of their new conquest. The conquerors turned back to settle in the land they had won, in the river valleys which scored the surface of the downs, in the tiny bends and grassy nooks of the vale of Avon, or in the meadows along the course of its affluent, the Wil or Wiley. It was probably in the last that the main body of the invaders fixed their home, for it was the Wiley, and the little township, or Wil-ton, which rose beside it, which gave them from this time their new name of Wil-sætas. From this time, indeed, the Gewissas, or West-Saxons, felt the need of local names for the peoples into which conquest broke them as they pushed over the country. But the character of these names shows the looseness of the bonds that held such 'folks' together. Each knew itself simply as a group of 'sætan' or 'set-

tlers' in the land it had won, Wiltsætan in the lands about the Wiley, Dor-sætan in the forest tract through which wound the 'dwr' or dark water of the Frome, Somer-sætan or Defna-sætan in lands yet more to the west.

But there was little to detain Cynric in the tiny vales and bare reaches of upland which his arms had as yet given him; and in 556, only four years after the fall of Old Sarum, he pushed forward again along a road that led from Winchester north-westward in the direction of Cirencester and the Severn. Descending the deep escarpment which forms the northern face of the Hampshire downs, he threaded his way through the woodlands of the Vale of Pewsey, whose relics survive in the Forest of Savernake, and again mounted the slopes on the further side of them. Here he made himself master of the town of Cunetio and of the upland which lay about it by a victory on the very brink of the downs at Barbury Hill. The ground, however, of which he thus became lord was far from affording any obstacle to further advance; on the contrary, its very character seemed to draw the Gewissas onward to new aggressions. The Marlborough Downs are in fact the starting-point from which the second and greatest of its chalk-ranges runs across Southern Britain. The upland trends to the north-east under the name of the Ilseley Downs till it reaches a gap through which the Thames strikes southward to its lower river-valley; then rising again in the Chilterns, it broadens at last into the Gwent in which the East-Anglians had found a home. In its earlier course this range naturally called Cynric's men to a fresh advance; for from the downs above Marlborough the high ground runs on without a break to the course of the Thames. This tract, however, like that which they had traversed in the Gwent, must have been a scantily-peopled one; and its invaders would turn with eagerness to the more tempting district which lay in the lower ground on either side of it. The northern face of the downs consists of a line of steep cliffs, looking out over a vale through which the stream of the Ock pours its waters into the Thames. On the face of this escarpment the traveller still sees, drawn white against the scanty turf, the gigantic form of a horse which gives the Vale of White Horse its name, and which tradition looks on as a work on the conquering Gewissas. Another monument of their winning of this district lingers in the rude stones called Weyland Smith's House, a cromlech of primæval times where the Saxons found a dwelling-place for the weird legend of a hero-smith which they brought with them from their German homeland.

The White Horse glimmers over a broad and fertile region, whose local names recall for us the settlement of the conquerors in hamlets that have grown into quiet little towns like Wantage, the future birth-place of Ælfred, or in homesteads that crowned the low rises or 'duns' which overlooked the valley, such as the dun where the Farrings planted their Farringdon, or another dun at the confluence of the Ock and the Thames, where the West-Saxon Abba chose the site for a dwelling-place which grew in later days into our Abingdon. On the south the downs fell in gentler slopes to the vale of the Kennet, whose silvery stream ran through masses of woodland, past the ford at Hungerford and the 'new burgh' of the conquerors which survives in Newbury, to the low and swampy meadows where it meets the Thames, as that river bursts from its cleft through the chalk-range to open out into its lower valley. In these meadows the house of the Readings planted a settlement which has grown into the busy town that preserves their name. Still further to the east the invaders pushed their way into the tangled woodland that stretched along the low clay flats which bordered the southern bank of the Thames, and where the predominance of the box, or bearroc, may have given in after days its name of 'Bearroc-shire' or Berkshire to the whole tract of valley and down which this fresh advance added to the dominions of the West-Saxons.

With its conquest the winning of the southern uplands was complete. And with the winning of these uplands the whole island lay open to the Gewissas; for the Andredsweald, which had held back the invader for half a century, was turned as soon as the West-Saxons stood masters of the southern Gwent, and their country now jutted forward like a huge bastion into the heart of unconquered Britain. Only on one side were the obstacles in their way still serious, where the woods of Dorset-shire, with the thick wedge of forest which blocked the valley of the Frome beneath the Wiltshire downs, were for long years to hold any western advance at bay. But elsewhere the land was open to their attack. On the north-west easy slopes led to the crest of the Cotswolds, from whence the Severn valley lay before them for their prey. On the north their march would find no natural obstacles as it passed up the Cherwell valley to penetrate either to the central plain of Britain or to the Wash. Above all, to the eastward opened before them the valley of the Thames. From its springs near the crest of the Cotswolds the river falls quietly to the low ground beneath the Marlborough Downs, and then turns abruptly to the south to hew a channel through the line of chalk uplands, and thus part the Berkshire heights from the

Chilterns. Once out of this narrow gorge it bends round the woodlands where the advanced guard of Cynric's men were feeling their way into the fastnesses about Windsor, and rolling in a slower and larger current eastward through the wide valley that lies between the North Downs and the East Anglian heights, after a course of two hundred miles it reaches its estuary and the sea.

No road can have seemed so tempting to the earlier invaders as this water-road of the Thames, leading as it did straight from the Channel to the heart of Britain through an open and fruitful country; and it was by this road that their advance seemed destined to be made when they settled on either side of its estuary in Essex and in Kent. But a century had passed since these settlements, and the Thames valley still remained untouched. Tempting as the road seemed, indeed, no inlet into Britain was more effectually barred. On either side the river-mouth, at but little distance from the coast on which East-Saxon and Kentishmen were encamped, long belts of woodland and fen stretched to the very brink of the Thames. On the south of it the fastnesses of the Weald found their line of defence prolonged by huge swamps that stretched to the river, and whose memory is still preserved by the local names as by the local floods of Rotherhithe and Bermondsey. To the north as formidable a line of defence presented itself in the tangled forest whose last relics survive in the woods of Epping and in the name of Hainault, and this barrier of woodland was backed by the swamps of the lower Lea to the rear of it. The one line of advance in fact open to an invader was the course of the Thames itself, and the course of the Thames was blocked by the fortress of London.

The commercial greatness of London has made men forget its military importance, but from the first moment of its history till late into the middle ages London was one of the strongest of our fortresses. Its site, indeed, must have been dictated, like that of most early cities, by the advantages which it presented as well for defence as for trade. It stood at the one point by which either merchant or invader could penetrate from the estuary into the valley of the Thames; and in its earlier days, before the great changes wrought by the embankment of the Romans, this was also the first point at which any rising ground for the site of such a town presented itself on either shore of the river. Nowhere has the hand of man moulded ground into shapes more strangely contrasted with its natural form than on the site of London. Even as late as the time of Cæsar the soil which a large part of it covers can have been little but a vast morass. Below Fulham the river

stretched at high tide over the ground that lies on either side of its present channel from the rises of Kensington and Hyde Park to the opposite shores of Peckham and Camberwell. All Pimlico and Westminster to the north, to the south all Battersea and Lambeth, all Newington and Kennington, all Bermondsey and Rotherhithe, formed a vast lagoon, broken only by little rises which became the 'eyes' and 'hithes,' the 'islands' and 'landing-rises,' of later settlements. Yet lower down to the eastward the swamp widened as the Lea poured its waters into the Thames in an estuary of its own, an estuary which ran far to the north over as wide an expanse of marsh and fen, while at its mouth it stretched its tidal waters over the mud flats which have been turned by embankment into the Isle of Dogs. Near the point where the two rivers meet, a traveller who was mounting the Thames from the sea saw the first dry land to which his bark could steer. The spot was in fact the extremity of a low line of rising ground which was thrown out from the heights of Hampstead that border the river valley to the north, and which passed over the sites of our Hyde Park and Holborn to thrust itself on the east into the great morass. This eastern portion of it, however, was severed from the rest of the rise by the deep gorge of a stream that fell from the northern hills, the stream of the Fleet, whose waters, long since lost in London sewers, ran in earlier days between steep banks—banks that still leave their impress in the local levels, and in local names like Snow Hill—to the Thames at Blackfriars.

The rise of 'dun' that stretched from this tidal channel of the Fleet to the spot now marked by the Tower, and which was destined to become the site of London, rose at its highest some fifty feet above the level of the tide, and was broken into two parts by a ravine through which ran the stream which has since been known as the Wallbrook. Such a position was admirably adapted for defence; it was indeed almost impregnable. Sheltered to east and south by the lagoons of the Lea and the Thames, guarded to westward by the deep cleft of the Fleet, it saw stretching along its northern border the broad fen whose name has survived in our modern Moorgate. Nor, as the first point at which merchants could land from the great river, was the spot less adapted for trade. But it was long before the trader found dwelling on its soil. Old as it is, London is far from being one of the oldest of British cities; till the coming of the Romans, indeed, the loneliness of its site seems to have been unbroken by any settlement whatever. The 'dun' was in fact the centre of a vast wilderness. Beyond the

marshes to the east lay the forest track of southern Essex. Across the lagoon to the south rose the woodlands of Sydenham and Forest Hill, themselves but advance guards of the fastnesses of the Weald. To the north the heights of Highgate and Hampstead were crowned with forest-masses, through which the boar and the wild ox wandered without fear of man down to the days of the Plantagenets. Even the open country to the west was but a waste. It seems to have formed the borderland between two British tribes who dwelt in Hertford and in Essex, and its barren clays were given over to solitude by the usages of primæval war.

With the coming of the Roman, however, this solitude passed away. We know nothing of the settlement of the town; but its advantages as the first landing-place along the Thames secured for it at once the command of all trading intercourse with Gaul, and through Gaul with the Empire at large. So rapid was its growth that only a few years after the landing of Claudius London had risen into a flourishing port, the massacre of whose foreign traders was the darkest blot on the British rising under Boadicea. But the town soon recovered from the blow. If York became the official capital of the province, London formed its actual centre, for by one of the many advantages of its site it was necessarily the point from which the roads of the conquerors radiated over the island. Such a point would naturally have been found at Richborough, where the line of communication with the body of the empire passed the Channel at its narrowest part. But Kent, as we have seen, was shut in by barriers which made communication with the rest of the island impracticable, save at the single spot where the road, thus drawn inland from Richborough, found a practicable passage over the Thames. And this spot was at London. For London was the lowest ground on the tidal waters of the river on which it was possible to build a bridge, and even before a bridge was built, it was the lowest ground where passage could be gained by a ferry. But once over the river, the difficulty of divergence was removed, and it was thus that roads struck from London to every quarter of Britain. As the meeting-point of these roads, the point of their contact with the lines of communication between the province and the empire, as well as the natural port for the bulk of its trade, which then lay exclusively with the Mediterranean and the Channel, London could not fail to grow fast in population and wealth.

From the traces of burial indeed, which we find over part of the ground, it seems almost certain that the earlier city was far from ex-

tending over the whole of the space embraced within the existing Roman walls. It is possible that Londinium at first only occupied the height to the eastward of the Wallbrook, which then ran in a deep channel to its little port at Dowgate, and that its northern bound was marked by a trench whose memory survives in the name of our 'Langbourne' Ward; while the ground to the westward as far as the Fleet was still open and used for interments. But buildings soon rose over the ground outside these narrow bounds. We find traces of villas and pavements stretching over the earlier grave-grounds; and by the close of the third century at latest London had spread over the whole area of the rise east of the Fleet between the Thames and the Moor. It was this London that was girt in by the massive walls which were probably raised by Theodosius, when the inroads of the Picts and the descents of the Saxons first made walls necessary for the security of towns in Britain.

But the city spread even beyond these wide bounds. Houses of citizens studded the country around its walls, and bordered the roads which struck westward along the hollow bourne or Holborn, and northward along our Gracechurch Street. Outside the walls too lay a ring of burial-places at Shoreditch and elsewhere; while a suburb rose across the river on the site of the present Southwark. One of the most laborious works of the Roman settlers was the embankment of the lower channels of the Thames and of the Lea; and it was on ground thus gained from the morass across the river at our Southwark that dwellings clustered whose number and wealth leave hardly a doubt that they were already linked by a bridge with the mother-city. Of London itself, however, we know little. Tradition places a temple of Diana on the spot where the Christian missionaries raised in after time the Church of St. Paul, and here on this higher ground some statelier public buildings may have clustered round it. But the scarcity of stone and abundance of clay in its neighbourhood were fatal to any architectural pretensions; and from the character of its remains the town seems to have been little more than a mass of brick houses and red-tiled roofs, pieced with a network of the narrow alleys which passed for streets in the Roman world, and cleft throughout its area by two wider roads from the bridge. One of these led by a gate near our Bishopsgate to the northern road, the other by a line which is partly represented in our Cannon Street to Newgate and the west. But if it fell far beneath many of the British towns in its outer seeming, as it fell beneath York in official rank, London surpassed all in population

and wealth. Middlesex possibly represents a district which depended on it in this earlier, as it certainly did in a later time; and the privileges of the chase, which its citizens enjoyed throughout the middle ages in the woodland that covered the heights of Hampstead and along the southern bank of the river as far as the Cray, may have been drawn from the rights of the Roman burghers.

In the downfall of the Imperial rule such a town would doubtless gain a virtual independence; but through the darkness of the time we catch only a passing glimpse of its life, when the Britons, after their rout at Crayford, fled from the Jutes to find shelter at 'Lundenbyryg.' Its power, however, was seen in the arrest of the invaders as they neared its southern suburb; for the western border of Kent represents, no doubt, fairly enough the point at which the Londoners were able to hold the 'Cantwara' at bay on the edge of the morass that stretched from Southwark to the Dulwich hills. Hardly were these southern assailants brought to a standstill when London must have had to struggle against assailants on the northern bank of the river. Here, however, the attack was probably a fainter one. Not only was the line of forest and marsh along the lower channel of the Lea impenetrable, but the woodland and mud flats of southern Essex offered little temptation to the settlers who might have pressed forward in this quarter. The energies of the East-Saxons were in fact long drawn elsewhere; for their settlements lay mainly in the north of the district to which they gave their name, where a clearer and more fertile country offered them homes in the valleys of the Colne and the Stour; and even here their numbers must have been too small to push inland, for half a century seems to have elapsed after their first settlement before they were strong enough to advance from the coast into the interior of the island.

When the time came for such an advance, it lay naturally up the river valleys in which they had settled; and these led through thinner woodland to a point in the downs where Saffron Walden still marks an open 'dene' that broke the thickets of the waste or 'Weald'. Once on these downs the East-Saxons found themselves encamped on the central uplands of the line of chalk heights whose extremities had already been seized by their brethren in Berkshire and by the Engle in the Eastern Counties. Though the tract was traversed by the great road which ran across Mid-Britain from London to Chester, the road to which the English gave its later name of Watling Street, it was a wild and lonely region, whose woodlands, even in the days of the Norman

kings, made travel through it a dangerous business. At this time it probably formed the district of Verulamium, a town which stood near the site of the present St. Alban's. Verulamium was one of the oldest towns in Britain; and, in spite of the wild tract in which it stood, its position on the main road from London across Mid-Britain gave it a wealth and importance which are still witnessed by the traces of an amphitheatre, the extent of its walls, and the expanse of ruins from which the Abbey and Abbey Church of later days were mainly constructed. Since Christianity had become the religion of the empire it had won celebrity as the scene of the martyrdom of a Christian soldier, Alban, who was said to have suffered under Diocletian, and whose church was a centre of Christian devotion. But neither its wealth nor its sanctity saved it from the invaders. Its fall was complete; and for centuries to come the broken and charred remains of the town were left in solitude without inhabitants.

The fall of Verulamium and the settlement of its conquerors in the downs about it must have fallen on London as a presage of ruin. A hundred years had passed away since Hengest's men had fallen back baffled from its neighbourhood; and in the long interval its burghers may have counted themselves safe from attack. But year by year the circle of invasion had been closing round the city. The conquest of Kent had broken its communications with the Continent; and whatever trade might struggle from the southern coast through the Weald had been cut off by the conquest of Sussex. That of the Gwent about Winchester closed the road to the south-west; while the capture of Cunetio interrupted all communication with the valley of the Severn and the rich country along its estuary. And now the occupation of Hertfordshire cut off the city from northern and central Britain, for it was over these chalk uplands that the Watling Street struck across the central plain to Chester and the north-west, and it was through Verulamium that travellers bent round the forest-block above London on their way to the north. Only along the Thames itself could London maintain any communication with what remained of Britain; and even this communication must have been threatened as the invaders crept down the slopes from the north through the woodland which crowned the rises of Hampstead and Highgate, or descended by the valleys of the Brent and the Colne on the tract which retains their name of Middle-Sexe. The settlers in this district, indeed, seem to have been unimportant; and the walls of the great city were still strong enough to defy any direct attack. But when once the invading force had closed

fairly round it, London like its fellow-towns must have yielded to the stress of a long blockade. Although no record remains of its capture or surrender, the course of events seems to give the date of its fall pretty clearly. It was certainly in English hands by the opening of the seventh century.

FREDERIC WILLIAM MAITLAND

1850–1906

The first passage is from Essay III, "The Hide," in Domesday Book and Beyond *(1896), and discusses the fundamental unit of land measurement in early medieval England. The second is from chapter 16, "The Anglican Settlement and the Scottish Reformation," which Acton asked the Downing Professor of English Law at Cambridge to write for volume 2 of the* Cambridge Modern History *(1907). It was the first venture of Maitland outside the sphere of legal history, and drew A. L. Smith to say that one cannot read it "without asking oneself whether, in losing Maitland, the English world has not lost one who might have made a great narrative historian."*

Apart from various obituary tributes (especially by P. Vinogradoff in the English Historical Review, *1907), see A. L. Smith,* F. W. Maitland *(1908), and R. L. Schuyler, "Maitland," in the* American Historical Review, *January, 1952.*

I

What was the hide? However unwilling we may be to face this dreary old question, we can not escape it. At first sight it may seem avoidable by those who are interested in the general drift of national life, but have no desire to solve petty problems or face unnecessary difficulties. The history of weights and measures, some may say, is probably very curious and no doubt is worth study; but we, who shall be amply satisfied if we understand the grand movements and the broad traits, must leave this little province, as we must leave much

else, to antiquarian specialists. Unfortunately, however, that question about the hide is 'pre-judicial' to all the great questions of early English history.

If our choice lay between 30 and 40 acres, or again between a long and a short hundred, then indeed we might refuse to take part in the conflict. But between the advocates of big hides of 120 acres or thereabouts and the advocates of little hides of 30 acres or thereabouts there should be no peace. In the construction of early English history we shall adopt one style of architecture if we are supplied with small hides, while if our materials consist of big hides an entirely different 'plan and elevation' must be chosen. Let us take one example. We find the kings giving away manses or hides by fives and tens. What are they really doing? Are they or are they not giving away whole villages? Obviously this question is pre-judicial to many another. Our whole conception of the Anglo-Saxon kingship will be profoundly affected by our attribution or our denial to the king of an alienable superiority over villages that are full of free landowners. This question, therefore, we should have upon our hands even if we thought that we could rear the fabric of political and constitutional history without first laying an economic foundation. But the day for such castles in the air is passing.

Howbeit, we must not talk in this pompous way of castles or foundations. We are not going to lay foundations, nor even to choose a site. We hope to test a few materials and perhaps to show how a site may some day be acquired. . . .

Now for a long time past there has been among historians and antiquaries a good deal of agreement in favour of this large hide, but against it appeal may be made to honoured names, such as those of Kemble and Eyton. Also it must be confessed that in favour of much smaller hides, or at least of much smaller hides for the earliest days, some weighty arguments may be advanced. In order that they may be understood, and perchance refuted, we must pursue a long and devious course and must raise by the way many questions, touching which we have no right to an opinion: questions about agriculture, questions about land measurement, perhaps even physiological questions. Also it is our misfortune that, as we stumble through the night, we must needs stumble against some of our fellow adventurers.

At the present moment there is no need for arguments which insist upon the immutable character of ancient agrarian arrangements. If we take up a map of a common field drawn in the eighteenth century,

the lines that we see upon it are in the main very old. The scheme seems fashioned for the purpose of resisting change and compelling the men of one age to till the land as their fathers tilled it. Nothing but an unanimous agreement among those who are not likely to agree can break up that prison-house of cells in which agriculture has been cramped and confined. Rather, it may be, the student who is perusing the 'estate map' and who is fascinated by the possession of a new tool for picking historical locks, should warn himself that, though there has been permanence, there has also been change, and that in a far-off time changes of a certain sort came quickly. True that in the current of agricultural progress there is a rapid acceleration as it flows towards our own day. We may easily go back to an age when the introduction of a new process or new implement was rare. On the other hand, if we fix our attention on the map of any one village and contemplate its strips and balks and virgates, the hazard involved in an assumption of their antiquity will increase swiftly when we have left behind us the advent of Duke William and are urging our inferential career towards Hengest, or, it may be, towards Caesar.

Let us look, for example, at the changes that take place in some Essex villages during the twenty years that precede the Domesday Inquest. The following table shows them:

	Villani	*Bordarii*	*Servi*	*Lord's teams*	*Men's teams*
Teidana, T.R.E.	5	3	4	2	4
T.R.W.	1	17	0	3	3
Waldena, T.R.E.	66	17	16	8	22
T.R.W.	46	40	20	10	22
Hame, T.R.E.	32	16	3	5	8
T.R.W.	48	79	3	4	12
Benefelda, T.R.E.	10	2	7	3	7
T.R.W.	9	11	4	3	4
Wimbeis, T.R.E.	26	18	6	3	21
T.R.W.	26	55	0	3	15

These are but specimens of the obscure little revolutions that are being accomplished in the Essex villages. In general there has been a marked increase in the number of *bordarii,* at the expense of the villeins on the one part and the serfs on the other, and this, whatever

else it may represent, must tell us of a redistribution of tenements, perhaps of a process that substitutes the half-virgate for the virgate as the average holding of an Essex peasant. The jar of conquest has made such revolutions easy.

But, it will be said, though the 'bundles' of strips be cut in half, the main features of the field remain constant. Let us, however, look at Yorkshire, where for fifteen years an immense tract of land has been lying 'waste.' Have we any reason to believe that when agriculture slowly steals back into this desert there will be a mere restoration of the defaced map? Surely not. If for a few years an 'open field' lies waste, there will be no mere restoration. For one thing many of the old outlines will have utterly vanished. Even if the acres were already divided by the so-called 'balks' (and we can not be sure that they always were), the balk was but a narrow strip of unploughed sward and would hardly be perceptible when the whole field was once more a sheet of grass and weeds. For another thing, new settlers would probably begin by ploughing only a small portion of the old field. It is likely enough that their measuring rod would not be even approximately equal to the rod employed in a previous century, and they would have ample opportunity for the introduction of novelties, for the substitution of three fields for two and for all that such a change implies. Now William's deliberate devastation of the north is but one final and grandiose exploit of an ancient kind of warfare. After his day agrarian history becomes more stable because invasions cease and the character of civil warfare changes. The strife between York and Lancaster, between King and Parliament, passes like a thunderstorm over the fields; it damages the crops; but that is all, and Bosworth 'Field' and Naseby 'Field' will next year be tilled in the same old way. A raid of the Danes, a feud between Angle and Saxon, was a different affair. The peasants fought. Men, women and children were sold as slaves. Also there was deliberate devastation. 'They make a wilderness and call it peace.' What else should they call it, when a foodless wilderness is the most scientific of frontiers? Readers of the English Chronicle will doubt whether there is any village in England that has not been once, or more than once, a deserted village. And if we must reckon with war, there is famine also to be reckoned with. When in a few brief words the English Chronicler tells us that in 1043 there was mickle hunger in the land so that the sestar of corn sold for sixty pence and even more, he is, like enough, telling us of a disaster which depopulated many a village and forced many a villager to bow his head

for meat in those evil days. Agrarian history becomes more catastrophic as we trace it backwards.

And, putting on one side the ravages of war and famine, we must call to mind the numerous hints that our map gives us of village colonization. Men did not make two contiguous villages at one time and call them both Hamton. Names are given to places in order that they may be distinguished from neighbouring places. So when we see two different villages, called Hamton and Other Hamton, lying next each other, we may be fairly certain that they are not of equal antiquity, and it is not unlikely that the one is the offshoot and daughter of the other. There are about one hundred and fifty Newtons and Newtowns in England. Every instance of colonization, every new settlement in the woods, gave scope for the introduction of novelties, such scope as was not to be found in after days when men stood thicker on the soil and all the best land was already tilled.

Therefore we must not trust a method of husbandry or a scheme of land-measures much further than we can see it. Nothing, for example, could be rasher than the assumption that the 'three-course system' of tillage was common in the England of the seventh century. We have a little evidence that it was practised in the eleventh, perhaps some evidence that it was not unknown in the ninth. But 'the two-course system' can be traced as far, and seems to have been as common, if not commoner, in the thirteenth century. If on a modern map we see a village with 'trinity fields,' we must not at once decide that those who laid them out sowed two in every year, for it is well within the bounds of possibility that two were left idle. An agriculture of this kind was not unknown in the Yorkshire of the fourteenth century, and indeed we read that in the eighteenth 'one crop and two fallows' was the traditional course in the open fieid of a Suffolk village.

We have time enough on our hands. Between Domesday Book and the withdrawal of the legions lies as long an interval as that which separates the Conqueror from Mr. Arthur Young. Also we have space enough on our hands. Any theory that would paint all England as plotted out for proprietary and agricultural purposes in accordance with a single pattern would be of all theories the least probable. We need not contrast Kent with Westmoreland, or Cornwall with Norfolk, for our maps seem to tell us that Somerset differed from Wiltshire and Dorset. The settlement of a heathen folk loosely banded together under a war-lord was one thing; the conquest of a new province by a Christian king who was advised by foreign bishops and had already

been taught that he had land to 'book,' would be another thing. If, as seems possible, we read in Ine's laws of a 'plantation' of some parts of Somerset effected by means of large allotments made to the king's gesiths, who undertake to put tillers on the soil, we must not at once infer that this is an old procedure, for it may be very new, and may have for its outcome an agrarian arrangement strikingly unlike that which existed in the heart of the older Wessex.

Moreover there are upon the face of our map many cases which seem to tell us that in the oldest days the smallest district that bore a name was often large, and therefore that the territory which subserved a single group of homesteads was often spacious. One example we will take from Norfolk. We find a block of land that now-a-days consists of eleven parishes, namely, Wiggenhall St. Mary the Virgin, Wiggenhall St. German, Wiggenhall St. Peter, Wiggenhall St. Mary Magdalen, Tilney cum Islington, Tilney All Saints, Tilney St. Lawrence, Terrington St. Clement, Terrington St. John, Walpole St. Peter, Walpole St. Andrew. In such a case we can hardly suppose that all these villages belong to the same age, even if we are not entitled to infer that the later villages were not founded until the day for parish churches had arrived. This being so, it is highly probable that some villages were formed at all stages of the feudalizing process, and therefore that a historical account of 'the' English township, or even of 'the' English nucleated village, would of necessity be untrue. And, while this East Anglian specimen is still before us, we may notice another interesting trait. In the Marshland Fen there is a considerable tract of ground which consists of 'detached portions' of these and other villages. Each has been given a block there, a fairly rectangular block. At one point the partition is minute. A space of less than 36 acres has been cut up so that no less than six villages shall have a piece, a rectangular piece of it. It seems very possible that this fen has at some time been common ground for all these villages, and, as already said, it is in this quarter that we may perhaps find traces of something that resembled the 'marks' of Germany. The science of village morphology is still very young, and we must not be led away into any discussion of its elements; but there is the more reason why we should take to heart those warnings that it already gives us, because what we can read of hides is to be found for the more part in documents proceeding from a central power, which, for governmental and fiscal purposes, endeavours to preserve fictitious continuity and uni-

formity in the midst of change and variety. However, we must draw nearer to our task.

As regards land measurement, we may be fairly certain that in the days before the Norman Conquest there was little real, though much nominal uniformity. The only measures for the size of things with which nature has equipped the natural man are his limbs. For the things that he handles he uses his thumb, span, cubit, ell; for the ground upon which he walks, his foot and his pace. For large spaces and long distances he must have recourse to 'time-labour-units', to the day's journey and the morning's ploughing. Then gradually, under the fostering care of government, steady equations are established between these units:—twelve thumbs, for instance, are to make a foot. Thus the measures for land are brought into connexion with the more delicate measures used for cloth and similar stuff. Then an attempt to obtain some standard less variable than the limb may forge a link between thumbs and grains of corn. Another device is the measuring rod. One rod will represent the arm of an average man; a longer rod may serve to mediate between the foot which is short and the acre or day's ploughing which is large. In laying out a field in such wise that it shall consist of equal pieces, each of which can be ploughed in a forenoon, we naturally use a rod. We say, for example, that to plough a strip that is 4 rods wide and 40 long is a fair day's work. For some while there is no reason why the rods employed in two neighbouring villages should be strictly or even approximately equal. Taxation is the great force that makes for standard land measures. Then a king declares how many thumbs there ought to be in the cloth-ell or cloth-yard. At a later time he actually makes cloth-ells or cloth-yards and distributes them, keeping an ultimate standard in his own palace. Thenceforward all other units tend to become mere fractions or multiples of this royal stick. The foot is a third, the thumb or inch a thirty-sixth part thereof. Five and a half cloth-measuring yards make a royal land-measuring rod. Plot out a space which is four rods by forty, you will have an acre.

The whole story, if ever it be told at length, will be intricate; but we believe that a general persuasion that land-measurements ought to be fixed by law and by reference to some one carefully preserved standard is much more modern than most people think. Real accuracy and the establishment of a measure that is to be common to the whole realm first emerge in connexion with the measurement of cloth

and such like. There is a delightful passage in the old Scotch laws which tells us that the ell ought to contain 37 inches meted by the thumbs of three men, 'that is to say, a mekill man and a man of messurabill statur and of a lytill man'. We have somewhere read that in Germany, if a perch of fifteen feet was to be manufactured, the first fifteen people who chanced to come out of church contributed each a foot towards the construction of the standard. At an early time, however, men were trying to find some class of small things which were of a fairly invariable length and hit upon barley-corns. This seems to have happened in England before the Norman Conquest. Instead of taking the 'thoume' of a 'man of messurabill statur' for your inch, you are to take three barley-corns, 'iii bear cornys gud and chosyn but tayllis (i.e. without the tails)'. But the twelfth century was drawing to an end before any decisive step was taken to secure uniformity even in the measurement of cloth. In Richard I's day guardians of weights and measures are to be appointed in every county, city and borough; they are to keep iron *ulnae*. At this time or a little later these *ulnae,* ells or cloth-yards were being delivered out by a royal officer to all who might require them, and that officer had the custody of the ultimate standards. We may doubt whether the laws which require in general terms that there shall be one measure throughout the realm had measures of land in view. A common standard is not nearly as necessary in this case as it is in the case of cloth. Even in our own day men do not buy land by the acre or the perch in the same sense as that in which they buy cloth or cotton by the yard. Very rarely will anyone name a price for a rood and leave it to the other bargainer to decide which out of many roods shall be included in the sale. Nevertheless, the distribution of iron *ulnae* was important. An equation was established between the cloth measure and the land measure: five-and-a-half *ulnae* or cloth-yards make one royal perch. After this we soon find that land is occasionally measured by the iron *ulna* of the king.

The scheme of computation that we know as 'superficial measure' was long in making itself part of the mental furniture of the ordinary man. Such terms as 'square rod' and 'square mile' were not current, nor such equations as that which tells us how 144 square inches make a square foot. Whatever may have been the attainments of some cloistered mathematicians, the man of business did not suppose that he could talk of size without talking of shape, and indeed a set of terms which speak of shapeless size is not very useful until men have enough

of geometry and trigonometry to measure spaces that are not rectangular parallelograms. The enlightened people of the thirteenth century can say that if an acre is *x* perches long it is *y* perches wide. They can compare the size of spaces if all the lines be straight and all the angles right; and for them an acre is no longer of necessity ten times as long as it is broad. But they will not tell us (and they do not think) that an acre contains *z* 'square perches.' This is of some importance to students of Domesday Book. Very often the size of a tract of land is indicated by the length of two lines:—The wood or the pasture is *x* leagues (furlongs, perches, feet) in length and *y* in breadth. Now, to say the least, we are hasty if we treat this as a statement which gives us size without shape. It is not all one to say that a wood is a league long and a league wide and to say that it is two leagues long and half a league wide. The jurors are not speaking of superficial content, they are speaking of length and breadth, and they are either giving us the extreme diameters of the irregularly shaped woods and pastures, or (and this seems more probable) they are making rough estimates of mean diameters. If we go back to an earlier time, the less we think of 'superficial measure' the better.

Let us recall the main features of our modern system, giving them the names that they bore in medieval Latin.

Linear Measure.

12 inches (*pollices*) = 1 foot (*pes*); 3 feet = 1 yard (*ulna*); 5.5 yards = 1 rod, pole, perch (*virga, pertica, perca*); 40 perches = 1 furlong (*quarentina*); 8 furlongs = 1 mile (*mille*); 12 furlongs = 1 *leuua, leuca, leuga* (league).

Superficial Measure.

144 square inches = 1 square foot; 9 square feet = 1 square yard; 30.25 square yards = 1 square perch; 40 square perches = 1 rood; 4 roods = 1 acre.

In the thirteenth century these outlines are already drawn; but, as we have seen, if we are to breathe the spirit of the time, we ought to say (while admitting that acres may be variously shaped) that the normal acre is 4 perches in width and 40 perches (= 1 furlong) in length. The only other space that we need consider is the quarter of an acre, our rood. That ought to be 1 perch in width and 1 furlong (= 40 perches) in length. The breadth of the acre is still known to all Englishmen, for it is the distance between the wickets.

II

Scotland had been slow to emerge from the Middle Age. A country which of all others demanded strong and steady government had been plagued by a series of infant Kings and contested Regencies. In the sixteenth century its barons still belonged to the twelfth, despite a thin veneer of French manners. Its institutions were rudimentary; its Parliaments were feudal assemblies. Since the close of the War of Independence there had been hardly anything that could properly be called constitutional growth. Sometimes there was a little imitation of England and sometimes a little imitation of France, the King appearing as a more or less radical reformer. But the King died young, leaving an infant son, and his feudatories had no desire for reformation. The Scottish monarchy, if monarchy it may be called, was indeed strictly limited; but the limits were set much rather by the power of certain noble families and their numerous retainers than by an assembly of Estates expressing the constant will of an organised community. The prelates, lords, and represented boroughs formed but one Chamber. Attempts to induce the lesser tenants-in-chief to choose representatives who would resemble the English knights of the shire had been abortive, and a bad habit prevailed of delegating the work of a Parliament to a committee known as "the Lords of the Articles." Normally the assembly of Estates was but the registrar of foregone conclusions. In troublous times (and the times were often troublous) the faction that was in power would hold a Parliament, and the other faction would prudently abstain from attendance. When in 1560 an unusually full, free and important Parliament was held for the reformation of religion, an elementary question concerning the right of the minor barons to sit and vote was still debateable, and for many years afterwards those who desire to see the true contribution of Scotland to the history of representative institutions will look, not to the blighted and stunted conclave of the three Estates with its titular Bishops and Abbots commendatory, but to the fresh and vigorous Assembly of the Presbyterian Church.

Steady taxation and all that it implies had been out of the question. The Scots were ready to fight for their King, unless they happened to be fighting against him; but they would not provide him with a revenue adequate for the maintenance of public order. He was expected "to live of his own" in medieval fashion, and his own was not enough to raise him high above his barons. Moreover, Douglases and

Hamiltons and others, hereditary sheriffs and possessors of "regalities," were slow to forget that these crowned stewards of Scotland were no better than themselves. What had "come with a lass" might "go with a lass," and was in no wise mysterious. We shall see Queen Mary, widow of a King of France, giving her hand first to a Lennox-Stewart whose mother is a Douglas and then to a Hepburn, while the heir presumptive to the throne is the head of the Hamiltons. We shall see Queen Elizabeth having trouble with northern earls, with Percies and Nevilles, who set up an altar which she had cast down, and belike would have cast down an altar which she had set up; but their power to disturb England was as nothing to the power of disturbing Scotland which was exercised by those near neighbours and like-minded fellows of theirs who joined the bellicose Congregation of Jesus Christ. And even in the briefest sketch we must not omit to notice that, as beyond England lay Scotland, so beyond the historic Scotland lay the unhistoric land of "the savages." The very means that had been taken by Scottish Kings to make Scotsmen of these "red-shanks" and to bring these savages within the pale of history had raised up new feudatories of almost royal rank and of more than baronial turbulence. Thenceforward, the King would have to reckon, not only with an Albany, an Angus, and an Arran, but also with an Argyll and with a Huntly. When we see these things we think of the dark age: of Charles the Simple and Rolf the Pirate.

Neither valorous feats of arms which overtaxed a people's strength nor a superabundance of earls and barons should conceal from us the nakedness of the land. It is more than probable that in the middle of the sixteenth century the whole of the Scottish nation, including untamable Highlanders, was not too large to be commodiously housed in the Glasgow of today. Life was short, and death was violent. It is true that many hopeful signs of increasing prosperity and enlightenment are visible in the days of James IV (1488–1513). But those days ended at Flodden. The flowers of the forest were once more mown down. The hand went back upon the dial towards poverty and barbarity. An aptitude for letters we may see. Of a brief springtime of song Scotland may fairly boast, for as yet no icy wind was blowing from Geneva. Universities we may see: more universities indeed than the country could well support. By a memorable, if futile, Act of Parliament James IV attempted to drive the sons of the gentry into the grammar-schools. But an all-pervading lack of wealth and of the habits that make for wealth was an impediment to every good endeavour. The

printing press had been in no hurry to reach England (1477); but thirty years more elapsed before it entered Scotland. An aptitude for jurisprudence we might infer from subsequent history; but it is matter of inference. Of lawyers who were not ecclesiastics, of temporal lawyers comparable to the professionally learned justices and serjeants of England, we can hardly read a word. When at length James V founded the College of Justice (1532), half the seats in it, and indeed one more, were allotted to the clergy, and in later days foreign science was imported from the continental universities to supply the deficiencies of an undeveloped system. Scotland had been no place for lawyers, and the temporal law that might be had there, though it came of an excellent stock, had for the more part been of the bookless kind. And as with jurisprudence, so with statesmanship. The Scottish statesman who was not a Bishop was a man of a new kind when Lethington began his correspondence with Cecil; for, even if we employ a medieval standard, we can hardly attribute statecraft or policy to the Albanys and Anguses and Arrans.

In this poor and sparsely peopled country the Church was wealthy; the clergy were numerous, laic, and lazy. The names of "dumb dogs" and "idle bellies" which the new preachers fixed upon them had not been unearned. Nowhere else was there a seed-plot better prepared for revolutionary ideas of a religious sort. Nowhere else would an intelligible Bible be a newer book, or a sermon kindle stranger fires. Nowhere else would the pious champions of the Catholic faith be compelled to say so much that was evil of those who should have been their pastors. Abuses which had been superficial and sporadic in England were widely spread and deeply rooted in the northern kingdom. In particular, the commendation of ecclesiastical benefices to laymen, to babies, had become a matter of course. The Lord James Stewart, the King's base-born son, who at the critical moment is Prior of St. Andrews and sits in Parliament as a member of the spiritual Estate, is a typical figure. The corslet had "clattered" beneath the Archbishop's cassock, and when Bishops and Abbots lie among the dead on Flodden field they have done no less but no more than their duty. We say that the Scottish Church was rich, and so it nominally was, for the kirk-lands were broad; but when the Protestant ministers, much to their own disappointment, had to be content with a very small fraction of the old ecclesiastical revenues, they had probably secured a larger share than had for a long time past been devoted to any purpose more

spiritual than the sustentation of royal, episcopal, and baronial families. We exclaim against the greedy nobles whose lust for the kirk-lands is one of the operative forces in the history of the Scottish Reformation. They might have said that they were only rearranging on a reasonable and modern basis what had long been for practical purposes the property of their class. Their doings send back our thoughts to far-off Carolingian days, when the "benefice" became the hereditary fief. To the King it was, no doubt, convenient that the power of those nobles who would leave heirs should be balanced by the power of other nobles, called prelates, whose children would not be legitimate. But such a system could not be stable, and might at any time provoke an overwhelming outcry for its destruction, if ever one bold man raised his voice against it. Men who are not themselves very moral can feel genuine indignation when they detect immorality among those who, though no worse than themselves, pretend to superior holiness. Prelates, and even primates of Scotland, who were bastards and the begetters of bastards, were the principal fore-runners and coadjutors of John Knox; and unfortunately they were debarred by professional rules from pleading that they, or the best among them, were in truth the respectable husbands of virtuous wives.

Lollardy too there had been, and in some corners of the land it had never been thoroughly extirpated. Also there had been a little burning, but far from enough to accustom the Scots to the sight of a heretic tortured by the flames. Then the German leaven began to work, and from 1528 onwards a few Lutherans were burnt. The protomartyr was Patrick Hamilton, the young and well born Abbot of Ferne. Like many another Scottish youth he had been at the University of Paris. Afterwards he had made a pilgrimage, if not to Wittenberg, at all events to Marburg. It is characteristic of time and place that historians have to consider whether a feud between Douglases and Hamiltons counts for nothing in his martyrdom. "The reek of Patrick Hamilton," we are told, infected many; and we can well believe it. The College of St. Leonard was tainted with humanism and new theology. Young men fled from Scotland and made fame elsewhere. Such were Alexander Aless, who as Alesius became the friend of Melanchthon, and John Macalpine, who as Machabaeus professed divinity at Copenhagen. Such also was George Buchanan, the humanist and the Calvinist, the tutor and the calumniator of Queen Mary. And we see the Wedderburns who are teaching Scotsmen to sing ballads of a novel kind, "good and godly

ballads," but such as priests are loth to hear. And we see Sir David Lindsay, the herald, the poet, the King's friend, scourging the lives and sometimes the beliefs of the clergy with verses which rich and poor will know by heart. In short, there was combustible material lying about in large quantities, and sparks were flying.

JOHN EMERICH EDWARD DALBERG, 1st BARON ACTON

1834–1902

Two volumes of Acton's Cambridge lectures were published, Lectures on Modern History *(1912) and* Lectures on the French Revolution *(1916); the latter were first delivered in the academic year 1895–96. "Robespierre," printed here, is number 19. The lectures on the French Revolution are the most energetic and colorful of his writings.*

The best essay on Acton is Herbert Butterfield's "Acton: His Training, Methods and Intellectual System," in Essays in Honour of G. P. Gooch, *edited by A. O. Sarkissian (1961); and see the same author's* Lord Acton, *Historical Association pamphlet (1948). Lionel Kochan has written on* Acton on History *(1954). The Creighton correspondence and the Inaugural Lecture are printed in* Essays on Freedom and Power, *edited by Gertrude Himmelfarb (Meridian Books, 1956).*

WE REACH the end of the Reign of Terror, on the 9th of Thermidor, the most auspicious date in modern history. In April Robespierre was absolute. He had sent Hébert to death because he promoted disorder, Chaumette because he suppressed religion, Danton because he had sought to restrain bloodshed. His policy was to keep order and authority by regulated terror, and to relax persecution. The governing power was concentrated in the Committee of Public Safety by abolishing the office of minister, instead of which there were twelve Boards of Ad-

ministration reporting to the Committee. That there might be no rival power, the municipality was remodelled and placed in the hands of men attached to Robespierre. The dualism remained between representation in the Assembly and the more direct action of the sovereign people in the Town Hall. When the tocsin rings, said a member of the Commune, the Convention ceases to exist. In other words, when the principal chooses to interfere, he supersedes his agent. The two notions of government are contradictory, and the bodies that incorporated them were naturally hostile. But their antagonism was suspended while Robespierre stood between.

The reformed Commune at once closed all clubs that were not Jacobin. All parties had been crushed: Royalists, Feuillants, Girondins, Cordeliers. What remained of them in the scattered prisons of France was now to be forwarded to Paris, and there gradually disposed of. But though there no longer existed an opposing party, there was still a class of men that had not been reduced or reconciled. This consisted chiefly of deputies who had been sent out to suppress the rising of the provinces in 1793. These Commissaries of the Convention had enjoyed the exercise of enormous authority; they had the uncontrolled power of life and death, and they had gathered spoil without scruple, from the living and the dead. On that account they were objects of suspicion to the austere personage at the head of the State; and they were known to be the most unscrupulous and the most determined of men.

Robespierre, who was nervously apprehensive, saw very early where the danger lay, and he knew which of these enemies there was most cause to dread. He never made up his mind how to meet the peril; he threatened before he struck; and the others combined and overthrew him. He had helped to unite them by introducing a conflict of ideas at a time when, apparently, and on the surface, there was none. Everybody was a Republican and a Jacobin, but Robespierre now insisted on the belief in God. He perished by the monstrous imposture of associating divine sanction with the crimes of his sanguinary reign. The scheme was not suggested by expediency, for he had been always true to the idea. In early life he had met Rousseau at Ermenonville, and he had adopted the indeterminate religion of the "vicaire Savoyard." In March 1792 he proposed a resolution, that the belief in Providence and a future life is a necessary condition of Jacobinism. In November, he argued that the decline of religious conviction left only a residue of ideas favourable to liberty and public virtue, and that the essential

principles of politics might be found in the sublime teaching of Christ. He objected to disendowment, because it is necessary to keep up reverence for an authority superior to man. Therefore, on December 5, he induced the Club to break in pieces the bust of Helvétius.

Although Rousseau, the great master, had been a Genevese Calvinist, nobody thought of preserving Christianity in a Protestant form. The Huguenot ministers themselves did nothing for it, and Robespierre had a peculiar dislike of them. Immediately after the execution of Danton and before the trial of Chaumette, the restoration of religion was foreshadowed by Couthon. A week later it was resolved that the remains of Rousseau, the father of the new church, should be transferred to the Pantheon.

On May 7, Robespierre brought forward his famous motion that the Convention acknowledge the existence of a Supreme Being. His argument, stripped of parliamentary trappings, was this. The secret of the life of a Republic is public and private virtue, that is, integrity, the consciousness of duty, the spirit of self-sacrifice, submission to the discipline of authority. These are the natural conditions of pure democracy; but in an advanced stage of civilisation they are difficult to maintain without the restraint of belief in God, in eternal life, in government by Providence. Society will be divided by passion and interest, unless it is reconciled and controlled by that which is the universal foundation of religions. By this appeal to a higher power Robespierre hoped to strengthen the State at home and abroad. In the latter purpose he succeeded; and the solemn renunciation of atheism impressed the world. It was very distinctly a step in the Conservative direction, for it promised religious liberty. There was to be no favour to churches, but also no persecution. Practically, the advantage was for the Christian part of the population, and irreligion, though not proscribed, was discouraged. The Revolution appeared to be turning backwards, and to seek its friends among those who had acquired their habits of life and thought under the fallen order. The change was undoubted; and it was a change imposed by the will of one man, unsupported by any current of opinion.

A month later, June 8, the Feast of the Supreme Being was held with all the solemnity of which Paris was capable. Robespierre walked in procession from the Tuileries to the Champ de Mars, at the head of the Convention. As the others fell back, he marched alone with his hair powdered, a large nosegay in his hands, wearing the sky-blue coat and nankeens by which he is remembered, for they reappeared in the

crisis of Thermidor. He had attained the loftiest summit of prosperity and greatness that was ever given to man. Not a monarch in Europe could compare with him in power. All that had stood in his way during the last five years had been swept to destruction; all that survived of the Revolution followed obedient at his heels. At the last election of a President in the Convention there had been 117 votes; but 485 had voted for Robespierre, that he might parade at their head that day. It was there, in that supreme and intoxicating moment, that a gulf opened before him, and he became aware of the extremity of his peril. For he could hear the hostile deputies in the front rank behind him, muttering curses and sneering at the enthusiasm with which he was received. Those fierce proconsuls who, at Lyons, Nevers, Nantes, Toulon, had crushed all that they were now forced to venerate by their master, vowed vengeance for their humiliation. They said that this was to be a starting-point for divine right, and the excuse for a new persecution. They felt that they were forging a weapon against themselves, and committing an act of suicide. The decree of the month before would have involved no such dire consequences; but the elaborate and aggressive ceremonial was felt as a declaration of war.

Experienced observers at once predicted that Robespierre would not last long. He lost no time in devising a precaution equal to the danger. He prepared what is known as the law of the 22nd of Prairial, which was presented by Couthon, and carried without a division on June 10, two days after the procession. It is the most tyrannical of all the acts of the Revolution, and is not surpassed by anything in the records of absolute monarchy. For the decree of Prairial suppressed the formalities of law in political trials. It was said by Couthon, that delays may be useful where only private interests are at stake, but there must be none where the interest of the entire public is to be vindicated. The public enemy has only to be identified. The State despatches him to save itself. Therefore the Committee was empowered to send whom it chose before the tribunal, and if the jury was satisfied, no time was to be lost with witnesses, written depositions, or arguments. Nobody whom Robespierre selected for execution would be allowed to delay judgment by defence; and that there might be no exception or immunity from arbitrary arrest and immediate sentence, all previous decrees in matter of procedure were revoked. That article contained the whole point, for it deprived the Convention of jurisdiction for the protection of its own members. Robespierre had only to send a deputy's name to the public accuser, and he would be in his grave next day.

The point had been so well concealed that nobody perceived it. Afterwards, the deputies, warned by the great jurist Merlin, saw what they had done, and on June 11, they stipulated that no member should be arrested without leave of the Convention. Couthon and Robespierre were not present. On the 12th, by threatening that the Committees would resign, they caused the decree of the previous day to be rescinded, but they assured the Assembly that it was superfluous, and their design had been misunderstood. They maintained their text, and gained their object; but the success was on the other side. The scheme had been exposed, and the Convention had resisted, for the first time. The opposing deputies had received warning, and showed that they understood. From that moment they were on the watch, and their enemy shrank from employing against them a clause the validity of which he had denied. He gave them time to combine. Over the rest of the nation he exerted his new power without control. The victims increased rapidly in number. Down to the middle of June, in fourteen months, the executions had been about 1200. In seven weeks, after the law of Prairial, they were 1376; that is, an average of 32 in a week rose to an average of 196. But the guillotine was removed to a distant part of the city, where a deep trench was dug to carry away such quantities of blood.

During this time the Tribunal was not acting against men actually in public life, and we are not compelled to study its judgments, as if they were making history. Whilst inoffensive people were suffering obscurely, the enemies of the tyrant were plotting to save themselves from the dreadful fate they saw so near them. Nothing bound them together but fear and a common hatred for the obtrusive dogmatist at the head of affairs; and it was not evident to each that they were acting in the same cause. But there was a man among them, still somewhat in the background, but gifted with an incredible dexterity, who hurled Napoleon from power in 1815 and Robespierre in 1794.

Fouché, formerly an Oratorian, had been one of the most unscrupulous deputies on missions, and had given the example of seizing the treasure of churches. For he said there were no laws, and they had gone back to the state of nature. After the execution of Hébert he was recalled from Lyons; and Robespierre, whose sister he had asked in marriage, defended him at the Jacobins on April 10. Being an unfrocked ecclesiastic, he was elected president of the Club on June 6, as a protest against the clerical tendencies of Robespierre. On the 11th, immediately after the procession, and the law of Prairial, Fouché

attacked him in a speech in which he said that it is to do homage to the Supreme Being to plunge a sword into the heart of a man who oppresses liberty. This was the first opening of hostilities, and it seems to be have been premature. Fouché was not supported by the club at the time, and some weeks later, when Robespierre called him the head of the conspiracy against him, he was expelled. He was a doomed man, carrying his life in his hand, and he adopted more subtle means of combat. July 19, five days after his expulsion, Collot was elected President of the Convention. He and Fouché were united in sacred bands of friendship, for they had put 1682 persons to death at Lyons. About the same day others joined the plotters, and on July 20, Barère, the orator of the Committee, who watched the turning of the tide, made an ambiguous declaration portending a breach. No plan of operations had been agreed upon, and there was yet time for Robespierre, now fully awake to the approaching danger, to strike an irresistible blow.

During the last few weeks the position of the country had undergone a change. On the 1st of June, Villaret Joyeuse had given battle to the English off Ushant. It was the beginning of that long series of fights at sea, in which the French were so often successful in single combat, and so often defeated in general actions. They lost the day, but not the object for which they fought, as the supplies of American grain were brought safely into port. That substantial success and the opportune legend of the Vengeur saved the government from reproach. At the end of the month St. Just brought news of the French victory over the Austrians at Fleurus, the scene of so many battles. It was due to Jourdan and his officers, and would have been lost if they had obeyed St. Just; but he arrived in time to tell his own story. Many years were to pass before an enemy's guns were again heard on the Belgian frontier. St. Just entreated his colleague to seize the opportunity, and to destroy his enemies while the people were rejoicing over victory. It appeared, afterwards, that the battle of Fleurus, the greatest which the French had won since the reign of Lewis XIV, rendered no service to the government under whom it was fought. The soil of France was safe for twenty years, and with the terror of invasion, the need for terror at home passed away. It had been borne while the danger lasted; and with the danger, it came to an end.

The Committee of Public Safety resented the law of Prairial; and when asked to authorise the proscription of deputies refused. Robespierre did nothing to conciliate the members, and had not the majority.

And he threatened and insulted Carnot. As the powers were then constituted he was helpless against his adversaries. The Commune and the Jacobins were true to him; but the Convention was on its guard, and the two Committees were divided. Lists of proscription had been discovered, and those who knew that their names were upon them made no surrender.

Two days after the speech which showed that Barère was wavering, when Collot had been chosen President, and Fouché was at work underground, a joint sitting of both committees was called at night. St. Just proposed that there should be a dictator. Robespierre was ready to accept, but there were only five votes in favour—three out of eleven on one Committee, two out of twelve on the other. The Jacobins sent a deputation to require that the Convention should strengthen the executive; it was dismissed with words by Barère. One resource remained. It might still be possible, disregarding the false move of Prairial, to obtain the authority of the Convention for the arrest, that is, for the trial and execution of some of its members. They had delivered up Danton and Desmoulins, Hérault and Chaumette. They would perhaps abandon Cambon or Fouché, Bourdon or Tallien, four months later.

The Committees had refused Robespierre, and were in open revolt against his will. His opponents there would oppose him in the Assembly. But the mass of the deputies, belonging not to the Mountain but to the Plain, were always on his side. They had no immediate cause for fear, and they had something to hope for. Seventy of their number had been under arrest ever since October, as being implicated in the fall of the Girondins. Robespierre had constantly refused to let them be sent to trial, and they owed him their lives. They were still in prison, still in his power. To save them, their friends in the Assembly were bound to refuse nothing that he asked for. They would not scruple to deliver over to him a few more ruffians as they had delivered over the others in the spring. That was the basis of his calculation. The Mountain would be divided; the honest men of the Plain would give him the majority, and would purge the earth of another batch of miscreants. On his last night at home he said to the friends with whom he lived, "We have nothing to fear, the Plain is with us."

Whilst Robespierre, repulsed by the committees which had so long obeyed him, sat down to compose the speech on which his victory and his existence depended, his enemies were maturing their plans. Fouché informed his sister at Nantes of what was in preparation. On the 21st of July he is expecting that they will triumph immediately. On the

23rd he writes: "Only a few days more, and honest men will have their turn.—Perhaps this very day the traitors will be unmasked." It is unlike so sagacious a man to have written these outspoken letters, for they were intercepted and sent to Paris for the information of Robespierre. But it shows how accurately Fouché timed his calculation, that when they arrived Robespierre was dead.

The importance of the neutral men of the Plain was as obvious to one side as to the other, and the Confederates attempted to negotiate with them. Their overtures were rejected; and when they were renewed, they were rejected a second time. The Plain were disabled by consideration for their friends, hostages in the grasp of Robespierre, and by the prospect of advantage for religion from his recent policy. They loaded him with adulation, and said that when he marched in the procession, with his blue coat and nosegay, he reminded them of Orpheus. They even thought it desirable that he should live to clear off a few more of the most detestable men in France, the very men who were making advances to them. They believed that time was on their side. Tallien, Collot, Fouché were baffled, and the rigid obstinacy of the Plain produced a moment of extreme and certain danger.

Whilst they hesitated, Tallien received a note in a remembered handwriting. That bit of paper saved unnumbered lives, and changed the fortune of France, for it contained these words: "Coward! I am to be tried to-morrow." At Bordeaux, Tallien had found a lady in prison, whose name was Madame de Fontenay, and who was the daughter of the Madrid banker Cabarrus. She was twenty-one, and people who saw her for the first time could not repress an exclamation of surprise at her extraordinary beauty. After her release, she divorced her husband, and married Tallien. In later years she became the Princesse de Chimay; but, for writing that note, she received the profane but unforgotten name of Notre Dame de Thermidor.

On the night of July 26, Tallien and his friends had a third Conference with Boissy d'Anglas and Durand de Maillane, and at last they gave way. But they made their terms. They gave their votes against Robespierre on condition that the Reign of Terror ended with him. There was no condition which the others would not have accepted in their extremity, and it is by that compact that the government of France, when it came into the hands of these men of blood, ceased to be sanguinary. It was high time, for, in the morning, Robespierre had delivered the accusing speech which he had been long preparing, and of which Daunou told Michelet that it was the only very fine

speech he ever made. He spoke of heaven, and of immortality, and of public virtue; he spoke of himself; he denounced his enemies, naming scarcely any but Cambon and Fouché. He did not conclude with any indictment, or with any demand that the Assembly would give up its guilty members. His aim was to conciliate the Plain, and to obtain votes from the Mountain, by causing alarm but not despair. The next stroke was reserved for the morrow, when the Convention, by voting the distribution of his oration, should have committed itself too far to recede. The Convention at once voted that 250,000 copies of the speech should be printed, and that it should be sent to every parish in France. That was the form in which acceptance, entire and unreserved acceptance, was expressed. Robespierre thus obtained all that he demanded for the day. The Assembly would be unable to refuse the sacrifice of its black sheep, when he reappeared with their names.

Then it was seen that, in naming Cambon, the orator had made a mistake. For Cambon, having had the self-command to wait until the Convention had passed its approving vote, rose to reply. He repelled the attack which Robespierre had made upon him, and turned the entire current of opinion by saying, "What paralyses the Republic is the man who has just spoken."

There is no record of a finer act of fortitude in all parliamentary history. The example proved contagious. The Assembly recalled its vote, and referred the speech to the Committee. Robespierre sank upon his seat and murmured, "I am a lost man". He saw that the Plain could no longer be trusted. His attack was foiled. If the Convention refused the first step, they would not take the second, which he was to ask for next day. He went to the Jacobin Club, and repeated his speech to a crowded meeting. He told them that it was his dying testament. The combination of evil men was too strong for him. He had thrown away his buckler, and was ready for the hemlock. Collot sat on the step below the president's chair, close to him. He said, "Why did you desert the Committee? Why did you make your views known in public without informing us?" Robespierre bit his nails in silence. For he had not consulted the Committee because it had refused the extension of powers, and his action that day had been to appeal to the Convention against them. The Club, divided at first, went over to him, gave him an ovation, and expelled Collot and Billaud-Varennes with violence and contumely. Robespierre, encouraged by his success, exhorted the Jacobins to purify the Convention by expelling bad men, as they had expelled the Girondins. It was his first appeal to the popular

forces. Coffinhal, who was a man of energy, implored him to strike at once. He went home to bed, after midnight, taking no further measures of precaution, and persuaded that he would recover the majority at the next sitting.

Collot and Billaud, both members of the supreme governing body, went to their place of meeting, after the stormy scene at the Club, and found St. Just writing intently. They fell upon him, and demanded to know whether he was preparing accusations against them. He answered that that was exactly the thing he was doing. When he had promised to submit his report to the Committee of Public Safety before he went to the Assembly, they let him go. In the morning, he sent word that he was too much hurt by their treatment of him to keep his promise. Barère meanwhile undertook to have a report ready against St. Just.

Before the Assembly began business on the morning of Sunday the 9th of Thermidor, Tallien was in the lobby cementing the alliance which secured the majority; and Bourdon came up and shook hands with Durand, saying, "Oh! the good men of the Right." When the sitting opened, St. Just at once mounted the tribune and began to read. Tallien, seeing him from outside, exclaimed, "Now is the moment, come and see. It is Robespierre's last day!" The report of St. Just was an attack on the committee. Tallien broke in, declaring that the absent men must be informed and summoned, before he could proceed. St. Just was not a ready speaker, and when he was defied and interrupted, he became silent. Robespierre endeavoured to bring him aid and encouragement; but Tallien would not be stopped. Billaud followed in the name of the government; Barère and Vadier continued, while Robespierre and St. Just insisted vainly on being heard. The interrupters were turbulent, aggressive, out of order, being desperate men fighting for life. Collot d'Herbois, the President, did not rebuke them, and having surrendered his place to a colleague whom he could trust, descended to take part in the fray. If the Convention was suffered once more to hear the dreaded voice of Robespierre, nobody could be sure that he would not recover his ascendency. These tactics succeeded. Both parties to the overnight convention were true to it, and Robespierre was not allowed to make his speech. The galleries had been filled from five in the morning. Barère moved to divide the command of Hanriot, the general of the Commune, on whose sword the triumvirs relied; and the Convention outlawed him and his second in command as the excitement increased. This was early in the afternoon; and it

was on learning this that the Commune called out its forces, and Paris began to rise.

All this time Robespierre had not been personally attacked. Decrees were only demanded, and passed, against his inferior agents. The struggle had lasted for hours; he thought that his adversaries faltered, and made a violent effort to reach the tribune. It had become known in the Assembly that his friends were arming, and they began to cry, "Down with the tyrant!" The President rang his bell and refused to let him speak. At last his voice failed him. A Montagnard exclaimed, "He is choking with the blood of Danton." Robespierre replied, "What! It is Danton you would avenge?" And he said it in a way that signified "Then why did you not defend him?" When he understood what the Mountain meant, and that a motive long repressed had recovered force, he appealed to the Plain, to the honest men who had been so long silent, and so long submissive. They had voted both ways the days before, but he knew nothing of the memorable compact that was to arrest the guillotine. But the Plain, who were not prepared with articulate arguments for their change of front, were content with the unanswerable cry, "Down with the tyrant!" That was evidently decisive; and when that declaration had been evoked by his direct appeal the end came speedily. An unknown deputy moved that Robespierre be arrested, nobody spoke against it; and his brother and several friends were taken into custody with him. None made any resistance or protest. The conflict, they knew, would be outside. The Commune of Paris, the Jacobin Club, the revolutionary tribunal were of their party; and how many of the armed multitude, nobody could tell. All was not lost until that was known. At five o'clock the Convention, weary with a heavy day's work, adjourned for dinner.

The Commune had its opportunity, and began to gain ground. Their troops collected slowly, and Hanriot was arrested. He was released, and brought back in triumph to the Hôtel de Ville, where the arrested deputies soon assembled. They had been sent to different prisons, but all the gaolers but one refused to admit them. Robespierre insisted on being imprisoned, but the turnkey at the Luxembourg was unmoved, and turned him out. He dreaded to be forced into a position of illegality and revolt, because it would enable his enemies to outlaw him. Once outlawed, there was nothing left but an insurrection, of which the issue was uncertain. There was less risk in going before the revolutionary tribunal, where every official was his creature and nominee, and had no hope of mercy from his adversaries, when he ceased to protect. The

gaoler who shut the prison door in his face sealed his fate; and it is supposed, but I do not know, that he had his instructions from Voulland, on the other side, in order that the prisoner might be driven into contumacy, against his will. Expelled from gaol, Robespierre still refused to be free, and went to the police office, where he was technically under arrest.

St. Just, who had seen war, and had made men wonder at his coolness under heavy fire, did not calculate with so much nicety, and repaired with the younger Robespierre, to the municipality, where a force of some thousands of men were assembled. They sent to summon their leader, but the leader declined to come. He felt safer under arrest; but he advised his friends at the Commune to ring the tocsin, close the barriers, stop the Press, seize the post, and arrest the deputies. The position of the man of peace encouraging his comrades to break the law, and explaining how to do it, was too absurd to be borne. Coffinhal, who was a much bigger man, came and carried him away by friendly compulsion.

About ten o'clock the arrested deputies were united. Couthon, who was a cripple, had gone home. The others sent for him, and Robespierre signed a letter by which he was informed that the insurrection was in full activity. This message, and the advice which he forwarded from his shelter with the police prove that he had made up his mind to fight, and did not die a martyr to legality. But if Robespierre was ready, at the last extremity, to fight, he did not know how to do it. The favourable moment was allowed to slip by; not a gun was fired, and the Convention, after several hours of inaction and danger, began to recover power. By Voulland's advice the prisoners out of prison were outlawed, and Barras was put at the head of the faithful forces. Twelve deputies were appointed to proclaim the decrees all over Paris. Mounted on police chargers, conspicuous in their tricolor scarves, and lighted by torches, they made known in every street that Robespierre was now an outlaw under sentence of death. This was at last effective, and Barras was able to report that the people were coming over to the legal authority. An ingenious story was spread about that Robespierre had a seal with the lilies of France. The western and wealthier half of Paris was for the Convention, but parts of the poorer quarters, north and east, went with the Commune. They made no fight. Legendre proceeded to the Jacobin Club, locked the door, and put the key in his pocket, while the members quietly dispersed. About one in the morning, Bourdon, at the head of the men from the district which had been

the stronghold of Chaumette made his way along the river to the Place de Grève. The insurgents drawn up before the Hôtel de Ville made no resistance, and the leaders who were gathered within knew that all was over.

The collapse was instantaneous. A little earlier, a messenger sent out by Gaudin, afterwards Duke of Gaëta and Napoleon's trusted finance minister, reported that he had found Robespierre triumphing and receiving congratulations. Even in those last moments he shrank from action. A warlike proclamation was drawn up, signed by his friends, and laid before him. He refused to sign unless it was in the name of the French people. "Then," said Couthon, "there is nothing to be done but to die." Robespierre, doubtful and hesitating, wrote the first two letters of his name. The rest is a splash of blood. When Bourdon, with a pistol in each hand, and the blade of his sword between his teeth, mounted the stairs of the Hôtel de Ville at the head of his troops, Lebas drew two pistols, handed one to Robespierre, and killed himself with the other. What followed is one of the most disputed facts of history. I believe that Robespierre shot himself in the head, only shattering the jaw. Many excellent critics think that the wound was inflicted by a gendarme who followed Bourdon. His brother took off his shoes and tried to escape by the cornice outside, but fell on to the pavement. Hanriot, the general, hid himself in a sewer, from which he was dragged next morning in a filthy condition. The energetic Coffinhal alone got away, and remained some time in concealment. The rest were captured without trouble.

Robespierre was carried to the Tuileries and laid on a table where, for some hours, people came and stared at him. Surgeons attended to his wound, and he bore his sufferings with tranquillity. From the moment when the shot was fired he never spoke; but at the Conciergerie he asked, by signs, for writing materials. They were denied him, and he went to death taking his secret with him out of the world. For there has always been a mysterious suspicion that the tale has been but half told, and that there is something deeper than the base and hollow criminal on the surface. Napoleon liked him, and believed that he meant well. Chambacérès, the arch-chancellor of the Empire, who governed France when the Emperor took the field, said to him one day, "It is a cause that was decided but was never argued."

Some of those who felled the tyrant, such as Cambon and Barère, long after repented their part in his fall. In the north of Europe, especially in Denmark, he had warm admirers. European society be-

lieved that he had affinity with it. It took him to be a man of authority, integrity, and order, an enemy of corruption and of war, who fell because he attempted to bar the progress of unbelief, which was the strongest current of the age. His private life was inoffensive and decent. He had been the equal of emperors and kings; an army of 700,000 men obeyed his word; he controlled millions of secret service money, and could have obtained what he liked for pardons, and he lived on a deputy's allowance of eighteen francs a day, leaving a fortune of less than twenty guineas in depreciated assignats. Admiring enemies assert that by legal confiscation, the division of properties, and the progressive taxation of wealth, he would have raised the revenue to twenty-two millions sterling, none of which would have been taken from the great body of small cultivators who would thus have been for ever bound to the Revolution. There is no doubt that he held fast to the doctrine of equality, which means government by the poor and payment by the rich. Also, he desired power, if it was only for self-preservation; and he held it by bloodshed, as Lewis XIV had done, and Peter the Great, and Frederic. Indifference to the destruction of human life, even the delight at the sight of blood, was common all round him, and had appeared before the Revolution began. The transformation of society as he imagined, if it cost a few thousand heads in a twelvemonth, was less deadly than a single day of Napoleon fighting for no worthier motive than ambition. His private note-book has been printed, but it does not show what he thought of the future. That is the problem which the guillotine left unsolved on the evening of June 28, 1794. Only this is certain, that he remains the most hateful character in the forefront of history since Machiavelli reduced to a code the wickedness of public men.

GEORGE MACAULAY TREVELYAN

1876–1961

This chapter, "Malplaquet," is from volume three, The Peace and the Protestant Succession, *of* England under Queen Anne. *It was first published in 1934.*

WHEN THE ALLIES, in the spring of 1709, refused to make peace on any reasonable terms, they were encouraged by the expectation that the resistance of the French army would soon be brought to an end by famine, and that the road to Paris would lie clear. The *Tatler* for June 4 amused the Town by an address to 'Lewis le Grand', taunting him with the poverty and starvation to which he had reduced France, and ending with the advice:

Then, sir, the present minute chuse
  Our armies are advancèd;
Those terms you at the Hague refuse
  At Paris won't be granted.

Consider this, and Dunkirk raze
  And Anna's title own;
Send one Pretender out to graze
  And call the other home.

The 'other' Pretender was his grandson, Philip V of Spain.

Indeed, the famine in France that year threatened to put an end

to the national resistance. The British Government made corn contraband, and in the summer an English Squadron under Sir John Norris was sent to the Sound to stop the exportation of corn to France in Scandinavian and other neutral bottoms. The cargoes thus stopped were not confiscated, but bought, for the Maritime Powers were throughout the war most anxious not to quarrel with the Baltic States. At the Hague the French negotiators confessed that they could no longer resist 'Famine, the hand of God.'

It was believed that the enemy forces were in a state of dissolution; and such, in truth, was the case when Villars first took over the command on the Franco-Belgian frontier. He himself tells us that, when he arrived at Tournai in March, the privates had sold their arms and jackets for bread and that even the subaltern officers were parting with their shirts. Men were fast drifting away from the colours in search of food. Hope and discipline were dead. If in April Marlborough could have gathered 80,000 men ready to attack, he could have marched to Versailles. But when he actually took the field at the end of June, 120,000 proved not enough: Paris had been saved by the customary six months' pause in military operations. During the spring and early summer a new French army had come into being, largely new in personnel and wholly new in spirit. How was this miracle accomplished?

All France knew that Villars was the only man who could stop Marlborough, as he had stopped him on the Moselle four years before. The French Marshal's air of jovial gasconade, expressive of unbounded self-confidence, was tonic to his depressed and anxious fellow-countrymen. Though always swaggering as if he alone had the secret of victory, he was no dupe of his own optimism; he seldom miscalculated chances and was far less rash in the presence of Marlborough than Marsin, Villeroi or Vendôme. He had, moreover, something of the equalitarian spirit of the French armies of the Republican age unborn. He was no courtier, no observer of persons, and seemed out of place in the *ancien régime.* He bullied Versailles till it sent bread to the army; he spoke in open scorn of the Marshals and Princes whose failures in the field had landed the country in this pass. It was his hour. Neither priests nor nobles dared murmur against, for he was their only hope. Madame de Maintenon supported him and he wrote her the frankest letters on the situation.

It might have been said of Villars as it had been said of Cromwell: 'In the dark perils of war, in the high places of the field, hope shone in him like a pillar of fire, when it had gone out in all the others.' And

from him it rekindled itself and spread. The habitual expression of his face was a smile in which were blended high spirits, self-approbation and sheer good humour. The soldiers saw in him their comrade, to whom they could speak man to man. The spirit of discipline could not have been restored in that army without confidence and the personal touch. He went round among the starving troops and heard their griefs, thanked them for their endurance, stirred their pride, awoke their expectations. Often, so he tells us, he promised them bread on such and such a day, when he did not in fact know whence it was coming. But the soldiers knew that at least he was making the most strenuous efforts to ransack France on their behalf. '*Monsieur le maréchal a raison*,' they would answer, '*il faut souffrir quelque fois*.' Others said to him, '*Nous vous demandons du pain: du reste nous nous passerons d'habits et de chemises*.'

King Louis, having named Villars to the command, supported him with all his might. The Provincial Governors were set on to furnish the army with bread at the expense of everyone else. The peasants starved, the rich ate black bread and sold their plate, that the soldiers might live. Villars gave rations to a regiment on the days when it marched; on days of repose it fasted. After this fashion they weathered that dreadful spring. When the peasants heard that food was to be had in the camp, sturdy youths came in by thousands to enlist and follow the bread waggons. The thinned ranks filled again. Frost and famine such as France had not known for a hundred years acted as recruiting sergeants for a force still dependent on voluntary enlistment.

And so, beneath the tattered flags, a hollow-cheeked army was formed under its gay commander. Men who had been through that experience would fight, under Villars, more stubbornly than the French of Ramillies and Oudenarde. Villars asked that some Princes of the Blood should come to share the campaign, but, suitably enough, none came except the gaunt young 'King of England', fit company for men in misfortune. Another exiled Prince had been found by Villars on his first arrival on the frontier, the Bavarian Elector, from whom he had parted in anger the year before Blenheim. 'I found him,' he wrote, 'in a very different condition from the brilliant surroundings where I had last seen him at Munich.' But in misfortune, the two men, both of them brave and generous, speedily forgot their old quarrels.

While Villars was thus at work, the Allies at the Hague were helping to revive the spirit of France. Their gross rejection of the almost abject terms which Louis offered as the price of peace, while it defeated

the hopes and disconcerted the politics of many quiet folk in England and Holland, put Louis in unity with his people. As early as October 1706 Vendôme had advised that the King should convoke the States General, in abeyance for a hundred years past, and 'expose to them the insolence of the foe.' The Grand Monarch could not stoop to that, but he took a new departure when in June 1709 he issued with great effect a proclamation to his subjects, setting out the case as it now stood between himself and his enemies, recounting the sacrifices he had offered to make and calling for 'new efforts, since the immense concessions I was ready to grant prove useless for the re-establishment of peace.' A war begun in the pride and world-ambition of a despot had been turned by the victories of Marlborough into the defence of a country by its citizens. The French spirit, sometimes so blind and overbearing, now appeared in its pure and legitimate shape.

On the other side an immense army was being assembled in the Spanish Netherlands to march on Paris under Marlborough and Eugene. The abnormal winter caused suffering throughout all Europe, but to nothing like the same extent as in exhausted and besieged France, where, moreover, the harvest prospects were worse affected than elsewhere by the power of the long-continued frost. Food and money were more plentiful among the Allies. Before the new year, the Whig Parliament had voted an increase of 10,000 men to the British contingent in Flanders. The Opposition dared only murmur that the decision might well have been left over till they learned what the Dutch were ready to do; and a few days later came the news that the States had decided to raise an additional 6000 men for 1709. The war-party was at length in full control of Holland, at the very moment when peace had become the most pressing need of the impoverished Republic. The greatest force ever yet raised by the Dutch was sent into the field under the charge of Deputies who, however little some of them like Goslinga loved the Duke, no longer dreamed of putting their veto on his use of the blue-coats in battle.

While Marlborough's command was thus increased, Eugene appeared beside him at the head of an unusually powerful German and Imperial contingent. The King of Prussia, according to his wont every winter, had grumbled and threatened to withdraw his troops, but had once more yielded to a personal letter of Marlborough and sent 5000 extra men.

And so, at the end of June, the Allied Army entered the plains of Lille some 120,000 strong, nearly twice the number that had triumphed

at Ramillies. Villars had by that time gathered 80,000 or 90,000 to oppose. Shortage of food for men and horses continued to hamper the French movements throughout the Campaign, but at least Villars was now in a condition to put up some resistance to the Allied advance.

Caution was still demanded of him: he was inferior in numbers, in supplies and in the prestige of victory, and his was the last army of France. Another Ramillies or Oudenarde would put an end to the war. He could not risk a battle in the open, yet he must stop the advance on Paris and he was well aware, as he tells of the truth of Turenne's dictum, that 'the general who is absolutely determined to avoid a battle surrenders his country to the general who appears to seek one.' He therefore adopted the system of field entrenchments, always dear to the soldiers of King Louis. As Uncle Toby said, from his experience of the wars of King William:

> If the French have the advantage of a wood, or you give them a moment's time to entrench themselves, they are a nation which will pop and pop for ever at you.

Combining caution with boldness, Villars constructed 'the Lines of La Bassée', forty miles long, from the neighbourhood of Aire to the neighbourhood of Douai. His own headquarters were in the centre at La Bassée only ten miles from the enemy's quarters at Lille. In spite, as he tells us, of 'the timorous counsels of several general officers,' he had constructed the Lines in the most advanced position that could be defended yielding to the invader as little as possible of the sacred soil. The marshy reaches of the upper Lys and Scarpe greatly added to the strength of the earthworks, and in some stretches altogether took their place. Heavy rains in June made the position more formidable, and the approach more difficult.

Cadogan, disguised it is said as a peasant, conducted a reconnaissance of the Lines of La Bassée, and his report was discouraging as to the chances of an attack. Marlborough and Eugene knew that they could not take such liberties with Villars as with Villeroi or Tallard. 'If it had been reasonable,' the Duke wrote to Sarah on June 27, 'this letter would have brought you news of a battle; but Prince Eugene, myself, and all the generals did not think it advisable to run so great a hazard.' They reluctantly turned instead to the siege of Tournai.

In a sense this decision was the crisis of the campaign and indeed of the whole last phase of the War of the Spanish Succession. For if instead of an immediate march to Paris, a long course of sieges was

after all necessary to clear the way, the chance was considerable that the patience or cohesion of the Alliance would be exhausted before the last frontier fortress was taken under the eyes of the vigilant Villars.

Having decided to besiege Tournai, Marlborough and Eugene deceived the French Marshal as to their real intentions, by a movement which seemed to threaten the north-western end of his Lines of La Bassée. To meet it he shuffled his troops, and withdrew a portion of the Tournai garrison. Then Marlborough, by a rapid turn of the Allied Army on its night march, invested the town before the men withdrawn from it could be sent back or the place itself revictualled.

Except Lille, that had fallen the year before, Tournai was the strongest fortress of the age. But the Allies hoped, in the circumstances, to take it in a month. It was, however, gallantly defended by its reduced and famished garrison of 6400 men, and more than two months elapsed before both town and citadel had fallen.

Next after Lille, Tournai afforded the siege of the war most interesting to professional soldiers. Its elaborate system of mines and underground galleries involved the attacking parties in a novel species of warfare in the dark, amid unseen dangers, 'more terrible than ever is met with in any other part of a soldier's duty.' 'Not a foot of the ground,' wrote Colonel Revett, 'that is not undermined and casemated,' in this 'the finest and strongest fortification in Europe.' 'Our miners,' wrote Marlborough, 'have discovered one of their galleries at each attack, but dare not advance to make the proper use of this discovery, because of the enemy's continual fire of small shot under ground. We are preparing to roll bombs into these galleries in order to dislodge them.' When at length the citadel fell on September 3, the Allies had lost over 5000 killed and wounded, including a large proportion of British.

The campaign had begun late, and when Tournai fell autumn was already at hand. Villars' Lines, which he had now extended eastward from the Scarpe to the Schelde above Condé, denied all approach to Valenciennes, Douai or Béthune on the route to Paris. Marlborough and Eugene decided that the best use they could make of the remainder of the year was to take Mons. Its capture would afford a pledge of some diplomatic value, but it would do little to open the road into France. Only if, to save Mons, Villars left his Lines to offer battle, could anything great be accomplished. It is probable that Marlborough now realized that nothing except a battle could put a

speedy end to the war, and that he was proportionately eager to bring one about.

Another skilful and secret movement, and a long circuitous route involving prodigies of marching by the Allied troops, placed them between the enemy and Mons. Villars arrived on the scene too late to throw in succours. But instead of returning at once to the shelter of the Lines of La Bassée, he remained to see what opportunity might occur of disturbing the progress of the siege.

Between the two armies lay a long screen of forest, which could be traversed either by the Gap of Boussu to the north, or near the southern end by the Gap of Malplaquet. Villars hung about behind the western edge of the trees, keeping the Allies in uncertainty and rendering it necessary for them to guard the debouchment of both the Gaps, lest he should attack them through one or the other. When, therefore, by a sudden march southwards he appeared in the Gap of Malplaquet, he caught Marlborough's Dutch and British army encamped near Blaregnies at some distance from Eugene's smaller German army, which was camped further north watching the Gap of Boussu. The French were in strong ground of woods and marshes, not yet reconnoitred by the Allies. Moreover, Marlborough's field artillery had not yet fully come up. Those authors, therefore, who have blamed him for not attacking Villars on September 9, when he first appeared in the Gap of Malplaquet, may well be mistaken.

But the opposite school of critics, who blamed Villars for not himself attacking the Allies on that day, may be equally unjust. His was the last army of France, and he had no right to risk the freedom of his country on such a hazard. It would have taken many hours to deploy his 80,000 men into line; and, after that, it would have been no light task to crush the enemy's best troops, fighting under Marlborough's eye. Before he had disposed of the Dutch and English, Eugene's Germans might have arrived like Blücher's at Waterloo, to overwhelm him with the superior numbers of the united Allied force. Moreover, the revived morale of his own troops was still unproven; his decision to test it behind entrenchments but not in the open field was very probably the salvation of France.

On the morning of September 10 Eugene's army was united to Marlborough's in face of the French, who were drawn up in the Gap of Malplaquet and in the parts of the forest contiguous on either side. It would have been possible for the Allies to refuse battle, to draw lines of contravallation against Villars, and proceed with the siege

of Mons under his nose; and some, though not all, of the British officers thought this would be the wiser course. But Marlborough and Eugene were playing for high stakes. There lay the enemy within their reach. Let them strike him as they had struck at Blenheim and at Oudenarde, and bring the war to an end.

It remained to be decided whether they should attack that day or wait till the morrow. The argument for delay was that eighteen battalions under General Withers were still on the march from Tournai and could join in the battle on the 11th but not on the 10th. Rightly or wrongly it was decided to give them time to come up. The extra day enabled Villars to render more formidable the system of field defences from which he derived so immense an advantage in the battle. After the event, it became usual to think that the decision to wait had been wrong, though nothing is certain in the might-have-beens of war.

At any rate, Villars used to good purpose the two nights and the whole day that passed between his arrival in the Gap of Malplaquet and the actual engagement. The army was set on to entrench itself in the open ground in the centre, and to fortify its woodland flanks with abatis of felled trees. In the Wood of Sars, line behind line of defences sprang into being. In the open country formidable earthworks were erected, with re-entrant angles, taking skilful advantage of the contours of the ground. Everyone, cavalry as well as infantry, toiled with a will. Only wherever Villars appeared, the soldiers dropped spades and axes and ran up to tell him how they meant to defend their handiwork next day.

A recent event had raised the enthusiasm of the army to its height. Boufflers had arrived in camp. The veteran of so many wars was the only other French Marshal whom Villars respected, and he had been wisely chosen by the King to go and strengthen his hands. Villars had responded generously and had offered to serve under his senior; but the old man had replied in the same spirit that he came only 'as a volunteer'. His presence and the manifest concord between the two best generals of France increased the ardour of the troops, as much as the notorious discord between Tallard and Marsin at Blenheim, and between Vendôme and Burgundy at Oudenarde had discouraged the temperamental and sensitive French *poilu*.

The plans of the Allied commanders to force this formidable position could not have been better laid. But they failed to reckon on the renewed spirit of the French soldiery: no doubt they expected a long

and hard struggle and grave losses all along the line as at Blenheim, to be followed once more by the moral disintegration of a large part of the French army when the day was lost, opening the road to Paris.

The ground in the French centre, between the woods, was strongly protected by a series of 'redans' and entrenched batteries. This part of the line was 'refused'—that is to say, withdrawn behind the protruding wings. In particular, the Wood of Sars was so situated that, until the Allies had occupied its skirts, they could not attack the French centre without being subjected to a devastating cross-fire. Orkney, therefore, with fifteen battalions of British infantry, stood motionless in the centre during the first half of the battle, gazing at the high 'redans' that he was ultimately to storm and so cut the French army in two.

But on both flanks an attack was to be begun in the morning, at seven by the Germans on the Allied right against the Wood of Sars, and half an hour later by the Dutch on the left. The great army of the States General nominally under the command of Count Tilly, but led and inspired that day by the gallant young Prince of Orange, was to assault the entrenchments on Villars' right, within and without the Wood of Laignières. But this operation, though it was to be pushed hard in order to hold the French forces in that quarter from being sent elsewhere, was only meant as a 'containing' attack, like that of Eugene on the enemy's northern flank at Blenheim.

The object of the Allied commanders was to break the enemy's left wing in the Wood of Sars, and to pierce his centre after it had been weakened by withdrawals of troops to strengthen the threatened flanks. To secure success, a fine strategic combination, unique in the wars of that period, was planned and effected; General Withers was coming up from Tournai with his eighteen battalions, partly of British infantry, accompanied by six squadrons of horse; he was ordered to join the main army on the field of battle, as he came into action on the extreme right wing. Indeed Withers was to approach the field by an isolated and dangerous route. He was to push through the forest belt by an undefended track to the north of the general battle, debouch on to the western or French side of the woods, and passing through the village of La Folie, fall on the left flank and rear of the enemy behind the Wood of Sars at the moment of crisis. This operation, requiring careful timing if it was not to lead to disaster, is of the same type as the arrival of the Prussians at Waterloo, or the junction of their two armies on the field of Königrätz. It succeeded to a nicety and won the day.

A dense blanket of morning fog enabled the Allies to deploy and begin their approach, unmolested by the enemy cannon. When it lifted, shortly after six o'clock, a majestic sight was disclosed. Line behind line in perfect order, the infantry three-deep, the cavalry behind them in the same formation, a hundred thousand men were moving to the attack, while over their heads flapped like sails a forest of huge flags, unfolding the blazonry of a score of the greatest States and Princes in Europe. The artillery, already mounted in earthwork batteries which the Allies had constructed overnight, were bombarding the French positions, and the enemy guns were replying as the mist rose. The sight thrilled spectators the more because nothing could be seen of the 80,000 defenders, except here and there a three-cornered hat showing above a parapet. The rest were hidden in the woods to left and right, or concealed in the centre behind the high entrenchments.

'It was hardly seven o'clock when we marched to attack,' wrote Orkney, 'and it really was a noble sight to see so many different bodies marching over the plain to a thick wood where you could see no men.' 'It was the most deliberate, solemn and well-ordered battle I ever saw,' wrote Colonel Blackader, second in command of the Cameronians that morning; 'a noble and fine disposition and as nobly executed . . . I never had a more pleasant day in my life. I was kept in perfect peace; my mind stayed, trusting in God.'

But, in bosoms less serene, more devilish passions were soon aroused. The failure to come to terms at the Hague had enraged the two armies against one another. Little quarter was asked or given, especially in the hand-to-hand struggle that raged in the deadly shadows of the Wood of Sars. The entrenchments along its edge had been carried by the high-hatted grenadiers charging at the head of their respective regiments; but deep in the heart of the forest stretched line behind line of felled trees, each shaped into a rough abatis, each to be defended, taken, retaken, and lost again, as hour after hour the glades re-echoed to the thunder of volleys and the crash of companies bursting through the trampled underwood.

Thirty-six battalions of Eugene's Germans had entered the forest on the north, supported by twenty-two battalions of Prussians, Hanoverians and British under Lottum. 'Before the end of the day,' writes Marlborough, 'we had eighty battalions in that wood, and I believe they had more.' The bulk of the British infantry were still waiting in the

centre under Orkney, but he detached his own regiment the Royals and a battalion of Guards, to join the Buffs in the Wood of Sars at a critical moment of the struggle for its possession. Under cover of fire from the Allied battery of forty guns, they forced their way in across a marsh, 'so that we got possession of the corner of the wood which flanked the retrenchments of the enemy.' There they found the Buffs, who were fighting behind their Colonel, the Duke of Argyll. As John Campbell was putting himself up as a rival to Marlborough, he felt all the more bound to lead the charges on foot, like the proud Highland Chieftain that he was. After one repulse from before a woodland abatis, he tore open his waistcoat and shirt to show each private of the Buffs that he wore no privileged breast-armour, and led them again to the attack. Indeed in this Homeric battle the leaders in all parts of the field exposed themselves to encourage their men. Before evening, Eugene and Villars had both been hit, and innumerable general officers and colonels on both sides were laid low.

Disputing every tree, the French were being driven back out of the Wood of Sars; Withers and his eighteen battalions were approaching their flank and rear through the village of La Folie, drawing Villars to that spot as the scene of crisis; and gradually the 'redans' in the centre were being stripped of defenders, hurried off to repel Withers or to hold the last corner of the woodland. And so, about one o'clock, Marlborough launched Orkney and his remaining thirteen British battalions at the 'redans'. Those formidable 'retrenchments upon the top of the hill,' Orkney tells us, were taken 'without firing a shot; for we found nothing to oppose us.' The key to the French position was won.

The Allied cavalry, following close behind, passed through the gaps in the 'redans' and formed up under cover of the fire of Orkney's infantry from the captured ramparts. Ten of the cannon from the forty-gun battery had been brought forward in the wake of the English foot, and now opened fire at close quarters on the French horse. The protection thus afforded to our horse was welcome, for they had to deploy on the far side of the entrenchments in face of the cavalry of France. The Maison du Roi, commanded by Boufflers in person, were drawn up, line behind line, across the wide heath of Malplaquet. A great cavalry action ensued on very even terms, that eventually ended in the defeat of the French.

Meanwhile on the Allied left, the Dutch army—the same splendid troops who had broken the resistance of the French at Ramillies—

moved up to the attack. They assaulted the trenches partly in the Wood of Laignières, but chiefly in the open ground near it. Led on by the young Prince of Orange, their infantry stormed the first line, but were broken before the second and chased back. Again and again they came on, but were each time repulsed 'with such a butchering that the oldest generall alive never saw the like.' The 'Blue Guards', beloved of William III, went down in swathes. The flower of the army of the States General was sacrificed in just such a way as the Field Deputies in years gone by had been wont to fear overmuch. But on this occasion the principal Deputy, Goslinga, was galloping gladly about the field, displaying a courage and presence of mind that won him golden opinions; neither before nor after the battle did he blame his old enemy Marlborough for making the attack. Nevertheless things went so ill with the Dutch that the Duke had to intervene in person with reserves in order to prevent a French advance.

About three o'clock the decision was reached upon the other wing. Withers, debouching from La Folie, made contact with the troops of Eugene and Lottum emerging on the west side of the conquered Wood of Sars. Some of the German artillery had been dragged right through the forest in the wake of the infantry and now came into action on the far side. The Irish 'Wild Geese' had been sent to repulse Withers, but the platoon firing of the Royal Irish broke the gallant charge of the exiles, and decision of the Boyne and Aghrim was repeated beside the Flemish wood.

It was at that critical point in the field that Villars, ever present where he was most wanted, received the wound in his knee that put him out of action. Boufflers, on whom the command devolved, drew off the army of France, defeated but neither demoralized nor pursued. They left behind most of their artillery, but very few prisoners, except some fifteen hundred of the wounded whom they had not been able to move. They returned to the Lines of La Bassée and left Mons to its fate. After forty days Villars was well enough to be moved to Paris. 'My passage through the towns on the way, lying on a stretcher, was a kind of triumph'—and, though it is he who tells us so, we can well believe it.

Marlborough, racked with headache as always after any great exertion, was kept hard at work for many days. He paid assiduous attention to the wounded of all nations. According to an excellent custom of that polite age, many of the enemy officers were sent back on parole to be cared for by their own folk. One of these, an Irish

adventurer named Peter Drake, has told us the tale of his personal appeal to the Duke upon the fields:

> I made shift to advance five or six yards toward his Grace, who, on seeing me in that condition, was so good as to stop and ask what was the matter. I told him as loud as I could that I had the honour to serve in the Gens d'Armes, and that I was a prisoner of war, very much wounded, and in danger of losing my life for want of a surgeon to dress my wounds, and begged he would please to take my parole of honour, which was a favour generally granted to prisoners of our corps, and to order some method to carry me to the French Army where I should be taken care of. He immediately called for Cardonnel who was his secretary and then at hand, and asked him how came all these poor gentlemen (meaning the prisoners) were not sent away, he having sent orders for that purpose, and desired carriages to be got ready for those that were not able to walk, for that there were no surgeons enough to dress our wounded.

As a result, Drake and his companions in misfortune were, as he tells us, sent to their friends at Bavay that very afternoon. But it is to be feared that, with the best will in the world, the regimental surgeons of the Allies could have done little enough for the wounded privates of all the nations, of whom nearly 15,000 must have remained upon their hands.

Meanwhile, pious Colonel Blackader, left at the head of the Cameronians by the death of Colonel Cranstoun in the battle,

> went to view the field to get a preaching from the dead, which might have been very edifying, for in all my life I have not seen the dead bodies lie so thick as they were in some places about the retrenchments, particularly at the battery where the Dutch Guards attacked. The Dutch have suffered most in the battle of any; their infantry is quite shattered so that it is a dear victory. It is a wonder to me the British escape so cheap, who are the most heaven-daring sinners in this army. But God's judgements are a great depth.

What would be the effect of Malplaquet upon opinion in Europe and England? The feelings of Orkney, a friend to Marlborough, were frankly expressed in a letter home to his brother five days after the action.

I can liken this last battle to nothing so much as an attack on a counterscarp from right to left, and I am sure you would have thought so if you had seen the field as I did the day after. In many places they lie as thick as ever did a flock of sheep. I really think I never saw the like; particularly where the Dutch Guards attacked it is a miracle. I hope in God it may be the last battle I may ever see. A very few of such would make both parties end the war very soon. The French are very proud they have done so well. I do not believe they have lost so many as we. I doubt it is with us as it was with the French at the battle of Landen . . . None alive ever saw such a battle. God send us a good peace.

'A good peace.' No word of a march to Paris!

The attacking force had lost between sixteen and eighteen thousand men; the defenders probably not much over 11,000. Yet the Allies had again asserted their military superiority, for they had driven the enemy from a position so strong that Marlborough, inspecting the captured lines next day, wondered at his success, especially since, to use his own words, 'the French have never, during this war, fought so well as this time.' If he had known beforehand that they would fight so well, would he have attacked such a position? Had he reckoned, wrong for once, that after a stout resistance they would give way to panic as so often before? These questions find no answer either in his letters or in his recorded conversations. If he had been Wellington, a word dropped to a friend in the ease of conversational retrospect would some day have let out the secret of his thought. But Marlborough was one who never boasted and who never confessed.

If such a field as Malplaquet had been won during the wars of William, England would have been all aglow with pride and joy. But Marlborough, by the glory of his deeds, had set up a standard of expectation not attained by a victory in which the victors lost more than the vanquished. Moreover, the battle had been fought when men were growing weary of the war. They had been disappointed by the Allies' refusal to make peace in the spring, and held that it would only be justified by a decisive battle and a march to Paris.

There was an element of sound political sense in the Tory outcry against Malplaquet, but as military criticism much of it was questionable. The 'butcher's bill', denounced as so extravagant, amounted for the British army to less than 600 killed and less than 1300 wounded,

out of 14,000 engaged. Our humane and enlightened generation slaughters ten times as many every year rather than limit the speed of its road traffic in time of peace; and it was a thirtieth part of the British losses in a single day of the Battle of the Somme. The Dutch, indeed, might have complained with better reason since more than 8000 of their troops had been killed or wounded; but the Tories who talked of the 'butcher's bill' cared nothing what happened to the Dutch.

If in 1709 England and Holland had still been fresh and eager to push their advantage, Malplaquet would, like one of Grant's costly victories, have helped to open the road to the enemy's capital in a few years' time. Professional military critics therefore regard the battle as being an Allied success—justly from their point of view. But there is always a diplomatic and political situation behind every act of war in relation to which it must be judged. So viewed, Malplaquet was a French success. Marlborough, by attacking had intended to destroy their army and it was not destroyed. Villars, by awaiting the attack, had intended to foster the nascent confidence of his troops, and on the whole they were more confident after the battle than before. But his success had only been relative to their former discouragement. The French made no further attempt to prevent the fall of Mons, and in no succeeding year did they dare give battle to Marlborough in the open field.

The first news of the storming of the enemy's Lines was received with joy in England. 'The guns went off all the afternoon,' we read, 'and the evening is concluding with bonfires.' Even St. John and Peterborough wrote to congratulate the Duke on his fourth great victory. But before the end of the month the losses were known and Malplaquet became a party question. The Tories began to talk of 'the late carnage,' and to declare that the battle would not have been fought in the way it was, 'could a great man have found in his heart to have parted with intelligence money,'—although in fact no General of the age was so well served with intelligence as Marlborough. Hearne, the Oxford Jacobite, had heard, unmoved, of Blenheim, Ramillies and Oudenarde, which find no mention in his voluminous daily jottings. But at the news of the slaughter at Malplaquet the learned diarist was all agog:

> As this has been the most obstinate so it has been the most direful battle to England that has yet happened, and there is not, in the opinion of all honest men, the least reason for bragging. Private

> letters frequently come which give most impartial accounts, and we are well assured that from the greatest to the meanest officer hardly one escaped but was either slain or very much wounded,

a statement which was grossly untrue, particularly of the British regiments.

The Whigs, on the other hand, carried through the national thanksgiving for the latest victory with pomp and cermony uncurtailed, hymned Marlborough to the skies and prophesied the speedy fall of Paris. A Malplaquet song was set to music:

> Now cannon smoke clouds all the sky,
> And through the gloomy wood
> From every trench the bougres fly,
> Besmeared with dust and blood.
> While valour's palm is our in fight,
> And Mons to terms we bring,
> Let bragging Boufflers vainly write
> False wonders to the King. . . .
>
> Monsieur, Monsieur, leave off Spain.
> To think to hold it is in vain,
> Thy warriors are too few.
> Then without more ado
> Be wise and strait call home little Anjou.

So sang the Whig politicians in their taverns, but it was no longer the full national chorus.

In one important quarter there was no weakening. The City, on whose goodwill the Government so largely depended, was still for 'No Peace without Spain.'

> Upon the strength of your victory [wrote Godolphin to Marlborough nine days after the battle] I spoke yesterday to the Bank, that, pursuant to the latitude given in the last session of Parliament, they would now contract with me for the circulation of £600,000 more in Exchequer bills to the carrying on the public service. What I said seemed to be pretty well received, and I hope it will succeed. But upon occasion Sir Gilbert Heathcote, who is Governor [of the Bank of England], said to me, 'Pray, My Lord, don't let's have a rotten peace.' 'Pray tell me,' I answered, 'what you call a rotten peace?' 'I call anything a rotten peace,' he said, 'unless we can have

Spain.' 'But, Sir Gilbert,' I said, 'I want you a little to consider the circumstances of the Duke of Marlborough and me; we are railed at every day for having a mind, as they call it, to perpetuate the war.' He replied very quick, 'They are a company of rotten rogues: I'll warrant you we'll stand by you.'

The policies of the Bank of England with regard to the disposal of the crown of Spain had not been forwarded by the events of the year's war in that country. So far from accomplishing anything in the Peninsula in 1709, the Allies had lost further ground, and by the autumn little outside Catalonia was left to the Austrian candidate, 'Charles III'. The last fortresses that still flew his flag along the coast of Valencia, under the partial protection of the English fleet, were falling one by one to the Bourbon armies. The French General D'Asfeld, a cruel man, skilful in siege warfare, put to the sword the Spanish adherents of Charles in one captured town after another. In November 1708 he had at last taken Denia, and subsequently Alicante after a five months' siege of the rock on which its Castle stood.

Alicante Castle was gallantly defended by 800 English and Huguenots under Major-General John Richards, who had first become known to fame as Peterborough's faithful but critical lieutenant. The rock was so tall and steep that it was useless to approach it by the ordinary methods of siege. D'Asfeld therefore spent three months in boring a mine fifty-six yards long in the living rock, at the end of which he placed 1200 barrels containing about 17,000 pounds of gunpowder, said to have been the greatest charge ever, till then, used in war. It was 216 feet below the parade ground of the castle. When all was ready, D'Asfeld called on Richards to surrender, inviting him to send officers to examine the mine. After carefully drawing up a paper of arguments in two columns 'for' and 'against', Richards decided to stand the shock; the explosion would be terrific, but its effect would be uncertain because the body of the rock was traversed in all directions by clefts. To encourage his men he determined to take his stand exactly over the mine. Some of his officers expostulated at his unnecessary self-immolation, but when he insisted they too claimed the right to stand by his side.

And so, on the morning of Monday, March 3, 1709, a little group of English and Huguenot officers, headed by the Governor, John Richards, in full regimentals, walked quietly into the middle of the parade ground and stood there, having ordered the privates of the guard to retire.

In the streets of the town below, the enemy could be seen running for shelter from the force of the coming explosion.

> The mine was blown up, and with little or no noise made an opening in the rock, on the very parade, of some yards in length about three feet wide, into which the Governor, Lt.-Colonel Thornicroft, Major Vignoles and other officers fell, and the opening instantly closing upon them, they all perished.

There were some who accused Richards of having sacrificed himself and his staff to 'a fond curiosity', but the more general feeling was awed appreciation of an incident recalling the leap of Curtius into the gulf rather than an actual incident of modern warfare. The garrison held out more than a month longer, and capitulated in the middle of April on honourable terms. Nothing else of importance happened that year in Spain.

In the year 1709 England had made her greatest effort in war, with no answering degree of success. But 'peace hath her victories . . .' While the red-coated grenadiers were playing their game of hide-and-seek with death in the charged chambers of Tournai and in the woodland alleys of Sars, the Londoners were eagerly buying and discussing a new wonder and delight, Steele's *Tatler,* born on April 12, and making its appearance every second week-day on a single unfolded sheet. Its influence, and that of the *Spectator* which grew out of it in two years' time, did more to launch Eighteenth Century civilization on its characteristic course than all the blood shed at Malplaquet. England's foreign wars, even at their most extravagant and burdensome height, did not in those happy days prevent the progressive softening of manners and the growth of the civilized arts in our island.

Addison wrote in the paper, but the idea and the enterprise were Steele's, who brought his friend's shy genius into play side by side with his own ever-marketable wares. Defoe's *Review* had shown the way in this style of publication, but the larger and better part of the *Review* had been political. Defoe's great gifts did not include the deft touch on social comedy which the Steele-Addison partnership gave to a delighted Town. And the *Tatler* was not only amusing but moral and rational—an unusual combination at that date. Humour changed sides and came to the rescue of good manners and good feeling. It was characteristic of the new influence that, in the summer of 1709, Steele preached in the *Tatler* a series of sermons against duelling—an unusual course for a man of fashion to take in those days. Most men

thought such a view fit only to be held by parsons, but here was an ex-soldier who had, in his day, been compelled unwillingly to 'pink' his brother officer, a Whig who supported the army against its clerical detractors, here was Dicky Steele taking up his pen against the duel. 'I shall talk very freely,' he wrote, 'on a custom which all men wish exploded, though no man has courage to resist it.' He denounced, in particular, the Gothic barbarism of the usage by which even the seconds were compelled to stab at one another, sometimes with fatal results, though busy as the Devil is, there was no pretence of quarrel between them. This attack on a practice peculiarly associated with military habits, being launched at the height of our war-effort by a supporter of the war, is an evidence of the essentially unmilitary character of English society, although more than a hundred years were to elapse before duelling completely disappeared from among our national customs.

R. H. TAWNEY

1880–1962

"The New Medicine for Poverty," given here in full, is one of the sections in the last part, "The Puritan Movement," of Religion and the Rise of Capitalism, *first published in 1926. The book was based on lectures given in 1922. It is important to note that Tawney is dealing here with Calvinism in the seventeenth century and after; he has earlier made it clear that Calvin himself was hardly, if at all, more favorable to economic individualism than the social teaching of the medieval church had been.*

Religion and the Rise of Capitalism *is available in a Pelican paperback (latest edition, 1961). There is an obituary article by Lawrence Stone in* Past and Present, *April, 1962. The gentry controversy is best explained in Professor J. H. Hexter's "Storm over the Gentry," reprinted in his* Reappraisals in History *(1961).*

To APPLAUD certain qualities is by implication to condemn the habits and institutions which appear to conflict with them. The recognition accorded by Puritan ethics to the economic virtues, in an age when such virtues were rarer than they are today, gave a timely stimulus to economic efficiency. But it naturally, if unintentionally, modified the traditional attitude towards social obligations. For the spontaneous, doctrineless individualism, which became the rule of English public life a century before the philosophy of it was propounded by Adam Smith, no single cause was responsible. But, simultaneously with the

obvious movements in the world of affairs—the discrediting of the ideal of a paternal, authoritarian Government, the breakdown of central control over local administration, the dislocation caused by the Civil War, the expansion of trade, and the shifting of industry from its accustomed seats—it is perhaps not fanciful to detect in the ethics of Puritanism one force contributing to the change in social policy which is noticeable after the middle of the century.

The loftiest teaching cannot escape from its own shadow. To urge that the Christian life must be lived in a zealous discharge of private duties—how necessary! Yet how readily perverted to the suggestion that there are no vital social obligations beyond and above them! To insist that the individual is responsible, that no man can save his brother, that the essence of religion is the contact of the soul with its Maker—how true and indispensable! But how easy to slip from that truth into the suggestion that society is without responsibility, that no man can help his brother, that the social order and its consequences are not even the scaffolding by which men may climb to greater heights, but something external, alien, and irrelevant—something, at best, indifferent to the life of the spirit, and, at worst, the sphere of the letter which killeth and of the reliance on works which ensnares the soul into the slumber of death! In emphasizing that God's Kingdom is not of this world, Puritanism did not always escape the suggestion that this world is no part of God's Kingdom. The complacent victim of that false antithesis between the social mechanism and the life of the spirit, which was to tyrannize over English religious thought for the next two centuries, it enthroned religion in the privacy of the individual soul, not without some sighs of sober satisfaction at its abdication from society. Professor Dicey has commented on the manner in which 'the appeal of the Evangelicals to personal religion corresponds with the appeal of Benthamite Liberals to individual energy'. The same affinity between religious and social interests found an even clearer expression in the Puritan movement of the seventeenth century. Individualism in religion led insensibly, if not quite logically, to an individualist morality, and an individualist morality to a disparagement of the significance of the social fabric as compared with personal character.

A practical example of that change of emphasis is given by the treatment accorded to the questions of Enclosure and of Pauperism. For a century and a half the progress of enclosing had been a burning issue, flaring up, from time to time, into acute agitation. During the greater part of that period, from Latimer in the thirties of the six-

teenth century to Laud in the thirties of the seventeenth, the attitude of religious teachers had been one of condemnation. Sermon after sermon and pamphlet after pamphlet—not to mention Statutes and Royal Commissions—had been launched against depopulation. The appeal had been, not merely to public policy, but to religion. Peasant and lord, in their different degrees, are members of one Christian commonwealth, within which the law of charity must bridle the corroding appetite for economic gain. In such a mystical corporation, knit together by mutual obligations, no man may press his advantage to the full, for no man may seek to live outside 'the body of the Church'.

Sabotaged by the unpaid magistracy of country gentlemen, who had been the obstructive agents of local administration, the practical application of such doctrines had always been intermittent, and, when the Long Parliament struck the weapon of administrative law from the hands of the Crown, it had ceased altogether. But the politics of Westminster were not those of village and borough. The events which seemed to aristocratic Parliamentarians to close the revolution seemed to the left wing of the victorious army only to begin it. In that earliest and most turbulent of English democracies, where buff-coat taught scripture politics to his general, the talk was not merely of political, but of social, reconstruction. The programme of the Levellers, who more than any other party could claim to express the aspirations of the unprivileged classes, included a demand, not only for annual or biennial Parliaments, manhood suffrage, a redistribution of seats in proportion to population, and the abolition of the veto of the House of Lords, but also that 'you would have laid open all enclosures of fens and other commons, or have them enclosed only or chiefly for the benefit of the poor'. Theoretical communism, repudiated by the leading Levellers, found its expression in the agitation of the Diggers, on whose behalf Winstanley argued that, 'seeing the common people of England, by joynt consent of person and purse, have caste out Charles, our Norman oppressour . . . the land now is to returne into the joynt hands of those who have conquered, that is the commonours', and that the victory over the King was incomplete, as long as 'we . . . remayne slaves still to the kingly power in the hands of lords of manors'.

Nor was it only from the visionary and the zealot that the pressure for redress proceeded. When the shattering of traditional authority seemed for a moment to make all things new, local grievances, buried beneath centuries of dull oppression, started to life, and in several Mid-

land counties the peasants rose to pull down the hated hedges. At Leicester, where in 1649 there were rumours of a popular movement to throw down the enclosures of the neighbouring forest, the City Council took the matter up. A petition was drafted, setting out the economic and social evils attending enclosure, and proposing the establishment of machinery to check it, consisting of a committee without whose assent enclosing was not to be permitted. A local minister was instructed to submit the petition to Parliament, 'which hath still a watchful eye and open ear to redress the common grievances of the nation'. The agent selected to present the city's case was the Rev. John Moore, a prolific pamphleteer, who for several years attacked the depopulating landlord with all the fervour of Latimer, though with even less than Latimer's success.

Half a century before, such commotions would have been followed by the passing of Depopulation Acts and the issue of a Royal Commission. But, in the ten years since the meeting of the Long Parliament, the whole attitude of public policy towards the movement had begun to change. Confiscations, compositions, and war taxation had effected a revolution in the distribution of property, similar, on a smaller scale, to that which had taken place at the Reformation. As land changed hands, customary relations were shaken and new interests were created. Enclosure, as Moore complained, was being pushed forward by means of law suits ending in Chancery decrees. It was not to be expected that City merchants and members of the Committee for Compounding, some of whom had found land speculation a profitable business, should hear with enthusiasm a proposal to revive the old policy of arresting enclosures by State interference, at which the gentry had grumbled for more than a century.

In these circumstances, it is not surprising that reformers should have found the open ear of Parliament impenetrably closed to agrarian grievances. Nor was it only the political and economic environment which had changed. The revolution in thought was equally profound. The theoretical basis of the policy of protecting the peasant by preventing enclosure had been a conception of landownership which regarded its rights and its duties as inextricably interwoven. Property was not merely a source of income, but a public function, and its use was limited by social obligations and necessities of State. With such a doctrine the classes who had taken the lead in the struggle against the monarchy could make no truce. Its last vestiges finally disappeared when the Restoration Parliament swept away military tenures, and

imposed on the nation, in the shape of an excise, the financial burden previously borne by themselves.

The theory which took its place, and which was to become in the eighteenth century almost a religion, was that expressed by Locke, when he described property as a right anterior to the existence of the State, and argued that 'the supreme power cannot take from any man any part of his property without his own consent'. But Locke merely poured into a philosophical mould ideas which had been hammered out in the stress of political struggles, and which were already the commonplace of landowners and merchant. The view of society held by that part of the Puritan movement which was socially and politically influential had been expressed by Ireton and Cromwell in their retort to the democrats in the army. It was that only the freeholders really constituted the body politic, and that they could use their property as they pleased, uncontrolled by obligations to any superior, or by the need of consulting the mass of men, who were mere tenants at will, with no fixed interest or share in the land of the kingdom.

Naturally, this change of ideas had profound reactions on agrarian policy. Formerly a course commending itself to all public-spirited persons, the prevention of enclosure was now discredited as the programme of a sect of religious and political radicals. When Major-General Whalley in 1656 introduced a measure to regulate and restrict the enclosure of commons, framed, apparently, on the lines proposed by the authorities of Leicester, there was an instant outcry from members that it would 'destroy property', and the bill was refused a second reading. After the Restoration the tide began to run more strongly in the same direction. Enclosure had already become the hobby of the country gentleman. Experts advocated it on economic grounds, and legislation to facilitate it was introduced into Parliament. Though its technique still remained to be elaborated, the attitude which was to be decisive in the eighteenth century had already been crystallized.

The change of policy was striking. The reason of it was not merely that political conditions made the landed gentry omnipotent, and that the Royalist squirearchy, who streamed back to their plundered manors in 1660, were in no mood to countenance a revival, by the Government of Charles II, of the administrative interference with the rights of property which had infuriated them in the Government of Charles I. It was that opinion as to social policy had changed, and changed not least among men of religion themselves. The pursuit of economic

self-interest, which is the law of nature, is already coming to be identified by the pious with the operation of the providential plan, which is the law of God. Enclosures will increase the output of wool and grain. Each man knows best what his land is suited to produce, and the general interest will be best served by leaving him free to produce it. 'It is an undeniable maxim that everyone by the light of nature and reason will do that which makes for his greatest advantage. . . . The advancement of private persons will be the advantage of the public.'

It is significant that such considerations were adduced, not by an economist, but by a minister. For the argument was ethical as well as economic, and, when Moore appealed to the precepts of traditional morality to bridle pecuniary interests, he provoked the retort that judicious attention to pecuniary interests was an essential part of an enlightened morality. What the poor need for their spiritual health is—to use the favourite catchword of the age—'regulation', and regulation is possible only if they work under the eye of an employer. In the eyes of the austere moralists of the Restoration, the first, and most neglected, virtue of the poor is industry. Common rights encourage idleness by offering a precarious and demoralizing livelihood to men who ought to be at work for a master. It is not surprising, therefore, that the admonitions of religious teachers against the wickedness of joining house to house and field to field should almost entirely cease. Long the typical example of uncharitable covetousness, enclosure is now considered, not merely economically expedient, but morally beneficial. Baxter, with all his scrupulousness—partly, perhaps, because of his scrupulousness—differs from most earlier divines, in giving a qualified approval to enclosure 'done in moderation by a pious man', for the characteristic reason that a master can establish a moral discipline among his employees, which they would miss if they worked for themselves. What matters, in short, is not their circumstances, but their character. If they lose as peasants, they will gain as Christians. Opportunities for spiritual edification are more important than the mere material environment. If only the material environment were not itself among the forces determining men's capacity to be edified!

The temper which deplored that the open-field village was not a school of the severer virtues turned on pauperism and poor relief an even more shattering criticism. There is no province of social life in which the fashioning of a new scale of social values on the Puritan anvil is more clearly revealed. In the little communities of peasants

and craftsmen which composed medieval England, all, when Heaven sent a bad harvest, had starved together, and the misery of the sick, the orphan, and the aged had appeared as a personal calamity, not as a social problem. Apart from a few precocious theorists, who hinted at the need for a universal and secular system of provision for distress, the teaching most characteristic of medieval writers had been that the relief of the needy was a primary obligation on those who had means. St Thomas, who in this matter is typical, quotes with approval the strong words of St Ambrose about those who cling to the bread of the starving, insists on the idea that property is stewardship, and concludes—a conclusion not always drawn from that well-worn phrase—that to withhold alms when there is evident and urgent necessity is mortal sin. Popular feeling had lent a half-mystical glamour, both to poverty and to the compassion by which poverty was relieved, for poor men were God's friends. At best, the poor were thought to represent our Lord in a peculiarly intimate way—'in that sect', as Langland said, 'our Saviour saved all mankind'—and it was necessary for the author of a religious manual to explain that the rich, as such, were not necessarily hateful to God. At worst, men reflected that the prayers of the poor availed much, and that the sinner had been saved from hell by throwing a loaf of bread to a beggar, even though a curse went with it. The alms bestowed today would be repaid a thousand-fold, when the soul took its dreadful journey amid rending briars and scorching flames.

> If ever thou gavest hosen and shoon,
> *Everie nighte and alle,*
> Sit thee down and put them on,
> *And Christe receive thy saule.*
>
> If hosen and shoon thou gavest nane,
> *Everie nighte and alle,*
> The whinnes shall pricke thee to the bare bane,
> *And Christe receive thy saule. . . .*
>
> If ever thou gavest meate or drinke,
> *Everie nighte and all,*
> The fire shall never make thee shrinke,
> *And Christe receive thy saule.*

If meate or drinke thou gavest nane,
Everie nighte and alle,
The fire will burne thee to the bare bane,
And Christe receive thy saule.

This ae nighte, this ae nighte,
Everie nighte and alle,
Fire, and sleete, and candle-lighte,
And Christe receive thy saule.

The social character of wealth, which had been the essence of the medieval doctrine, was asserted by English divines in the sixteenth century with redoubled emphasis, precisely because the growing individualism of the age menaced the traditional conception. 'The poor man', preached Latimer, 'hath title to the rich man's goods; so that the rich man ought to let the poor man have part of his riches to help and to comfort him withal.' Nor had that sovereign indifference to the rigours of the economic calculus disappeared, when, under the influence partly of humanitarian representatives of the Renaissance like Vives, partly of religious reformers, partly of their own ambition to gather all the threads of social administration into their own hands, the statesmen of the sixteenth century set themselves to organize a secular system of poor relief. In England, after three generations in which the attempt was made to stamp out vagrancy by police measures of hideous brutality, the momentous admission was made that its cause was economic distress, not merely personal idleness, and that the whip had no terrors for the man who must either tramp or starve. The result was the celebrated Acts imposing a compulsory poor-rate and requiring the able-bodied man to be set on work. The Privy Council, alert to prevent disorder, drove lethargic justices hard, and down to the Civil War the system was administered with fair regularity. But the Elizabethan Poor Law was never designed to be what, with disastrous results, it became in the eighteenth and early nineteenth centuries, the sole measure for coping with economic distress. While it provided relief, it was but the last link in a chain of measures—the prevention of evictions, the control of food supplies and prices, the attempt to stabilize employment and to check unnecessary dismissals of workmen —intended to mitigate the forces which made relief necessary. Apart

from the Poor Law, the first forty years of the seventeenth century were prolific in the private charity which founded alms-houses and hospitals, and established funds to provide employment or to aid struggling tradesmen. The appeal was still to religion, which owed to poverty a kind of reverence.

> It was Thy choice, whilst Thou on earth didst stay,
> And hadst not whereupon Thy head to lay.

'What, speak you of such things?' said Nicholas Ferrar on his death-bed to one who commended his charities; 'it would have been but a suitable return for me to have given all I had, and not to have scattered a few crumbs of alms here and there.'

It was inevitable that, in the anarchy of the Civil War, both private charity and public relief should fall on evil days. In London, charitable endowments seem to have suffered from more than ordinary malversation, and there were complaints that the income both of Bridewell and of the Hospitals was seriously reduced. In the country, the records of Quarter Sessions paint a picture of confusion, in which the machinery of presentment by constables to justices has broken down, and a long wail arises, that thieves are multiplied, the poor are neglected, and vagrants wander to and fro at their will. The administrative collapse of the Elizabethan Poor Law continued after the Restoration, and twenty-three years later Sir Matthew Hale complained that the sections in it relating to the provision of employment were a dead letter. Always unpopular with the local authorities, whom they involved in considerable trouble and expense, it is not surprising that, with the cessation of pressure by the Central Government, they should, except here and there, have been neglected. What is more significant, however, than the practical deficiencies in the administration of relief, was the rise of a new school of opinion, which regarded with repugnance the whole body of social theory of which both private charity and public relief had been the expression.

'The generall rule of all England', wrote a pamphleteer in 1646, 'is to whip and punish the wandring beggars . . . and so many justices execute one branch of that good Statute (which is the point of justice), but as for the point of charitie, they leave [it] undone, which is to provide houses and convenient places to set the poore to work.' The House of Commons appears to have been conscious that the complaint had some foundation; in 1649 it ordered that the country justices should be required to see that stocks of material were provided as the

law required, and the question of preparing new legislation to ensure that persons in distress should be found employment was on several occasions referred to committees of the House. Nothing seems, however, to have come of these proposals, nor was the Elizabethan policy of 'setting the poor on work' that which was most congenial to the temper of the time. Upon the admission that distress was the result, not of personal deficiencies, but of economic causes, with its corollary that its victims had a legal right to be maintained by society, the growing individualism of the age turned the same frigid scepticism as was later directed against the Speenhamland policy by the reformers of 1834. Like the friends of Job, it saw in misfortune, not the chastisement of love, but the punishment for sin. The result was that, while the penalties on the vagrant were redoubled, religious opinion laid less emphasis on the obligation of charity than upon the duty of work, and that the admonitions which had formerly been turned upon uncharitable covetousness were now directed against improvidence and idleness. The characteristic sentiment was that of Milton's friend, Hartlib: 'The law of God saith, "he that will not work, let him not eat". This would be a sore scourge and smart whip for idle persons if . . . none should be suffered to eat till they had wrought for it.'

The new attitude found expression in the rare bursts of public activity provoked by the growth of pauperism between 1640 and 1660. The idea of dealing with it on sound business principles, by means of a corporation which would combine profit with philanthropy, was being sedulously preached by a small group of reformers. Parliament took it up, and in 1649 passed an Act for the relief and employment of the poor and the punishment of beggars, under which a company was to be established with power to apprehend vagrants, to offer them the choice between work and whipping, and to set to compulsory labour all other poor persons, including children, without means of maintenance. Eight years later the prevalence of vagrancy produced an Act of such extreme severity as almost to recall the suggestion made a generation later by Fletcher of Saltoun, that vagrants should be sent to the galleys. It provided that, since offenders could rarely be taken in the act, any vagrant who failed to satisfy the justices that he had a good reason for being on the roads should be arrested and punished as a sturdy beggar, whether actually begging or not.

The protest against indiscriminate almsgiving, as the parade of a spurious religion, which sacrificed character to a formal piety, was older than the Reformation, but it had been given a new emphasis

by the reformers. Luther had denounced the demands of beggars as blackmail, and the Swiss reformers had stamped out the remnants of monastic charity as a bribe ministered by Popery to dissoluteness and demoralization. 'I conclude that all the large givings of the papists,' preached an English divine in the reign of Elizabeth, 'of which at this day many make so great brags, because they be not done in a reverent regard of the commandment of the Lord, in love, and of an inward being touched with the calamities of the needy, but for to be well reported of before men whilst they are alive, and to be prayed for after they are dead . . . are indeed no alms, but pharisaical trumpets.' The rise of a commercial civilization, the reaction against the authoritarian social policy of the Tudors, and the progress of Puritanism among the middle classes, all combined in the next half-century to sharpen the edge of that doctrine. Nurtured in a tradition which made the discipline of character by industry and self-denial the centre of its ethical scheme, the Puritan moralist was undisturbed by any doubts as to whether even the seed of the righteous might not sometimes be constrained to beg its bread, and met the taunt that the repudiation of good works was the cloak for a conscienceless egoism with the retort that the easy-going open-handedness of the sentimentalist was not less selfish in its motives and was more corrupting to its objects. 'As for idle beggars,' wrote Steele, 'happy for them if fewer people spent their foolish pity upon their bodies, and if more shewed some wise compassion upon their souls. That the greatest of evils is idleness, that the poor are the victims, not of circumstances, but of their own 'idle, irregular, and wicked courses', that the truest charity is not to enervate them by relief, but so to reform their characters that relief may be unnecessary—such doctrines turned severity from a sin into a duty, and froze the impulse of natural pity with the assurance that, if indulged, it would perpetuate the suffering which it sought to allay.

Few tricks of the unsophisticated intellect are more curious than the naïve psychology of the business man, who ascribes his achievements to his own unaided efforts, in bland unconsciousness of a social order without whose continuous support and vigilant protection he would be as a lamb bleating in the desert. That individualist complex owes part of its self-assurance to the suggestion of Puritan moralists, that practical success is at once the sign and the reward of ethical superiority. 'No question', argued a Puritan pamphleteer, 'but it [riches] should be the portion rather of the godly than of the wicked, were it good for them; for godliness hath the promises of this life as

well as of the life to come.' The demonstration that distress is a proof of demerit, though a singular commentary on the lives of Christian saints and sages, has always been popular with the prosperous. By the lusty plutocracy of the Restoration, roaring after its meat, and not indisposed, if it could not find it elsewhere, to seek it from God, it was welcomed with a shout of applause.

A society which reverences the attainment of riches as the supreme felicity will naturally be disposed to regard the poor as damned in the next world, if only to justify itself for making their life a hell in this. Advanced by men of religion as a tonic for the soul, the doctrine of the danger of pampering poverty was hailed by the rising school of Political Arithmeticians as a sovereign cure for the ills of society. For, if the theme of the moralist was that an easy-going indulgence undermined character, the theme of the economist was that it was economically disastrous and financially ruinous. The Poor Law is the mother of idleness, 'men and women growing so idle and proud that they will not work, but lie upon the parish wherein they dwell for maintenance'. It discourages thrift; 'if shame or fear of punishment makes him earn his dayly bread, he will do no more; his children are the charge of the parish and his old age his recess from labour or care'. It keeps up wages, since 'it encourages wilful and evil-disposed persons to impose what wages they please upon their labours; and herein they are so refractory to reason and the benefit of the nation that, when corn and provisions are cheap, they will not work for less wages than when they were dear'. To the landowner who cursed the poor-rates, and the clothier who grumbled at the high cost of labour, one school of religious thought now brought the comforting assurance that morality itself would be favoured by a reduction of both.

As the history of the Poor Law in the nineteenth century was to prove, there is no touchstone, except the treatment of childhood, which reveals the true character of a social philosophy more clearly than the spirit in which it regards the misfortunes of those of its members who fall by the way. Such utterances on the subject of poverty were merely one example of a general attitude, which appeared at times to consign to collective perdition almost the whole of the wage-earning population. It was partly that, in an age which worshipped property as the foundation of the social order, the mere labourer seemed something less than a full citizen. It was partly the result of the greatly increased influence on thought and public affairs acquired at the Restoration by the commercial classes, whose temper was a

ruthless materialism, determined at all costs to conquer world-markets from France and Holland, and prepared to sacrifice every other consideration to their economic ambitions. It was partly that, in spite of a century of large-scale production in textiles, the problems of capitalist industry and of a propertyless proletariat were still too novel for their essential features to be appreciated. Even those writers, like Baxter and Bunyan, who continued to insist on the wickedness of extortionate prices and unconscionable interest, rarely thought of applying their principles to the subject of wages. Their social theory had been designed for an age of petty agriculture and industry, in which personal relations had not yet been superseded by the cash nexus, and the craftsman or peasant farmer was but little removed in economic status from the half-dozen journeymen or labourers whom he employed. In a world increasingly dominated by great clothiers, iron-masters, and mine-owners, they still adhered to the antiquated categories of master and servant, with the same obstinate indifference to economic realities, as leads the twentieth century to talk of employers and employed, long after the individual employer has been converted into an impersonal corporation.

In a famous passage of the *Communist Manifesto,* Marx observes that 'the *bourgeoisie,* wherever it got the upper hand, put an end to all feudal, patriarchal, idyllic relations, pitilessly tore asunder the motley feudal ties that bound man to his "natural superiors", and left remaining no other bond between man and man than naked self-interest and callous cash payment'. An interesting illustration of his thesis might be found in the discussions of the economics of employment by English writers of the period between 1660 and 1760. Their characteristic was an attitude towards the new industrial proletariat noticeably harsher than that general in the first half of the seventeenth century, and which has no modern parallel except in the behaviour of the less reputable of white colonists towards coloured labour. The denunciations of the 'luxury, pride, and sloth' of the English wage-earners of the seventeenth and eighteenth centuries are, indeed, almost exactly identical with those directed against African natives today. It is complained that, compared with the Dutch, they are self-indulgent and idle; that they want no more than a bare subsistence, and will cease work the moment they obtain it; that, the higher their wages, the more—'so licentious are they'—they spend upon drink; that high prices, therefore, are not a misfortune, but a blessing, since they compel the wage-earner to be more industrious; and that high wages are

not a blessing, but a misfortune, since they merely conduce to 'weekly debauches'.

When such doctrines were general, it was natural that the rigours of economic exploitation should be preached as a public duty, and, with a few exceptions, the writers of the period differed only as to the methods by which severity could most advantageously be organized. Pollexfen and Walter Harris thought that salvation might be found by reducing the number of days kept as holidays. Bishop Berkeley, with the conditions of Ireland before his eyes, suggested that 'sturdy beggars should . . . be seized and made slaves to the public for a certain term of years'. Thomas Alcock, who was shocked at the workman's taste for snuff, tea, and ribbons, proposed the revival of sumptuary legislation. The writers who advanced schemes for reformed workhouses, which should be places at once of punishment and of training, were innumerable. All were agreed that, on moral no less than on economic grounds, it was vital that wages should be reduced. The doctrine afterwards expressed by Arthur Young, when he wrote, 'every one but an idiot knows that the lower classes must be kept poor, or they will never be industrious', was the tritest commonplace of Restoration economists. It was not argued; it was accepted as self-evident.

When philanthropists were inquiring whether it might not be desirable to re-establish slavery, it was not to be expected that the sufferings of the destitute would wring their hearts with social compunction. The most curious feature in the whole discussion, and that which is most sharply in contrast with the long debate on pauperism carried on in the sixteenth century, was the resolute refusal to admit that society had any responsibility for the causes of distress. Tudor divines and statesmen had little mercy for idle rogues. But the former always, and the latter ultimately, regarded pauperism primarily as a social phenomenon produced by economic dislocation, and the embarrassing question put by the genial Harrison—'at whose handes shall the bloude of these men be required?'—was never far from the minds of the most cynical. Their successors after the Restoration were apparently quite unconscious that it was even conceivable that there might be any other cause of poverty than the moral failings of the poor. The practical conclusion to be drawn from so comfortable a creed was at once extremely simple and extremely agreeable. It was not to find employment under the Act of 1601, for to do that was only 'to render the poor more bold'. It was to surround the right to relief with obstacles such as those contained in the Act of 1662, to give it, when it could

not be avoided, in a workhouse or house of correction, and, for the rest, to increase the demand for labour by reducing wages.

The grand discovery of a commercial age, that relief might be so administered as not merely to relieve, but also to deter, still remained to be made by Utilitarian philosophers. But the theory that distress was due, not to economic circumstances, but to what the Poor Law Commissioners of 1834 called 'individual improvidence and vice', was firmly established, and the criticism on the Elizabethan system which was to inspire the new Poor Law had already been formulated. The essence of that system was admirably expressed a century later by a Scottish divine, as 'the principle that each man, simply because he exists, holds a right on other men or on society for existence'. Dr Chalmers' attack upon it was the echo of a note long struck by Puritan moralists. And the views of Dr Chalmers had impressed themselves on Nassau Senior, before he set his hand to that brilliant, influential, and wildly unhistorical Report, which, after provoking something like a rebellion in the north of England, was to be one of the pillars of the social policy of the nineteenth century.

It would be misleading to dwell on the limitations of Puritan ethics without emphasizing the enormous contribution of Puritanism to political freedom and social progress. The foundation of democracy is the sense of spiritual independence, which nerves the individual to stand alone against the powers of this world, and in England, where squire and parson, lifting arrogant eyebrows at the insolence of the lower orders, combined to crush popular agitation, as a menace at once to society and to the Church, it is probable that democracy owes more to Nonconformity than to any other single movement. The virtues of enterprise, diligence, and thrift are the indispensable foundation of any complex and vigorous civilization. It was Puritanism which, by investing them with a supernatural sanction, turned them from an unsocial eccentricity into a habit and a religion. Nor would it be difficult to find notable representatives of the Puritan spirit, in whom the personal austerity, which was the noblest aspect of the new ideal, was combined with a profound consciousness of social solidarity, which was the noblest aspect of that which it displaced. Firmin the philanthropist, and Bellers the Quaker, whom Owen more than a century later hailed as the father of his doctrines, were pioneers of Poor Law reform. The Society of Friends, in an age when the divorce between religion and social ethics was almost complete, met the prevalent doctrine that it was permissible to take such gain as the market

offered, by insisting on the obligation of good conscience and forbearance in economic transactions, and on the duty to make the honourable maintenance of the brother in distress a common charge.

The general climate and character of a country are not altered, however, by the fact that here and there it has peaks which rise into an ampler air. The distinctive note of Puritan teaching was different. It was individual responsibility, not social obligation. Training its pupils to the mastery of others through the mastery of self, it prized as a crown of glory the qualities which arm the spiritual athlete for his solitary contest with a hostile world, and dismissed concern with the social order as the prop of weaklings and the Capua of the soul. Both the excellences and the defects of that attitude were momentous for the future. It is sometimes suggested that the astonishing outburst of industrial activity, which took place after 1760, created a new type of economic character, as well as a new system of economic organization. In reality, the ideal which was later to carry all before it, in the person of the inventor and engineer and captain of industry, was well established among Englishmen before the end of the seventeenth century. Among the numerous forces which had gone to form it, some not inconsiderable part may reasonably be ascribed to the emphasis on the life of business enterprise as the appropriate field for Christian endeavour, and on the qualities needed for success in it, which was characteristic of Puritanism. These qualities, and the admiration of them, remained, when the religious reference, and the restraints which it imposed, had weakened or disappeared.

SIR LEWIS NAMIER

1888–1960

This essay, "King George III: A Study of Personality," was published in Personalities and Powers *in 1955. H. R. Winkler has written a useful account of Namier's life and writings: "Sir Lewis Namier,"* Journal of Modern History, *March, 1963.*

THERE WERE three large pictures of George III at the exhibition of Royal portraits arranged by the Academy of Arts in the Spring of 1953. Looking at the first, by Reynolds, painted when the King was 41, I was struck by the immaturity of expression. The second, by Lawrence, painted in 1792 at the age of 54, depicts him in Garter robes; face and posture seem to attempt in a naive, ineffective, and almost engaging manner to live up to a grandeur which the sitter feels incumbent on him. The third, by Stroehling, painted in November 1807, at the age of nearly 70, shows a sad old man, looking dimly at a world in which he has no pleasure, and which he soon will not be able to see or comprehend.

A picture in a different medium of the King and his story presents itself to the student when in the Royal Archives at Windsor he surveys the papers of George III. They stand on the shelves in boxes, each marked on a white label with the year or years which it covers. The eye runs over that array, and crucial dates recall events: 1760, '65 and '67, '74 and '75, '82 and '83, 1789, '93, '96, 1802, 1805—the series breaks off in 1810; and brown-backed volumes follow, unlabelled:

they contain the medical reports on a man shut off from time, which means the world and its life.

Fate had made George III ruler when kings were still expected to govern; and his active reign covered half a century during which the American conflict posed the problem of Imperial relations, while at home political practice constantly ran up against the contradiction inherent in the then much belauded 'mixed form of government': personal monarchy served by Ministers whose tenure of office was contested in Parliament. Neither the Imperial nor the constitutional problem could have been solved in the terms in which the overwhelming majority of the politically minded public in this country considered them at the time; but George III has been blamed ever since for not having thought of Dominion status and parliamentary government when constitutional theory and the facts of the situation as yet admitted of neither.

In the catalogue, *Kings and Queens,* on sale at the exhibition, the introduction dealing with the reign of George III gave the traditional view of his reign:

> Conscientious and ambitious, he tried to restore the political influence of the Crown, but his intervention ended with the humiliating American War of Independence.

Conscientious he certainly was, painstakingly, almost painfully, conscientious. But was he ambitious? Did he try to exercise powers which his predecessors had relinquished, or claim an influence which was not universally conceded to him? And was it the assertion of Royal, and not of Parliamentary, authority over America which brought on the conflict and disrupted the First British Empire?

Let us place ourselves in March 1782. Dismal, humiliating failure has turned public opinion, and the House of Commons is resolved to cut losses and abandon the struggle; it is all over; Lord North's government has fallen; and the King is contemplating abdication. He has drafted a message to Parliament (which was never sent); here are its first two paragraphs:

> His Majesty during the twenty-one years he has sate on the throne of Great Britain, has had no object so much at heart as the maintainance of the British Constitution, of which the difficulties he has at times met with from his scrupulous attachment to the rights of Parliament are sufficient proofs.

> His Majesty is convinced that the sudden change of sentiments of one branch of the legislature has totally incapacitated him from either conducting the war with effect, or from obtaining any peace but on conditions which would prove destructive to the commerce as well as essential rights of the British nation.

In the first paragraph the King declares his unswerving devotion to the British Constitution, and shows himself conscious of his difficulties in America having arisen through 'his scrupulous attachment to the rights of Parliament'; the second paragraph pointedly refers to the Commons as 'one branch of the legislature', and gives the King's view of the American war: he is defending there the vital interests and essential rights of the British nation.

A year later, in March 1783, when faced by the necessity of accepting a Government formed by the Fox-North coalition, George III once more contemplated abdication; and in a letter (which again was never sent) he wrote to the Prince of Wales:

> The situation of the times are such that I must, if I attempt to carry on the business of the nation, give up every political principle on which I have acted, which I should think very unjustifiable, as I have always attempted to act agreable to my duty; and must form a Ministry from among men who know I cannot trust them and therefore who will not accept office without making me a kind of slave; this undoubtedly is a cruel dilemma, and leaves me but one step to take without the destruction of my principles and honour; the resigning my Crown, my dear Son to you, quitting this my native country for ever and returning to the dominions of my forefathers.
>
> Your difficulties will not be the same. You have never been in a situation to form any political system, therefore, are open to addopt what the times may make necessary; and no set of men can ever have offended you or made it impossible for you to employ them.

Alongside this consider the following passage from a letter which George III wrote on 26 December 1783, after having dismissed the Coalition and while he was trying to rally support for the newly formed Administration of the younger Pitt:

> The times are of the most serious nature, the political struggle is not as formerly between two factions for power; but it is no less than whether a desperate faction shall not reduce the Sovereign to a mere tool in its hands: though I have too much principle ever

> to infringe the rights of others, yet that must ever equaly prevent my submitting to the Executive power being in any other hands, than where the Constitution has placed it. I therefore must call on the assistance of every honest man . . . to support Government on the present most critical occasion.

Note in these two passages the King's honest conviction that he has always attempted to do his duty; that he has been mindful not to infringe the rights of others; but that it would be equally wrong in him to submit 'to the Executive power being in any other hands, than where the Constitution has placed it.' And while I do not for a moment suggest that these things could not have been done in a happier manner, I contend that the King's statements quoted above are substantially correct.

In the eighteenth century, a proper balance between King, Lords, and Commons, that is, the monarchical, aristocratic, and representative elements of the Constitution acting as checks on each other, was supposed to safeguard the property and privileges, the lives and liberty of the subjects. Single-Chamber government would have been no less abhorrent to the century than Royal autocracy. The Executive was the King's as truly as it is now of the President in the United States; he, too, had to choose his Ministers: but from among Parliamentary leaders. And while aspirants to office swore by the 'independency' of the Crown and disclaimed all wish to force themselves on the King, if left out they did their level best to embarrass and upset their successful rivals. The technique of Parliamentary opposition was fully established long before its most essential aim, which is to force a change of government, was recognized as legitimate; and because that aim could not be avowed in its innocent purity, deadly dangers threatening the Constitution, nay the life of the country, had to be alleged for justification. Robert Walpole as 'sole Minister' was accused of arrogating to himself the powers of both King and Parliament; the very tame Pelhams, of keeping George II 'in fetters'; Bute, who bore the name of Stuart, of 'raising the standard of Royal prerogative'; and George III of ruling not through the Ministers of his own choice whom he avowed in public, but through a hidden gang of obscure and sinister 'King's friends'. It is obviously impossible here to trace the origin and growth of that story, or to disprove it by establishing the true facts of the transactions to which it has become attached—it was a figment so beautifully elaborated by Burke's fertile imagination that

the Rockinghams themselves finished by believing it, and it grew into an obsession with them. In reality the constitutional practice of George III differed little from that of George I and George II. William Wyndham was proscribed by the first two Georges as a dangerous Jacobite, and C. J. Fox by the third as a dangerous Jacobin; while the elder Pitt was long kept out by both George II and George III on personal grounds. But for some the Royal veto and Royal influence in politics lose their sting if exercised in favour of successful monopolists in Whiggery.

I go one step further: in the eighteenth century the King had to intervene in politics and was bound to exercise his political influence, for the party system, which is the basis of Parliamentary government, did not exist. Of the House of Commons itself probably less than half thought and acted in party terms. About one-third of the House consisted of Members who looked to the King for guidance and for permanency of employment: epigoni of earlier Courts or forerunners of the modern Civil Service; and if they thus pursued their own interest, there is no reason to treat them as more corrupt than if they had done so by attaching themselves to a group of politicians. Another one-fifth of the House consisted of independent country gentlemen, ready to support the King's Government so long as this was compatible with their conscience, but averse to tying themselves up with political groups: they did not desire office, honours, or profits, but prided themselves on the disinterested and independent line they were pursuing; and they rightly claimed to be the authentic voice of the nation. In the centre of the arena stood the politicians, their orators and leaders fighting for the highest prizes of Parliamentary life. They alone could supply the façade of governments: the front benches in Parliament. But to achieve stability a Government required the active support of the Crown and the good opinion of the country. On matters about which public opinion felt strongly, its will would prevail; but with the House constituted as it was, with the electoral structure of the unreformed Parliament, and an electorate which neither thought nor voted on party lines, it is idle to assume that modern Parliamentary government was possible.

I pass to the next point: was George III correct in saying that it was 'his scrupulous attachment to the rights of Parliament' which caused him the difficulties in America? Undoubtedly yes. It was not Royal claims that the Americans objected to, but the claims of 'subjects in one part of the King's dominions to be sovereigns over their fellow-

subjects in another part of his dominions.' 'The sovereignty of the Crown I understand,' wrote Benjamin Franklin; 'the sovereignty of Britain I do not understand. . . . We have the same King, but not the same legislature.' Had George III aspired to independent Royal Power nothing could have suited him better than to be Sovereign in America, the West Indies, and possibly in Ireland, independent of the British Parliament; and the foremost champions of the rights of Parliament, recalling the way in which the Stuarts had played off Ireland and Scotland against England, would have been the first to protest. But in fact it would be difficult to imagine a King simultaneously exercising in several independent countries executive powers in conjunction with Parliamentary leaders. It will suffice to remember the difficulties and jealousies which Hanover caused although itself politically inert. The two problems which George III is unjustly accused of having mismanaged, those of Imperial and constitutional relations, were interconnected: only after responsible government had arisen did Dominion status within the Commonwealth become possible. Lastly, of the measures which brought on the American conflict none was of the King's making: neither George Grenville's Stamp Act, nor the Declaratory Act of the Rockinghams, nor the Townshend Duties. All that can be said against him is that once the struggle had started, he, completely identifying himself with this country, obstinately persevered in it. He wrote on 14 November 1778:

> If Lord North can see with the same degree of enthusiasm I do, the beauty, excellence, and perfection of the British Constitution as by law established, and consider that if any one branch of the Empire is alowed to cast off its dependency, that the others will infalably follow the example . . . he . . . will resolve with vigour to meet every obstacle . . . or the State will be ruined.

And again on 11 June 1779, expecting that the West Indies and Ireland would follow:

> Then this island would be reduced to itself, and soon would be a poor island indeed.

On 7 March 1780:

> I can never suppose this country so far lost to all ideas of self importance as to be willing to grant America independence, if that could ever be universally adopted, I shall despair of this country

being ever preserved from a state of inferiority and consequently falling into a very low class among the European States . . .

And on 26 September 1780:

. . . giving up the game would be total ruin, a small State may certainly subsist, but a great one mouldering cannot get into an inferior situation but must be annihilated.

When all was over, Lord North wrote to the King on 18 March 1782:

Your Majesty is well apprized that, in this country, the Prince on the Throne, cannot, with prudence, oppose the deliberate resolution of the House of Commons . . . Your Majesty has graciously and steadily supported the servants you approve, as long as they could be supported: Your Majesty has firmly and resolutely maintained what appeared to you essential to the welfare and dignity of this country, as long as this country itself thought proper to maintain it. The Parliament have altered their sentiments, and as their sentiments whether just or erroneous, must ultimately prevail, Your Majesty . . . can lose no honour if you yield at length . . .

Your Majesty's goodness encourages me . . . to submit whether it will not be for Your Majesty's welfare, and even glory, to sacrifice, at this moment, former opinions, displeasures and apprehensions (though never so well-founded) to . . . the public safety.

The King replied:

I could not but be hurt at your letter of last night. Every man must be the sole judge of his feelings, therefore whatever you or any man can say on that subject has no avail with me.

What George III had never learnt was to give in with grace: but this was at the most a defect of character.

2

Lord Waldegrave, who had been Governor to the Prince of Wales 1752–6, wrote in 1758 a character sketch of him so penetrating and just that it deserves quoting almost in full.

The Prince of Wales is entering into his 21st year, and it would be unfair to decide upon his character in the early stages of life, when there is so much time for improvement.

A wise preamble: yet a long and eventful life was to change him very little. Every feature singled out by Waldegrave finds copious illustration in the fifty years that followed (in one case in a superficially inverted form).

> His parts, though not excellent, will be found very tolerable, if ever they are properly exercised.
>
> He is strictly honest, but wants that frank and open behaviour which makes honesty appear amiable. . . .
>
> His religion is free from all hypocrisy, but is not of the most charitable sort; he has rather too much attention to the sins of his neighbour.
>
> He has spirit, but not of the active kind; and does not want resolution, but it is mixed with too much obstinacy.
>
> He has great command of his passions, and will seldom do wrong, except when he mistakes wrong for right; but as often as this shall happen, it will be difficult to undeceive him, because he is uncommonly indolent, and has strong prejudices.
>
> His want of application and aversion to business would be far less dangerous, was he eager in the pursuit of pleasure; for the transition from pleasure to business is both shorter and easier than from a state of total inaction.
>
> He has a kind of unhappiness in his temper, which, if it be not conquered before it has taken too deep a root, will be a source of frequent anxiety. Whenever he is displeased, his anger does not break out with heat and violence; but he becomes sullen and silent, and retires to his closet; not to compose his mind by study or contemplation, but merely to indulge the melancholy enjoyment of his own ill humour. Even when the fit is ended, unfavourable symptoms very frequently return, which indicate that on certain occasions his Royal Highness has too correct a memory.

Waldegrave's own endeavour was to give the Prince 'true notions of common things.' But these he never acquired: which is perhaps the deepest cause of his tragedy.

The defect Waldegrave dwells upon most is the Prince's 'uncommon indolence', his 'want of application and aversion to business'. This is borne out by other evidence, best of all by the Prince's own letters to Bute:

> *July 1st,* 1756: I will throw off that indolence which if I don't soon get the better of will be my ruin.

> *March 25th,* 1757: I am conscious of my own indolence . . . I do here in the most solemn manner declare, that I will throw aside this my greatest enemy . . .
> *September 25th,* 1758: . . . . that incomprehensible indolence, inattention and heedlessness that reigns within me . . .

And he says of his good resolutions: 'as many as I have made I have regularly broke'; but adds a new one: 'I mean to attempt to regain the many years I have fruitlessly spent.'

> *December 19th,* 1758: . . . through the negligence, if not the wickedness of those around me in my earlier days, and since perhaps through my own indolence of temper, I have not that degree of knowledge and experience in business, one of my age might reasonably have acquir'd . . .
> *March* 1760: . . . my natural indolence . . . has been encreas'd by a kind of indifference to the world, owing to the number of bad characters I daily see . . .

By shifting the blame on to others, he tries to relieve the bitter consciousness of failure: which is one source of that excessive 'attention to the sins of his neighbour' mentioned by Waldegrave. Indeed, George III's letters, both before and after his accession are full of it: 'the great depravity of the age', 'the wickedest age that ever was seen', 'a degenerate age', 'probity and every other virtue absorb'd into vice, and dissipation'; etc. 'An ungrateful, wicked people' and individual statesmen alike receive castigation (*in absentia*) from this very young Old Testament prophet. Pitt 'is the blackest of hearts', 'the most dishonourable of men', and plays 'an infamous and ungrateful part'; Lord Temple, an 'ungrateful arrogant and self-sufficient man'; Charles Townshend is 'a man void of every quality', 'the worst man that lives', 'vermin'; Henry Fox, a man of 'bad character', 'void of principles'; Lord Mansfield is 'but half a man'; the Duke of Bedford's character 'contains nothing but passion and absurdity'; etc. As for George II, the Prince felt ashamed of being his grandson. And on 23 April 1760, half a year before his accession, aged twenty-two he wrote to Bute: '. . . as to honesty, I have already lived long enough to know you are the only man who possesses that quality . . .'

In Bute he thought he had found the tutelary spirit who would enable him to live up to his future high vocation. Here are further excerpts from the Prince's letters to him:

July 1st 1756: My friend is . . . attack'd in the most cruel and horrid manner . . . because he is my friend . . . and because he is a friend to the bless'd liberties of his country and not to arbitrary notions . . .

By . . . your friendship . . . I have reap'd great advantage, but not the improvement I should if I had follow'd your advice . . . I will exactly follow your advice, without which I shall inevitably sink.

March 25th, 1757: I am resolved . . . to act the man in everything, to repeat whatever I am to say with spirit and not blushing and afraid as I have hitherto . . . my conduct shall convince you that I am mortified at what I have done and that I despise myself . . . I hope this will persuade you not to leave me when all is at stake, when nobody but you can stear me through this difficult, though glorious path.

In June 1757 Leicester House were alarmed by rumours of an alliance between the Duke of Newcastle and Henry Fox, and were ascribing fantastic schemes to the Duke of Cumberland. The Prince already saw himself compelled to meet force by force or to 'yield up the Crown',

for I would only accept it with the hopes of restoring my much beloved country to her antient state of liberty; of seeing her . . . again famous for being the residence of true piety and virtue, I say if these hopes were lost, I should with an eye of pleasure look on retiring to some uninhabited cavern as this would prevent me from seeing the sufferings of my countrymen, and the total destruction of this Monarchy . . .

August 20th, 1758: . . . by . . . attempting with vigour to restore religion and virtue when I mount the throne this great country will probably regain her antient state of lustre.

Was this a Prince nurtured in 'arbitrary notions', ambitious to make his own will prevail? or a man with a 'mission', striving after naively visionary aims? No doubt, since early childhood it must have been rammed into him, especially when he was being reproved, to what high station he was born; and disparaging comparisons are said to have been drawn between him and his younger brother. He grew up with a painful consciousness of his inadequacy: 'though I act wrong perhaps in most things', he wrote on one occasion. Excessive demands on a child, complete with wholesome exhortations, are fit to reduce it to a state of hebetude from which it is not easy to recover. A great deal of the pattern of George III's behaviour throughout life can be traced back to his up-bringing.

He spent his young years cut off from intercourse with boys of his own age, till he himself ceased to desire it. Bubb Dodington notes in his *Diary* on 15 October 1752, that the Princess Dowager of Wales

> did not observe the Prince to take very particularly to anybody about him, but to his brother Edward, and she was glad of it, for the young of quality were so ill-educated and so vicious that they frightened her.

And so they did him for the rest of his life. Isolation by itself would be apt to suggest to a child that there was something wrong with those he had to shun; but this he was probably told in so many words. On 18 December 1753, Dodington records another talk with the Princess:

> I said, it was to be wished he could have more company. She seemed averse to the young people, from the excessive bad education they had, and from the bad examples they gave.

So the boy spent joyless years in a well-regulated nursery, the nearest approach to a concentration camp: lonely but never alone, constantly watched and discussed, never safe from the wisdom and goodness of the grown-ups: never with anyone on terms of equality, exalted yet oppressed by deferential adults. The silent, sullen anger noted by Waldegrave, was natural to one who could not hit back or speak freely his mind, as a child would among children: he could merely retire, and nuture his griefs and grievances—and this again he continued through life. On 3 May 1766, during a political crisis, he wrote to Bute: 'I can neither eat nor sleep, nothing pleases me but musing on my cruel situation.' Nor could he, always with adults, develop self-reliance: at nineteen he dreamt of reforming the nation, but his idea of acting the man was to repeat without blushing or fear what he had to say.

For the pious works which were 'to make this great nation happy' Bute's 'sagacious councils' were therefore indispensable. When in December 1758 Bute expressed doubts whether he should take office in the future reign, the Prince in a panic searched his own conscience:

> Perhaps it is the fear you have I shall not speak firmly enough to my Ministers, or that I shall be stagger'd if they say anything unexpected; as to the former I can with great certainty assure that they, nor no one else shall see a want of steadiness either in my manner of acting or speaking, and as to the latter, I may give fifty sort of puts off, till I have with you thoroughly consider'd what part will be proper to be taken . . .

George III adhered to this programme. On his grandfather's death he waited to hear from Bute what 'must be done'. When expecting Pitt at a critical juncture: 'I would wish to know what I had best say. . . .' With regard to measures or appointments: 'I have put that off till I hear my Dear Friend's opinion'; 'If this [is] agreeable to my D. Friend I will order it to day . . .'; 'I desire my D. Friend to consider what I have here wrote, if he is of a contrary opinion, I will with pleasure embrace it'. And when in November 1762 Bute declared he would retire on conclusion of peace:

> I had flattered myself [wrote the King] when peace was once established that my D. Friend would have assisted me in purging out corruption . . . ; . . . now . . . the Ministry remains compos'd of the most abandon'd men that ever had those offices; thus instead of reformation the Ministers being vicious this country will grow if possible worse; let me attack the irreligious, the covetous &c. as much as I please, that will be of no effect . . . Ministers being of that stamp . . .

Two years on the throne had worked little if any change in his ideas and language; nor did the next twenty. The same high claims on himself, and the same incapacity to meet real situations he was faced with: hence his continued dependence on others. By 1765 he saw that Bute could not help him, by the summer of 1766 he had written off Bute altogether. In the spring of 1765 he turned to the Duke of Cumberland, the bugbear of his young years: 'Dear Uncle, the very friendly and warm part you have taken has given me real satisfaction. . . .' And to Pitt, 'the blackest of hearts': 'My friend for so the part you have acted deserves of me. . . .' In July 1765 Cumberland formed for him the Rockingham Administration and presided over it a quasi-Viceroy; but a few months later Cumberland was dead. In July 1766 Chatham formed his Administration; but a few months later his health broke down completely. Still George III clung to him like a molusc (a molusc who never found his rock). 'Under a health so broken,' wrote Chatham, 'as renders at present application of mind totally impossible. . . .' After nearly two years of waiting for his recovery, the King still wrote: 'I think I have a right to insist on your remaining in my service.' Next he clung to the ineffective Grafton who longed to be relieved of office; and when Grafton resigned, the King wrote to him on 27 January 1770:

> My heart is so full at the thought of your retiring from your situation that I think it best not to say more as I know the expressing it would give you pain.

Then came North. Totally unequal to the difficulties of the American crisis, in letter after letter he begged the King to let him resign. Thus in March 1778:

> Lord North cannot conceive what can induce His Majesty, after so many proofs of Lord North's unfitness for his situation to determine at all events to keep him at the head of the Administration, though the almost certain consequences of His Majesty's resolution will be the ruin of his affairs, and though it can not ward off for a month that arrangement which His Majesty seems to apprehend.

But the King would not hear of it. July 2nd, 1779: 'no man has a right to talk of leaving me at this hour. . . .' October 25th, 1780: he expects North 'will show that zeal for which he has been conspicuous from the hour of the Duke of Grafton's desertion.'

George III's attitude to North conformed to the regular pattern of his behaviour. So did also the way in which after a while he turned against North in bitter disappointment. By the '70s the King spoke disparagingly of Bute and Chatham; and in time his imagination enabled him to remember how on the day of his accession he had given the slip to them both. A month after Grafton had resigned, George III wrote to him: 'I . . . see anew that the sincere regard and friendship I have for you is properly placed. . . .' Somewhat later his resignation changed into 'desertion'. When North resigned: 'I ever did and ever shall look on you as a friend as well as a faithful servant. . . .' But incensed at the new situation he soon started attacking North, and treated him niggardly and unfairly over his secret service accounts. George III's attachment was never deep: it was that of a drunken man to railings—mechanical rather than emotional. Egocentric and rigid, stunted in feelings, unable to adjust himself to events, flustered by sudden change, he could meet situations only in a negative manner, clinging to men and measures with disastrous obstinacy. But he himself mistook that defensive apparatus for courage, drive, and vigour, from which it was as far removed as anything could be. Of his own mental processes he sometimes gave discerning though embellished accounts. Thus to Bute in 1762: 'I . . . am apt to despise what I am not accustom'd to . . .' And on 2 March 1797, to the younger Pitt when criticizing the way measures were weakened in passing through Parliament:

> My nature is quite different I never assent till I am convinced what is proposed is right, and then . . . I never allow that to be destroyed by after-thoughts which on all subjects tend to weaken never to strengthen the original proposal.

In short: no after-thoughts, no reconsideration—only desperate, clinging perseverance.

Still it might be said: at least he broke through his indolence. Yes, indeed: from pathologically indolent he turned pathologically industrious—and never again could let off working; but there was little sense of values, no perspective, no detachment. There is a legend about a homunculus whose maker not knowing what to do with him, bid him count poppy-seed in a bag. That George III was doing with his own busy self. His innumerable letters which he copied in his own hand, or the long documents transcribed by him (he never employed an amanuensis till his eye-sight began to fail) contain some shrewd perceptions or remarks, evidence of 'very tolerable parts if . . . properly exercised'. But most of his letters merely repeat approvingly what some Minister, big or small, has suggested. 'Lord A. is very right . . .'; 'General B. has acted very properly . . .'; 'the minute of Cabinet meets with my fullest concurrence . . .'; 'Nothing can more deserve my approbation than' —whatever it was. But if a basic change is suggested, his obstinacy and prejudices appear. On 15 March 1778, in a letter to Lord North, he makes an unusual and startling admission:

> I will only add to put before your eyes my most inmost thoughts, that no advantage to this country nor personal danger can ever make me address myself for assistance either to Lord Chatham or any other branch of the Opposition. . . .

As a rule he would sincerely assert, perhaps with somewhat excessive ostentation, that first and foremost he considered the good of the country. When told by Bute that it would be improper for him to marry Lady Sarah Lennox, he replied: 'the interest of my country ever shall be my first care, my own inclinations shall ever submit to it' (and he added: 'I should wish we could next summer . . . get some account of the various Princesses in Germany'—and he settled down to 'looking in the New Berlin Almanack for Princesses'). When considering withdrawal from the German War, he wrote (with a sidelong glance at the late King) about the superiority of his love 'to this my native country over any private interest of my own. . . .' He was 'a King of a free

people'; 'I rely on the hearts of my subjects, the only true support of the Crown,' he wrote in November 1760. They will not desert him—

> if they could be so ungrateful to me who love them beyond anything else in life, I should then I realy believe fall into the deepest melancholy which would soon deprive me of the vexations of this life.

The same note, of love for his country and trust that his subjects would therefore stand by him, continues for almost twenty years. But gradually other overtones begin to mix with it. He had become the target of virulent attacks and unjust suspicions which he deeply resented. Thus to Lord North on 7 March 1780: '. . . however I am treated I must love this country.' And to the Prince of Wales on 14 August 1780:

> The numberless trials and constant torments I meet with in public life, must certainly affect any man, and more poignantly me, as I have no other wish but to fulfill my various duties; the experience of now twenty years has convinced me that however long it may please the Almighty to extend my days, yet I have no reason to expect any diminution of my public anxiety; where am I therefore to turn for comfort, but into the bosom of my own family?

And he appealed to his son, the future George IV, to connect himself only with young men of respectable character, and by his example help 'to restore this country to its former lustre'—the old tune once more. And, in another letter:

> From your childhood I have ever said that I can only try to save my country, but it must be by the co-operation of my children only that I can effect it.

In the 1780s there is a more than usually heavy crop of bitter complaints about the age by one 'righteous overmuch': 'it has been my lot to reign in the most profligate age', 'depravity of such times as we live in', 'knavery and indolence perhaps I might add the timidity of the times. . . .' And then:

> I thank Heaven my morals and course of life have but little resembled those too prevalent in the present age, and certainly of all objects in this life the one I have most at heart, is to form my children that they may be useful examples and worthy of imitation . . .

With the King's disappointments in country and son another note enters his letters. He warns the Prince—

> in other countries national pride makes the inhabitants wish to paint their Princes in the most favourable light, and consequently be silent on any indiscretion; but here most persons if not concerned in laying ungrounded blame, are ready to trumpet any speck they can find out.

And he writes of the 'unalterable attachment' which his Electoral subjects have shown to their Princes. When George III went mad in 1788, he wanted to go back to Hanover. Deep down there was a good deal of the Hanoverian in him.

His insanity was a form of manic-depression. The first recorded fit in March 1765 was of short duration, though there may have been a slight relapse in May; and a year later he wrote to Bute—

> if I am to continue the life of agitation I have these three years, the next year there will be a Council [of] Regency to assist in that undertaking.

During the next twenty-three years he preserved his normal personality. The attack in 1788 lasted about half a year: the King was over fifty, and age rendered complete recovery more difficult. His self-control weakened and his irritability increased. He was conscious of a growing weakness. Yet there was something about him which more and more endeared him to the people. He was never popular with London society or the London mob; he was much beloved in the provinces—perhaps it was his deeper kindness, his real piety, and sincere wish to do good which evoked those feelings. These appear strikingly, for instance, in his own account of his journey to Portsmouth in 1788, and in Fanny Burney's account of his progress through Wiltshire in 1789. He was not a politician, and certainly not a statesman. But in things which he could judge without passion or preconceived ideas, there appears basic honesty and the will to do the right thing. I shall limit myself to two examples. When in 1781 a new Provost was to be appointed at Eton, George III insisted on choosing a man 'whose literary tallents might make the appointment respectable . . . for Eton should not be bestowed by favour, but merit'. And when in 1787 a new Lord Lieutenant had to be chosen for Ireland, the King wrote to the younger Pitt about the necessity

> of looking out for the person most likely to conduct himself with temper, judgement, and an avowed resolution to avoid partiality and

> employ the favours he has to recommend to with the justice due to my service and to the public. . . . When I have stated this Mr. Pitt must understand that I do not lean to any particular person . . . when I state that a Lord Lieutenant should have no predelection but to advance the public good I should be ashamed to act in a contrary manner.

I have given here a picture of George III as seen in his letters, 'warts and all'. What I have never been able to find is the man arrogating power to himself, the ambitious schemer out to dominate, the intriguer dealing in an underhand fashion with his Ministers; in short, any evidence for the stories circulated about him by very clever and eloquent contemporaries. He had a high, indeed an exaggerated, notion of royalty but in terms of mission and duties rather than of power; and trying to live up to this idealized concept, he made unreasonable demands on himself. Setting himself unattainable standards, he could never truly come to grips with reality: which condemned him to remain immature, permanency of inner conflict precluding growth. Aware of his inadequacy, he turned to others and expected them to enable him to realize his visionary program (this appears clearest in his relations with Bute); and he bitterly reproached them in his own mind, and blamed the age in which he lived, for his own inevitable failure. The tension between his notions and reality, and the resulting frustration, account to a high degree for his irritability, his deep-seated resentments, and his suppressed anger—for situations intolerable and disastrous for himself and others; and it may have been a contributory factor in his mental breakdowns. The desire to escape from that unbearable conflict repeatedly shows itself in thoughts of abdication which must not be deemed insincere because never acted upon (men of his type cannot renounce their treadmill). He himself did not understand the nature and depth of his tragedy; still less could others. There was therefore room for the growth of an injurious legend which made that heavy-burdened man a much maligned ruler; and which has long been accepted as history.

ABOUT THE AUTHOR

J. R. HALE was born in Ashford, Kent, England, in 1923. He attended Eastbourne College and was a Scholar of Jesus College, Oxford, from 1945 to 1948. Between 1948 and 1949 he did graduate work at Johns Hopkins University and Harvard University on a Commonwealth Fund Fellowship. Since 1949 he has been a Fellow of Jesus College, Oxford, and a Tutor in Modern History. Recently he was made a Professor of History at the University of Warwick. He is the author of *England and the Italian Renaissance, Machiavelli and Renaissance Italy,* and *The Literary Works of Machiavelli.*

D0310901